APM

Early Proceedings of The Association of Professors of Mission

Volume I
Biennial Meetings from 1956 to 1958

First Fruits Press
Wilmore, Ky
c2018

Early Proceedings of the Association of Professors of Mission.
First Fruits Press, © 2018

ISBN: 9781621715610 (vol. 1 print), 9781621715627 (vol. 1 digital), 9781621715634 (vol. 1 kindle) 9781621712886 (vol. 2 print), 9781621712862 (vol. 2 digital), 9781621712879 (vol. 2 kindle)

Digital versions at (vol. 1) http://place.asburyseminary.edu/academicbooks/26/
(vol. 2) http://place.asburyseminary.edu/academicbooks/27/

Early proceedings of the Association of Professors of Mission.
Wilmore, KY : First Fruits Press, ©2018.

2 volumes ; cm.

Reprint. Previously published: [Place of Publication not identified] : Association of Professors of Mission, 1956-1974.
Volume 1. 1956 to 1958 – volume 2. 1962 to 1974.

ISBN: 9781621715610 (vol. 1 : pbk.)
ISBN: 9781621712886 (vol. 2 : pbk.)

1.Missions--Study and teaching--Congresses. 2. Missions--Theory--Congresses. 3. Religion and social problems--Congresses. 4. Association of Professors of Mission. I. Association of Professors of Mission. II. Proceedings of the Association of Professors of Mission.

BV2020.A875

Cover design by Jon Ramsay

asburyseminary.edu
800.2ASBURY
204 North Lexington Avenue
Wilmore, Kentucky 40390

First Fruits
THE ACADEMIC OPEN PRESS OF ASBURY SEMINARY

First Fruits Press

The Academic Open Press of Asbury Theological Seminary

204 N. Lexington Ave., Wilmore, KY 40390

859-858-2236

first.fruits@asburyseminary.edu

asbury.to/firstfruits

About the Association of Professors of Mission

The Association of Professors of Mission (APM) was officially organized in June of 1952 at a meeting held at Southern Baptist Seminary in Louisville, Kentucky. This meeting was the result of a desire to bring together mission teachers from seminaries, colleges, and Bible schools to share papers and discuss issues related to Christian missions and especially the teaching of missions.[1] From 1952 to 1972, the APM met biennially, usually in conjunction with the American Association of Theological Schools (AATS) meetings.

Papers and research were shared and discussed at these meetings, and this work was often mimeographed and bound, along with minutes and other reports, to be distributed to members and sold to a few institutions or other interested parties. By the 1960s it became standard to present papers from the three traditions of the APM- conciliar Protestant, Roman Catholic, and conservative-evangelical Protestant. Horner notes, "The APM was thus in some important respects the most widely ecumenical body in North America at that time."[2]

Today these papers are hard to find and rather rare, often located within institutional archives. In the interest of preserving this heritage and the unique perspectives of missionary professionals over such an important time period in mission history, the APM decided to reprint these papers and make them available digitally as well. Proceedings were not made or preserved for the 1952 or 1954 meetings, so they are not included in this collection. In addition the papers presented at the fifth biennial meeting in

---

1   For a thorough discussion of the development of the Association of Professors of Mission see Norman A. Horner's excellent article "The Association of Professors of Mission: The First Thirty-five Years, 1952- 1987" in the *International Bulletin of Missionary Research* 11(3): 120 – 124, July 1987.

2   *Ibid.*, page 121.

i

1960 were published as a separate book,[3] so they are likewise not included here. The remaining nine proceedings from 1956 to 1974 are presented here in their entirety, with minutes and additional reports being placed in appendices for those interested in these documents from an historical perspective.

In 1972, members of the APM worked to found a more inclusive organization focused on Christian Missions, and so the American Society of Missiology (ASM) was born, and in 1974 began the tradition of having the APM meet jointly with the larger ASM at their annual meeting, with future papers to be published through the ASM journal, *Missiology: An International Review*. As the APM/ASM has continued to grow, both parts have continued to thrive, with the APM continuing to focus on the teaching and educational side of mission. Many professors of mission are the only professors in this field in their institutions, so the APM continues to offer a place for these professors to find fellowship as well as pedagogical ideas to further their course design and content. Beginning in 2013 the APM once again began producing its proceedings in a digital online format, with print copies available through a print-on-demand source at a low cost in order to promote the teaching of missions to a wider global audience.[4]

Of the APM, R. Pierce Beaver once wrote,

> Our Association of Professors of Missions came into existence... not as an expression of the old missionary triumphalism but as an attempt to build a lifeboat for floundering brothers and sisters. It really marks the beginning of a new era rather than a climax of the older development. The biennial reports of the Association reveal the wrestling we have done over our reason for

---

3   Wilber C. Harr, editor, *Frontiers of the Christian World Mission since 1938: Essays in Honor of Kenneth Scott Latourette*, New York: Harper & Brothers, 1962.

4   The 2013 proceedings is entitled *Social Engagement: The Challenge of the Social in Missiological Education* (http://place.asburyseminary.edu/academicbooks/3/), and the 2014 proceedings is entitled *Transforming Teaching for Mission: Educational Theory and Practice* (http://place.asburyseminary.edu/academicbooks/10/).

being, curriculum, and teaching methods during the past twenty-odd years.[5]

It is the earnest hope of the APM that these historic documents can continue to add to our growing knowledge of mission history by being made more accessible for both members of the APM and scholars in the field of Christian missions all over the world. It is also our hope to allow professors and teachers of mission all over the globe the ability to access material that can help make them more effective educators for the kingdom of God.

Robert Danielson
Advisory Committee Member

---

5   R. Pierce Beaver, "The American Theological Seminary and Missions: An Historical Survey," in APM, *Proceedings, Twelfth Biennial Meeting* (Wheaton, IL, June 9-10, 1974), pgs. 7-14.

Table of Contents

APM

Christianity and the Non-Christian Religions: Historical Review of Thought and Literature

3rd Biennial Meeting
Evangelical Theological Seminary
Naperville, Illinois
June 7-9, 1956

Preface

It is altogether fitting that a brief word of appreciation be given honoring a number of people who made this set of papers possible. The names of persons preparing the papers appear in the index. Others carried on after the biennial meeting had ended. Miss Ruth Hirsch as secretary to Pierce Beaver did an immense amount of the mimeography. Norvin Hein assisted in having secretarial help at Yale do his paper. The International Missionary Council mimeographed the paper presented by M. Searle Bates. Several persons have helped us here in Naperville, gradually getting the papers ready for assembly.

We believe you will enjoy and appreciate the papers. Their quality reaffirms the fact so prosaically stated in the minutes that we want to meet again.

Wilber C. Harr

Secretary-Treasurer

Introduction

Joseph M. Kitagawa

My assigned topic was to present an historical review of thought and literature on either Christianity and Buddhism or Christianity and Far Eastern Religions in general. After some reflection, I have redefined my task as an "Historical Review of Thought and Literature on Christianity and Buddhism in the Far Eastern Religious Context."

A comprehensive subject such as this requires a considerable amount of discrimination and structuring of the materials. Our concern, if I understand it correctly, is not a technical study of each religion involved, but rather the "relations" among these religions. Numerous books and articles have been written in this general area. Historians, social scientists, and students of religion continually discuss this difficult question of the relation among religions. One cannot help but feel, however, that many books on the subject, competent and useful as they may be, do not face the main issues of our concern. Many scholars have a notion, developed during the heyday of the so-called "Comparative Religions" approach, that it is possible to depict the essential qualities of each religion in a systematic and orderly manner, and somehow discuss them according to a neat comparative method. Today, the assumptions of the comparative method have come to be questioned, and many of us are groping for a new perspective with which to approach the study of world religions.

CULTURAL RELIGIONS AND SUPRA-CULTURAL RELIGIONS

The late Professor Van der Leeuw, at the Seventh Congress of the History of Religions held in 1950 at Amsterdam, stressed two main tasks of the history of religions: (1) the need of a friendly relationship between theology and the history of religions, and (2) the importance of contacts with other branches of learning, such as philosophy, archaeology, anthropology, ethnology, psychology and sociology. What he was advocating was some kind of a "synthetic view" of the study of religions. [1] In fact, such a multi-dimensional concern was reflected in the theme of the Amsterdam Congress namely, "the mythical-ritual pattern in civilization." Various papers presented at the Congress discussed religious patterns and the inter-relations between religions and cultures.

Obviously there are different ways to study the inter-relations of religions and cultures. Increasingly, students of history, the social sciences, cultures and missions are taking keen interest in the role and function of religions in various cultures. In a recent publication entitled *Cultural Patterns and Technical Change*, it is stated that:

> a culture is a systematic and integrated whole, "Culture" ... is an abstraction from the body of learned behavior which a group of people who share the same tradition transmit entire to their children, and, in part, to adult immigrants who become members of the society. It covers not only the arts and sciences, religions and philosophies, to which the word "culture" has historically applied, but also the system of technology, the political practices, the small intimate habits of daily life... as well as the method of electing a prime minister or changing the constitution. [2]

> Within the confines of the cultural pattern each individual responds in terms of his own constitution and life-experiences ... Cultural forms, as human beings have so far developed them, while inclusive enough so that most of the human beings who survive within them can live in terms of their institutions and values, are not sufficiently varied and flexible to protect and express all of the individual personalities -- each an organized whole -- in the society. [3]

The flexible and yet sufficiently rigid pattern of culture conditions the character and development of religion. In turn, however, religion

---

[1] *Proceedings of the 7th Congress for the History of Religions* (Amsterdam: North-Holland Publishing Co., 1951), P. 20.

[2] Margaret Mead, ed,. *Cultural Patterns and Technical Change* (New York: The New American Library, 1955), PP. 12-13.

[3] *Ibid.*, p, 13.

influences all aspects of culture. For example, Buddhism affects the standard of living in Burma.

> The best way of spending money, the expression of a "high" standard of living, was to give, as an act of merit not for the sake of others, but for one's own enhancement, for the strengthening of the clan. If there was enough money, one built a pagoda; for less, one could establish a shelter near a pagoda for the devout, or a rest-house on the mountain-side... The hoarding of money was regarded as evil; spiritual merit was accumulated, rather than material wealth.[4]

The fact that religion penetrates all aspects of culture makes it difficult to treat religion merely as one ingredient of culture. Therefore we are compelled to re-examine our understanding of the relation between religion and culture with greater sensitivity than ever before. A similar question has been raised by ethnolinguists in recent years. For example, Whorf asserts that language patterns and cultural patterns have grown up together, constantly influencing each other.[5]

For our purpose, methodologically at least, we might do well to articulate our concepts of "cultural patterns" and "religious patterns" respectively, and then proceed to examine the relation between the two. Our tentative hypothesis is that living religions may be divided into two main groups. The first may be termed "cultural religions," and refers to religions which accept and support, in the main, the mythical-ritual patterns of the culture in which they exist. For instance, both Hinduism and Indian culture are grounded in the caste system. The second group may be called "supracultural religions," which are not rooted in the mythical-ritual patterns of any particular culture.

A significant fact about supra-cultural religions is that two of them -- Christianity and Buddhism -- show a remarkable contrast in their approach to local religions. Hocking observes that:

> Christianity has been as a rule more belligerent toward the local religions. Professing to supply all the religious needs of Mankind, it has called for singleness of allegiance. Buddhism in China presented the paradox of a religion

---

[4] *Ibid.*, p. 27.

[5] B. L. Whorf, "The Relation of Habitual Thought and Behavior to Language," in *Language, Culture and Personality* (Menasha, Wisconsin, 1941), p. 91.

with no God and at the same time with many divine figures, Buddha's, Bodhisattvas, and saints. A multiform system can flexibly add to its number or find cross-identities, whereas a monotheism... must set itself against the whole apparatus of polytheistic worship, especially the images of the gods. The march of Christianity has therefore been a demand for either-or decisions; the temples and idols of the "heathen" have had to fall. But here also the conflict has not extended to the ground level of the local structure. The tenacity of folk-custom and festival has led to many local amalgamations, and the sagacity especially of the Catholic missionaries has seen possibilities of conserving rather than destroying many a local observance within the body of the new faith. Hence the Christianities of the German forests, the Eruid countries, the Mexican mountains, the old Spanish Southwest, are markedly different in temper: they are variations on a common theme.[6]

As Hocking observes, Buddhism did not pretend to be a contestant, but rather, a supplement to existing local religions. [7] Thus, in Burma Buddhism lives side by side with Nat worship, in China with Confucianism and Taoism, in Tibet with Bon religion, and in Japan with Shinto.

My main task today is an analysis of the relation between these two different supra-cultural religions -- Christianity and Buddhism -- historically and in their contemporary settings. First, however, let us look at cultural religions in the Far East and see how Buddhism has related itself to them. We shall take China as an example.

CULTURAL PATTERNS AND RELIGIOUS PATTERNS IN CHINA

Several years ago, Hajima Nakamura of Tokyo University attempted to compere the modes of thought of the Indians, Chinese, Japanese, and Tibetans.[8] The importance of his work is pointed out by Arthur Wright:

---

[6] W. E. Hocking, "Living Religions and a World Faith," in *The Asian Legacy and American Life*, ed. by A. E. Christy (New York: John Day, 1942), p. 207.

[7] *Ibid.*, p, 206.

[8] Hajime Nakamura, *Toyojin Shii Hoo* (2 vols. Tokyo, 1948-49).

What is new and interesting…is his study of Chinese thought in interaction with the alien ideas of Indian Buddhism. By this means he attempts to show which indigenous thought patterns changed under its influence and in what ways and which proved resistant both to change and to assimilation with alien ideas. He thus uses Buddhism as a device for isolating or precipitating that which is most persistent, and unchanging in Chinese thought- It might be that one of the other alien systems which has come to China could be similarly used…[9]

Although our attempt is not as ambitious as that of Nakamura, we might first discuss the cultural patterns and religious patterns of China, and then try to relate the two.

First, Chinese culture and society are based on the principle of "familism," based on the notion of filial piety, No further comment is required on this well known subject, except to mention that a family is a religious as well as a sociological unit and that the nation traditionally has been understood as an extension of the family. Second, Chinese culture has been kept intact by the same written language even though the spoken language has been divided into numerous dialects. Third, culture and religions are closely identified.

There are some obvious, external characteristics of Chinese religions. Scholars usually cite the following features as central: (1) belief in spirits, (2) worship of Shang-ti, (3) ancestor worship, (4) veneration of Confucius, and (5) rationalistic and humanistic temperament. However, religion is more than the obvious, external so-called "religious" activities.

The genius of the Chinese was their refusal to make a distinction between the sacred and the secular. The only significant distinction made was between ceremonial and ordinary everyday activities. Here, we must not hastily equate religion with the "ceremonial," as many people are inclined to do. Creel, in discussing the public and home life of the Chinese, stated that the latter was more important and, thus, taken more seriously. Similarly, the religious ethos of the Chinese must be found in the midst of their ordinary, everyday life, instead of in their ceremonial activities, though the latter certainly should not be overlooked. In other words, the

---

[9]   Arthur F. Wright, ed. *Studies in Chinese Thought* (Chicago: The University of Chicago Press, 1953), p. 13.

meaning of life was sought in the whole of life, not confined to any section of it called "religious," As Lin Yutang puts it:

> There is no doubt that the Chinese are in love with life…They are in love with life, which is so sad and yet so beautiful, and in which moments of happiness are so precious because they are so transient. They are in love with life, with its kings and beggars, robbers and monks, funerals and weddings and childbirths and sickness and glowing sunsets and rainy nights… Yes, life (is) so poignantly beautiful… down to its lowliest details.[10]

But this life, which the Chinese love so dearly, was understood in its cosmological setting, and not as something independent of and superior to nature. If the ancient Greeks thought of man as a political being, the Chinese thought of him as a cosmological being. This is true even of the so-called humanistic tradition in China. "Man" in China, says Derk Bodde, "is not the supremely important creature he seems to Westerners; he is but a vital part of the universe as a whole."[11] As such, the world of man and that of nature constitute one great indivisible unity.

Even though the ancient Chinese sages did not develop meta - physical theories of this indivisibility of the world of man and the world of nature, the metaphysical implications nevertheless were taken for granted. In fact, a metaphysical concern was the central theme in the Ying-Yang system, which was a sort of hybrid of astronomy and astrology, science and magic, and metaphysical and physics. For lack of better terminology, we use de Groot's expression, "Universism,"[12] to describe this implicit metaphysical structure, namely, that the Chinese operate from the point of view of the whole, treating nature (and man) as integral, instead of starting from particulars and deriving laws by way of induction or generalization, [13] "Thus, the highest category of the Chinese apprehension of the world and life is "Totality," or the Eternal Order (Tao), which is the molding

---

[10]   Lin Yutang, *My Country and My People* (New York: John Day, 1935), pp. 103-104.

[11]   Derk Bodde, "Dominant Ideas," In *China*, ed. by H.F. MacNair (Berkley: University of California Press, 1946), p. 20.

[12]   J. J. M. de Groot, *Religion in China; Universism* (London: G, P, Putnam's Sons, 1912).

[13]   Gi-ming Shien, "Being and Nothingness in Greek and Ancient Philosophy," in *Philosophy East and West*, Vol. 1, No. 2, July, 1951, pp. 16-17.

principle of the universe.[14] Tao realizes itself in the ordered life of man, and *vice versa*. How to keep this harmony intact and how to actualize it in everyday life has been the real "religious concern" of the Chinese .

In this connection, it may be useful for us to depend on Martin Buber's distinction between "I-Thou" and "I-It" relationships. Seen from an "I-Thou" perspective, anything -- world, man, or a thing -- can be an object of religious relationship, while seen from an "I-It" perspective, even gods can not enter into a religious relationship. The so-called "Cult of Shang-ti" is a case in point.

Most books regard the cult of Shang-ti as a central feature of Chinese religious life. And certainly in the external, ceremonial dimension, it has a prominent place. However, seen from the religious perspective of the Chinese, the cult of Shang-ti, with all its drama and paraphernalia, implies "distance" and "remoteness"[15], rather than an "I-Thou relationship". The Chinese followed the sage's teaching: "To be earnestly occupied in rendering full justice to man, to show reverence for demons and gods, but to keep oneself at a *distance from them*, may well be called wisdom."[16] To be sure, in one sense, Shang-ti was regarded as sacred, super-human, or even divine, but only in the ceremonial dimension; he was celebrated but always kept at a distance.

As stated before, the highest category of the Chinese apprehension of the world and of life is the Eternal Dynamic Order (Tao). Religious questions have been raised, not in the form of "what is Tao?" so much as "how to realize Tao?" Here, this question is approached differently in the two cultural religions of China-Taoism and Confucianism.

The Taoistic tradition emphasizes an "I-Thou relationship" with Nature, while the Confucian tradition emphasizes an "I-Thou relationship" among human beings, as symbolized in the Five Relationships with reciprocal obligations and duties. Confucianism, which is grounded in "Cosmic-human Monism," views man as a cosmic being and attempts to actualize Tao in the form of an immanental theocracy in human society. Viewed in this way, Taoism, which may be characterized as a "Naturalistic

---

[14] H. Kraemer, *The Christian Message in a Non-Christian World* (London: The Edinburgh House Press, 1938), p. I84.

[15] G. Van Der Leeuw, *Religion in Essence and Manifestation*, tr. By J.E.Turner (London: George Allen & Unwin, Ltd ., 193 3) > P. 597.

[16] Quoted in Ibid., p, 598; also, cf. Lin Yutang, op. cit., p, II6,

Monism," and Confucianism are not too far apart in their philosophic apprehension of the world and man.

But in the area of practical affairs, Confucianism and Taoism are miles apart. To put it simply, Taoism is concerned with "cosmic engineering," and Confucianism with "socio-political engineering." This explains why Taoism in a later period was easily invaded by witchcraft and superstitions.

The "socio-political engineering" of Confucianism linked the Cosmic Order (Tao) with the family -- which was the dynamic, stable unit of society -- and with the State, which was the extension of the family. In actual practice, however, "to live according to Tao" was understood by many to "live according to the traditional rules and etiquette. "[17] Also, as Bodde points out, Confucianists "sometimes fell into the common error of assuming that morality can be realized automatically, through the preaching of lofty doctrines, without regard for the practical difficulties that lie in the way of realization of these doctrines."[18]

Now, let us turn our attention to Buddhism. While the traditionally accepted date for the introduction of Buddhism in China is 67 A.D., recent scholarship points out that Buddhism must have been practiced in China long before this legendary date. For our purpose, two observations will suffice: (1) In the course of time, Buddhism discovered a new creative impulse and developed a unique form in the climate and soil of China, (2) Buddhism did not replace Confucianism and Taoism, but it did change the tenor of these cultural religions. Johnston once remarked:

> As to the form of Buddhism which prevails in China, perhaps we may fairly say that it is not only both a religion and philosophy, but that it embraces many religions and many philosophies, and that these are not always consistent with themselves or with one another.[19]

More recently, Wing-tsit Chan has said: "Chinese Buddhism has followed the Cha'an (or Zen) and Pure Land Schools in practice and has adhered to the T'ien-T'ai and Hua-yen schools in doctrine."[20]

---

[17] Kraemer, op. cit., p. 184.

[18] Bodde, op cit,, p, 23.

[19] Reginald F. Johnston, *Buddhist China* (London: I, Murray, 1913) p.17.

[20] Wing-tsit Chan, *Religious Trends In Modern China* (New York: Columbia University Press, 1953)j pp. 94-95.

At the expense of oversimplification, we may depict three philosophical trends in Chinese Buddhism: (1) Every effort is made to save the world of appearance, thus changing the historic tenor of Buddhism, (2) Elements of existence are understood to emerge from the Mind (which is not the psychological mind as taught by Mencius, but the metaphysical Mind.) (3) Mind and nature is understood to be interdependent and interpenetrated.

Although metaphysics and epistemology were important, the chief concern of Chinese Buddhism has been the practical problem of salvation. [21] Here, we can only mention three main approaches. First, is the Gospel of salvation by faith, emphasized by the Pure Land schools, "It accepts the idea that Nirvana has neither space nor time, neither life nor death. But it interprets this as nothing other than the land of the Buddha of Infinite Light and Infinite Life, that is, the Pure Land.[22] "Second is the mystical approach of Mantra Buddhism known as the True-Word School. This school treats the universe as the spiritual body of the Buddha, which manifests itself in the static (Diamond) and the dynamic realms. These two realms are regarded as interdependent, much as in the Ying-Yang system. This school teaches that one can become Buddha in this very body. Another characteristic is the use of arts and symbolism such as mandalas and dharanis. Third, and the most "Chinese," is the Meditation school, Ch'an, better known in the West as Zen. Zen, in short, tries to attain the same goal as the Mantra school, but by a radically different method. The difference between these two forms of Buddhism is somewhat analogous to the difference between Catholicism and Quakerism in Christianity; Zen is basically a method of "direct intuition into the heart to find the Buddha nature,"[23] rejecting traditional Buddhist scriptures, teachings, and symbolism.

Understandably, the development of Chinese Buddhism exerted a tremendous influence on Chinese thought, philosophy, art, literature, and cultural religion. Here, we need only mention that Neo-Confucianism, which arose in the 11th century, in part as a protest against Buddhism, nevertheless was deeply influenced by Buddhism. Fung Yu-lan attributes the Neo-Confucianist idea of the Universal Mind to Buddhism, in the following quotation: "Before the introduction of Buddhism, there was

---

[21] Ibid., p, 99.

[22] Wing-tsit Chan, "Story of Chinese Philosophy" in *Philosophy – East and West* (Princeton: Princeton University Press, 1906), p, 50

[23] Ibid.

in Chinese philosophy only the mind, but not *the mind*."[24] He further comments:

> The Neo-Confucianists developed a point of view from which all the moral activities valued by the Confucianists acquire a further value that is super-moral. They all have in them that quality that the Ch'annists (Zen) called the wonderful Tao. It is in this sense that Neo-Confucianism is actually a further development of (Zen).[25]

It has even been said that Neo-Confucianism resembled "Confucianism externally, but Buddhism internally."[26] This does not imply, however, that Buddhism converted Confucianism. Rather, Buddhism which in the Chinese cultural environment developed a unique Chinese form, in turn changed the character of Confucianism, to the extent that these two, together with Taoism, could co-exist together harmoniously. Thus, in China, the two cultural-religions -- Taoism and Confucianism -- were supplemented by the supra-cultural religion: Buddhism.

BUDDHISM IN THE FAR EAST

Several years ago, Northrop wrote that Asiatic religions are "reared almost exclusively on a philosophy grounded predominantly in the aesthetic components alone," and thus these religions can merge quite happily.[27] But, as we have seen in the case of China, the fact is that they do not "merge," Rather, after a long process of mutual influence and re-interpretation, Asiatic religions have developed patterns of co-existence or "plural belongingness"[28] -- in different localities. And if there is anything like a thread which runs through the co-existence of diverse religious traditions, it may be attributed to the role played by Buddhism. Surveying the long history of Buddhist expansion in Asia, one is struck by the fact that Buddhism, which has allowed itself to be influenced by local religions

---

[24] Fung Yu'lan, *A Short History of Chinese Philosophy* (New York: The Macmillan Co., 1950), p. 254.

[25] Ibid., p. 280.

[26] Wing-tsit Chan, "Neo-Confucianism," in *China*, ed. by H. F. MacNair (Berkeley: University of California Press 1925), p. 260.

[27] F. S. C. Northrop, *The Meeting of East and West* (New York: The Macmillan Co. 1946) p. 437.

[28] W, E, Hocking, *Living Religions and a World Faith* (New York: The Macmillan Co., 1940), p. 69.

and cultures, has nevertheless had the tenacity to maintain its own identity despite its "plural belongingness." What is the nature of this supra-cultural religion, which is both so inclusive and exclusive at the same time?

Whitehead once remarked that while Christianity was a religion which developed a philosophy. Buddhism was a philosophy which developed into a religion. In reality, however, Buddhism was a genuine religion from its beginning. The earliest creedal formula of Buddhism was:

"I take refuge in Buddha; I take refuge in Dharma; and I take refuge in Sangha." All Buddhist schools, which for the sake of brevity may be grouped into (1) Hinayana, (2) Mahiayana, and (3) Mantrayana, subscribe to Buddha, Dharma, and Sanghah.

Buddha has been understood differently by different Buddhist schools. To the Hinayanist, the historic Buddha, Sakyamuni, alone is entitled to be called the Buddha. He was the Enlightened. His followers can attain arhat-ship or sainthood but can never attain Buddhahood. To the Mahayanist, the historic Buddha is not important; what is emphasized is Buddha-ness or the truth, Sakyamuni was a revealer of the truth in the sense that his personality was so transparent that he, and other Buddha's, could be equated with the truth. According to this tradition, Sakyamuni's followers may follow his footsteps and become bodhisattvas or semi-Buddha's. To the Mantrayanist, the entire cosmos alone is the Buddha-body; all beings have the potentialities to become Buddhas.

Actually, little is known about the founder of Buddhism, Streeter writes:

> Sakyamuni, the Buddha, was born five and a half centuries before Christ; yet there is much in his outlook upon life which is curiously modern. In certain respects it is distinctly more "modern" than that of Jesus... The modernity of his outlook was the direct result of personal experience. [29]

What Sakyamuni experienced tinder a Bodhi-tree: is known as *sad-dharma* or Good Law. In his understanding of the truth, Buddha rejected the classical Vedic notion of atman (substance) being the basic reality. In the words of Murti:

> ... Buddha came to deny the soul, a permanent substantial entity, precisely because he took his stand on the reality of moral consciousness and the efficacy of Karma... Denial

---

[29]   B. H. Streeter, The Buddha and the Christ (London, Macmillan, 1932), P. 53.

of Satkaya (atman or Substance) is the very pivot of the Buddhist metaphysics and doctrine of salvation. [30]

While Buddhist doctrines have been expressed in negative terminology, positive affirmations are implicit in them, Melamed rightly points out:

> Although Buddha insisted that the universe is governed by necessity and causation, his conception of causation is much more refreshing than that of Spinoza, His causation, far from excluding evolution, presupposes it because its effects are not the mechanical succession of motion, but organic evolution in which one state is developing itself to another state. In a certain sense this evolution is actually creative, for it necessitates growth and "the operating of -the inner forces, in which we behold something that grows out of the seed. Hence, the world is one continuous, organic development, and not a series of chance phenomena without any inner unity.[31]

Historically, the doctrine of the Reality has undergone several stages of reinterpretation. Without violating the classic theory of "no substance, no duration, and no bliss except Nirvana," all Buddhist schools attempted to affirm the reality of the phenomenal world to a certain extent. We may follow Stcherbatsky's outline of the development of the Buddhist conception of the Absolute:

> 1. Buddha… accepted a system denying the existence of an eternal Soul, and reducing phenomenal existence to a congeries of separate elements evolving gradually towards final extinction.

> 2. To this ideal of a lifeless Nirvana and an extinct Buddha some schools alone remained faithful. A tendency to convert Buddha into a superhuman, eternally living, principle manifested itself early among his followers and led to a schism.

---

[30] T. R. V. Murti, The Central Philosophy of Buddhism (London: George Allen & Unwin Ltd., 1955), p. 17.

[31] S.M. Melamed, Spinoza and Buddha (Chicago: The University of Chicago Press, 1933), p. 261.

3. This tendency gradually developed until in the 1st century A.D. it ended in the production of ... a new canonical literature. It then adopted... the brahmanical idea of a pantheistic Absolute, of a spiritual and monistic character...(then) the Buddha was converted into a full-blown *brahman* and its personification worshipped under the names of a Cosmical Body (dharmakuya), Samantabhadra, Vairocana and others.

4. The philosophical doctrine of the old church stuck to the central conception of separate elements of Matter, Mind, and Forces, composed lists of them with a view to investigate the method of their gradual extinction in the Absolute.

5. Among the early schools of the Mahasamghikafs, Vatsiputriyas and others already assumed a kind of consciousness surviving in Nirvana.

6. They were followed by a school with critical tendencies, the Sautrantikas, which cut down the list of artificially constructed elements, cut down Nirvana itself as a separate entity and transferred the Absolute into the living world, thus constituting a transition to Mahayana.

7. The philosophy of the new religion (Mahayana) is an adaptation of the Vedanta system. It forsook the pluralistic principal altogether and became emphatically monistic.

8. It then took a double course. It either assumed the existence of a store-consciousness of which all phenomenal life was but a manifestation. This school in the sequel cultivated logic. The other school denied the possibility of cognizing the Absolute by logical methods, it declared all plurality to be an illusion, and nothing short of the whole to be the Reality directly cognized in mystic intuition.

9. The transitional school of the Sautrantikas coalesced in the 5th century A.D. with the idealistic school of the Mahayana and produced India's greatest philosophers, Dignaga and Dharmakirti. With regard to Nirvana it assumed the existence of a pure spiritual principle, in which object and subject coalesced, and along with it, a

force of transcendental illusion (vasana) producing the phenomenal world.

10. Contemporaneously with this highest development of Buddhist philosophy, in the 7th century A.D., the relativist school of early Mahayana received a fresh impulse and a revival of popularity. This led to the formation of new hybrid schools.

11. ... both the idealistic and relativistic schools of Buddhism...(influenced) all philosophical circles of India, and we see in the next period the old Vedanta remodeled and equipped with fresh arguments by an adaptation to it of the methods elaborated in the Vijnravada and Sunyavada schools of Buddliism.[32]

It must be added, however, that the truth advocated by Buddhism was more than sheer philosophy. Ultimately, the truth was understood to be a means to achieve Nirvana. Sakyamuni himself was a tireless evangelist of this Good Law, and he commissioned his disciples to proclaim the Gospel for the conversion of the whole world.

From the beginning, the Sangha or monastic fellowship was considered the normative path for the followers of the Buddha. According to Geden:

The monastic order in Buddhism... was not essentially a new creation in India, but was derived from ancient Hindu usage and practice...The distinctive feature of the Buddhist order, in which it was differentiated from its predecessors, and to which, in large part at least, it owed its wide extension and success, was the removal of all restrictions of caste...The community of monks as a whole was known as the Sangha, or order, and with the Buddha himself and the Dharma, the sacred rule or law, formed a Buddhist triad, each member of which was idealized and invested with a sacred character, and ultimately became the object of a definite worship.[33]

---

[32] Th. Stcherbatsky, *The Conception of Buddhist Nirvana* (Leningrad, 1927), pp. 60-62,

[33] A. S. Geden, *"Monasticism (Buddhism),"* in E. R. E., Vol. VIII, p. 797.

Originally, Sakyamuni in creating the *Sangha* took the name and the constitutional form of the political *sangha* which was practiced in northeastern India in his time.[34] To him, the ecclesiastical Sangha and the political sangha existed side by side in mutual trust and harmony. The gradual institutionalization of the Buddhist Sangha necessitated the formulation of regulations governing the relation between the Sangha and society. In the course of time, Buddhist monastic law (vinaya) was recognized by the secular authorities in India.[35] As Buddhism penetrated other parts of Asia, it helped interpret existing political orders in Buddhist terms, even though it never articulated what might be termed a Buddhist political theory. In the main, Buddhism modified and sanctioned existing political orders throughout Asia. One might view the Buddhist expansion as a process of "secularization." However, it also had the effect of narrowing the gulf between the Sangha and culture.

Some scholars claim that "only the Monastic Orders could be called specifically Buddhist at any time."[36] However, from the beginning the lay disciples were regarded as something like associate members of the Sangha. Gradually the laity began to play an important role in ecclesiastical affairs, and in the Mahayana countries the Sangha came to embrace all of the faithful, monastic or otherwise.

The institutional Sangha, however, does not exhaust the religious meaning of the Sangha. Different traditions of Buddhism -- Hinayana, Mahayana, and Mantrayana -- all subscribe to the "theological" concept of the Sangha universal, of which the empirical Sangha is but an incomplete manifestation. Ultimately, Buddhism rises or falls with its triad- Buddha, Dharma, and Sangha. Among the three, the most crucial is the Sangha, precisely because it is rooted in two realms -- in faith and in the concrete institutional structure. A reconciliation of these two realms of the Sangha is an urgent task of Buddhists in the contemporary world. This is one of the underlying themes of the Sixth Great Buddhist Council, which is being held in Rangoon today.

---

[34] Richard A. Gard, *Buddhist Influence on the Political Thought and Institutions of India and Japan* (Claremont; Society for Oriental Studies, 1949), pp. 2-3 and 4-9.

[35] Ibid, p. 12.

[36] T. R. V. Murti, "Radhakrishnan and Buddhism," in *The Philosophy of Sarvepalli Radhakrishnan* (Mew York: Tudor, 1952), p,604.

CHRISTIANITY AND BUDDHISM IN THE CONTEMPORARY WORLD

In discussing the relation of Christianity and Buddhism, a student of religions cannot talk in abstract terms. Thus, it may be helpful to use Morrison's definition of Christianity:

> ... instead of seeking a definition of Christianity in terms of its essence, we seek to define it as a phenomenon. Can we lay hold of Christianity as a concrete and objective phenomenon, having an identifiable integrity and continuity despite all its inner changes and despite the multiplicity of its "essences" and the inexhaustible richness of its contents? If our problem is thus stated and if we then ask, "What is Christianity?" we shall not be primarily concerned with its specific doctrines, or its institutional forms, or its particular experiences, or its ethical standards, or any other of its specific contents. What we wish to know is, what is it that contains these contents. [37]

For Morrison, the container of the Christian contents is the Christian community. However, we like to think that the Church is the container of the Christian contents, inasmuch as the Church is more than the empirical, historical community of the faithful. Indeed, as Trinterud rightly points out:

> The Church of Jesus Christ, in all ages, and under all-historical circumstances has in the final analysis regarded itself as a people of God, a people related to God by the redemption which comes through Jesus Christ. This then is the Church Catholic -- in every age, in all situations, and beyond all those institutional forms in which it finds expression -- redemption through Christ under the circumstances of historical existence. Where there is redemption through Christ in history, there is the Church his Body. [38]

---

[37] C. C. Morrison, *What is Christianity?* (Chiciago: Clark & Co., 1940), pp. 10-11.

[38] L. J. Trinterud, "The Task of the American Church Historian," *Church History*, Vol. XXV, No. 3, March, 1956, pp, 3-15.

From the beginning, the Church had a dual character. The paradoxical nature of the church was already foreshadowed in the pre-Christian Hebrew church. The Israelites were both the "socio-cultural assembly of the people of God" and the "covenanted-worshipping community," In the New Testament, we find two events corresponding to these two aspects of the church. One is Jesus' commissioning of the twelve disciples, and the other the Pentecost. When Jesus called the twelve, he did not call men of like-minded disposition, nor did he create monastic fellowship. The twelve were the Israel -- the assembly of the people. Then, on the day of Pentecost, these disciples as the assembly of the people received the gift of the Spirit. Here the spiritual and communal bonds were woven together. These two events -- the commissioning of the twelve and the Pentecost -- must be seen together in order to appreciate the paradoxical nature of the church. Here the spiritual covenant and the sociocultural community are fused into a new unity. And the conviction of the historic Christian community has been that both the worshipping group and the socio-cultural community owe their allegiance ultimately to God, the Lord of history and of nature. [39] Thus, according to Van Der Leeuw:

> A church actually exists solely in Christianity; for neither the Buddhist monastic community, nor that of Islam resting on the principle of mere agreement and conformity, nor again the Judaic assembly of the people, merits the title of church. This historic fact, still further, is intimately connected with the church's essential nature, since it arose from the concrete historical situation which the Jews' rejection of Christ, and the subsequent turning towards the heathen, brought in their train. In this concrete situation, then, there subsists on the one hand the transition from community to covenant, but on the other the concentration of the heathen religious consciousness, already manifested in various types of covenant, into a community given in a new manner...in its essence the church is the Body of Christ...The church is therefore visible-invisible at once humanly organized and mystically animated, spiritual and cosmic.[40]

---

[39] Van der Leeuw, op cit., p. 265.

[40] Ibid, p. 266 also cf. L. S. Thornton, *The Common Life in the Body of Christ* (London: Dacre Press, 1942.}

From the beginning, Christians believed that the Body of Christ becomes concretized in the local church. With the gradual institutionalization of the empirical church, tradition began to play an important role. In this connection, Flesseman reminds us that tradition for the Apostolic Fathers was "the preaching of the church as the way in which revelation reaches man."[41]

> Conceived in this way tradition is ... the very essence and life of the church. For the church is where the revelation becomes actual, in proclamation (including the sacraments) and teaching ... Church and tradition are indissolubly bound together and determine each other. For wherever revelation is really transmitted, i.e., is proclaimed and taught, there is church. But also: the real church in her message transmits necessarily the revelation and gives voice to it. All this, however, is unqualifiedly true only as long as we remain conscious of the fact that church and tradition are matters of faiths ... In the visible church and her doctrine expressing itself in preaching and teaching, we recognize by faith, and in no other way, the church which transmits the apostolic tradition. [42]

In A.D. 313, by the Edict of Milan, the persecuted church became the church of the empire. The inevitable secularization of the church together with the rise of monasticism introduced a principle of duality. As Neill observes:

> Where monasticism is regarded as a special vocation within a Christian society which in its totality is redemptive, the integrity of the Church is preserved. If, however, the ascetic vocation is regarded as essentially higher than the vocation of the Christian in the world, still more if it is regarded as the only effective means of salvation, the Church outside the cloister is in danger of losing its sense of obligation to be salt and leaven...[43]

It is a matter of interest to note that while Buddhism, which started as a monastic movement, eventually developed into an all-

---

[41]   E. Flesseman-Van Leer, *Tradition and Scripture in the Early Church*, (Assen: Van Gorcum, 1954), 186.

[42]   Ibid. pp. 186-187.

[43]   Stephen Neill, *The Christian Society* (New York: Harper, 1952), pp. 55-56.

embracing Sangha, Christianity which started as a lay movement developed monasticism within it.

The complex development of the Christian church has been ably treated by Troeltsch,[44] despite his own conviction that Christianity and Western culture are inseparable. Time does not allow us to discuss the historic relation between the church and culture. Suffice it to mention H. Richard Niebuhr's penetrating work, *Christ and Culture,* which discusses the five alternative ways in which the historic church wrestled with the problem of relating the church and cultural society, under the suggestive headings: (1) Christ against culture, (2) The Christ of culture, (3) Christ above culture, (4) Christ and culture in paradox, and (5) Christ the transformer of culture.[45]

For a long time the church was coterminous with European culture. Western Christendom did not extend its influence outside Europe until the 16th century. The early Protestant Reformers did not take an active part in missionary work among non-Christians. Organized Christian missionary work outside Europe was initiated by the Counter Reformers, notably the Jesuits. By the 18th century, however, Protestant missionary work began to supersede the Roman Catholic missionary program. Ironically, the Protestant missionary movement coincided with Deism and Rationalism in Europe and Great Britain. In the words of Dawson:

> The dynamic force in the new movement (of Rationalism) came not from the critical rationalism of Voltaire and his friends, but from the romantic humanitarianism of Rousseau… He provided the new social gospel which was to take the place of orthodox Christianity as the moral basis of Western society and the spiritual inspiration of Western culture… No doubt this creed differed little in formal content from the beliefs of the rationalists. It was equally hostile to religious authority and tradition, and it shared with the Deists their doctrine of Natural Religion …

---

[44] Ernst Troeltsch, *The Social Teachings of the Christian Churches*, tr. by Olive Wyon (New York: Macmillan Co., 1531).

[45] H. Richard Niebuhr, *Christ and Culture* (New York: Harper, 1951).

... One wing of the rationalist movement went on towards scientific materialism, while the other turned back towards philosophic intellectualism. [46]

In a sense, Pietism, which motivated the Protestant missionary movement, was a reaction against rationalism as well as Protestant scholasticism. Thus, while European rationalists were enchanted by the discovery of Natural Religion in China and India, Pietists were determined to save the heathens from hellfire.

It must be remembered that the Protestant churches in Europe developed, in the main, as state churches, and that the spiritual care of colonial peoples was considered a responsibility of the temporal ruler. This explains why, in the 18th century, many of the private missionary societies did not receive much encouragement from the official church bodies in Europe. Nor did they receive much cooperation from colonial officials. Only in the 19th century, when Western colonial powers became conscious of spreading the gospel of Western culture in their colonies, did the colonial rulers begin to look upon the work of missionaries with favor. There is no doubt that, by and large, missionaries found it convenient to carry on their work under the umbrella of colonial powers, even though a few of them such as Hudson Taylor did not consciously take advantage of the prestige of the West. Thus, European colonial interests and missionary interests became interdependent in the mission field.

In the meantime, a totally different development was taking place in American Protestantism. American Protestant bodies may be characterized by their biblicism in theological temperament,[47] and "denominational type" in institutional form.[48] The combined effect of Biblicism and a voluntaristic, denominational structure made American Protestant churches gigantic missionary organizations. After the turn of the century, American Protestants played an increasingly important role in the mission field, and two schools of thought in American Protestantism – the Social Gospel and Fundamentalism -- left their marks on their daughter-churches in Asia and Africa.

---

[46] Christopher Dawson, *Enquiries into Religion and Culture* (New York: Sheed & Ward, 1933), pp. 150-151.

[47] Jerald C. Brauer, *Protestantism in America* (Philadelphia: The Westminster Press, 1953), pp. 7-8.

[48] Joachim Wach, *Types of Religious Experience* (Chicago: The University of Chicago Press, 1951), Chap, IX, "Church, Denomination and Sect," pp. 187-208.

Toynbee argues that in the recent encounter of the East and the West, it was the advance of the West which awakened the East from its centuries long slumber,[49] and there is a great deal of truth in his observation. However, it might be more accurate to say that the advance of the West coincided with the general decline of Eastern cultures in the 18th and 19th centuries, and that the East was in a peculiarly receptive mood to Western influence until the beginning of the 20th century. During this period, Christian missionary policy unconsciously assumed the eventual Westernization of the East. Therefore, initially Western missionaries established the so-called "Mission Compound," in which new native converts were isolated from their pagan surroundings. For all practical purposes these mission compounds were regarded as cultural colonies of the West. Unfortunately, the mission compounds developed into self-perpetuating institutions, identified as the norm of the Christian church in many parts of Asia. Even today, many native Christians in Asia feel closer emotionally to Western Christians than to their non-Christian neighbors. We must understand the strength and weakness of the so-called younger churches in this historic setting.[50]

The situation since the turn of the century has been very complex. Easterners, who previously felt helpless in the wake of the advance of Western culture and civilization have begun to aspire for equality and self-determination in politics and economics, as well as in other spheres of life. The issue is no longer defined in terms of the acceptance or rejection of Western technology, but of the life or death of Eastern spiritual heritage.

> ... It is not yet certain what will be the upshot of this impact of East and West, this tremendous spiritual struggle which is taking place.
>
> What is the struggle about?... The spirit which comes from the West is forcing an entrance, and can no longer be withstood, the 'new flood of thought' permeates irresistibly all departments of life; not even the innermost region of the religious life re mains untouched. It affects man's whole being. The question is whether in the end the man of the East will have lost himself, whether he will be hopelessly subservient to the spirit of the West or whether

---

[49] Arnold Toynbee, *The World and the West* (New York: Oxford University Press, 1953).

[50] Joseph Kitagawa, "The Case of the Younger Churches," in *Pastoral Psychology*, Vol. 5, No.45 June, 1954, pp. 27-31.

he will emerge from the encounter a new man, who has found the way to a peculiar, creative, reshaping of his life, *as a nation and as a person.* In this sense it is a question of life or death. Only as a new man can the man of the East dominate the tremendous crisis which has come on him and which in breadth and depth is unparalleled in the history of mankind. [51]

In the spiritual struggle of the East, however, the man of the East must be understood, not only "as a man and as a nation" but as a member of religious communities.

It has been said that Asia is undergoing a three-fold revolution today; first, a revolt against colonialism; second, a social and economic revolution; and third, a determination that Asia will be its own master.[52] In this situation, it is too superficial to say, as many do, that the resurgence of Eastern religions is motivated solely by the spirit of nationalism. Undoubtedly, the newly gained political independence of many of the Asiatic nations is an important asset to Eastern religions. But we will do a gross injustice if we do not feel the pulse of the dynamic spiritual awakening in Asia. In this sense, the Sixth Great Buddhist Council is a symbol of new Asia, which with all its independent nation-states is attempting to find a unified religious institutionalized form.

In surveying the situation in Asia today, we cannot help but feel alarmed at the rapid growth of Communism in China and elsewhere. However, we should remind ourselves that:

> Communism is not the same as the social revolution which is shaking... our complacent world of traditional values. Nor have Communists brought it about. What the Communists claim to do is to explain the revolution and to have the right of leading it to a successful end. [53]

Indeed, Communism presents a serious challenge both to the Christian Church and to non-Christian religions. The leaders of the Buddhist Sangha, together with leaders of other Eastern religions, are

---

[51] Walter Freytag, *Spiritual Revolution in the East*, tr. by L, M. Stalker (London: Lutterworth Press, I940), pp. 18-19.

[52] W. MacMahon Ball, *Nationalism and Communism in East Asia*, Melbourne; Melbourne University Press, 1952), p. 1.

[53] *Communism and the Social Revolution in India*, ed, by P. D. Devanandan & M. M. Thomas (Calcutta: Y.M. C.A, Publishing House, 1953), p. 7.

making a serious attempt to address themselves to the social, economic, and political issues, and to translate their doctrines into a concrete program. On this score., Christians in Asia feel the disadvantage of being a minority and of not having participated in shouldering political responsibilities in their native lands.

The problem of the relation between Christianity and Buddhism in the Far Eastern religious context may be stated in terms of the relation between the Church and the Sangha. Today, the Sangha is digging deep into its doctrine, cult, and tradition to define an adequate relation between the Sangha Universal and the empirical Buddhist communities which are involved in multi-dimensional problems in various parts of Asia. The Christian Church is also trying to rediscover the nature of its being, both in the Ecumenical Movement and in global confessionalism, even though these two forces often drive the younger churches to a schizophrenic solution. Basically, both Buddhism and Christianity are supracultural religions, despite their historic conditioning factors.

In recent years, various theories have been advanced concerning the Christian approach to non-Christians.[54] Also, many non-Christians have advocated their views of Christianity. [55]But the problem is not confined to doctrinal matters. For instance, both Christianity and Buddhism are historic communities of faith, involved to be sure in all aspects of cultures both in the West and East. No one can predict the future of the relation of these supra-cultural religions, I do not subscribe to either "continuity or discontinuity," I cannot discuss the relation between Christianity and Buddhism in abstract terms. The fact is plain: both Christianity and Buddhism are destined to relate their messages to the same cultures, and establish their churches and sanghas in the same cultural areas. Undoubtedly, there will be some mutual borrowing and mutual influencing. But as for me, believing as a member of the Body of Christ, I can only witness to the presence of the Church Catholic. In the words of Newman:

> The phenomenon, admitted on all hands is this: That a great portion of what is generally received as Christian truth is, in its rudiments or in its separate parts, to be found

---

[54] E. C. Devdck, *The Christian Attitude to Other Religions* (Cambridge: The University Press, 1949)| Kraemer, op. cit, Rajah B, Mairikam, ed., *Christianity and the Asian Revolution* (New York: Friendship Press, 1954), Chap, VI," "The Christian Approach to Non-Christian Religions," pp. 185-209.

[55] Cf. S. Kadhakrishnan. *Recovery of Faith* (New York: Harper, 1955), D. T. Suzuki, *Living by Zen* (New York: Rider, 1950).

in heathen philosophies and religions...Mr. Milman argues from it, "These things are in heathenism, therefore they are not Christian"; we, on the contrary, prefer to say, "These things are in Christianity, therefore they are not heathen." That is, we prefer to say, and we think that Scripture bears us out in saying, that from the beginning the Moral Governor of the world has scattered the seeds of truth far and wide over its extent; that these have variously taken root, and grown up as in the wilderness, wild plants indeed but living...

What man is amid the brute creation, such is the Church among the schools of the world; and as Adam gave names to the animals about him, so has the Church from the first looked round upon the earth, noting and visiting the doctrines she found there. She began in Chaldea, and then sojourned among the Canaanites, and went down into Egypt, and thence passed into Arabia, till she rested in her own land. Next she encountered the merchants of Tyre, and the wisdom of the East country, and the luxury of Sheba. Then she was carried away to Babylon, and wandered to the schools of Greece. And wherever she went, in trouble or in triumph, still she was a living spirit, the mind and voice of the Most High; "sitting in the midst of the doctors, both hearing them and asking them questions;" claiming to herself what they said rightly, correcting their errors, supplying their defects, completing their beginnings, expanding their surmises, and thus gradually by means of them enlarging the range and refining the sense of her own teaching. So far, then, from her creed being of doubtful credit because it resembles foreign theologies, we even hold that one special way in which Providence has imparted divine knowledge to us has been by enabling us to draw and collect it together out of the world and, in this sense, as in others, to "suck the milk of the Gentiles and to suck the breast of kings." [56]

---

[56] John Henry Newman, *Essays Critical and Historical* (New York: Longmans, Green and Co., 1897), vol. II,, pp. 231-232.

Early Protestant Views of Hinduism: 1600 - 1825

Norvin Hein
Yale Divinity School

The question of the Christian view of Hinduism remains as acute as ever for the church today, externally and internally. In foreign missions there is no consensus on this matter, and within Christian lands certain forms of Hinduism stand almost alone in power to attract respectful attention of thinking western people to eastern religion. Our greatest modern books on Christianity and the non-Christian religions are based primarily on Hinduism or deal prominently with that faith. Their authors could not have done otherwise.

This paper attempts to make a historian's contribution to the discussion of the problem. It undertakes a survey of how Protestant writers have described and interpreted Hinduism during the earlier part of the three and a half centuries in which Protestants and Hindus have been in contact. We shall confine our attention to authors who were avowedly Christian in training and occupation, who were acquainted with Indian religion at first hand, and who wrote on Hinduism in some detail, We stop with the year 1825 because our present tradition of Protestant missions in India was well-begun by that time, and the nature of Protestant thinking about Hinduism thereafter is likely to be relatively well known to students of the history of missions. The time of pristine impressionability among Protestants was then past, also. Distinctive attitudes were already established. Some were of recent formation, and some had been long developing in generations of writers whose works we seldom hear of, and almost never read. Our concern here is with those early books, now yellow and crumbling, whoso influence upon us calls for recognition precisely because it has been forgotten.

We do not foolishly suppose that this survey of past attitudes will enable us to produce, by totaling and averaging, the definitive Christian view of Hinduism, or be in itself the creative reconsideration of the matter which our age demands. But fresh thinking begins with self -knowledge. Discussion of the direction we should take will be more pertinent and productive when we realize that we travel in tracks worn deep by our predecessors, know where the grooves of inherited predisposition run, and why.

Protestant interpretation of Hinduism begins only with the seventeenth century. Only after the defeat of the Spanish Armada had upset the Iberian control of the seas could groups in Protestant lands dream of organized communication with India. Between 1600 and 1618 commercial companies were formed in England, Holland, and Denmark to establish trade relations. The first Protestants in India were not missionaries but merchants and diplomats engaged in commercial negotiations. But with the trading fleets and ambassadorial parties came chaplains. Being men of literary education, and having a personal interest in religion, these clergymen sometimes turned their pens from writing sermons to describing the non-Christian religious life they saw about them. Therefore our chronological account of treatises on the "Gentiles" of India begins with the writings of the chaplains.

1. EDWARD TORRY, 1590-1660.

The Reverand Edward Terry, just out of Oxford, took a chaplaincy with a fleet of the East India Company and served in India for three years with the diplomatic party of Sir Thomas Roe, at the court of the Emperor Jehangir. When home again, he wrote up his India experiences and presented them in 1622 to Prince Charles. When this account was printed in 1625 in Samuel Purchas' *Pilgrimes*,[1] Protestantism received its first eyewitness account of Hinduism from one of its own. His chapter on the "Gentiles," though a sensible document, is neither very extensive nor very profound. With no helps save his two eyes and a smattering of Persian, he managed to get into his notes only a miscellany of observations on external Hindu life and customs. The Hindu widows practice of burning themselves alive

---

[1]   Samuel Purchas, *Pilgrimes* (London, 1625), II, 1464-1482; published again in Terry's *A Voyage to East India.*, 1655, 2nd ed. 1777. Translated into French in 1696 and into Dutch in 1707. Also in William Foster, ed., *Early Travels in India* (Humphrey Milford, Oxford University Press, 1921), pp. 288-332.

with their husband's bodies -- a "hellish sacrifice" -- drew his shocked attention, like that of all western visitors since the earliest times. The rest of his reporting is unexcited and unexciting. Terry confesses that he has not gotten far with the religious doctrines of the Brahmans. These priests, he says, are illiterate, and "scarce know what they hold." Consequently he is helpless to give an account of what he calls the twenty-four sects, whose beliefs "had oftentimes filled me with wonder, but that I know Satan (the father of division) to be the seducer of them all." Despite this reference to the devil, Terry's general description of Hinduism is not hostile. Neither is it much given to applying Christian standards of criticism. At the end of the chapter he enters his one specific complaint, from the standpoint of a man of the Renaissances:

> The summe is that both Mahometans and Gentiles ground their opinions upon tradition, not reason; and are content to perish with their forefathers...never ruminating on what they maintain, like unclean beasts which chew not the cud. [2]

2. HENRY LORD, B. 1563.

Henry Lord was chaplain of the East India Company post at Surat from 1624 to 1629. In 1630 he published his *Display of Two Forraigne Sects in the East Indies*, [3] dealing with the Parsi faith as well as with the "Banian religion", or Hinduism, This work is the first full-scale treatise on Indian religion written by a Protestant, In his introduction Lord tells us how he gathered his data: he approached certain Brahmans of Surat through interpreters and by their assistance made his collection "out of a book of theirs called the SHASTER, which is to them as their Bible..." Fourteen chapters follow which claim to describe the contents of their books of ceremonial and moral law and to set forth the teaching of the Hindus regarding the creation of the world by "the great God," the peopling of the earth with men of the four castes, the history of the ages before and after the Flood, and the future judgment of the world by fire.

---

[2]   Foster, op. cit., p. 325.

[3]   (London, Francis Constable, 1630). Republished in French, Paris, 1667, and in English in Bernard Picart, *The Religious Ceremonies and Customs of the Several Nations of the Known World*, III, (London, Nicholas Provost, 1731, pp. 273-308; in Awnsham Churchill, *A Collection of Voyages and Travels*, VI (London, 1732), pp. 299-342; and in John Pinkerton, *A General Collection of the Best and Most Interesting Voyages and Travels in All Parts of the World*, VIII London, Longman etc., 1811, pp. 523 -555.

In reading Lord's pages one senses that he has listened, more or less, to the relation of some genuine cosmological material from the puranas: the many unrecognizable proper names in his text have an Indian sound, and he weaves a number of authentic Hindu concepts into the fabric of his tale. But it is clear enough that Lord did not understand the half of what was told him, and that he made good what he had missed with the help of the Bible, the classics, and a mind filled with seventeenth-century ideas on the origin and history of religion. He imposed upon the mass of material which he had assembled a form which he borrowed from the Pentateuch, and turned out as his final product a fabulous, convivial cosmological romance. It served as an effective piece of recruiting literature for the East India Company for many a day.

Purusha and Prakriti, the two primordial principles of the Samkchya philosophy, appear in Lord's fantasia as the Adam and Eve of the Hindu Genesis, the parents of four sons who begat the principal castes, Brahma is the Hindu Moses, and in the midst of a dark cloud on Mount Meru (his Sinai) he receives the *sastra* from the Lord God Almighty! When he undertakes to give the content of those sastras he actually describes the visible moral and ritual observances of his own time, and presents some pages of relatively sober and factual observation. On the whole the book is an excellent example of the human tendency to force strange ideas through the die of established concepts and understand the utterly new in terms of the familiar.

Mr. Lord tells his tale with such gusto that he seldom pauses to register a reaction to what he relates. He offers a refutation of Hindu vegetarianism and tee-totaling, but on the basis of the classics rather than Christian principles. He says in his brief conclusion that the study of these superstitious fictions show "how Satan leadeth those that are out of the pale of the church, a round, in the maze of error and gentilisme." The chief profit to be gained from it is "to settle us in the solidnesse of our own faith, which is purged of all such leuities…" *The Dictionary of National Biography* says that Lord dedicated the original edition to the Archbishop of Canterbury, expressing a hope that His Grace might see fit to suppress such idolatries.

The reader will recognize from all that has been said that in 1630 grave and responsible writing on Hinduism had not yet begun.

3. ABRAHAM ROGER, D. 1649

Intensive Protestant study of Hinduism begins with the work of a Dutch Calvinist minister named Abraham Roger or Rogcrius, Roger was the first chaplain of the Dutch East India Company's station at Paliacatta (Pulicat) north of Madras. He served there from 1631 to 1641, spent five additional years in Java, and retired to Holland in 1647. Two years later he died leaving an unpublished manuscript. Through the efforts of his widow it was published posthumously in Leiden in 1651 as *De Open-Deurc tot hot Vorborgen Heydendom.*[4]

Roger had developed a happy and fruitful cooperation in Paliacatta with a Portuguese-speaking Brahman of the place named Padmanäbha. Though Roger was not entirely ignorant of Tamil, evidently he was in no position to use its literature. Again and again he acknowledges in his book his total dependence on his Brahman friend for extensive areas of information. Roger contributed a wide curiosity and a thoroughness and fairness of mind, and produced a book which honors both its collaborators. A model of comprehensive and compact information, it is still profitable reading for those interested in traditional South Indian Hinduism.

The first twenty chapters of the book describe the life and manners of the Bradmans. First we have an almost modern sociological description of the caste hierarchy and of the contemporary sects of Brahman householders and sannyasis. We are told what the Brahmans' prerogatives and incomes are, their customs in childhood, marriage, and keeping house, and their funeral rites. The second half of the book details the Brahman beliefs: on God and on the gods; on Vishnu's incarnations, the cosmic ages, man's soul and the afterlife; and it describes the manner in which Hindus build temples, observe their festivals, and go on pilgrimages. Through Padmanabha Roger is able to append to his work a translation of the *Vairägyasatakam* of Bhartrihari -- the first Sanskrit work to be translated into any European language.

---

[4]   (Leyden, Franyoys Hackos, 1651). New Dutch od. by W. Caland, ('s-Gravcnhage, Martinus Nijhoff, 1915). German tr., *Abraham Rogers Offne Thür zur dem Verborgenen Heydenthum* (Nürnberg, J.A.Enders, 1663. French tr. by Thomas La Grue, *Le theatre de l'idolatrie, ou la porte ouverte pour parvenir a la cognoissance du paganisme cache* (Amsterdam, Joan   Schipper, 16707. Abridged English version (unreliable in text and translation) in Bernard Picart, *The Religious Ceremonies and Customs of the Several Nations of the Known World*, III (London, Nicholas "Provost, 1731) pp. 309-364.

Roger's first and fundamental accomplishment was his success in breaking through the barrier of mutual irritation and contempt which separated Christians and Brahmans throughout all this early period. Almost all writers of the time complain of how arrogant and aloof are the proud Brahmans, and of how few of them are educated well enough to be informative even if they are willing. In Padmanabha, Roger was fortunate in finding a broad-minded, intelligent and cooperative pandit of better-than-average education. At only a few points did his information fail. The account of the four Vedas which he gave to Roger bears no relation to the facts: Padmanabha could not read the Vedas and was misinformed about them himself. Also, being exclusively a Vaishnava and a theist by education and conviction, he gave Roger no hint that a powerful non-theistic monism exists among Hindus. Thus he left Roger with a too-simple certainty that all Indians adhere to a monotheism much like our own:

> No one must think that these heathen are just like beasts. On the contrary, we should testify to the opposite. Navigation has made known to us that there is no people so brutal and deprived of sense and judgment that they do not know that there is one God, and have no religion. Thus those pagans also recognize one God. We have said in Part I Chapter 3 that the Vaishnavas say that Vishnu, who is also named Perumäl and a thousand other names, is the sovereign God; but the Saivas say that it is not Vishnu but Isvara, whom they name by a thousand names also, that is the sovereign God; so that they acknowledge not only that there is one God, but that there is one sovereign God who is sole and unique, with none superior to Him or like Him.[5]

Much water was yet to go over the mill before any European would become familiar with the total range of Hindu theologies and philosophies and be in a sound position to discuss whether Hindus are or are not believers in the One God.

Roger's descriptions are starkly factual; he does not inject evaluations into them. Yet when a strong criticism is called for, he neither hesitates to make it, nor lingers to scandalize over it. In the twentieth chapter of Part One he gives full descriptive details of how Brahman widows are burned. "An inhuman cruelty!" he exclaims, "One can't even

---

[5]   From La Gruo's French version, pp. 139-141, cf. Caland's Dutch text, p. 86.

think without horror of these cruel and frightful things. Yet they are true, and are practiced in that place!" then he goes on to the next topic.

Roger in no place explains what his views are on the relationship between Christianity and Hinduism. The devil is not mentioned anywhere as Hinduism's special patron.[6] Perhaps death deprived Roger of the opportunity to explain his theological perspective. One Andreas Wissowatius, Netherlands lawyer and friend, provided a theological introduction to the first edition in which he credits the Hindus with a natural knowledge, but not a saving knowledge, of God. Though the doctrine we find in this introduction is not out of keeping with the general tone of Roger's text, we have no assurance that it expresses his views.

4. Philip Baldaeus, 1632-1672

The Reformed clergy of the Netherlands produced in the next generation a worthy successor to Roger in Philip Baldaeus. Beginning in 1656 he served as chaplain to the Dutch forces engaged in wresting dominance from the Portuguese in Indian waters. From 1661 to 1666 he was settled down at Jafna as pastor in charge of the churches of that northern outpost of Ceylon. He published in 1672 an extensive and valuable account of the historical events in which he had been involved; his *Naauwkeurige Beschrijvinge van Malabar en Choromandel en het Eylandt Ceylon, nevens de Afgoderije der Oost-Indiche Heydenen.*[7] The final part of this work is, in itself, a major treatise on Hinduism. It is primarily a compendium of myths of the more important gods of South Indian polytheism. The ten *avatäras* of Vishnu -- and especially the Krishna incarnation -- are described in detail. For the first time, we find a synopsis of the story of the Mahäbhärata.

---

[6]   La Gruo's French edition of 1670 shows in its frontispiece a scene of the devil hovering in the air and rejoicing over a widow burning. Roger was not the source of this picture, of course. Neither was Roger responsible for an interpolation, existing in the English version only (p. 347), saying that Hindu marriage is no better than prostitution because it is not sanctified by Christian rites.

[7]   Amsterdam, J. J. van Waesberge, 1672). Modern Dutch edition of the portion on Hinduism by Albert Johannes deJong, *Afgderije der Oost-Indischo Heydcmon* ('s-Gravenhagc, M. Nijhoff, 1917). German tr., *Wahräftaftigo Ausführliche Beschreibung der Berühmten Oost-indischen Kusten der Malabar und Coromandel* (Amsterdam, van Waesberge, 1672). Slightly Abridged English translation in Awrsham and John Churchill, *A Collection of Voyages and Travels*, II [London 1704), pp. 562-901.

There is a great deal more of confusion in this book than in Roger's, because Baldaeus was drawing upon a multiplicity of sources instead of one, and had no better linguistic equipment than his predecessor for resolving conflicts in what he heard. Baldaeus complains that the press of ecclesiastical duties left him with little time for study of the Malabar (Tamil) tongue, and in consequence "...I was forced to be content with what part thereof I could attain..."[8] He says that in preparing his work he has made wide enquiries with the help of a Ceylonese member of his church named Francis de Fonscca; and he has consulted much with a Bengali Brahman who resided in Jafna. Also he uses certain "Portuguese histories" left on the island by his Jesuit predecessors. He knows Roger's book and comments on its information. Occasionally he cites the published comments of other Europeans regarding Indian customs.

The Bengali Brahman was his source for an ample account of all the sports of Krishna, more or less after the Bhagavata Purana. His tales of the other gods show many a departure from the classical literary versions that must have been picked up from the local traditions. About the content of the Vedas he can neither add to, nor subtract from, Roger's misinformation. Like Roger also, he has heard of no level of Hindu though above the mythological. He is at a loss in writing Indian names. They come to him from at least the Sanskrit, Tamil, and Malayalam languages, and they come in the disguise of romanizations that sometimes represent Portuguese sound values and sometimes Dutch. He is therefore found referring to Parasurāma as "Prassaram" and "Siri Parexi Rama" on the same page,[9] and hesitates between Dasserat, Daseratha, and Daexareda as the name of Rāma's father. He docs not recognize that "Ramtzander" is identical with the "Ram" whose career as seventh incarnation of Vishnu he has just described. Not knowing adequately any of the languages which contribute to this Babel, he can not avoid confusions of identity nor develop a consistent system of spelling Indian names.

But even after noting all these shortcomings, we must still credit Baldaeus with adding significantly to Europe's knowledge of Hinduism. He ranks with Roger because he used Roger's method, continued his virtues, and added no shortcomings of which Roger would not have been guilty in the same circumstances. These two men, together, represent the maximum achievement that was possible, humanly speaking, by the method of enquiry in a foreign language. They effected what industry, carefulness, and good judgment could accomplish under this handicap.

---

[8]   Churchill, op. cit., p. 663.

[9]   ibid., p. 858.

Baldaeus' treatment of Hinduism is generally objective, and at critical points, kindly. In relating certain Krishna-myths he often ignores a sensational alternative form of the story, or a scandalous interpretation which was surely known to him. He makes no capital of such opportunities. Like other Europeans, he yellows a little at the sight of devout Hindus obtaining and sipping cow's urine, and is shocked by various uses of dung: "The Malabar women, the otherwise pretty cleanly, yet are so intoxicated to this Superstition, that they cleanse their Chambers and their Cisterns with Cowdung."[10] (From the first, the Indian uses of cow excreta degraded Hinduism in most Western eyes.) Baldaeus spares the Hindus any extensive expose of "that most barbarous custom" of sati, but uses the occasion to close "with a hearty wish, that these poor wretches, quite entangled in the darkness of paganism, may thro his mercy, and with the assistance of such magistrates as ought to keep a watchful eye over their actions, be in time brought to the true knowledge of the Gospel."[11]

Baldaeus seems to regard the Hindus as monotheists in some sense, since he asserts there is no nation that does not acknowledge a God or Supreme Being. [12] He considers that various Hindu teachings show that in the past some confused report of Jesus Christ has been heard in India: the fact that Brahmä is regarded as creator of the world, determiner of the duration of created things, Son of God, possessor of a human nature, and Governor of Angels;[13] the similarity of certain infancy tales of Krishna to the Biblical flight into Egypt and the murder of the innocents; [14] the belief that "Ramtzander" delivered his people from the giants, and that the Buddha is invisible and was born without father and mother. [15] He does not label any part of Hinduism as the work of the devil. Although he does not discuss the theological status of Hinduism, in these respects he evidences a rather positive view.

However, in one interesting instance he prefers to interpret a similarity between eastern and western belief as evidence that paganism has crept into Christianity, rather than that paganism possesses Christian

---

[10] Churchill, op. cit., p. 895.

[11] ibid., p. 901.

[12] ibid., p. 830.

[13] ibid., p. 891.

[14] ibid., p. 868.

[15] ibid., p, 888. (Though Baldaeus lives on the coast of Ceylon, he lists the Buddha among the incarnations without a flicker of recognition nor does he identify anywhere the dominant religion of Ceylon.)

truth. Narrating how Draupadï in the Indian epic purified herself of the guilt of polyandry by passing through fire, he comments that "...it is evident, that the Pagans ascribed to Fire a purifying Quality; from whom the Jews question less took that Doctrine, and the Roman Catholics their Purgatory,"[16] Doughty Protestant that he is, Baldaeus sees proof here that Jews and Catholics are in some degree pagan!

5. Bartholomaous Ziegenbalg, 1683-1719

Ziegenbalg, the first Protestant clergyman to come to India exclusively for mission work among the Hindus, was born in Germany and educated (briefly) at Halle. He arrived in Tranquebar on the Madras coast in 1706 as a missionary of the Danish Lutheran Church. He lived and worked there continuously, save for one visit to Europe, until his early death. His fame as a pioneer Protestant missionary is widely known. It is little known that he was the author of several studies of Hinduism which are a landmark in the technique of Indie studies.

In one of his earliest letters from India, published under the title "Of the gross and blind idolatry of the Malabarians". Ziegenbalg shows that he has perceived at once the importance of getting a thorough knowledge of the prevailing religion.[17] He sat down to a program of intensive study. Two years later, in 1708, he showed the first fruits of his efforts by sending home to Europe translations of three books of moralistic proverbs from the Tamil: the *Nidawunpa,* the *Kondei Wenden,* and the *Ulaganïdi,* with introductions written by himself.[18] His *magnum opus* followed in 1711, the *Ausführliche Beschreibung des Malabarischen Heidenthums* -- a comprehensive survey of the literature, beliefs, and cultic practices of the Hindus of the Tamil country.[19] Two years later he supplemented this general study with another major work, the *Genealogie der Malabarischen Götter,-* which deals especially with the South Indian pantheon and its mythology.[20]

---

[16]   ibid., p. 386.

[17]   Ziegenbalg, *Propagation of the Gospel in the East,* tr. Joseph Downing, 3rd ed., (London, 1718), pp. 19-25.

[18]   W. Caland, ed., *B. Ziegenbalg's Kleinere Schriften* (Amsterdam, Vcrhandelingen der Koninklijkc Akademie van Wetenschappen, Afdeeling Letterkunde, Nieuwe Reeks, Decl XXIX, No. 2, 1930.)

[19]   Caland, ed., *Ziegenbalg's Malabarischen Heidenthums* (Amsterdam, Vcrhandelingen (etc.) Deal XXV No. 3, 1926)

[20]   Wilhelm Germann, ed., (Madras, the editor, 1867).

Though for special reasons Ziegenbalg gained little credit by these writings, they represent a great advance over everything that had been written by Europeans up to his time. Complete mastery of an Indian language made the difference. He says in his *Ausführliche Beschreibung...* that when he first arrived he trusted Baldaeus for his information on Hinduism, but soon found him to be almost always incorrect in his use of names and often erroneous in his facts, for the obvious reason that he had only a weak knowledge of the Malabar language. Determined not to be guilty of the same failing, Ziegenbalg applied himself strenuously to the study of Tamil, collected a sizeable Tamil library, and spent his time in it night and day. Now this work, he says in his introduction, is not a *Sehmierewerek* taken from other authors, but everything in it has either been heard orally again and again from intelligent Hindus in their own tongue, or it has been translated into German word for word from Tamil books.[21] He could have made the same boast in the introduction to every writing of his save his first letter. The chapters of his major works often contain a topical anthology, practically, of selections translated from Tamil religious literature. Here we find reporting that rests on a new and wider base. Europe had never received from India before anything so extensive and so accurate in its information. Roger had been a man of judicious mind and was a man of great orderliness and industry, but even he had looked in upon Hinduism from outside the gates of literacy. Ziegenbalg knows Tamil only, but it is seldom that he attempts to tell of things beyond the Tamil heathendom and the Tamil gods. His one venture into the field of Sanskrit literature -- his attempt to outline the content of the four Vedas -- is a total failure. The philosophical *darsanas*, including the very name of Vedänta, seem to be unknown to him. But in his own field -- the popular religion of South Indian polytheism and of the great theistic sects -- his books have not even now lost their worth.

Very few persons during the past two hundred fifty years have read his volumes or even known of their existence. The first to be printed, the *Genealogie der Malabarischen Götter*, appeared only in 1867 after a century and a half of neglect. His other mature works have waited until the present century to make their appearance in a learned journal. None have been made available outside their original language. In short, these books, which might have advanced western knowledge of Hinduism by something like a century, were suppressed until the age of their greatest usefulness had passed. Apparently this loss was caused by the narrow-mindedness of the superiors in Denmark and Germany to whom he sent his manuscripts. Professor A. H. Grancke wrote, after reading his *Genealogie...* that

---

21   Caland, ed., Ausführliche Beschreibung... , p. 14f.

printing the book was out of the question: missionaries are sent to root out heathenism, not to spread pagan nonsense in Europe.[22] Similar comments must have sent his other manuscripts to the dusty files rather than to the printer. It is hard to say what may have been in the minds of those who buried those works. They may have been disturbed by the praise which our author accords the Hindus in certain matters, which we shall notice later. They may have feared the books would encourage fantastic theological speculation. They may have merely failed to see the importance of such publications for the mission enterprise.

Whatever the home authorities may have thought, Ziegenbalg wrote as a devout Christian and missionary, for the sake of the progress of the gospel. He says in his introductions that he writes in order that his successors may know how to communicate with the heathen effectively so that the mission leaders at home may understand the problems of mission work and contribute their advice; and so that European Christians may sympathize with the heathen in their plight and be moved to share the gospel with them. He is not content merely to write detached scholarly descriptions of Hindu beliefs and practice: his Christian evaluations precede or follow. He does not permit his pronounced attitudes to blur his power to discern the facts, however, and he does not attack any aspect of Hinduism unless he has seen it clearly and perceived in it a genuine opposition to an essential point of Christianity.

Though Ziegenbalg never deals with the theological problem of Christianity and Hinduism intensively and systematically, many scattered comments indicate that he was a man of some theological concern. He provides us with more material than any other Protestant of our period.

Ziegenbalg's attitude toward Hinduism remained always quite negative at the central point. He never regarded Hinduism as a whole as anything other than a corrupted and ineffective system of religion which does not effect man's salvation and which ought to be replaced. His letter of September 2, 1706, mentioned above, shows that he arrived from Europe with a predisposition toward a severe view of Hinduism: he says he is writing "to lay open the folly and falsity of their worship" and to give "a short smack of their ridiculous theology"-- which he does, on the slender basis of his reading and his first impressions, until he tires of rehearsing "so much of this useless trash." The garbled information and callow judgments of this letter soon came under Ziegenbalg's own critical re-examination. In his later writings he does not allow sharp and sweeping

---

[22]   Wilhelm Germann, ed. , *Genealogie...*, p. vii.

condemnations of this kind to stand alone. But he remains ever a staunch evangelical Christian championing the true religion against a false one. In the introduction and conclusion of his last work, his *Genealogie...* of 1713, he wishes to make it clear to his readers that he does not write about the gods because he is happy to spend his time with such foolishness, but because it is a necessity of his work. He despises those gods, prays that God will annihilate them and bring the heathens from darkness to light, from the power of Satan to Himself. [23] The popular polytheism he finds particularly offensive, with its imputation to God of trivial and sinful mythological doings which offend against the divine justice, wisdom, truth, and holiness. Truly the heathen must be blind when they bow down and worship the perpetrators of such deeds!

At some points Ziegenbalg's later attitude was more exclusive than the one with which he came to India. In the above-mentioned letter of 1706 he was inclined to think that the Hindus might have heard of the Holy Trinity, because they attribute to Brahmä a human nature and other characteristics of Jesus Christ. Their beliefs about the incarnations of Vishnu, too, indicated to him "that this deluded people have heard some imperfect Rumor of Christ, but talking it all in a huddle, have interlaced it with a World of Fables and Fictions." The *kalkï* incarnation that is yet to come indicated, he thought, some imperfect notion of the Day of Judgment.[24] But when he wrote his introduction to the *Nidiwunpa* two years later he could no longer agree that the Christian God could be referred to by a trinity of any such personalities as Brahrmä, Vishnu and Siva, lewd and quarrelsome as they are. [25] And regarding the allegation that it was for the salvation of men that Vishnu became incarnate, that god's motive in taking the form of the Dwarf was to take away Mahäbali's kingdom by trickery, as he read the story in a Tamil book. Thus his earlier tracing of certain Hindu beliefs to a source in God's revealed Word did not stand up under the test of study as far as he was concerned.

Yet we have not done justice to Ziegenbalg's rich and sophisticated insight if we report only that in the end he rejected the rightfulness of Hinduism's claim upon men. In the seven years of his study and writing, his acquaintance with Hinduism went deep. He became aware of the vast variety within that faith, of the need for separate judgments, and of the inhumanity of absolute generalization.

---

[23] Germann, ed., *Genealogic...*, pp. 3, 288.

[24] Ziegcnbalg, *Propagation of the Gospel in the East*, pp. 19-25.

[25] Caland, ed., ...*Kleinere Schriften*, p. 22.

Again and again Ziegenbalg sought to counteract European prejudice by testifying to the great accomplishments of the "Malabarians" in the virtues. He writes in 1703 that he is sending his examples of the Hindu moralistic literature in order to show how far the heathen have been able to go in the ethical life unaided by the Word of God.[26] He hopes to change the notions of Europeans, he says, who generally think the Malabar heathens are a very barbarous folk, a sort of *schwarze hunde* knowing nothing of erudition or moral propriety. [27] Such conclusions are drawn from outward appearances only, and are based upon ignorance of their language. Ziegenbalg confesses that when he first arrived among them he could not imagine that their language might be a rationally structured one, their social life a very human one guided by civil and moral law. He was gradually freed of such notions, he says, as he started to read their language. And when he gained full competency and discovered they followed the same philosophical disciplines the learned of Europe had known, and possessed regular written authorities in theological matters, he was astonished, and worked eagerly to become thoroughly instructed in their heathenism. [28] As a result of these studies he has been convinced that the Malabar people equal the ancient Latin and Greek heathen in knowledge of the moral law -- indeed, quite surpass them.[29] The books which he is forwarding, he says, will give adequate evidence of this. Also he can say from observation that they are very sympathetic toward travellers and the poor. Everywhere they have built special houses to provide these needy people with rest and alms. At some monastic establishments the poor are fed in thousands. The quantity of alms the Malabar people give puts Christians to shame. They believe alms-giving to be very important for salvation -- and they have such a great concern for their future blessedness that many give up property, house, and family and retire to the wilderness to do severe penances. Seeing what a high attainment they have made in the virtuous life without the aid of either the revealed Word or the peculiar support of the Holy Spirit, we Christians are warned of how much more shall be expected of us who enjoy every advantage! [30]

Nor has Ziegenbalg found among the Hindus any atheist who denies there is a God and a future life.[31] "Every one of those heathen

---

[26] ibid., pp. 25, 53, 71.

[27] ibid., p. 15.

[28] ibid., p. 11.

[29] ibid. , p. 25.

[30] Caland, ed,... .*Kleinere Schriften*, p. 25f .

[31] ibid. , p. 23.

knows that there is one divine being by whom all was created and on whom all in heaven and on earth depends, and they hold this truth in no way in doubt. This Supreme Being or Ens Entium is called by them Baräbara-wastu, a designation which may be read here and there in their books, and heard in their discourses."[32] He presents in translation a number of striking monotheistic passages from his Tamil books and then exclaims:

> Where in the writings of the ancient Greek and Latin heathens does one find such convincing utterances regarding God? Why, when I first read such things in their books, I became quite convinced that by some chance their authors were Christians, since they not only reject the plurality of gods, but also criticize all the other heathenish ways and put them down as foolishness![33]

But his enquiries showed that those writers were esteemed highly by the Hindus, who regarded them as their own. They had traversed all the Hindu paths and had arrived at these opinions by their own natural light.

Ziegenbalg sets down here and there in passing his thoughts on how these truths regarding the nature of virtue and the existence of the One God came to be known among the Hindus. Evidently he never dismissed completely the idea that the Hindus may yet have some small remnant of the primeval revelation of Genesis, or that they may have received in the course of history some remote influences from the people of the Biblical faith. We still find the idea in the introduction to his *Genealogie...*, where he invites the reader to notice for himself what is preserved in the heathen traditions from the Word of God, "and how this and that Old Testament story and such-and-such scriptural articles of faith and godly truths have been turned upside down and distorted by the poets through the cunning of the devil."[34] In all other instances Ziegenbalg discusses this problem in terms of a theory of natural light. In the introduction to his *Ausführliche Beschreibung. . .* he says that his readers will be able to perceive, in his description of Hindu beliefs and disciplines,

> ...on the one hand the devil's great deception and the dreadful errors to which such heathens are given, and on the other hand how far they have been brought, by their light of reason, in the knowledge of God and of natural

---

[32]   Caland, ed., *Ausführliche Beschreibung . . .* , p. 39.3

[33]   ibid. , p. 42.

[34]   Germann, ed., Genealogie..., p. 2.

things, and how they often put many Christians to shame
in virtuous living, and often feel a much greater aspiration
toward the future life than they. [35]

Elsewhere Ziegenbalg adds that though these pagans do not have
the true law, yet their consciences convince them that they should avoid
sins and do good. Now if they were to do these things out of gratitude
toward God and with faith in Jesus Christ, rather than in order to raise up
their own righteousness, they could be called doers of truly good works.
As it is, they are found wanting. But we Christians can see in them how
much men can achieve by their natural powers and their natural light, and
be ashamed. [36]

Having seen how generously Ziegenbalg could praise certain
doctrinal and moral achievements of the Hindus, we must now be sure to
note how inadequately equipped he finds them on both these counts in
the final analysis. He finds their impressive moral effort corrupted at the
root, as we have seen, because it is self -centered rather than God-centered.
Because the Hindus rely upon their own merits rather than on those of
Christ, even their sincere urge toward virtuous life results in external
propriety and civility only, and is ineffective.[37] Sunk in error, they cannot
realize their own condition nor find their way out unless compassionate
Christians communicate to them the light given by the Father in Jesus
Christ. [38]

With regard to true belief, the situation of the Hindus is no better.
Hindu books mention the One God, and some Hindus therefore read
about Him and talk about Him -- but there are very few who reverence
and seek Him. They know the bare name, not the Being himself; they
know the name Barabaravastu and can say that it represents the Being of
All Beings. That is all. Their religious books prescribe the worship of the
many gods only, and in their preoccupation with idols the heathen as a
whole have quite forgotten the One God. [39] They say that the Supreme
Being is too high to be troubled by the affairs of the many worlds and that
He has therefore created inferior gods to be their rulers. The scriptures
continue to draw a line between the Ens Entium and the created gods, but

---

[35] Caland, ed., *Ausführliche Beschreibung. . .* , p. llf .

[36] Caland, ed., *Ausführliche Beschreibung...* p. 79.

[37] ibid., pp. 79, 235.

[38] ibid., p. 176.

[39] ibid., p. 39.

the common people worship every god as the highest.[40] Some so degrade monotheism as to say that there are three hundred thirty million gods! [41]

The omnipresent polytheism which dominates Hindu religious practice can be understood by Ziegenbalg only as a degradation wrought by the devil; "...these heathen have allowed themselves to be misled into polytheism by the devil and by their old poets, through whom they have wandered from the path of the One God to such a degree that they do not know how to find it again."[42] Their belief in rebirth and their demand for superstitious wonders are the devil's cunning work to hold them back from conversion.[43] Satan has spared himself no trouble to extinguish the natural light of these people and to turn it more and more into thick darkness in which only small remnants of knowledge of the Divine Being remain.[44]

Any effort to sum up and interpret Ziegenbalg's attitude toward Hinduism cannot fail to note that he ascribed practically the whole of Hindu religious practice to the devil. Such language means a most emphatic rejection, however one may look at it. It is the ultimate in negative evaluation.

Yet it needs interpretation. First, we must observe that there are aspects of Hinduism to which the condemnation does not apply. He does not impute a diabolical disposition to the Hindus themselves nor call any non-Christian an agent of the devil. Dupes of the devil they may be, but there is a difference. He does not question the sincerity of their intentions. Their situation is tragic rather than blameworthy. There is no indication that his relationships with the Hindus about him was ever rancorous. On the contrary, he can say of one with whom he was engaged in dispute, "I grew very fond of the man..."[45] So it is not Hindu persons that are demonic, but the greater part of their religious ideas and practices, Ziegenbalg's talk of the devil is not, as in so much of modern usage, a part of the language of angry personal abuse.

Another necessary observation is that he does not put the brand of the devil on quite the entirety of the Hindu intellectual system. Hindu thinkers are not wholly ignorant of the true God. There are points of light

---

[40] Caland, ed., ...*Kleinere Schriften*, pp. 10-13.

[41] --*Ausführliche Beschreibung...*, p. 43.

[42] ibid.

[43] -- ...*Kleinere Schriften*, p. 21

[44] Germann, cd. , *Genealogie..*, p. 26.

[45] Caland, ed.,. . .*Kleinere Schrifton*, p. 17.

-- not bright nor adequate lights, nor are they set in central places, but they are *there*, and they are sufficient to keep the relationship between Christian and Hindu faith from being one of utter contrast between absolute light and absolute darkness.

Absolute contrast is prevented by yet another consideration: the devil's operations are not confined to India. Ziegenbalg acknowledges in one of his introductions that Satan is active in all four of the great world-religions; and although the Christian religion is founded on the Word of God and is the one true and holy faith, even in it the devil has caused Christians to divide into many quarrelsome sects which fall from one error into another.[46] This consideration does not seem to enter into his thoughts very persistently as he ponders the relation between Christianity and Hinduism at other times, but it is significant that he acknowledges at any time that the devil operates in the church to some degree as well as in the temple.

Therefore it would be a serious misrepresentation to say of Ziegenbalg that he held Christianity to be entirely of divine origin and Hinduism to be entirely of the devil. Not only does the devil operate in both, but the knowledge of God and the good which Hindus have achieved by their natural light is valid, even if feeble.

If Ziegenbalg's works had been used fully by Protestants, their attitudes would have been broadened as well as their knowledge. He applied to Hinduism a more reflective and persistent Christian criticism than had any of his predecessors. He made a perceptive distinction between a Hinduism that is higher and a Hinduism that is lower from a Christian point of view. His judgment upon the latter, while severe, was not unfair when properly understood.

Ziegenbalg hoped that his writings would be used as handbooks by succeeding generations of missionaries. Nothing more useful for the purpose was to be written for at least a hundred years. As things turned out, they were to lie in oblivion during the period of their greatest potential usefulness. Only now do we know what he achieved and how it was wasted. At the beginning of the nineteenth century, when Protestant missions expanded into a broad continuous movement, the Protestant effort to understand Hinduism factually and theologically made an independent start.

---

[46] Caland, cd. , *Ausführliche Beschreibung…*, p. 9f.

6. WILLIAM WARD, 1769-1823.

After Ziegenbalg's time, his mission produced a well-informed student of Hinduism in Frederick Schwartz, but no new writings of importance in this field. In the last quarter of the eighteenth century great advances in general knowledge of Hindu culture began to be made in Bengal by a small group of enthusiastic Englishmen who had taken up the study of Sanskrit language and literature. Sir William Jones, Charles Wilkins, Nathaniel Halhed, Henry Thomas Colebrooke and others organized in Calcutta in 1764 an association of vast importance for the future of oriental studies, the Asiatic Society of Bengal. The contagious interest in the study of the classical Indian languages which this group generated spread eventually to the western universities, where it continues to this day. The founders of this society were Protestant by religion, but they studied the Hindu heritage primarily as historians and men of literature. They were neither active church men nor did they contribute much, directly, to the theological interpretation of Hinduism in the churches. Their movement was not anti-Christian, but many who were opposed to Christian missions for one reason or another found ammunition for their cause in the impressive classics of Hindu literature published by the Asiatic Society.

Until almost the end of the eighteenth century the Lutheran mission in Danish Tranquebar remained perforce the only Protestant mission in India. The British East India Company had refused through out its history to tolerate missionary activities in its territories, nor was any liberalization of this policy in sight as the century drew toward a close. However, in the last decade, William Carey managed to begin a quiet Baptist missionary activity in Bengal, and in 1799 William Ward, accompanied by Joshua Marshman, came out from England to join him. Ward had been in his childhood a printer's apprentice, then a proof-reader, and, after some years of self-education in these roles, a rather successful country editor. Now he became an essential member of the famous missionary trio of Serampore, contributing his special professional skills from 1800 until his death in 1823.

Ward's principal responsibility in Serampore was the supervision of the mission's extensive printing and publishing enterprises. But he became also the Scrampore teams principal writer on Hinduism. He was fluent in spoken Bengali; he had a journalist's understanding of the importance of observing, enquiring, and taking notes; and he had at his disposal the help of numerous literate Hindus employed in the translating and printing work centered at the mission press. In 1811 he published his voluminous and detailed *Account of the Writings, Religion and Manners of the Hindoos.*[47] The many later editions of this work bear the title *A View of the History, Literature, and Mythology of the Hindus,* [48] and usually include an extensive introduction summarizing and interpreting the material. Later, Ward expressed his general views on Hinduism again very forcefully in *Farewell Letters to a Few Friends in Britain and America on Returning to Bengal in 1821.* [49]

Ward's *Account...* is almost an encyclopedia of the most varied information on the religious and social traditions of Bengal. The volumes include a history of India, summaries of major Hindu books, catalogs of Hindu deities, accounts of prominent temples, festivals, and pilgrimage-places. He describes the personal and family ceremonies, the castes, the major sects and monastic orders, and the schools of philosophy. As he acknowledges, his "translations" from Sanskrit literature are really English renderings of versions communicated to him in Bengali by his pandits. Usually they are paraphrases or summaries, perfunctorily done. In explaining Hindu philosophy, his information and also his aptitude are poor. He is often factually mistaken when he makes generalizations about the whole of Hinduism or writes of situations outside Bengal. But when he writes of the castes, customs, institutions, ceremonies and deities of his own province, he presents a rich collection of facts about the life and worship of the masses. Even in this field, however, his selection of materials is affected by an extremist attitude toward Hinduism.

In all of Ward's writings we find a deprecation of Hinduism, both theological and practical, of an intensity not to be found in any of his Protestant predecessors. It is not his hostility toward polytheism and idolatry that puts him in a separate category, for all shared by all. What makes him stand alone is the great difficulty he has in finding any mote of noble truth or any shred of redeeming virtue in any aspect of Indian thought and life that is in any way associated with Hinduism. The Hindus have "...no morality, for how should a people be moral, whose gods are monsters of vice; whose priests are their ringleaders in crime, whose scriptures encourage pride, impurity, falsehood, revenge, and murder;

---

[47] (4 v., Serampore, Mission Press, 1811).

[48] Second edition, Seramporce Mission Press, 1815-18; 3rd ed., London, Black Parbury and Allen, 1817; 4th ed. , London, Kingsbury Parbury & Allen, 1822; Hartford, J. Huntingdon Jr., 1824. (from the 2nd ed.); 5th ed., Madras, J. Higginbotham, 1863.

[49] (N.Y., E. Bliss & White, 1821; 2 editions, London, 1821; Lexington KY., T. T. Skillman, 1822.)

whose worship is connected with indescribable abominations, and whose heaven is a brothel?"[50] ". . . amidst a pretty large acquaintance with the heathen in India, *I have never seen one man* who appeared to 'fear God and work righteousness,'" says Ward. "Their throat is an open Sepulchre. (The impurity of their conversation is beyond description.)" "... their feet are swift to shed blood. (Oh, how strikingly is this exemplified in the eagerness with which the Hindoos go into the work of immolating the poor widows and other human victims."[51] They drag their dying relations to the river banks at all seasons without remorse; they burn their bodies there in an inhuman manner, "Nor do any Hindoos die with the hope of even temporary happiness, except those who drown or burn themselves alive."[52] They have never built an alms-house or a hospital, and they let their fellows die of want before their very doors.[53] "...in ignorance, in vice, and immorality the Hindoos are far below the most savage nations ...the Hindoo females have not a spark of maternal tenderness toward their off spring."[54] They "...murder their own children, by burying them alive, throwing them to the alligators, or hanging them up alive in trees for the ants and crows before their own doors, or by sacrificing them to the Ganges."[55] The Rajputs, all families, we are assured, butcher all their female children.[56] The Hindus do not affirm, as the Muslims do, that women have no souls, but they *treat* them as if they had none.[57] In view of the worship in the temples of "the lecher Krishna and his concubine Radhä"[58] and the existence in the shrines of the lewd emblem of Siva, it is not surprising "that a chaste woman, faithful to her husband, is scarcely to be found among all the millions of Hindus."[59] "..fidelity to marriage vows is almost unknown among the Hindoos; the intercourse of the sexes approaches very near to that of the irrational animals."[60]

---

[50] Ward, *Farewell Letters...*, (N.Y., 1821), p, 57.

[51] Ward, *Farewell Letters ...* (N.Y., 1821), p. 37.

[52] Ibid., p. 50.

[53] Ward, *A View...* (3rd ed.), I, pp lvi, lvii, xcv.

[54] Quoted from a pamphlet of Ward's by J. A. Dubois, *Letters on the State of Christianity in India* (London, Longman etc., 1823), p.148.

[55] *A View...*, I, p. lvi.

[56] *Farewell Letters...* , pp.6lf, 78f.

[57] *Farewell Letters. . .*, p. 65.

[58] ibid., p. 52.

[59] *A View...*, I, p. xxix.

[60] ibid., xcivf, cf. *Letters* p. 92.

Nor is there in Hindu thought, as distinct from moral life, anything true or good. Though the Hindus do believe in the unity of God, this belief has no place whatever in the actual religion of the country. They worship the 330,000,000 gods, and the general belief is that each of the many idols is a real deity.[61] In all of India there stands not a single temple to the One God.[62] Not even a distant allusion to Christian truth is to be found in their absurd philosophical systems. [63]Their greatest minds have been feeling after the Supreme Being for ages with complete ineffectiveness in knowing Him.[64]

> There is scarcely anything in Hindooism, when truly known, in which a learned man can delight, or of which a benevolent man can approve; and I am fully persuaded that there will soon be but one opinion on the subject, and that this opinion will be, that the Hindoo system is less ancient than the Egyptian, and that it is the most puerile, impure, and bloody of any system of idolatry that was ever established on earth.[65]

In short, even such appreciations and acknowledgments as the staunch Ziegenbalg willingly made, Ward withholds.

The theological standing of Hinduism is discussed by Ward only in a few scattered remarks. However, they make his position fairly clear. He does not give a moment's consideration to any notion that a positive divine initiative may be at work in any sense whatever in Hinduism. The relation between Christianity and Hinduism, as he sees it, is at best analogous to the relation between the one true God and fallen man. Man rejected the doctrine of the divine unity and chose for his worship images suggested by his darkness and his passion.[66] "And what agreement hath the temple of God with idols?"[67] And yet in his view the idolatry of the heathen is not merely the work of man; Hinduism is a part of a revolt against God inspired by Satan, who leads an organized rebellion based on an alliance of

---

[61]   ibid. , p. 1f, xlviii,

[62]   *Farewell Letters...*, p. 50.

[63]   *Farewell Letters..*, p. 88.

[64]   *A View...*, I, p. 1xxxvii.

[65]   *A View ...*, I, p. ciii.

[66]   Ward, *A View...* (3rd. ed.), I, p. xiii.

[67]   ibid,, p. cii.

...Three mighty powers, marshaled under the prince of darkness, having for their subordinate leaders the Roman pontiff, Mahomet, and all the gods of the heathen.[68]

Thus, Christianity is not merely as different from Hinduism as God is different from man: the two religions stand on opposite sides of the chasm which separates God and Satan. They are related only as opposites, Hinduism is demonic in toto.[69]

Ward's picture of Hinduism had immense outreach and influence. His original volumes of 1811 were English-speaking Protestantism's first report on the subject from its first India missionaries. His *Farewell Letters* went through at least four editions in the 1820's, as noted earlier. Editions of *A View of the History, Literature and Mythology of the Hindus* were published at Serampore in 1815, in London in 1817 and 1822, at Hartford in 1824, and in Madras in 1863. The work had some critics from the start, but their voices in no way hindered its heavy circulation nor kept it from occupying a prominent place in the libraries of nineteenth-century missionaries. In his missionary manual of 1847, T. Phillips includes it on his recommended list as "...this work so well known and probably to be found in every missionary home."[70] Mr. Phillips acknowledges that Ward makes errors outside his field of special competence but upholds his work as being of unexcelled accuracy so far as practical Hinduism in Bengal

---

[68] Ward, *Farewell Letters...* (N.Y., 1821), p. 179.

[69] The demon theory seems to have been general at Serampore. In Joshua Marshman's *Thoughts on Propagating Christianity by mere Effectual among the Heathens* (2nd ed., Serampore, 1827, p. 6) we find:

"India has been, from the earliest ages, the seat of the grossest delusion that has over pervaded the mind of man. Here the prince of darkness has reigned in the most triumphant manner and from thence has he sent forth those streams of delusion, under the name of Buddhism, which, on the one side, have deluged Ceylon, Boutan, and Tibet, and, on the other, all the notions beyond the Ganges, even to China and Japan."

Henry Martyn's reaction on seeing in Serampore, for the first time, the public worship of an image, shows the views with which evangelical Protestants sometimes arrived in India in Ward's time: "I shivered at being in the neighborhood of hell; my heart was ready to burst at the dreadful state to which the Devil had brought my poor follow creatures. I would have given the world to have known the language and to have preached to them" (J.N. Ogilvie, *The Apostles of India*, London 1915, p. 357.)

[70] T. Phillips, *The Missionary's Vade Mecum* (Calcutta, Baptist Mission Press, 1847), p. 257.

is concerned. He feels it his duty "to defend the memory of so judicious and worthy a man from the charge of prejudice,"[71] in the fifth edition of Madras, the writer of the introduction admits that the book cannot be altogether acquitted of being too prudish and condemnatory, but is inclined in view the author's faults as those of immoderate expression rather than of substance: "Deduct something for the heat of controversy, and the Missionary's views escape censure." And he adds that the atrocities of the mutiny of 1857 have done much to substantiate Ward's view of the Hindu moral character. [72]

Since Ward was clearly an influential guide, it is important that we evaluate the temperateness of the guidance he gave. Were his verbal observations based solidly on his visual observations? Did he write with serious intent to describe with precision, and justly?

People of this generation may easily fail to realize how much ground for unfavorable report the religious life of India presented to a firm Christian one hundred fifty years ago. Hindu intellectual life and Hindu social morality were at a low ebb, all agree. For centuries both theistic and non-theistic religious groups had been devoting themselves largely to providing wholesale escapes and compensations for a people constantly frustrated by outsiders and by their own rigid institutions. The activities carried out in the name of the gods were often coarse in specific content, and in their function they were ethically non-constructive. To any Christian thoroughly trained in the biblical conception of God and His place in life, the views of deity implicit in the Bengal practices of 1800 could irritate like the intolerable defamation of a revered friend. "I have found no traces of God's immaculate purity, or inflexible justice, in any part of the Hindoo writings, nor amongst the great number of intelligent Hindoos with whom I have conversed," says Ward -- and those words could have been said after a considerable search; "How unworthy those ideas are of God, and how infinitely short they fall of the scripture idea of God, every person blessed with a Christian education is competent to decide."[73] Ward perceived truly that the popular cults of Bengal in his time had little or nothing to do with morality, and he had a right to protest against what, to a Christian, can be only a dishonoring travesty upon the Divine nature.

But to charge that *no* morality is found among the Hindu people, or to imply that they had lived for centuries "in a state of perfect brutality

---

[71] Ibid. , p. xi, xii.

[72] Ward, *A View. . .* (5th ed.), p. 11f (by W. O. Simpson).

[73] Ward, *An Account...* (1811), IV, pp. 275, 277.

and crime"[74] is quite a different kind of accusation. His many swooping condemnations of Hindu life as something wholly vile raises the question of whether Ward was an unbalanced emotional man, full of hostility in his general relationships.

Gross tendencies of this kind are not indicated by the common biographical material on Ward. John Clark Marshman, who is rather frank in his character sketches, and who certainly knew Ward well, writes of him as amiable, affectionate, habitually sweet of disposition, a man who "never made an enemy."[75] He was the Serampore group's foremost advocate of interdenominational fellowship among Christians.[76] Furthermore, he evidently had no deep hostility toward aspects of Hindu culture not connected with the doctrine, worship, and morality of the Hindu religion, because he joined with his associates in insisting that converts keep their Indian dress, food, domestic habits, language, and even their Hindu names. An intemperate, fanatical individual is not suggested by any of these facts.

On the other hand there may be significance in the fact that of all the Protestant writers we have studied he had the least formal schooling, and that even his primary education was obtained in editorial offices at a time when journalists wrote with pens dipped in vitriol. As a young sympathizer with the republican ideas of the French Revolution, Ward himself had written an editorial for the *Derby Mercury* for which the newspaper had been prosecuted. This brush with the law certainly proves nothing ignoble in the editorialist, but it probably does indicate a capacity for violent utterance.

As one would expect of a man of his background. Ward was aware of the processes and power of publicity, and he was capable of using selected material with a given propagandistic purpose in mind. While in England in 1819 he carried on a campaign directed toward the admirable end of procuring a measure for the legal prohibition of widow burning. As to means, "We must inundate England with these horrid tales," he said, "till the practice can be tolerated no longer."[77]

There are indications in his book on the Hindus that here, too, he is working not in the scholarly spirit of impartial description, but with a

---

[74] Ibid

[75] John Clark Marshman, *The Story of Carey Marshman and Ward* (London, Alexander Strahan and Co., 1864), pp. 196, 318.

[76] ibid,, p. 96f.

[77] ibid., p. 293.

view to the maximum impact in a competition for the molding of opinion, "I fear a very unjust and unhappy impression has been made on the public mind," he says in his 1811 edition, "by the encomiums which have been so lavishly bestowed on the Hindoo writings."[78] He mentions his irritation with Nathaniel Halhed, who in 1776 in his *Code of Gentoo Laws* accepted the Brahman chronologies and set the rationalists of Europe to raving for years over the incomparable antiquity of Hindu culture. He protests at the fact that President Ezra Stiles of Yale College in America, though a devout Christian, was so taken in by this that he actually wrote Sir William Jones asking him to look for the books of Adam in India! Yet Ward approves of the work of the orientalists, basically his wrath is directed rather against persons who are using their discoveries to give substance to a rosy picture of the character of Hinduism in general, saying that the Hindu religion teaches sublime doctrines, inculcates pure morality, recognizes the One God and is not really idolatrous, etc., etc. [79]

Now, current discussions in the press about the virtues of the Hindu religion had a significance for the missionaries in the little Danish settlement of Serampore that was more than academic. During the entire time in which Ward was working on his first edition it was illegal, technically, for him or any missionary to stop across the boundary into British India. The view of the established merchants and empire builders was that mission work was dangerous to security, and they meant to see the policy of exclusion of missionaries maintained when the East India Company's charter came up for renewal in Parliament in 1812. In a campaign of speaking, publishing, and pamphleteering, the old India hands were promoting the view that efforts to convert the Hindus to Christianity were not only impolitic, but also impertinent, since the Hindu religion was so lofty and its morality so refined that Hindus had nothing to gain from Christianity. [80] A journalist like Ward recognized the importance of impressing upon the English reading public the fact that the Hindus did indeed have need of Christian morality. Quite aside from the political crisis of 1812, there was a continuing need to justify the mission work in the face of the extravagantly eulogistic literature on Hinduism that had been put into circulation.

A missionary book giving due attention to the deficiencies of everyday Hinduism was required by truth itself at this time. Ward's

---

[78]   Ward, *An Account...* (Serampore, 1811), I, 303.

[79]   Ward, *A View...* (3rd ed.), I, xcvii-ci,

[80]   Marshman, *op. cit*, pp, 214-238, gives the substance of the arguments used in these crucial debates.

writings were certainly effective in counteracting the romantic fictions about Hinduism that were current and in making Hindu shortcomings known. But when he had finished, had truth and justice been served? Or is the picture which he created as artificially distorted as the view which he demolished?

Ward's dark generalizations upon Hinduism aren't easily tested for factuality and fairness at this distance in time. Nothing is settled by our impression that he is an extremist in his judgments and reckless in his methods: we were not there. His accuracy and impartiality must be checked through persons who *were* there.

The first witness is Ward himself. The sweeping indictments quoted from the third edition of 1817 and from his letters of 1821 are summary statements upon aspects of Hindu life which he had described in detail in his *Account...* of 1811. By examining the body of factual know ledge out of which his accusations rise, we can note how fairly he draws his conclusions from the evidence.

Take for instance his accusation that the Hindus "murder their children, by burying them alive, throwing them to the alligators, or hanging them alive in trees for the ants and crows before their doors..." The reference to burying children alive seems to be a gratuitous exuberance. If any Hindus bury their children alive, he has not informed us of the practice in four exhaustive volumes which seldom miss a detail of this sort. His basis may be a reference to certain yogis and certain Vaishnavas who practice burial and whose widows were sometimes buried alive with their deceased mates.[81] If so, his memory has confused the identity of the victims.

The allusion to throwing children to the alligators and to sacrificing them to the Ganges refer to a single practice covered in a section of the 1811 publication which says that mothers sometimes abandon their children to the river in compliance with a vow, and that the island of Gangä-sägara at the mouth of the Hooghly is one of the places where this is done.[82] "This custom is not commanded by any shastru, and is principally practiced by persons who come from the Eastern parts of Bengal, and from the vicinity of Midnapoor," he says in 1811. The crocodiles do not appear on the scene at all in this early version. Ward could not have witnessed the practice after 1802, because the British Government in that year prohibited such

---

[81]   Ward, *An Account...*, II, p. 56lf .
[82]   Ibid., pp. 572-574.

sacrifices by law, and, as John Clark Marshman reports, "...they ceased at once without any disturbance, and with-out even a murmur."[83] Ward is aware of this fact, and recognizes in one note in his third edition, and elsewhere, that "This is now prevented by a guard of sepoys sent by government." Nevertheless, in his frequent catalogs of the abominations of present-day Hinduism he continues to mention the sacrifice of babies at Ganga-sagara in the context of the present tense. Spealcing in a letter of 1821 of the beastly callousness of the heart of the Hindu mother, he exclaims, "See the cow butting her horns, and threatening the person who dares to approach her offspring. See woman in India (at Saugur Island) throwing her living child into the outstretched jaws of the alligator!"[84] The alligators, introduced thus late into the scene, are used with tremendous effect in another letter which inserts a concessive "formerly" into the account, but goes on to transfer the force of the events into a current situation:

> At Saugur island, formerly, mothers were seen casting their living offspring amongst a number of alligators, and standing to gaze at those monsters quarrelling for their prey, beholding the writhing infant in the jaws of the successful animal, and standing motionless while it was breaking the bones and sucking the blood of the poor innocent! What must be the superstition, which can thus transform a being, whoso distinguishing quality is tenderness, into a monster more unnatural than the tiger prowling through the forest for its prey![85]

In a pamphlet Ward seems to have built up this story into something even more substantial, for in 1823 the Abbe Dubois quotes him as follows:

> What must be the state of the female mind when *millions* are found throwing the children of their vows into the sea?[86]

Thus we see that Ward is willing to take accounts of a practice which on his own testimony never happened with more than limited frequency and which ceased absolutely twenty years before, and to refurbish it with

---

[83] Marshman, *op. cit*, p. 76.

[84] *Farewell Letters.* . (N.Y. 1821), p.62.

[85] Ibid., p. 79.

[86] Dubois, *op. cit*, p. 203.

now horrors and multiply it to the millions in order to create in his readers' minds a revolting impression of the current behavior of Hindu mothers.

With regard to the hanging of children in the trees alive for the food, presumably, of ants and crows, we have descriptive coverage in Section 41 of the 1811 edition under "Exposing of children to be starved to death."[87] Newborn children who refused the breast, it appears, were in certain areas sometimes actually hung on trees in baskets for three days to live or die, before another attempt was made to suckle them. Regarding the frequency and distribution of this custom Ward says, "This is a barbarous custom, not commanded by any of the shastras, and wholly confined to the lower classes of the people," "The custom is unknown in many places, but, it is to be feared, it is too common in many others," Mr. Ward is well aware of how universal this practice is -- or rather is *not* -- but in the passage under discussion he allows the foreign reader to suppose that babies are thus fed to the birds and insects all over India.

We have noticed above Ward's remark that Hindus can have no morality because, among other reasons, their heaven is a brothel. We find a detailed description of the Hindu heavens in twenty-five pages of his work of 1811.[88] They contain no factual support for such violent language beyond a general remark that the happiness of several of the heavens consists of "sensual pleasures," and a repetition of the charge that these heavens "are houses of ill-fame" like the paradise of Muhammad. The details he gives of these celestial abodes are naive and morally crude, but they do not support his use of the word "brothel."

The complaint against Mr. Ward's methods is not that his charges are absolute fabrications, but that he does not hesitate to represent past abuses as present, the local as the universal, and the rare as the typical. He seems to make these misrepresentations knowingly; or it may be nearer the facts to suppose that in the moment of impetuous attack on what he hates he gives himself over entirely to his feelings; his scruples are submerged, like those of a boy in a snowball fight who packs into his misslies whatever casual stones he happens to scoop up.

In a criminal case, the accused may well be guilty as charged even though the prosecutor exaggerates or deliberately falsifies in order to get a conviction. Though Ward makes many charges that have next to nothing to them, may his overall generalization regarding an almost totally depraved

---

[87] Ward, *An Account...*, II, p. 574.
[88] Ibid., IV, pp. 279-282, 316-338.

Hindu social life be a fair representation of the facts nevertheless? Let us introduce the judgment of a contemporary, the Abbe J. A. Dubois, whose *Hindu Manners, Customs and Ceremonies* is still much read. In his *Letters on the State of Christianity* in India we find a treatise entitled "Vindication of the Hindoos, both males and females, in answer to the attacks made upon both by the Reverend _____." Quotations from the unnamed cleric identify the object of the rebuttal as the Reverend William Ward, "...the severity with which he treats these poor Hindoos," says Dubois, "is far from being a subject of edification to me." Until recently, he goes on, "everyone regarded the Hindus as mild, sober, industrious, patient and submissive people with a reasonably high achievement in the scale of civilization; but now we have a shocking account of a people polluted by every kind of wickedness, barbarians in deepest ignorance and immorality, below most savage nations, nearer brute than human." "I cannot disguise to you that their exaggerations and misrepresentations (not to use harsher terms) respecting the Hindoos have been to me a subject of scandal, and have, in several instances, roused may indignation to a high degree." Dubois then admits that he has often denounced the Brahmans himself for their pride and imposture, and the common people for their monstrous worship, but this blackest picture of an entire people depraved below the brutes is pure malevolence: the ordinary Hindu is not inferior to the ordinary European in devotion to duty, sobriety, industry, patience, or peacefulness. Though several Rajput clans have practiced infanticide, the charge that every Rajput mother puts her female child to death is an odious slander. Throwing children into the sea and the like is a rare practice, now illegal. Hindu women suffer inequalities, but their position in the home is not that of a domestic animal, as Ward suggests; and regarding the charge that a chaste female is almost unknown among the Hindus, "I can confidently affirm that this shameful accusation is unfounded." [89]

Now, the Abbe may have had a natural tendency to disapprove of Protestants and all their works. And, having spent most of his life in Madras and Mysore, he may have witnessed a Hindu moral life less deteriorated than that of Bengal. But he had the confidence of many non-Catholics, he had travelled in India at least as widely as Ward, and he had been in the country seven years longer. And he considered Ward's picture of the Hindus an outrage. That "Ward's description was unreasonably hostile seems fairly obvious. Possibly no two judges could over agree on the precise degree of distortion in his picture. Therefore lot us conclude our discussion of Ward with two observations that are fairly objective and demonstrable. First, Ward's injustice goes beyond mere immoderation of

---

[89]   Dubois, *op. cit*, pp. 145-208.

language; he often distorts his facts. Second, in comparison with all earlier Protestant writers he is an extremist in every sense of the word. In his total condemnation of Hindu moral life, and in his utter rejection of the possibility of any doctrinal truth in Hinduism, he was the most severe of the severe.

GENERAL CONCLUSION

Six writers on Hinduism in the course of more than two centuries are not a great many. But the number of Protestant chaplains in India during this period was few, and the missionaries were fewer. In view of this fact, the accomplishment is not insignificant. Furthermore, save the two earliest, the writings were substantial.

In mastery of Indian languages our Protestant writers left room for improvement. The chaplains in their short terms in the trading posts had not time for great accomplishments. Our two missionary authors with their serious lifetime commitment mastered the local vernaculars to their great advantage, and ours. No Protestant worker acquired a knowledge of Sanskrit during this period, and for this lack alone the penetration of all our writers into Indian thought was superficial. Even the theologies of the relatively accessible theistic sects were necessarily presented without the aid of their basic theological documents.

Theological thinking on the relationship between Hinduism and Christianity is remarkable for its scarcity. Nowhere do we find two consecutive pages of systematic discussion of the problem. The most persistent idea is that Hinduism manifests Satanic influence in whole or in part. Roger and Baldaeus, alone, do not employ the concept, Ziegenbalg ascribes to the devil the polytheism and idolatry which dominate in Hindu practice, but finds a residue which must be attributed to a more constructive source. Ward finds in living Hinduism nothing but polytheism and idolatry, and nothing not of ultimate Satanic inspiration.

Baldaeus sees in Hinduism indications that revealed truths have been imparted at some time or other from the biblical faiths, and Ziegenbalg is willing to entertain the notion. But Ward, recognizing nothing remotely like Biblical religion in Hinduism, has no use for a theory that borrowing from revelation has occurred. Ziegenbalg alone holds an avowed belief in the universal human possession of a "natural light" which guides the Hindus positively in the moral life and enables some of them to comprehend the truth of monotheism. Since for Ward the Hindus have neither any moral sense nor any living monotheistic faith, he has no place for a theory of natural light.

The prevalence of the devil-theory gives the early Protestant views of Hinduism a rather harsh tone. But there are differences of great importance. The harshest in every way is the latest, William Ward, who can find no common factor or point of contact whatsoever between Hinduism and Christianity. Despite Ziegenbalg's powerful evangelical interest, it is he who develops the most appreciative theory of all. But Ziegenbalg's influence passed into quick oblivion along with his neglected books, and it was Ward's writings which were available for the reading of the nineteenth-century missionaries. We are part of a tradition that is under the remote influence, at least, of Ward. At the outset of our thinking we should understand how his descriptions are related to the objective facts of Hinduism, and how his interpretations are related to other Protestant interpretations.

(Suggestions and criticisms will be welcomed.)

--N. H.

The Meeting of Muslim and Christian

Kenneth Cragg

In 1948 in Algiers there appeared a French novel by Malek Bennabi, one of the most articulate of Algerian Muslim writers. It concerned the conversion to the state of Islamic 'Falah' or good-in life, of a drunkard youth from Bone in Algeria, where the story opened. Pilgrims from the Maghreb had gathered in the seaport and the boat for Mecca was leaving on the morrow. The harbor-town had been busy with farewells and a festive air hung over the evening. Those not fortunate enough to go on pilgrimage had petitioned the happy ones to remember them at the well of Zamzam. Brahim, the hero of the story, had been oblivious of these pious aspirations all around him. He staggered home at midnight -- drunk as usual. Unable in his stupefaction to turn the key in the lock, Brahim had roused his uncle Muhammad in the midst of the night prayers. Remonstrating with his nephew, as often before, the uncle recalled the pious parents of the youth whose memory was now so wantonly desecrated.

Mumbling that his lot was 'Maktüb' Brahim stumbled to his bed and fell into a heavy sleep. But in the early morning he awoke after a dream of the Ka'bah where he had seen himself in the *Ihräm* garment of the pilgrim throngs. In a reverie he surveys his past life -- the drunken charcoal-seller of Bone. Into his reflections breaks the raucous *Hayyä' alä-l-Fälah* of the morning muezzin. "Come ye unto the good," Brahim impulsively decides to go to the mosque and in his unaccustomed prayers he resolves to make the pilgrimage. Since the boat is to leave that very afternoon rapid action is called for. But uncle Muhammad, overjoyed at the strange turn of events, aids him with the necessary papers and the sudden resolve becomes a reality.

Bennabi describes life aboard the pilgrim ship with insight. But his main theme is the regeneration of a soul, Brahim befriends a street urchin who has stowed away on the ship and his solicitude for this lad plays a part in his own transformation. After the pilgrimage Brahim decides to stay in Medina, where the story leaves him as a cafe-waiter reconciled with his former wife, who had divorced him for his drunkenness, but who now comes to the Prophet' s city to rejoin him. The title of the novel, significantly, is *Labbaika*, the word with which the pilgrim repeatedly announces his advent to the *Haramain*, "Here I am before thee O God," The study behind the title is a study of a man's reclamation by the good to which, in God, Islam bears witness.

We begin with Bennabi only to leave him at once. Our purpose is not to evaluate his thinking, nor to suggest that Brahim' s remaining in Medina is perhaps regrettable if Bone is where he lived in wrong. Nor do we want here to explore the question whether the novel does not suggest somehow that it is easy to be good or that a man's retrieval need not involve redemption. The sole purpose in using Bennabi here at the outset of our theme is the assurance his novel provides that the things the Christian Gospel means and says have an immediate relevance to universal man. Indeed that there is a commonness about humanity and that the significance of the Gospel is an inclusive significance, since it is about precisely those things which are the burden of all existence and the ultimate concern of *all* religion.

These truths may sound trite and indisputable. Yet such has been the general course of Muslim-Christian relations that it is often this very confidence in the relevance of the Christian thing to the Muslim best which has been doubted or obscured. The encounter has too often looked like an academic barter, or banter, of competitive metaphysical systems or a kind of abstruse theological exchange of total alternatives where we have seemingly conceived that what we had to gain was a debating victory, rather than a spiritual awakening and that we had to work against rather than through Islamic concepts. Because, however, of the long legacy of Muslim-Christian relations it is good that we should be fortified at the beginning with the realization that beneath all that may have seemed barren and tedious there abides a real and an attainable mutuality of significance. He who goes into the world with the Gospel of Christ need never fear that what he takes is not already in positive relation to the religious meanings he encounters, however much he himself may fail in serving that relation. Nor, in the same world as God, need we ever lose heart.

A hopeful attitude, then, even despite the legacies and precedents of the past is not only our first need but our proper right. No implication is meant here against the massive loyalty and dogged erudition with which the great Muslim-Christian controversy in earlier centuries was served. Every generation owes much to its position in the sequence and none has right to graceless reproach of those that went before. Our debt to past controversialists is immense -- and not only for the lessons of mistakes. Moreover, Islam itself has been transformed and the visage of much of Islam today differs profoundly from that which scorned Henry Martyn's mission or expressed itself in Ibn Hazm. If we are to be rightly critical of the history of Muslim-Christian controversy we must be rightly grateful for what by its painstaking it exempts us from, for what by its concentrations it frees us for.

No attempt is to be made here to examine in detail the course or content of that long controversy. I hope I am interpreting aright your wishes in trying to concentrate on the contemporary scene. But a few general remarks on the historical may perhaps be made as a prelude to our main concern. The story itself has been well traced by Harry Dorman in his doctoral study at Columbia *Towards Understanding Islam*. Professor Sweetman's volumes, especially the third in the series *Islam and Christian Theology*, offer a wealth of detail on the themes and pre-occupations of Christian writers and polemicists vis-a-vis Islam from John of Damascus, through Ricoldo of Monte Crucis and Ramon Lull. More recently, Gottfried Pfander's monumental *Balance of Truth* is still available, the number of its editions bearing witness to its esteem.

But through all these classic exponents of the Christian controversy with Islam, -- in Abu Qurra, Al-Kindl, Peter the Venerable and Nicholas of Gusa -- we find recurring patterns of argument that dominate the course of thought. And the Muslim reaction, though it varies in tone profoundly, as between Ibn Hazm for example and Al-Ghazali, revolves around the business of reciprocating defense and is not really sent self-critically into the heart of its own inward heritage. It is provoked, or inspired, to find Muslim resources for Christian antagonism, but rarely Muslim reasons for Christian openness. It is these latter surely that we must seek to explore as they lie latent in such thoughts as those of Malek Bennabi, and other Muslim self-expression to which we shall turn below.

The classic Christian controversy seems, however, to have left the Muslim much as he was inwardly and more vigilant outwardly. There are three important characteristics of the great controversy which may perhaps be noted: its scriptural pre-occupation, its comparative history and its metaphysical abstraction. The word 'scriptural' is purposely used here with a small ' s' to indicate the competitive authorities of recorded revelation. There is a clash of the Biblical and the Quranic. Pfander, to take a late example, explores what should be the criteria of the true revelation, then finds them vindicated ideally in the Bible and dismally unvindicated in the Quran. Henry Martyn ventures on a similar argument. The very earliest writers on the Christian side emphasize the prophetic fulfillment of the Bible and the lack of prophecy for Muhammad. Rarely does the discussion penetrate into the basic issue of the appropriateness of the auricular revelation of Muhammad's experience over against the concept of personality as the supremely proper vehicle of the self-disclosure of God. Rather the disputants assert the authority of their traditional volumes and when their claims are returned in kind, they develop more and more acumen in discovering flaws in the other's book or rebuffing allegations which their own provocation has done something to sharpen. Was it not in part the form of Christian controversy over Muhammad as the non-prophesied Prophet which engendered the complicating Muslim habit of searching curiously for Biblical precedents and parallels for the Arabian founder of Islam? It is true that certain features of the Islamic notion of the inter-relatedness of *Taurah*, *Zabür* and *Injïl* explains this in part. But much of the liability of this kind of discussion, still with us in the Ahmadiyyah movement, we owe to the ineptitude of much Christian custodianship of Biblical faith.

Then there was the instinctive comparison of histories, touching to the quick the Muslim susceptibilities about the nature of Muhammad and his role in history, sacred and mundane. All too often those comparisons gravitated to the least important areas having to do with wars and marriages, more than anything else. Not that these do not have their place. The trouble was that they tended to monopolize debate and so to obscure the deeper questions of which they formed only part. Muhammad was taken to task, at once too much and too little, castigated on the one side and so in turn vindicated on the other by criteria that had not plumbed the depths of their duties to the absolutes of every age. At its worst this kind of controversy provoked Muslims into wild and sometimes irrelevant discussions of western patterns of sexual behavior, or at other times it stimulated certain Muslim minds to condemn as weakness, or even effeminacy, the qualities of the Jesus of the Gospels. When this happened Muslims had been carried far from the traditional veneration for Jesus which, looking upon Him as the prince of pilgrims, or the Imam of the homeless (*Imäm al-Sä' ihïn*), did not normally associate Him with any compromise of manliness. In this way the form of Christian controversy in some sense contributed to the obscuring of the very Gospel picture itself, in a way that cannot wholly be attributed to malice on the other side.

Since all religious systems, being, as Martin Buber finely said, molds into which the spirit of man is poured, tend to react defensively to alternatives that present themselves aggressively. The Christian concentration on the reprehensibility's of Muhammad and of Muslim history frequently evoked a self-vindicating reaction of the 'tu quoque' kind, or else a hardening of alienation. Only rarely did they lead the Muslim mind back into an examination of its own heritage. It is not without significance that the Aljmadiyyah Movement as one of the most expressive and assertive elements in contemporary Islam was largely generated in a context, at Qadian, of conscious anti-Christian militancy. The areas in which it has been ready for compromise of Muslim orthodoxy have been areas involving a sharpened resistance to the Church, in an effort to render Islam -- even at the price of unorthodoxy -- more independent of Christian eschatology. It is this defensive reaction against missions which largely explains why Mirza Ghulam re-interpreted the Quranic account of the crucifixion to allow of Christ's being nailed on the Cross without dying, and then buried Him in Kashmir. In this way, his heavenly 'rapture' was eliminated and Islam is emancipated- from any further expectation vis-a-vis Christ. Is this way, it would appear, Mirza Ghulam Ahmad wished to fortify a Muslim sense of distinctiveness and self-sufficiency. But the immediate point is that he was responding negatively to Christian mission. This is a paradox we do well to ponder. It returns in part to that sense of menace to Islam which Christian expression aroused when it centered itself so much on historical controversial assessments of a delinquent Muhammad.

When this emphasis on history was extended into comparative discussion of Muslim Empire it was always in danger of being forced into the role of the Devil's advocate, in the sense that it was necessary to dwell on the sinister and unsavory aspects of historic Islam in order to prove the point. This of course is not a situation unique to missionary writing. Politicians have been guilty too. When Lord Cromer, for example, wrote that "Islam reformed is Islam no longer" he coined a foolish phrase which really meant that he wanted the essential Islam to remain the atrophied thing he thought it was. This may have been an easy way since it obviates the need to reckon with change and the unfamiliar. But it is entirely inappropriate to its subject. Temple Gairdner of Cairo in his writing on Islam was always acutely aware of this danger of seeming to want Islam at its worst just in order to have a readier, more devastating case to make for an alternative. He always sought to avoid it, since it invariably provokes from the other side some form of the retort: "But this is not that: Islam is not the thing you accuse it of being." It is a very obvious further step to dismiss the interpreter of the Gospel as the calumniator of Islam. Such is the dilemma to which an over-controversial historical pre-occupation seems often led.

An undue confidence in metaphysical debate was the third point in our analysis. This need hardly be illustrated here. One can find documented in Sweetman with more fullness than one can readily digest the Christological niceties and minutiae of Muslim-Christian controversy. Doubtless numerous factors made for this. But alike in Ramon Lull and Henry Martyn we find this -- to us -- strange confidence in the power of dialectic, this excessively logical and terminological approach. When perpetuated into our times it sets many inter Muslim-Christian themes in areas where they have no meaning for the average devotee on either side, or in realms that are abstrusely remote from the business of the new social and national context.

Yet having assessed the classic exposition of Christian truth for Muslims as unduly 'scriptural,' historical and ontological, in the senses indicated, we must beware the impression that these areas of meeting are dispensable or avoidable. When Professor Christy Wilson, in his *Christian Message to Islam* a few years ago, wrote that the whole Muslim-Christian controversy had passed into the limbo of forgotten things, he surely overstated the case. It is not so much *Whither* controversy?, since the Gospel in the profoundest sense is always controversial. The question is perhaps rather *Whither* controversy? or How? and Whence? It may be said that the most ultimately controversial is never provocatively so. The controversy of Christ with the soul is not always in or through the controversy of the Christian with the system. Yet it is through Christians, concerned about systems, that Christ works. Here is the heart of our problem. It is no use calling for things like Biblical realism and assuming that by a phrase we have banished the besetting needs -- or sins -- of controversy. When the Madras report on evangelism appealed in the Near East section for "the winning way to the Muslim heart" and identified it as the way of witness and the sharing of experience it was profoundly right. But the accompanying implication that thereby all sharpness of issue could be eliminated was mistaken. We may rightly desire to escape Christological subtleties as an exercise in scholasticism. But personal witness to God in Christ cannot be sincere without also being doctrinal. This then is the inescapability, and yet the liability, of the controversial. How to transmit, without compromising the mood of hospitality without which no transmission is likely, how to join issues without separating contact, how to be adequately Christian in terms both of truth and love: these are our needs.

We are of course seeking in these paragraphs a valid contemporary form of Muslim-Christian meeting. We are doing so in implicit recognition that only the Holy Spirit guides and only by His wisdom is ours not foolishness. But the Apostles themselves wrote on one occasion about matters seeming "good to the Holy Ghost and us." We should not pretend to that claim but at least the apostolic precedent for it encourages the belief that the Holy Spirit may be working in the instrumental thinking of such as we are, provided we are humble enough to be just instrumental. Such at any rate must be the aspiration in all such discussion as we are engaged on here. In that understanding let's turn to the present, fortified as we are by the long and probing lessons of many precedents.

Back for a moment to Malek Bennabi and his 'converted' charcoal seller. Must we not strive to address our ministry to felt needs within Islam and to deepening their feltness? Can we leave aside for the moment the question whether 'conversion' *has* to be patterned as we know it in Christ, through the Cross and unto the Church, and gratefully explore with any Muslims who will join us the corollaries of men's remaking as they see it from the minaret and through the muezzin's call? Let us strive to open up the whole rich meanings of the Christian understanding of man on the basis of where alert Muslims already find him. Let us mediate the Christian understanding of Christ from the starting point of the Muslim understanding of God, for there are so many points in the latter, which argue up into the former. Indeed, how often in studying Islam does the awakened Christian mind find itself saying in the words of Jesus: 'Ye believe in God, believe also in Me.' How can we interpret the force of this 'also' -- the necessity of somebody like Christ to any valid sense of a good omnipotence?

These are only a few of the queries that have to do with the vistas opened up by a mission to Islam that begins with what Muslims already believe and goes forward in terms of Muslim concepts -- their implications and their corollaries, it may be inconsistencies. "Let the word of Christ," said St. Paul, "dwell in you richly in all wisdom." Let the Christian message, he surely implied, be so deeply implanted in the mind that it controls all thinking and inspires all responses. Let it so enter into the collective body of the faithful that it really makes a home for itself in their minds, secure enough to be hospitable to all that need it in the context and as expressive, by that very hospitality, as any true home is, of its inmost nature. This, in Pauline metaphor is what we have in mind. Not, that is, to think of the Christian mission as going out to do battle, but going out to take in guests, to give itself and so its message in a genuine openness to all the aspirations and dilemmas of the world, not holding them indubiety because they start outside the Church, but ripening them by ministry to the maturity of their promise.

We will not stay here to discuss the agencies through which this can be done, the institutions, publications, forms, through which this hospitably dwelling word of Christ in us invites men to its wealth of wisdom. In the end all those means turn on persons, people in whose hearts Christ Himself has taken up His abode. Instead our duty here in the time that remains is simply to try to illustrate a few out of many central ideas in contemporary Islam in terms of which we may hope that "the word of Christ might dwell in us richly."

Let us take first what we will risk here calling the problem of evil, not however in the sense of a theological discussion as to its origin, nor yet a theodicy in face of it, still less an evaluation of human freedom and Divine responsibility. Rather take the problem of evil as a dilemma of the new Muslim societies. May not some people come into a sense of the wrongness of the soul through the wrongness of the soul through the wrongness of society? The second at least is a phenomenon that events and thoughts in some circles in Islam are making paramount. Consider for a moment the obvious fact of new political self-responsibility through most of the Muslim world. This development is a feature of our own generation too familiar to require elaboration. But notice how, for the thinking person, the new independence is obliged to turn the human giagnosis inward. The old external alibis are no longer convincing. It is true that some features of the Pakistani or the Egyptian or the Indonesian scene may still be blamed on the lengthening entail of British or Dutch occupation. A balanced view of imperialism is not something to be looked for in the present mood of self-awareness. But the range and validity of these alibis are steadily diminished as the years recede. Not only independence but wrongness is more and more seen to be one's own. The negative cast of mind, the external militancy necessary to oust the foreigner, these must gradually give way to self-constructiveness. The transference is not easy. But all that is necessary for our point here is that it has to be made. The more people become responsible for themselves the more the minds of their thinkers are confronted by the puzzles of their human nature – puzzles which were formerly veiled in measure because the inclusive diagnosis of the ills about men went indubitably and unerringly to the foreigner. The problem of evil is now a more domestic problem. Moreover, it is one which Islam in its new recovery of destiny believes itself not only competent, but designed, to solve.

So it is that we see religious ideology in measure underlying new movements of social reform sustained by the new nationalisms. It is true that in most Muslim countries the forces in power are not representative of conservative Islam. But they are surely in temper and intention deeply Muslim. The Egyptian Regime offers the most obvious and instructive example. It is dealing in effect with the problem of evil -- the evil of debauched monarchy, of corrupt politics, of social injustice and inequality, of national compromise with selfishness. Hence its internal revolution, while inspired in measure by Quranic concepts, is also deeply concerned about one sorry aspect of the earlier 'evil' in Egypt, namely its tolerance of a state of gross self-interest that led directly to the Arab defeat in the Palestine War of 1948-49. Indeed it is just this Arab view of that Arab debacle, as a part of the evil of its past, that underlies the impermanence in the Arab mind of the present state of truce. Israel, so to speak, bettered itself territorially and now wants to perpetuate that advantage, -- all as a concomitant of a tragic Arab political compromise of the true virtues of Islam. However this may seem to us, it is the way the Arabs see it. Palestine becomes a kind of symbol of what ought not to have been, not simply in the sense that peoples ought not to get defeated, but that they should not have gone into it already self-defeated by their own wrongness. So the problem of evil is real to the thinking Arab in the Near East, even if he passionately merges the one awareness with the other antipathy to Israel, into whose hands the deeper maladies actually played. But how many peoples before in history have always been able to distinguish clearly between the occasions of their failure and its causes?

Internally, then, and externally, this problem of why men are what they are, themselves their own worst foes, is present or latent in many Muslim minds. Nor is it a theory that is wanted but a remedy. It is worth pausing to remark that the problem of evil is all the entire sharper in a system like Islam which believes in the givenness of the good. Men's recalcitrance cannot be credited to ignorance. For the perfect revelation is in hand. Nor does exhortation to the revelation provide the answer, for such exhortation goes on all the time. The mystery is man' s competence to ignore it. His recalcitrance *is* recalcitrance, not weakness or ignorance. And how does this non-submission, this non-*Islam*, this won't-power, this insubordination, relate itself to God, who is presumably deified, at least by implication, when the law of which He is the source, is flouted? Here are doors wide open to the Christian meanings of redemption, insofar as the word of Christ dwells in us sensitively.

Glance sometime at Abd al-Nàsir' s little book *Falsafat-al-Thaurah* (English translation: "Egypt's Liberation.") He refers there eloquently ' to the need of a remaking of human nature, beyond a change of political regime. What he sought for, he writes, on the morrow of the revolution was for a single Egyptian who was not asserting his 'I' and scheming to make personal advantage out of the new occasion. But how does one come by these new men? How does one inject into the body social the inestimable benefit of disinterested unselfish souls, the stuff of national recovery and the sinew of social action? These are the questions to which the Church must speak, and speak as it must in the assurance that what it has to say is not a depredatory thing against which Islam does well to be guarded, but a meaning central to man's deepest hopes.

How, again, does one properly correct a situation like that of Israel as the Arab sees it? How does one react to the sense of being wronged? With destructive recrimination in which one also involves and blights oneself? Or with a recognition that only good, positive good, casts out evil, and only love builds and redeems? "Can Satan cast out Satan" is perhaps the profoundest of the Gospel sayings. To get to rights the situation as it is in the Middle Eastern world is infinitely costly because it cannot be repaired without its acceptance as it is. It is just this costliness of setting the world to rights which the Cross so eloquently proclaims, not as some arbitrarily constructed scheme of atonement, but as the central and inclusive expression of the forgivingness that assures forgiveness. So in being lifted up Christ draws all men unto Himself, gathers into His own passion the clue and the cost of their redemption. I do not suggest that all men can see this, now or soon. Still less that the Arab world is poised for a great act of magnanimity such as would retrieve the entail of its own and other's wrongs and make reconciliation a door of hope. But what we must say is that these are the real meanings of the place where men find themselves and that this is what Christ says to their situation. This is the true shape, surely, of His controversy with men. For all occasions, if only we interpret their fullness, are schoolmasters to bring us unto Christ.

I am not, of course, suggesting here that the Western ministrant can broach evangelism among Arab Muslims from the starting point of co-existence with Israel. Nothing so inane. At best he will only win the retort that as a Westerner he is anxious to see the liquidation of a situation that troubles his conscience. At worst much else. But what is meant here is that we must help the minds of men to think into the deepest meanings of their own dilemmas and that as they do so they will be learning the mind of Christ.

Are there any signs that these dilemmas are really searched? I think so. It is hard to know how much weight to attach to Abd al-Näsir's little book. But taken at its face value it goes deep into these realms of man and evil, as all sincere political reformers must. There is some evidence also in Arab circles of a new interest in the person of Christ and not least in the Cross. One striking item here is the recent study by Muhaammad Kämil Husain, a member of the Arab Academy, called *Qaryah Zälimah*, "City of Wrong." There is no time to discuss it fully here and perhaps no need since a contributor to the April and July issues of *The Muslin World*, 1956, has analyzed it carefully. Let me simply add that the orthodox view of the Quran on the Cross not only allows but requires the antagonism of the Jews to Jesus, which *willed* He should be crucified. What it disallows is the consummation of that purpose, which God thwarted by having the Jews crucify mistakenly a likeness to Jesus, while He escaped from the Garden to Heaven but the Passion, so to speak, up to Gethsemane, is all there, even in the Quranic denial that Jesus was crucified. He was at least One whom men intended to crucify. Even Abbäs al Aqqäd in his 1952 study on "The Genius of Christ" referred to the opposition suffered by Jesus as the bitterest accorded to any Prophet. So Muhammad Husain finds in the passions and reasoning's of Jews, and Romans, culminating in the sentence against Jesus, an index to the wrongness of humanity. These sins, he says, are re-committed day by day across the world. They were not isolated or confined to Jews and Romans. Indeed that Friday when Jesus was sentenced to suffer, men willed to crucify the conscience of mankind. Let me commend to you this book, as one of the most penetrating expressions of Muslim openness to the meaning of the Gospel that I have ever encountered. Nowhere of course does the author explicitly state that the Cross happened. But all that he writes is destined to shattering anti-climax unless he is prepared to concede that there was a self -offering of Jesus in a situation of contradiction (as Hebrews calls it) whereby men are shown to themselves for what they are. Surely to grasp this truth of the Cross as an index to humanity is to be on the way to a sense of its meaning as an index to God. One has only to pass beyond Jesus teaching by what He said (so as to arouse the enmity that made the Cross) to Jesus teaching by what He did with that enmity. Here surely the clues go together. To have seen the one is to be on the way to the other. We may be coming to a time in our missionary lifetime when the historicity of the Crucifixion will cease to be merely a matter of academic debate and become a theme of genuine understanding. If that happens we will be a long way to turning the flank of lots of the old Christological and Trinitarian controversies. For in the end the meaning of the Trinity is that God cares enough to redeem.

There is perhaps space for one other, somewhat different illustration of how we may search for a new and active Muslim awareness of what is distinctive in Christianity -- the sort of awareness that stays to ponder before it moves to disprove. Let me refer briefly to the basic Muslim concept of *Shirk* on which I ventured to write in a short discussion in the January issue of *The Muslim World* (to which I refer only to excuse the present brevity). *Shirk* as you remember is the deadly sin of association with God, the associating, rather, of anything with God so that it receives worship, attributes, functions, or ascriptions proper only to the One God. *Shirk* is the antithesis of *Tauhïd*. The One God is militantly so, intolerant of all usurpation, implied or actual, of His uniqueness. It may take many forms, but the one most popularly in mind when the term is used is of course idolatry, or plurality of deities. It is under the invalidity of *Shirk* that Islam condemns the Christian faith in the Divinity of Christ. It reprobates the classic Christian doctrine as a piece of idolatry it was designed to destroy. Yet nothing could be more polar in its contrast than idolatry is from Christology properly understood.

This business of association, as the Quran forbids it, is of course, association by men with God. It is deifying it deplores, it does not (though the average Muslim does not stay to think this out)-- it does not exclude an association which the Divine wills with some human place, agent or time. Indeed revelation and religion alike would be impossible if God had no access to, no instrumentalities in, the world of men. Islam itself has many such loci of the Divine action – Muhammad and Mecca in particular. These are the focal points, historically and geographically, of a Divine enterprise of revelation. In pilgrimage the Muslim comes to greet them both and says as he does so: "Here I am O God before Thee." In this revelatory sense the Divine is emphatically 'associated' with the human, though not of course so as to make the human Divine. But the human is certainly caught up into the counsels and intent of the Divine. Now of course the Christian understanding of Christ arises in just this realm of the Divine action. The great difference is that there are certain Divine purposes which the faith understands to be so rich and real that only God can truly undertake them. They are incapable of delegation. It takes God, we say, to reveal God, so when God is revealed it is God also Who is revealing. Man's redemption, being a deed of love such as only God has, must necessarily be God's deed. The crowning of prophetic revelation in the Son, the crowning of the Divine Compassion in the Cross, these are tasks so tremendous as to be inalienably Divine, both in their concept and their doing. So properly seen, the Christian understanding of Christ is not a part or an instance of the *Shirk* Islam decries, but a part -- the instance -- of that Divine involvement in the human which the Quran posits only through *tanzīl* to the Prophet. Christian faith about Christ is not deification. The direction is all the other way. Essential man is not made God by human superstition. The Word is made flesh. We on our side are recognizing a Divine involvement in our world that is inalienably Divine precisely because in its Self-giving it has no limits that withhold it.

Islam in effect 'withholds' God from such totality of involvement and does so in the interests of what it understands to be the Divine transcendence. But the Divine coming is no compromise of the Divine majesty, so long as it is Self-willed and so long as one obeys Divine, and not human, criteria, of what is fitting to God. These reflections merge into many more themes upon which there is no space here to enlarge: how the Divine prerogative of forgiveness, in which Islam believes, should be conceived to be at work: how the *Rahmān* becomes the *Rahīm*, how the revelation of a sovereign law involves the action of a sovereign grace, unless evil is to leave us with an unresolved dichotomy. There is also the question whether idolatry, which errs mathematically, is as heinous a form of *Shirk*, as men's defiance, which errs morally. Men who make themselves, their systems or their races, into ultimate's do more to flout the Oneness of God in ways that matter than does the simple pagan, who often multiplies deities out of a sense either of worshipfulness or fear.

But these questions we must leave. My purpose in raising the query about *Shirk* is simply that I feel a proper understanding of what it does, and what it cannot, mean helps to pave the way for a Muslim understanding of Christ from within his own sense of Divine sovereignty and activity towards man. There are signs in some quarters both in the Arab world and Pakistan that Muslims themselves are aware of the deep significance of the Muslim idea of *Shirk* as something much more inclusive than anti-idolatry in its Arabian form. Indeed they say there are conceivably senses in which even Islam itself in some forms is a kind of *Shirk*, if and when nomocracy, or community, or Islam for its own sake, usurp the role that only God should play in the lives of His creatures. But all that I mean to say here is that the more Muslims explore the feasible connotations of this most basic of all Muslim concepts, the further they will get from devalidating Christianity on such score. And positively, they may learn the Christian form of that Divine human inter-relatedness without which all religion would be farce and fantasy.

Many thanks for your patience. I do wish a more normal situation allowed me to be with you. The foregoing is a poor gesture towards a vast problem, but as long as men are men and Muslims are Muslims and Christ is Christ we'll be putting our minds and wills to these themes. God be with you.

The Christian Faith And Other Religions: The Present Phase

R. Pierce Beaver

The Madras Conference of 1938 stimulated vigorous discussion of the relationship of Christianity to other religions, but the advent of the Second World War soon brought other concerns to the fore, and the subject receded into the background. The political religion of nationalism in its Nazi, Fascist, and Japanese forms, received more attention than the old religions and the Christian confrontation of them. After the War had passed, the rise of a new political religion, Communism, drew major attention. However, new movements were stirring in the old faiths, and within a few years it became evident that they were experiencing a renaissance or resurgence. Allied with nationalism, the ancient religions were soon confronting young churches and western missions with a challenge in the form both of practical obstacles and an apologetic literature. Consequently the relation of the Christian revelation to the other faiths has now become one of the livest issues in theology and in strategy currently demanding the attention of the Christian world mission.

The confrontation of vital religious forces by the Christian mission today is no mere academic concern, nor is it simple. It leads directly to the basic theological issue: What is that *mission* to which the whole Church throughout the world, and not just the Western Church, is called in unity? It poses the urgent questions of the life and message to be communicated, the "how" of communicating them, the indigenous expression of universals, fostering the growth of new churches in a manner which imparts evangelistic zeal, and a host of other questions. Both global strategy and local evangelistic methods await illumination by the answers to these questions.

There are at least five ways in which the mission agencies of the Church are presently responding to the contemporary revival of religions. These are: fostering Christian scholarship, technically competent and sufficient in numbers to provide the Church with the data and insights needed for meeting the challenge of this radically new situation; trying to understand what is actually occurring within the various religions; preparing to meet the apologetic put forth by old religions newly become missionary; studying seriously the problem of the Gospel in relation to other religions; and experimenting in the approach, or witness, to devout adherents of other faiths.

FOSTERING SCHOLARSHIP

A quarter of a century ago the opinion spread among missionaries that the Eastern religions were moribund and would eventually die out. They were considered no longer to be a challenge to the expansion of Christianity. Mission boards and societies then saw little reason to urge their missionaries to devote time and talent to the study of these religions. Moreover, scholarly interest in general appears to have waned among missionaries after World War I. Consequently neither the young churches nor the missionary societies have more than a meager handful of experts in the history of religions who can supply the information and the insights now desperately needed for an understanding of these religions, which are so important an ingredient of nationalism, which hold the key to the understanding of national and regional cultures, and which are satisfying the spiritual hunger of millions. This situation is in marked contrast to -that of earlier periods of mission history, when missionaries like James Legge, William E. Soothill, S. Wells Williams, and Timothy Richards--to name a few scholars in one country only -- were the principal authorities on the cultures and religions of Asian lands.

Scholars are not entirely lacking among missionaries, to be sure, and a few are constantly at work. A small stream of books has come from the press since World War II. Islam, more than any other religion, attracts missionary scholarship, despite the fact that the mission to Arab lands is an infinitely smaller operation in the quantity of men and money involved than any other segment of the world mission. The total mission among Muslims everywhere is not large. Since the end of World War II there have appeared, for example, the first three volumes of *Islam and Christian Theology* by J. Windrow Sweetman, professor of Islamics at the Selly Oak

Colleges.[1] J. Spencer Trimingham has published three studies *The Christian Approach to Islam in the Sudan* (1948), *Islam in Ethiopia* (1952), and *The Christian Church and Islam in West Africa* (pamphlet, 1955).[2] He also has in preparation a book on Islam in West Africa *Islam in East Africa*, by Lyndon Harries,[3] is another regional study but not as high in quality. There have been published also such works as: *Toward Understanding Islam*, by Harold G. Dorman, Jr.;[4] *How to Lead Moslems to Christ*, by George K. Harris;[5] *Islam*, by Emmanuel Kellerhals;[6] *Mohammod at Mecca*, by W. Montgomery Watt;[7] and *The Christian Message to Islam*, by J. Christy Wilson.[8] *The Call of the Minaret*, by Kenneth Cragg, is in press.

Hinduism follows Islam as the next most intensive field of study, and publications of this recent period include: *The Christian Message to the Hindu*, by A. G. Hogg;[9] *The Religion of Tagore in the Light of the Gospel*, by Sigrid Eastborn;[10] *Two Religions : A Comparative Study of Some Distinctive*

---

[1]   Sweetman, J. Windrow, *Islam and Christian Theology*, London: Lutterworth, 1947.

[2]   Trimingham, J. Spencer, *The Christian Approach to Islam in the Sudan,* London: Oxford University Press, 1948. *Islam in Ethiopia*, London: Oxford University Press, 1952, *The Christian Church and Islam in West Africa,* (I.M.C, Research Pamphlets No, 3) London: S.C.M. Press, 1955.

————————. *Islam in Ethiopia.* London: Oxford University Press, 1952.

————————. *The Christian Church and Islam in West Africa.* (I.M.C. Research Pamphlets No. 3) London: S. C. M. Press, 1955.

[3]   Harries, Lyndon P. *Islam in East Africa*, London: U.M.C.A., 1955.

[4]   Dorman, Harold G., Jr. *Toward Understanding Islam*, New York: Columbia University Press, 1948.

[5]   Harris, George K. *How to Lead Moslems to Christ*, London: China Island Mission, 1947.

[6]   Kellerhals, Emanuel, *Islam*, Basel: Easier Missionsbuchhandlung, 1945.

[7]   Watt, W. Montgomery, *Mohammed at Mecca*, London: Oxford University Press, 1953.

[8]   Wilson, J. Christy. *The Christian Message to Islam*, New York: Revell, 1950.

[9]   Hogg, A. G., *The Christian Message to the Hindu.* London: S. C. M. Press, 1947.

[10] Estborn, Sigrid, *The Religion of Tagore in the Light of the Gospel.* Madras: C. L. S., for India, 1940.

Ideas and Ideals in Hinduism and Christianity, by John MacKenzie; [11] and *Social Ethics in Modern Hinduism*, by Roland W.Scott. [12]

A few studies in Buddhism have been published since the end of World War II, including *Paradox and Nirvana*, by Robert Lawson Slater, [13] and *Man in Buddhism and Christianity*, by Bryan de Kretser.[14] Chinese religions in general have been treated by Francis Cho-min Wei in *The Spirit of Chinese Culture* [15] and by Karl Ludwig Reichelt in *Religion in a Chinese Garment* (translated by Joseph Tetlie). [16]

These recent studies, it will be seen, fall into two types. There are analytical and interpretative works on aspects of particular religions, and there are a number of studies in the confrontation of specific religions by Christianity. The latter type reveals an increasing concern with central theological issues; and the problem of the Christian faith in relation to others is taken up in a large perspective in a small number of able studies. Hendrick Kraemer's *Christian Message in a Non-Christian World* has a reading many times as large as that following publication nearly twenty years ago, and is now being reprinted. [17] His new book, *Religion and the Christian Faith*, will be published this month in England and next fall in America. Other titles include: *Religious Truth and the Relation Between Religions*, by D. G. Moses; [18] *The Christian Interpretation of Religion*, by Edward J. Jurhi; [19] and

---

[11] McKenzie, John. *Two Religions: A Comparative Study of Some Distinctive Ideas in Hinduism and Christianity*, London: Lutterworth, 1950.

[12] Scott, Roland W. *Social Ethics in Modern Hinduism*, Calcutta: Y. M. C. A., Printing House, 1953.

[13] Slater, Robert Lawson, *Paradox and Nirvana*, Chicago: University of Chicago Press, 1952.

[14] De Kretser, Bryan, *Man in Buddhism and Christianity*, Calcutta: Y.M.C.A. Publishing House, 1954.

[15] Wei, Francis C. M. *The Spirit of Chinese Culture*, New York: Scribner's, 1947.

[16] Reichelt, Karl Ludwig, *Religion in a Chinese Garment*, translated by Joseph Tetlie, London: Lutterworth Press, 1951.

[17] Kramer, Hendrick, *The Christian Message in a Non-Christian World*, New York: Harper & Brothers for the T. M. C., 1930.

[18] Moses, D. G. *Religious Truth and the Relation Between Religions*, Madras: C. L. S. 1950 (London: Lutterworth).

[19] Jurji, Edward J. *The Christian Interpretation of Religion*, New York: Macmillan, 1952.

The Christian Attitude Towards Other Religions, by E. C. Dewicke.[20] These will be treated in a later section. The outstanding example of the current German mission practice of endeavoring to comprehend the whole of the religions of mankind from the standpoint of the Gospel is *Evangelische Religionskundes* by Gerhard Rosenkranz.[21] Intensive study in the problem of the Christian revelation in relation to truth in other religious systems can be fruitful and can gain the respect of scholars only if they combine with biblical and theological competence a thorough grounding in the methodology and phenomenology of *Religionswissenschaft* along with specialized knowledge of specific religious systems.

The Roman Catholic missionary enterprise has been more far sighted than the Protestant missions, and the mission orders and societies have regularly set aside scholars for continuous study. A steady stream of publications has come from their pens and these are available to us. The same is to be said for the scholarly labors of the experts in the universities, although most of them, regarding religion only sociologically, have been hostile to missions. Now, however, new university departments of the history of religions are appearing all over the country, less doctrinaire than older ones and stressing modern movements rather than narrow preoccupation with the ancient classical aspects of the faiths, and many of the new scholars can be drawn into friendly collaboration.

One hears it repeated often that if each missionary agency or young church would devote one per cent of its budget to scholarship in this field the need would be fulfilled. Whatever the figure may be, a small portion of missionary financial resources so invested would return large dividends. And although it is hard to get the funds designated for the purpose, it is much easier to secure the money than to find the right persons to train for the task. Few administrators realize how long and arduous is the task of attaining expert status in this field, even for a member of a young church living in a non-Christian environment. Remedying the present lack of scholars cannot be accomplished in a day. Concern about this need has led through three or four years of discussion to a movement under the auspices of the International Missionary Council for the establishment of institutes for study and training. There will be set up in India next year a new Christian Institute for the Study of Hinduism, under the direction of Dr. Paul D. Devanandan. A similar Institute for the Study of Buddhism is operating in Ceylon and another is being created in Burma. There is soon

---

[20] Dewick, E. C. *The Christian Attitude to Other Religions*. London: Cambridge University Press, 1953.

[21] Rosenkranz, Gerhard, *Evangelische Religionskunde*. Tübingen: Mohr, 1951.

to be set up at Hongkong another such Institute for the study of Chinese religions, especially religion among the overseas Chinese. Another new study center is being projected for Japan. Professor Kenneth Cragg will later this summer begin an experimental approach, with a non-institutional program for the present, in the Near East under the joint sponsorship of the Near East Christian Council, the International Missionary-Council, and the Overseas Missions Council of the Church of England. The Henry Martyn School of Islamics under its new director, Dr. Akbar Abdul Haqq, is said to show new vigor and promise. In addition to the older provisions for study in this field in the United States and Canada, such as Hartford, new resources are developing, such as Cantwell Smith's program in Islamics at McGill University and a new Center for the Study of the Christian World Mission at the University of Chicago, which will put strong emphasis on the problem of the relationship and approach of Christianity to other faiths and also, at the outset, stress the study of Theravadin and Mahayana Buddhism. Thus it is evident that a determined effort is under way to foster the growth of missionary scholarship in the history of religions. If, in the next ten years, half-a-dozen first-rate scholars can be trained up, it will make a tremendous difference in the illumination available to evangelists and will stimulate a deeper probing into the meaning of the Gospel.

THE RESURGENCE OF RELIGIONS

A group of Asian churchmen prepared for the Evanston Assembly a book entitled *Christianity and the Asian Revolution*. [22] One hundred out of its less than three hundred pages are devoted to a section, "Resurgent Religions," and many more pages elsewhere in the book are given to that subject. Every visitor to South and East Asia reports the revival of Buddhism. The modernizing of Hinduism is fascinating to behold. A multitude of new Buddhist, Shinto, and messianic sects have erupted in Japan. [23] Islam is in ferment from the Straits of Gibraltar to Indonesia. Religion is a force in world affairs to a degree not known for many decades.

The revived religions are allied with nationalism. Really a new secular religion, nationalism has succeeded in drawing to itself the blessing

---

[22] Manikam, Rajah B., ed. *Christianity and the Asian Revolution*, [Madras] Joint Secretariat of the International Missionary Council and World Council of Churches, 1954.

[23] See: Ariga, Tetsutaro, "The So-Called 'Newly Arisen Sects' in Japan" in the Missionary Research Library, *Occasional Bulletin*, Vol. V, No. 4 (March 29, 1954).

and the support of the ancient ethnic faiths. Political leaders support the old religions because they have been the integrating force in, and the preserver of, the old indigenous culture, and it is advantageous to associate the sacred traditions of the past with a dynamic program for the present. However, it would be a grave mistake to suppose that the religious revival is due primarily to political manipulation. There is a groundswell of new spiritual life in the Eastern countries, and the politicians who make use of that fact are most frequently also caught up in it personally as practicing believers. Premier U Nu of Burma is an example. Most of the numerous journalistic articles about him, while stressing his political astuteness in making use of Buddhism, nevertheless usually impart also a conviction about his sincerity and devotion as a religious man. Santha Rama Rau reports him as saying, "You think my political position is strong? It is because my religious position is stronger."[24] After reading many of his speeches one seems to hear in this statement as much personal sincerity as political canniness. This is notable in other Asian statesmen as well. Christians in Burma and Ceylon feel political pressures exerted in the name of Buddhism as the national faith, but if they believed that the revival were only political, they would deal with the matter within the National Christian Councils and in the organs of the churches as subjects of strategy. They would not be so keen on establishing permanent study institutions if they did not believe that there were profound spiritual depths in the revival.

Professor Devanandan, writing in the book just mentioned above, states:

> "This is an age of religious revival. The ancient peoples of Asia are passing through revolutionary social changes; they have made rapid advances as independent nations. They turn to their ancestral religions with a new hope. They realize that a good deal of their national culture is closely related to their religious heritage, and that a cultural reintegration necessarily involves a religious reconstruction. Thus, in recent times, the ancient religions of Hinduism, Buddhism, and Islam have become very real forces in the life aid thought of Asian Peoples."[25]

---

[24] Rau, Santha Rama. "Peace, Rice, Friendship and the Burma of U Nu," *Reporter*, Vol. XIV (April 19, 1956).

[25] Manikam, Rajah B., ed. *Christianity and the Asian Revolution*. [Madras] Joint Secretariat of the International Missionary Council and World Council of Churches, 1954.

He goes to the heart of the matter with keen discernment, when he states: "The environment, however stimulating, cannot of itself initiate such movements in religious life and thought unless there is a corresponding responsive reaction on the part of the religion itself. For any response presupposes a certain vitality and 'aliveness' on the part of the responding organism."[26] The new missionary impulse in Buddhism and Islam, for example, is evidence of vitality welling up from within G. R. Jackson states: "The modern missionary movement in Buddhism, though yet unorganized, is one of the most powerful of the many dynamic factors in the Asian revolution."[27]

Not the least significant and interesting phenomenon in the entire religious picture is the rise of a multitude of new movements, religions, and sects from Vietnam to Korea,-- some of them variants of the old religions, some syncretistic products, some apparently *sui generis* in character. Taken together with the movements within the ethnic religions, they strongly reinforce the impression that Asia is in spiritual ferment.

Some observers, on the contrary, come away from Asian countries with an impression of the state of religion quite contrary to that of vigorous revival. Due to the particular persons with whom they associated, they report an espousal of secularism and a turning away from religion. This seems to be especially true among young intellectuals and technologists in India. The fact that a revolt against religion accompanies the revival of religion, only serves to emphasize how complicated is the situation.

Moreover, within the religious ferment of Asia one finds elements of reaction as well as of modernization. There is the Dar-ul-Islam among Moslems and the Mahasabha among the Hindus. Such movements can indicate vitality; they can also indicate the frantic rear-guard delaying actions of despair.

New movements, modernization, reaction, revolt; they all indicate activity and change and focus attention on the present in contrast to the classic philosophies and cultus of the past. These things have immediate bearing on evangelism. There may be no abandonment of the foundation studies in the fostering of scholarship; and Pali, Sanskrit, and Wenli are still important tools for the expert; but the primary stress must now be, as far as missionary scholars are concerned, on the actual present state of the religions as living forces in society. Sociology, cultural anthropology,

---

[26] Ibid., p. 118.

[27] Ibid, p, 140.

economics, political science, modern history and psychology are to be added to the traditional tools and methods of the historian of religion. Attention should be given to description and analysis of the contemporary trends and movements with respect to relationships to the national cultural renaissance and national political aspirations, with regard to their influence in international and intercultural affairs, and with reference to genuine spiritual renewal. Within the focus of study come developments in theology, philosophy, religious literature both technical and popular, *belles-lettres* and journalism, art, education, agencies of propaganda, philanthropy, technical services, and foreign missionary movements.

THE NEW MISSION MOVEMENTS AND APOLOGETICS

An almost entirely new dimension of meeting between Christianity and other religions has been created in the last few years due to the missionary invasion of the post-Christian West by Eastern religions and by the enlarged volume of their apologetic literature directed towards Christians and secularized Westerners. Although Christianity has been encountering an Islamic advance in Africa for several decades and the Ramakrishna-Vivekananda Mission has long worked with American intellectuals in some of our big cities, the presence of missionary agents of Islam and Buddhism pressing for conversions among our people presents a development distinctly new. They must be accorded the same religious liberty, including the right of propagation, which Christian agents claim. Such efforts will probably not be numerically large, but they do bring the challenge of the revived faiths directly to some of our rank and file church members and they present a new opportunity for Christian witness in conversations with their agents. Propaganda directed to the Christian minority in Asia is far more intense.

Far more important at the moment to the world mission than the propagation of Oriental religions in our midst by a few missionary agents, is the apologetic literature addressed towards Christianity. And today this is just as effective and demands just as much attention by the Christian Church in America as in Asia. There is an unprecedented interest in religion among students and intellectuals, John Noss's textbook, *Man's Religion*, [28] has had an extraordinary sale and is now coming out in a revised edition. Other publishers are hurrying books into print in order to cash in on this popularity. Lectures on Oriental religions are popular. Even boys in prep schools are reported to be setting up voluntarily

---

[28] Noss, John B. *Man's Religions*. New York: Macmillan, 1949.

seminars on comparative religions. However, the popularity of such books as Schuon's *The Transcendental Unity of Religions* and *Spiritual Perspectives and Human Facts* [29] and the picture book *Truth Is One*, by Forman and Gammon, [30] indicates the prevailing viewpoint. A kind of Neo-Vedantist outlook has captured a large section of our so-called intelligentsia. All religions are equated as routes to a unity of truth, but there is a tendency to think of Christianity as antiquated and premodern, and what is Eastern is supposed to have some sort of superiority. The less discerning feed upon such books as Akhilananda's *A Hindu View of Christ*, [31] while the more able are attracted to the persuasive reasoning of a work of real stature, like the *Recovery of Faith*, by Radhakrishnan.[32] Buddhism's apology contra Christianity on the grounds of our faith's responsibility for the broken peace of the world and the claim of Buddhism to be able best to provide a spiritual basis for world peace have a strong appeal in both East and West.

The new missionary movements and the apologetic literature of the Asian religions extend the encounter from Asia and Africa into Europe and America. This is one more reason why the mission is a world mission. Pastors and theologians in America and Europe who have thought of the missionary encounter of faiths as something remote ought now acknowledge their front line position and become actively engaged. And perhaps the most significant fact about this new development is that after having been on the defensive against Christian aggression for a very long time, these religions have turned about face, are claiming both spiritual and moral superiority and have put Christianity on the defensive. Canon E. C. Bewick writes: "... some of the non-Christian religions, ancient and modern, are today putting forth claims to absolute supremacy and universality, very similar in essence to those of the political totalitarianisms, and others, while they are admitting that they are not absolutely perfect,

[29] Schuon, Fritjof. *The Transcendental Unity of Religions*. New York: Pantheon, 1953.

_____. *Spiritual Perspectives and Human Facts*. London: Faber, 1954.

[30] Forman, Henry James and Roland Gammon. *Truth Is One*, New York: Harper, 1954.

[31] Akhilananda, Swami. *A Hindu View of Christ*, New York: Philosophical Library, 1949.

[32] Radhakrishnan, Sarvepalli. *Recovery of Faith*, New York: Harper & Brothers Publishers, 1955.

still maintain that they can offer alternatives to Christianity which are move satisfying to the moral and spiritual needs of mankind."[33]

The Gospel and Religions: The Central Issue

The general resurgence of religions and their new missionary activities require that Christian missionary scholarship give high priority to the problem of the relation of the Christian revelation to other systems of religion and to the related question of the approach to adherents of other religions.

It must be recognized that for thousands of missionaries there is no problem. It is with them, as it was with the majority of the missionaries of the nineteenth century, simply a matter of destroying heathenism and replacing it with Christianity. Professor Hocking well characterized this as the concept of radical displacement. Moreover, most of that enormous number of missionaries who have gone out under very conservative faith missions since World War II have a similar idea of "heathenism," but do not look forward to complete displacement. They expect the end before the goal might be achieved, and hope to pluck individual brands from the burning while there is yet time. Both decades of experience in meeting adherents of other religions and objective study by missionary scholars laid bare the wrong perspective and the distortion involved in the usual attitude towards the "heathen," and the majority of missionaries after the beginning of the 20th Century were increasingly uncomfortable about holding such a view. The unhappiest thing about such an attitude is that it tends to magnify in the missionary that un-Christlike spiritual pride to which he appears to be unusually susceptible. During the course of a joint faculty seminar on the Christian mission in which social scientists and theologians participated, references to the pride of missionaries in cultural relations were numerous, and the cumulative effect was painful.

The period roughly from the Edinburgh Conference of 1910 to the Madras Conference of 1938 witnessed the gradual growth to primacy, among English-speaking missionaries at least, of the "fulfillment concept." This is the view that God has never left any of his children orphaned and has in every generation granted the saving revelation of His truth and grace, so that deposits of divine truth are found in the various religious systems. They are, however, "broken lights," containing a mixture of truth and error. All that is good, noble, and true in them is to be gathered up, comprehended, and fulfilled in Christianity, while the error is to be cast

---

[33] Dewick, *The Christian Attitude Towards Other Religions*, p, 39.

off. Thomistic and Anglican theology, relying strongly on ideas of natural theology and general revelation, find such a concept naturally attractive. The book, *Mankind and the Church*,[34] written by a group of English bishops, was a pioneer work in this field. Dr. J. N. Farquhar's notable book, *The Crown of Hinduism*,[35] generally regarded as the typical expression of this viewpoint. His attitude is summed up in these words: "Christ provides the fulfillment of the highest aspirations of Hinduism… He is the Crown of the Faith of India,"The writings of Bishop Appasamy, Kenneth J. Saunders, and Daniel J. Fleming are other examples of this school of thought, and generally hold that whatever is true, good, and noble in the thought and practice of the religions can be transformed, adapted, or sublimated to the worship and service of Christ and made a living part of the experience of the Christians.[36] Dr. Karl Reichelt not only wrote along these lines, but also put his theories into practice in the Christian Mission to Buddhists at the celebrated monastery of Tao Feng Shan.[37] Such an attitude was reflected in the papers and discussions of the Jerusalem Conference of 1928, where a concern over the menace of secularism led many to advocate some degree of a common front against a common enemy.[38]

There were certain persons, especially some American humanists, who were prepared to go far beyond the concept of fulfillment. It came

---

[34] Montgomery, H. H. *Mankind and the Church*, London: Longmans, Green, and Co,, 1907.

[35] Farquhar, J. N. *The Crown of Hinduism*, London: Oxford University Press, 1913.

[36] Appasamy, A. J. *Christianity as Bhakti Marga*. London: Macmillan & Co., 1927.

_____. *The Cross and Hindu Thought*, Madras: 1932.

Saunders, Kenneth J. *The Gospel for Asia*. New York: Macmillan, 1928.

Fleming, Daniel J. *Christian Contacts with Non-Christian Cultures*, New York: Doran, 1923.

_____. *Attitudes Towards Other Faiths*. New York: Association Press, 1928.

_____. *Ways of Sharing with Other Faiths*. New York: Association Press, 1929.

[37] See: Holth, Sverre, *Karl Ludwig Reichelt*, Oslo: Egede Institutet, 1952. This pamphlet presents a sketch of Reichelt's life and work and a bibliography.

[38] See: *The Jerusalem Meeting of the International Missionary Council*, 1928, Vol. I. New York: I. M. C. 1928.

into the open in the report volume of the Laymen' s Foreign Mission Inquiry, entitled *Re-Thinking Missions*, published in 1932. The furor over the theological viewpoint there expressed led to an almost complete disregard of the remainder of the report. Professor William Ernest Hocking, the chairman of the Laymen's Inquiry, developed his ideas fully in a subsequent work entitled, *Living Religions and a World Faith*, [39] and Hugh Vernon White contributed much to the same school of thought in *A Theology for Christian Missions and A Working Faith for the World*.[40] Hocking called his attitude "the concept of reconception," His idea is essentially that by friendly cooperation with other faiths Christianity will discover and develop neglected aspects of its own inherent truth; that the effect on the other religions will be similar; and that eventually then Christianity will become in fact the world faith which it is now potentially, and that the other religions will remain and revolve around Christianity as regional satellites. Professor Arnold Toynbee appears to revive some of these ideas today.

A major challenge to both the prevailing Anglo-Saxon viewpoint and Hocking's concept of reconception was presented by *The Christian Message in a Non-Christian World*, prepared for the Madras Conference by Professor Hendrick Kraemer. [41] No summary of this famous book needs to be given to members of the Association of Professors of Missions. The key words in this work are "Biblical Realism" and "Discontinuity." Biblical Realism demands the conclusion that Christ is *sui generis*, that Christian revelation places itself over against all other efforts to apprehend the totality of existence, that the only possible relation between Christianity and the other religions is one of "discontinuity." It is impossible to compare Christianity and other religions; there are no genuine points of contact or bridges; and the other religions are irrelevant to salvation. Relatively little attention was paid to Professor Kraemer's assertion that empirical Christianity as well as other religious systems stands under the judgment of the revelation in Christ, and still less to his guidance in approach to the other religions.

---

[39] Hocking, William Ernest. *Living Religions and a World Faith*, New York: Macmillan, 1940.

[40] White, Hugh Vernon. *A Theology for Christian Missions*, New York & Chicago: Willett & clark, 1937.

_____. *A Working Faith in the World*, New York: Harper, 1938.

[41] See note 17 above. A new reprint is now being brought out by Feature Publishing Service.

Continental theologians and missionaries supported Kraemer in the debate at Madras and in subsequent books, such as *The Gospel, Christianity and other Faiths*, by Heinrich Frick, [42] and *Mission als Theologische Problem*, by Karl Hartenstein.[43] Most English-speaking missionaries at the time rejected Kraemer's view as decisively as that of Hocking and occupied a middle ground between them. There was lively debate of the issues for a short time after the Madras Conference, but then, as was noted earlier, the advent of the Second World War threw the subject into the background and brought other issues into prominence. Apart from the activities of the so-called Bangalore Continuation Committee, under the leadership of P. Chenchiah, who wrote *Re-Thinking Christianity in India*, [44] little interest was shown in the matter until almost a decade after the end of the war, when the resurgence of the religions had made it a burning issue once more.

One of the first indications of the reemergence of the problem was the publication of *The Gospel and Other Faiths* by Canon E. C. Dewick in 1948, followed by his Hulsean Lectures of 1949 on "The Christian Attitude to Other Religions."[45] The lectures were published under the same title in 1953. *The Impact of Christianity on the Non-Christian World* by J. H. Bavinck appeared simultaneously with Dewick's first book.[46] Then came *Religious Truth and the Relation Between Religions*, by David G. Moses in 1950, [47] and other works including *The Christian Interpretation of Religion*, by Edward J. Jurji, [48] and the section on "Resurgent Religions," in particular J. R. Chandran's chapter on "The Christian Approach to

---

[42]   Frick, Heinrich. *The Gospel, Christianity and Other Faiths*, London: Oxford University Press, 1938. (English Translation).

[43]   Hartenstein, Karl. *Mission als Theologische Problem*, Berlin: Furche-verlag, 1933.

[44]   Chenchiah, P. *Rethinking Christianity in India*, Madras: A. N. Sudarisanam, 1938.

[45]   Dewick, Canon E. C. *The Gospel and Other Faiths*, London: Canterbury Press, 1948.

_____. *The Christian Attitude to Other Religions.* Cambridge University Press, 1953.

[46]   Bavinck, J. H. *The Impact of Christianity on the Non-Christian World*, Grand Rapids, Eerdmans, 1948.

[47]   Moses, *Religious Truth and the Relation Between Religions*, Madras: C. L. S. 1950, (London: Lutterworth).

[48]   Jurji, *The Christian Interpretation of Religion*, New York: Macmillan, 1952.

Non-Christian Religions," in *Christianity and the Asian Revolution*.[49] Now Professor Kraemer's great book is being reissued and his new work, *Religion and the Christian Faith* will be published this month in England and next autumn in America. Most significantly theologians not directly participating in the mission have also begun to be attracted by this central issue of Christian concern, and notable contributions are being made by Karl Barth, Paul Tillich, Herbert H. Farmer, and others. It is to be hoped that participation in the discussions will become even more extensive and profound. However, this is not a field of study and discussion in which the systematic theologian can work in the realm of pure theory. He must be supplemented by the experience and insights of the theologian-evangelist who does his thinking about the issue on the frontline of the encounter. More over, both of them require the partnership of the historian of religions who adds to his knowledge of recognized methodology in his field a fair measure of competence in Christian theology. Neither the theologian *qua* theologian, nor the historian of religions *qua* historian can accomplish this task alone. The former is likely to fall into the trap of spiritual pride if he works alone.

Some attention was given to the problem in the discussions of the Commission on Evangelism at the Second Assembly of the World Council of Churches at Evanston; and, since this was a matter of grave personal concern to Dr. D. T. Niles, the secretary of the Department of Evangelism, he began to make plans for taking up again what he called "The Tambaram Debate." Consequently a Consultation on Christianity and the Non-Christian Religions was held at Davos, Switzerland, July 21-25, 1955, under the joint sponsorship of the Department of Evangelism and the Department of Missionary Studies. There was a review of thinking in the field since the Madras Conference, various aspects of the problem were discussed, and it was recommended that the two departments jointly initiate a series of studies under the title, "The Gospel and Religions," involving contributions by individual authors and group consultations. Planning for such study is now in progress. Thus the subject has once again become a very live one, in which there is participation by individual scholars working independently on their own projects and by agencies including the World Council of Churches, the International Missionary Council, and the various National Christian Councils.

The situation at the moment is this: it is futile to speak of taking up the "Tambaram Debate." Hocking vs. Kraemer is not a live option. The study and discussion are to be taken up at a point some where beyond

---

49   Dewick, *The Christian Attitude Towards Other Religions*, p, 202.

this. It is hoped that the topic, "The Gospel and Religions" will provide a framework within which that is possible. Hardly a voice is now raised either among the young churches or in missionary circles on behalf of complete continuity. There is much appreciation of aspects of the various religions, but there is a deathly fear of syncretism. Views based on natural theology and general revelation are still strong among English-speaking people, and Dewick is typical of the best spokesmen of this group. He holds: 49 "that through Jesus Christ, God has given a revelation of truth that is central, distinctive, supreme, and satisfying for all mankind," but that this does not exclude the possibility that God may also have spoken to men truly through other channels; that when religious systems are tested by the principles of Jesus Christ's teachings it is impossible to claim that they are all alike or of equal value; and that Christians, realizing those differences, may prayerfully engage in inter-religious conversations, expecting the Holy Spirit to lead them into fuller light. Professor Kraemer has an increasingly large following accepting the concept of "discontinuity," especially Continental missionaries, but also more and more English-speaking missionaries. This view, however, seems to assume that God did indeed leave some of His children orphaned, and that in all His dealings with them He did not let His right hand know what His left hand was doing. It leads to the sin of spiritual pride, which Dr. Kraemer would be the first to condemn. Kraemer is challenged chiefly in Europe by a group of conservative Dutch theologians -- including Bavinck, Korf and Berkauer -- who reject "discontinuity," saying that while man in his sinfulness always resists God and rebels against Him, the love and grace of God in His outreach to them is stronger than their resistance, and that He breaks through it with His revelation, consequently leaving deposits of His truth which can be identified and used as bridges. A variety of other views shading into one or another of these main types are to be found. Some of them are briefly described in Dewick's book and in Chandran's chapter in *Christianity and the Asian Revolution*. Fresh treatments of the subject are now needed in order to present all the valid live options, and in order to make the exponents of the various schools of thought probe deeper. Any concept newly set forth will of necessity have to be supported by sound biblical, theological, and history-of-religions scholarship if it is to be influential.

THE APPROACH OF THE APOLOGIST

Study into the problems of the relation and attitude of the Christian faith to other religious systems is to the Christian mission by no means a mere academic exercise. It is rather the provision of a foundation for a

Christian apologetic adequate to this new period of world mission and of revived Asian religions now also embarking upon a world mission of their own. Like everything else connected with the mission in this day, theology has an ultimately evangelistic purpose. In the final analysis much of the effectiveness of the frontline evangelist's witness will be dependent upon the expert scholar's efforts, but it is not the scholar's job to instruct him in the tactics of evangelism. The scholar's task is to prepare the apologetic approach which will be effective. The local churchmen and evangelists will then form their tactics in the light of the scholar's findings. And, of course, the apologetic literature can be used directly in witnessing to intellectuals and to professional representatives of other faiths.

The scholarly apologist and the local evangelist ought to share certain attitudes as they take up their respective tasks. Above all, they must approach those to whom they witness in humility, shorn of spiritual pride, acknowledging themselves debtors "both to Greeks and to barbarians," identifying themselves with all men as God's children and as sinners before Him. The shortcomings and corruptions of organized Christianity and the vanity, pomp and arrogance of the Church must weigh heavily on their hearts. It is required that they recognize that their task is to witness, not to convert, since conversion is the work of the Holy Spirit alone. But along with all their humility and penitence they must have the joyous conviction that God is in Christ reconciling the world unto Himself, and that their ministry is a sharing in His work of redemption.

There seems to be a consensus among recent writers that both the apologist and the evangelist are witnessing to people -- individuals and communities -- and not to religions or ideological systems. For example, Professor Bavinck stated at the Davos Consultation last summer:

> We must distinguish between a religion as a body of tradition, rites, and doctrines, and as the personal experience of individuals. The religion of the individual may be deeper and richer than the official religion. Moreover, in our approach we are not meeting religions but persons having individual religious experience.

Similarly, Principal Chandran writes:

> The Christian apologist is primarily concerned with People -- Hindus, Muslims, Buddhists, Communists -- rather than with the religious systems they represent. But one cannot really understand a person without a thorough

knowledge of the religious system which has moulded his life.[50]

Canon Warren at the Davos Consultation advocated an "experimental approach" to the problem of truth and revelation, that is, to truth as it is involved in the evangelistic task rather than as an abstraction. He stated that truth for the evangelist is primarily a personal relationship and only secondarily propositions about the Person to whom he endeavors to introduce the inquirer. His attitude is not one of "I have the truth," but rather of, "Let me introduce you to a Person whom to know is to live in a new dimension." There are four steps in making the introduction: telling the story of Jesus, interpreting the story in relevant terms, demonstrating Jesus' spirit through *agape* and *diakonia* in the Christian community, and presenting an invitation to focus one's capacity for faith on Jesus Christ. Writers on Christianity and Hinduism call attention to the necessity of witness in and through the community as a safeguard against syncretism.

The apologetic task in interpreting Christ is well described by Principal J. Russell Chandran of Bangalore, and this survey of the subject will be closed with a summary of his statement. He states:

> The main task of the Christian apologist is to see how the truth of the Gospel can be so interpreted that the non-Christian is able to understand the wisdom of accepting Christ as "the Way, the Truth, and the Life," and to find in Christ the truth that judges, fulfills and redeems his own religious life. This task involves the presentation of the Christian truth through doctrinal exposition and indigenous expression, and through the demonstration of the relevancy of the Gospel to concrete human situations.[51]

He goes on to point out that in Christian faith the primary emphasis is not on revelation and truth, but on the person of Jesus Christ, and that truth is not known in the form of propositions about the nature of reality but in the person and work of Jesus Christ. All other ideas of revelation and knowledge of God should be examined in the light of this faith in the self-disclosure of God in His saving act in Christ. In this perspective the apologist examines the various doctrines of God, man, the world, sin, life after death, etc., saying both a yes and a no to the truth in

---

50 Chandran, J, R, "The Christian Approach to Non-Christian Religions," in *Christianity and the Asian Revolution*, p. 199.

51 Ibid., p. 199.

other religions, eliminating what is false in them, upholding what is true. The use of indigenous expressions is another kind of apologetics, for the Westernized form of presentation of Christianity is often an offence to the non-Christian. Apologetic literature should be addressed directly to the individual Hindu, Muslim, or Buddhist, and not clothed in unintelligible language or expressed as an impersonal analysis of some religious system. Finally, Christianity must be presented as relevant to the life of Asia today, the Church taking seriously its responsibility to society at every level, and particularly at the most local one of the congregation. The apologist has to find the relevance of Christ's words, "I came not to destroy but to fulfill," as he considers the relations of Christianity to other faiths.

The present phase of Christian confrontation of other religions is manifold. The resurgence of the ancient religions presents a new opportunity for witness at the same time when these revived faiths have put Christianity on the defensive. There is a new role for theological scholarship in the world mission. An effective apology awaits the combined efforts of the systematic theologian and the historian of religion, with considerable help from the church historian and the cultural anthropologist.

African Religious Beliefs And The Christian Faith

Eduardo C. Mondlane

"Christianity in its approach to the African will be most effective when the message of life in Christ Jesus has become thoroughly naturalized, that is, has been so related to the African's own spiritual experience that he recognizes it as a fulfillment of the best that he knows and feels, an impregnating of the beliefs and longings of his traditional religion with the creative power of Christ."[1]

The above statement is an excerpt from the findings of an interdenominational missionary conference held in South Africa in 1934. It is obvious that this is an ideal hardly capable of being achieved by any single missionary or group of missionaries in any single field of work. But all the same, it is worthy of an attempt. The ideal represents about the most enlightened view of what all sincere and dedicated servants of God should always strive to do. In this paper we shall not attempt to cover all of Africa, for even if we were qualified to do so (which we are not), there is not sufficient time available to us. Therefore, as a compromise, we shall content ourselves with discussing a small phase of only one aspect of African cultural and social life, and relate it to Christian work.

It is common knowledge that most of the people of Africa south of the Sahara worship their ancestral spirits. We shall not enter into the discussion of the controversial question as to whether the African ancestral spirits are worshipped or simply venerated by those who believe in them. While it may be an important one for semanticists and others, we prefer to put it aside and deal with the problem with which we are interested,

---

[1] *The South African Outlook,* June 15, 1934.

namely the general attitude of the Africans toward their ancestors as it is related to the Christian belief.

ANCESTOR WORSHIP

We would like to introduce a few key concepts describing the major units of organization in Bantu African life. The order in which these concepts appear does not suggest a hierarchical ordering in terms of value standing. We list them in this order following their quantitative correlates, namely, from the smallest to the largest in the number of individuals involved. The first of these is the *family*. This includes husband and wife (or wives), children, their wives, and grandchildren of the male side of the unit. Then follows the *kinship group*, which is a conglomeration of families linked to each other by blood ties, always following the male side of the line, A *clan* includes all the individuals who share a common ancestral background. These do not necessarily have to compose a tribe.[2] A *tribe* is a cultural, linguistic, as well as political unit composed of people who belong to several clans and kinship groups.

Ancestor worship, i.e. "rites carried out by members of a larger or smaller lineage...with reference to the deceased members of the lineage," is, without doubt, the actual religion of the peoples of South East Africa.[3] The deceased ancestors are the real gods. In a way, one can say that the deceased persons rule the community life of the Bantu peoples of South East Africa. According to the Bantu, the dead are interested in the living; they take part in the life of the tribe in a real way. The dead member lives in the memory of the living person of his family in a dynamic and real way, and so he becomes an active force, participating in their daily activities. The communion with the ancestral spirits of the family and those of the tribes guarantees the normal course of existence; such blessings as rain, sunshine, the growth of crops, and the thriving of the animals, the health of the family members and the harmony within a tribe, are the result of this relationship. The social position of the head of the family as well as that of the chief depends to a large extent on the ancestral spirits. The family, clan or tribal circle into which an individual is born is not merely a group of

---

2   Junod, H. A., *The Life of a South African Tribe*, I, p. 89 ff.; and also Pettersson, O., Chiefs and Gods, CWK, Gleerup, Lund, 1953, pp. 13-14.

3   Schapera, I., *The Old Bantu Culture, Western Civilization and the Natives of South Africa*, Capetown, 1953, pp. 3-36; cf. Junod, H, A., "Le Sacrifice dans l'ancestrolatrie sud-africaine," *Archives de Psychologie*, Geneve, 1932, pp. 305-35.

kinsfolk and fellow citizens, but it also embraces the ancestor spirits. These divine members of the family or tribe are supposed to dwell in the world of other dead members of the same tribe, organized according to mundane principles, and at the same time capable of constant communication with the living family and tribe. The presence of the dead individual's personality is always felt by the living. In this paper, we will discuss the sociological implications of the religious beliefs of the African people, especially as they relate to the Christian faith.

According to Driberg, the idea behind the ancestor worship is simply a social one;[4] he maintains that ancestor worship is founded on the fact that the deceased person has acquired a new status[5] and that, though he is physically separated from his tribe, he still belongs to it, takes part in its councils and shows an interest in it, just as he did during his life time.[6] However, Smith, in *The Golden Stool*, presents an opposite viewpoint, namely, that the basis of African social life is of an evident religious character. He maintains, unlike Driberg, that the ancestor worship is a religious manifestation of the living toward the dead members of the tribe.[7] As one who has had some experience in both the ancestral and the Christian faiths, I choose to believe that the former is more of a religious phenomenon than a social one. As Shropshire says, "The very atmosphere of this (the ancestor) worship, even if homely, free and easy, and without constraint, is religious."[8] And as Pettersson states, "The ancestor cult is a religious phenomenon because the object of this cult, the dead, has a supranatural, a nonmundane status."[9] The Bantu people look to their "unseen relatives for good health, and for protection of the village and its children," and great care is taken with regard to the correctness of the ceremonial, and in connection with this cult there are rites which very clearly show that they belong within the sphere of the holy, the sacral.[10] The point we would like to stress in this discussion is that, regardless of whether ancestor worship is primarily religious or a social phenomenon, the fact remains that it (ancestor worship) acts as a uniting factor within the family and that, through the worship of the common ancestors, the

---

4   Hobby, C. W., *Bantu Beliefs and Magic*, London, 1938.

5   Thurnwald, R. C. *Black and White in East Africa*, London, 1935.

6   Driberg, J. H., *The Secular Aspects of Ancestor-Worship in Africa*, Supplement to Journal of the African Society, London, 1935.

7   Smith, E. W., *The Golden Stool*, London, 1927, p. 190, ff.

8   Shropshire, D. W., T*he Church and Primitive Peoples*, London, 1938, p. 192.

9   Pettersson, O., op. cit., p. 136.

10   Smith, E. W., op. cit., p. 192,

living are knit together into a closed unity to which also the dead belong.[11] According to the Bantu, there is no fixed boundary between life and death; and this may very well be the reason for the social import of the ancestral spirits. [12] When the old die, their burial is the object of different rites, and later on they are placed in a new status, superior to that of the living old, but within the bounds of the individual family units. Later, when their sons die, the old dead automatically move up a step in the order of precedence, and so on. In a society where this kind of religious outlook is predominant, the family, the clan, the tribe form a strong community with deep roots in the past. [13] The individual has his rights and duties to both the living and the dead. Through the rites which take place within the tribe, the kinship group, and the family, this solidarity is strengthened, i.e., "the complex system of sentiment towards the family, the clan or the tribe, its history, its present and future are kept alive and are strengthened."[14] It is perhaps safe to say that among all African peoples there is a strong dependence upon the ancestors. There is a strong belief among Africans that the individual receives every thing from the ancestral spirits: children, wealth, and what one might call "good fortune;" in short, they provide for his general well-being. [15] But the ancestors also watch his behavior and if he fails in his duties toward his family or tribe, the ancestors can send sickness and other misfortunes to him, to punish him for his misdemeanor. The member of the family cannot stand alone and depend only upon himself. He must depend on both the living and the dead. [16] But, of course, the power of any ancestral spirit over any one individual or family is relative to the relationship and social status, which existed during their lives on earth. Generally, the dead have power over their own children and descendants in the male line.[17] The dead person's status during his life on earth is to a great extent decisive for the attitude of the living toward him, when he has become an ancestor god. The ancestor worship sanctions the respect of rank and age. [18] "The whole of the political and social life of the

---

[11] Wilson, M., *Good Company*, London, 1951.

[12] Driberg, J. H., op. cit., p. 10.

[13] Radcliffe-Brown, A. R., "Religion and Society," *The Journal of the Royal Anthropological Society*, London, 1949, pp. 33-1131

[14] Pettersson, 0., op. cit., p. 136.

[15] Radcliffe-Brown, A. R., op. cit., p. 43.

[16] Leaver, K. D., "Native Religion; its Constitution," *The Southern Rhodesia Native Affairs Department Annual, Salisbury*, 1941, pp. 46-48.

[17] Hunter, M., *Reaction to Conquest*, London, 1936, p. 233.

[18] Hunter, M., Ibid., p. 266.

Bantu is founded on this respect and loyalty. The younger members yield to the older ones who will become ancestor-gods to them. If they did not do so, the older members would become dangerous to their descendants after their death."[19] So one can safely say that the ancestor worship serves as a bastion of moral life, and in society as a conservative factor in the positive sense of the word. The dead man is still a member of the group of relatives; he has never been torn away from the social bonds, never been released through the promise of immortality.[20] The communalistic spirit also appears in the cult. When the living father addresses himself to his dead father, one gets the impression that two living individuals are talking to each other and each one represents a group of people, the living and the dead.

The man who has been excluded from the family community cannot become an ancestor god. In order to become an ancestor god he must also accept his obligations as a member of the community. It is possible at this point to venture the hypothesis that the ancestor cult is responsible for the low rate of crime in areas where the African culture is still unadulterated, as compared to Westernized areas. As the processes of industrialization and urbanization are progressing in Africa, one is likely to ask, in view of what we have discussed above, what is going to happen to the African individual? As a matter of fact, the processes of change are taking place now. In many parts of Africa, especially Southern Africa, family ties are fast disintegrating. In Mozambique alone, over 300,000 able-bodied men leave their homes every year to work in the Union of South Africa and Rhodesia for periods ranging from two to four years. Many of these men never return to their traditional homes. The consequences of this isolation have served as themes for several descriptive novels, and we need not belabor them here. However, we would like to point out one or two of the most important results. There is an apparent failure of the economic and political institutions to provide means whereby individuals who migrate from traditional to industrial areas could surround themselves with the necessary cultural environment. One reason for the disintegration of the African religious life could be assigned to the fact that Africans have lost the power to organize and order their lives. This power has been taken over by Europeans. This has far reaching consequences. A people whose economic and political affairs are in the hands of an outside group cannot be expected to organize themselves to cope with even the most elementary problems.

---

[19] Pettersson, O., op. cit., p. 137.

[20] Kuper, H., *An African Aristocracy*, Oxford, 1947, p. 196.

Another reason for this social malaise is the development of individualism which seems to accompany the modern capitalistic economy. Maybe individualism is a good thing for Western Europe and North America. But it is doubtful whether it serves the immediate social needs of the African people. Even if, in the long run, Africans could adjust to it, at the present stage it is doubtful if this individualization fulfills basic human needs. We suspect that even the most industrialized of Western nations are not as happy with individualism as they often boast to be. Assuming that they are, why is it that we still hear of serious family, personal, and group maladjustments, as exemplified by high divorce rates, mental diseases, high suicide rates, high frequency of serious juvenile and adult crimes, and so on? The development of slum conditions along with high accumulation of wealth, and extremisms in inter-racial, inter-ethnic and inter-class tensions, are indications that all is not well in Western civilization.

In a way, the Christian churches are as responsible for these changes as the economic and political institution. Secularization has progressed very far in Western society, especially among the industrial countries of northern, western and central Europe, and North America. Although religion still plays an important part in the life of a great many people in North America, it must constantly compete with other institutions, which also claim priority in the attention of those who accept it. Religion plays a more basic role in African cultures than in Euro-American culture. It is, for instance, practically impossible to discuss methods of producing food in Africa -without taking into account religion. One may not understand the African systems of property rights, husband and wife relationships, parent and child relationships, etc., without understanding the African's beliefs in ancestor-gods, and their function in interpersonal relations.

Ancestor Worship and the Christian Preacher

If I were to make any recommendations to Christian preachers in reference to African culture and society, I would stress the points implied in the opening sentences of this paper, quoted from the South African churches: Christianity must give to the African what he has lost in his traditional religion. Unfortunately, Christian missionaries in the past tended to ignore the African beliefs, considering them as simply primitive. The spirit of community, embodied in ancestor worship, and as it suffuses the rest of life, including economics, politics, and social relations, was also basic for the early Christian church. Its revival in the Western Christian church will mark a turning point from crass individualism to cooperative living.

While the African communal life was exclusive in that it cared for the individuals who had a status within the extended family, and as such it was limited in its outlook, the Christian religion should be more inclusive. But, alas, this is seldom the case. The Christian church in Africa is divided not only along denominational lines but also along racial lines. If the Church were to return to the attitude of its founder it might be able to say with Him, "Whosoever will come, let him follow me." But instead what we often hear in Africa is, "Whosoever will come, let him believe in: Anglicanism, Reformism, Baptism, Methodism, Roman Catholicism, etc." For most Africans brought up in the systems discussed above, this is not difficult, for they have been following family and clan gods. The difference may be in the names. There is the implication that God only communicates with people of a certain denominational brand, just as the ancestors spoke to and communicated with persons belonging to certain families, kinship groups, and tribes. Here, then, we see two important dangers for the Christian church in Africa, namely, 1) in its eagerness to destroy the traditional, family-oriented religion, the Christian church will land to pull the individual from his social milieu, and 2) the tendency to develop sectarianism which often undermines the very basis of Christianity, The experience of the Christian church in both Europe and America ought to be an eye opener. The African has a rich religious background, which enabled him to live a fairly well integrated life; one within a community which combined both worlds. The Christian church, accompanied by its industrial and urban normlessness and confusion, is tending to disintegrate the communal life of the African.

In the West, life is no longer whole. This is a theme about which, of late, many scholars have written. This lack of wholeness of Western society is being brought to Africa. As Dr. Emory Ross says, "We need it (i.e., wholeness) in the West. Africa has not lost it. But Africa cannot bring it in its ancient form into its new life. In helping Africa hold, adapt and use it we may be furthering our own search for a unifying wholeness for ourselves in the West."[21]

When you Western Christian missionaries come to Africa, you should always remember that we Africans are a people with a traditional religion which for centuries has provided us with the moral codes necessary for a normal human existence. If you, in your eagerness to preach the Gospel

---

[21]   Ross, Emory, "Africa's Need of Wholeness," in Isaacs, H. R., Africa; *New Crisis in the Making*, from *Headline Series, Foreign Policy Association*, No. 91, 1952, p. 62.

of Jesus Christ, destroy this religion without substituting something as concrete, you are likely to do more harm than good.

The Expression Of Christianity In The Arts And Customs Of Asian Cultures

Apologia By Way of Preface

Malcolm Pitt

The following are a few random statements each of which might be forged into a thesis for the construction of this paper:

1. The problem of the naturalization of Christianity has as many facets as there are aspects of social and ecclesiastical life.

2. The problem is a universal one. It is more dramatic perhaps as it signalizes the penetration of Christianity into a "new" culture, but the difficulty of avoiding both syncretism on the one hand and aridity on the other is as vital to the Church in Western cultures as it is to those in the Oriental or African areas.

3. Both communication and vitality are at stake. This is essentially a missionary problem, but not primarily the problem of the "foreign" missionary. His function is one of:

   a) A realization of his own limitations, imposed upon him by his background.

   b) A realization of the issues at stake.

   c) An eager encouragement of indigenous movements involving a trust and confidence in his national colleagues.

    d) Any aid in the interpretation of fundamental theological issues involved historically in the naturalization process.

    e) A recognition of the worth of social patterns, organization, and cultural expressions among the people.

4. We are still in the self-conscious stage of naturalization. Question - Is the end ever accomplished by such a deliberate approach or must there be only spontaneity? The element of the self-conscious is valuable. It is that which perhaps we have lost in our approach to the problem in the United States.

5. A distinction could readily be made in the areas of adaptation, between those external things wherein we have perhaps "arrived" to a certain extent, and the more fundamental understanding and use of the sources of the life of a people. In this latter, we have not gone so far, although there are many signs that we are eager to make the grade. In this we witness the liturgy of the Church of South India and the report of the commission on the indigenization of worship in India.

6. A study might be made of splinter sects and dissenting movements, on the basis of the interpretation of Churches as ecclesiastical imperialism from their sources.

7. A distinction could be made between the twin motivations of the Church, for its own inner vitality and for communication to the outside. One thing that has appalled the writer of this paper has been the apparent indifference to the former aspect of the naturalization of Christianity and the use of indigenization as only the handmaid, and a very inconvenient one at best, a questionable one even, for the purpose of arresting the attention of others, so that a more essential job, after the initial stages, can be done in conversion to a non-indigenized church.

8. It would be a great joy to this writer to consider the whole subject from the point of view of the symphony of Christian voices as it is raised from all cultural areas of the Christian Church. I believe it essential for the universal comprehension of Christianity that all peoples shall offer their treasures before the Throne of God.

Even with a profound belief in the above statement, there is no degree of self-conscious analysis that can predetermine the contribution that any geographic area of the Christian Church is to make. This must be free and spontaneous and it will, of necessity, be a naturalized Christianity if it is to make a vital contribution.

9. Studies are being made by Christian scholars of society and thought to comprehend more accurately and realistically the backgrounds of their own heritage, and the modern forces playing upon these back grounds, such as The Christian Institute for the Study of Society), with a view to defining their implication for the statement of Christian theology and the involvement of the Christian.

I welcome with deep gratitude the opportunity to address you on the subject that you have assigned to me. As I have contemplated the approach to this area of mission thinking, however, I have thought increasingly how presumptuous it is for me to attempt this at all, for it is indeed taking cocoanuts to Kerala. Any adequate treatment of this subject should necessarily spring from long research, on the spot, in many areas of the world. I have envied the editor of *Liturgical Arts*, a quarterly of the Liturgical Arts Society of the Roman Catholic Church, who has completed in fairly recent date, a world tour of the Catholic Church to investigate one area of our study, namely, the extent to which there has been adaptation, particularly in the art forms, centering in ecclesiastical necessities and activity. He has produced a series of numbers of *Liturgical Arts* which to me are some of the finest expressions of the mission problem as we fact it in the matter of indigenization or, I would rather call it, the naturalization of the Church in its many culture settings.

We usually relegate this problem to the areas of the so-called mission fields. May I say, however, that I think it is a universal problem of the Church wherever it is found, and is one of those areas of thought and life, which must necessarily have restatement at all periods of the changing life of the world. It was not at all accident that the Abbe Godet discovered that the parish churches of France were by no means flexible enough to meet the changing cultural situation in France, particularly among the workers, and the institution of the pretre ouyrier came into being. This activity on the part of the Abbe Godet and his associates raised the inevitable problem which we all face in the matter of adaptation of expressional forms, of a fundamental theological approach to the matter of the incarnation of the word in forms other than language. There is with us perpetually the question of steering a very narrow course between the dangers of over-adaptation to a cultural situation, and the equally present dangers of the stagnation of the life of the Church or the Christian life of the individual, if no adaptation whatever is made and it is found an alien thing in a setting completely uncongenial to it.

Years ago, when committees were working on material preparatory to the Tambaram Conference, I was for some reason or other placed on a committee to prepare a report on the faith by which the Church had lived. This was the American Committee, of course. I took this commission seriously with one intent. I wanted to get in there some kind of statement of the faith of the American churches; that we had confidence in the maturity of the churches that had come into being in fellowship with us abroad and that we were waiting with great eagerness for the contribution that they would be able to make to us in the consideration of our Christian problems as we met the modern world and as we sought to express God's word in a world setting. I hoped that we were eager to see the new insights that the implanting of the Christian message would being forth among the peoples of ancient cultures. In the course of the meetings of this committee, I made this proposal in a way in which I thought it would be understood. And I discovered that I was thinking entirely outside the bounds of any realism, because so far as that committee was concerned at least, that was not one of the items in the faith by which the Church in the United States lived. The attitude in this area has changed considerably since the days of that meeting, but certainly from the point of view of some of the "younger churches," there is a sense of responsibility to us that they have in the communication of their view of the Christian message to the Christian world. As one Christian Indian has put it;

> "The Church in India has come of age. We are deeply conscious of the role we are called to play, not only of the destinies of our own country, but also in virtue of our Christian vocation, in the general life of the Church so that one and all may see her standing, in gilded clothing, surrounded with variety. Naturally we feel greatly encouraged if other countries take cognizance of our ideals and achievements. We shall be enriched by a communication and exchange of experiences and endeavors. The East has been called mysterious only because it is too little known. It will shed a great deal of its mysteriousness in the measure in which its treasures are being made more and more known to the outside world. The process has begun and is gaining strength."

I have been presented throughout my whole teaching life with a series of frustrations in this regard. First of all, I believe that the missionary should be aware of the dangers on both sides, that of syncretism and that of non-life, and I have felt that the way to try to instill the feeling of the necessity for naturalization is through the aesthetic rather than through the rational, critical approach of the West. I have been interested therefore, that my students who are to spend their lives among the Indian people, should be able to move freely within the thought-forms of India and be able to criticize, as it were, from the inside, and to feel the necessity for an expression in terms of that life, not only in the most accurate linguistic patterns possible, but also in patterns of life and expression through the necessary arts of the Church: through architecture, through sculpture as it may be used, through painting, and through music. I have therefore felt an urge to have these young people become aware of the finest products of India in these various fields. To me, it is not sufficient that Indianization will occur simply by putting saris on the madonnas. There is something much more fundamental to the Indian theory of art that is definitely the handmaid of Christian expression quite as vitally as is that of language itself. To me, it parallels the job that I was doing in India, which was the teaching of the Greek New Testament. I was always aware of the extreme difficulty of translation and particularly aware of the limitations of the way in which I was seeking to instill the ideas necessary to translation in my Indian students. It pained me that I was teaching the Greek New Testament in English, and although I did teach Greek on a comparative basis with Sanskrit, and sought to bring something of the necessity for knowing the original settings of words which were used in translation of New Testament ideas, we were still obliged to search for an exactness of expression *in English*. I realized that these students, who would go out to preach the word among their people, would have a still more difficult transition to make in removing this translation another precarious step to the spoken language of their audience. This they had to do without benefit of any help from me except awareness on my part of the difficulties which they faced. It may be for this reason that many have felt that those trained in the English-speaking theological colleges in India had equipment that was scarcely relevant to the people to whom they preached. Some of those who were most acutely aware of the necessity of reaching the Indian on the basis of his own felt religious need would find it almost impossible to use students so trained, however brilliantly they could supplement their mm imagination and their own appreciation of the life of the Indian intellectual or Indian villager.

What applies to words also applies to the other forms of expression and interpretation in the life of the country. Particularly is it true that the understanding of most of the civilizations of the world involves an understanding of the peoples who are more closely integrated in their total approach to life than are the civilizations from which the missionary comes. Civilizations, and our own, are undergoing radical processes of change. At the same time, there is a necessary link with a past integration which gives vitality to the success and the continuance of the Christian Church in the areas.

In this paper I should like to lay stress on the expressions in the fine arts of the Christian complex of life as it is expressed on the so-called mission fields. I have said before that this is not merely a matter of putting saris on madonnas or in illustrations of bible stories that substitute architecture and clothing and facial aspects of the countries or cultures in which they grow up. There is a necessity of the understanding of the fundamental aims and ideals of the art forms as they have been traditionally regarded in these areas, with a sense of their true meaning to those who contemplate them.

I must confess to an inordinate sense of the existential reality of such works of art in the Christian realm when they loom suddenly upon my horizon. I shall never forget, for instance, more or less accidentally tuning in to one of our better radio stations as they were broadcasting a Mass from a Cathedral in Elizabethville. This Mass was beautifully sung with drums in a traditional (?) African style. The most arresting thing about it, however, was that when there was a musical climax beyond which the human voice could take neither the choir or the congregation, the talking drums took up the theme. I shall long cherish the exultation of the Gloria, particularly after the voices had left words and the drums took up the theme. Another unforgettable experience was seeing the doors of the Anglican Cathedral in Port-au-Prince in Haiti opened to reveal the most staggering riot of color that I have ever seen in any ecclesiastical edifice. The young Bishop of Haiti had had imagination and consecration enough to turn over to the young primitive artists, who were reveling in newfound artistic experience, a Cathedral to hallow their work. The Chancel was decorated by four young Haitians who had cooperated in the three panels and the ceiling of the Chancel. Since I saw it, the rest of the Cathedral has been given over to murals by this group. I may say that the Catholic editor of *Liturgical Arts*, although equally staggered by the beauty and reality of this, wonders whether or not there has been too much syncretism with the voodoo aspects of Haitian religion really to find a place in a Christian Cathedral. He gives, however, his hesitant approval to such a move. I also remember with great joy a recent visit to Bangkok where we looked over most of the ecclesiastical establishments in that city. We saw a number of new churches, thriving churches no doubt, but churches that might have been at almost any crossroads in Iowa. They were modern, they were well-equipped, they were probably adequate to the situation. But then suddenly, on the outskirts of town, we came upon a church, a Catholic Church this time, and there was the very soul of the religious architecture of Thailand without any of its non-Christian symbols, but standing in an intrinsic beauty of its own with a very real sense of belonging in the situation in which it was.

This type of experience has certainly come to all of us at some time or other, and not only as "interesting experiments" but as something having profound reality in current church history.

For a statement of the perspective and the problem involved in these movements I should like to acquaint you with an article in *L'Art d'Eglise*, a Belgian Catholic periodical, called the Paradox of Adaptation. Here are some quotations in translation from the article written by Dom Samuel Steaman:

"We are condemned, it seems to us, to misunderstand the role of Christian art in missionary countries, and we shall not find a solution if we do not realize it is a missionary problem rather than a question of art. According to the definition we give to art, one or other of these aspects is likely to be stressed."

"If we consider it exclusively from the aesthetic standpoint, we shall have to admit that from the missionary point of view, it can only be secondary. It becomes little more than a matter of presentation which, in any case, ought to be attractive, since we can admit a form of beauty which is more than a mere pleasure for the eye, something that contains a message which elevates and makes part of a spiritual education. Such a view is not false but it is incomplete, indeed seriously incomplete, since it lacks all that is essential."

"The missionary's duty is to bring stable truths to those he visits, truth which is comprehensible and not over-complicated. His standpoint is above all, one of utility. He requires churches, ritual objects, drawings, paintings, sculpture. All these should, at least, be suitable to their purpose. If to do this he adds an artistic (aesthetic) value, so much the better because beauty can convey homage to the Creator in the same manner as the flowers on the altar, and when the eye is pleased, the faithful will worship all the better. One can even venture to go some way in this respect so the taste of the people be satisfied as much as possible. We can, therefore, encourage all attempts at adaptation. However, so long as such questions are not a matter of Faith and Morality, they are of secondary importance. As a missionary, I know well enough what I ought to teach -- Faith and Morality..."

"The problem lies in artistic and poetic sources. The real drama of adaptation lies in this -- we are not adapted to art in itself, apart from exotic art which is always genuine. The primitive peoples which we contact, still posses, even when they have not finished to elaborate it, what we have lost, the intelligence which is derived from the art process, what one might call the poetic sense. The Chinese and the Japanese know far more than we in such matters. We are now little more than the barbarians of a technical civilization and the primitive African who marks out the entrance to his hut with a row of stones is much nearer to the Egyptian temple than we, with our modern churches in the form of garages."

"After all, the question is quite a simple one. The art process is not merely a matter of art but, as we have said, concerns all human activities and particularly those which are social. Its temperature can be taken in the streets. We have only to compare a student of the Sorbonne in shorts with a Negro in his loincloth. The first no longer dresses and the other is not yet dressed. On the one hand, we have a civilization which is coming to an end. On the other, one which is just beginning. Our civilization in shorts has nothing to offer the civilization of the loincloth which it resembles much as a stupid old man in his second childhood resembles a vigorous youth. We are too late for a world which is too young."

"What is to be done? One of two things. Either we fail to adapt ourselves and take our civilization along with us, with its decadence and mixture of sterilized values and many foolish aberrations or we come to adapt ourselves by respecting the indigenous genius in which we only appreciate the surface aspects and aesthetic qualities. We discover its forms, and at the best, its spirit. But the forms are circumstantial and the spirit implicit. That is to say, it is beyond our grasp. In this way we come to flatter the native artist on his spectacular and exterior side. We call it "exotic and picturesque" and offer him as a guide. What is little more than a smoke screen. The conclusion to all of this is somewhat paradoxical. It is we who have to learn from these native races who now possess a more authentic civilization than ours, by our contact with them and also we must admit, by their example. We have to discover what is universal in our own civilization. But you say our civilization is Christian? It was in the past but it can only become so again when it once more becomes human. And so only our art, our Christian art, will find its regeneration."

"In culture, as in art, Occident is a missionary field full of promises for the Pagans. We bring them the knowledge of the true God, the least we can expect is that they reciprocate by bringing us back the knowledge of Man."

This is an extreme statement, but it holds many aspects of truth. When I think that the criteria of Christian expression which seems to be most prevalent in most of our Christian Churches consists of the left-over Sunday School golden text pictures, well-thumbed and torn, which have been sent from American Churches to Sunday Schools abroad, I can only think with some degree of apprehension of what it is that we are communicating through the things we have brought to it.

Actually the problem is not the problem of the missionary although it is profoundly a missionary problem. Both we ourselves as missionaries and those who have been trained as we have been trained are in what we might call the self-conscious stage of this business of indigenization. Even the reports of those who are studying the process of indigenization are still saying many of the same things that were said in the earlier days. The chapter on the Christian approach to non-Christian religions in Rajah Manikam's *Christianity and the Asian Revolution* restates many of the principles on which we have been working for some time. Some of these are external, but even those which seem to be external, such as the use of congenial music and architecture and congenial forms of linguistic expressions and so forth, have perhaps a profounder significance than we have given them in earlier days. "What difference can these externals make?" has always been the question asked. And yet these externals are symbols of something much more profound which means that there has not been, as yet, the proper naturalization of the Christian Church. In India, I believe that I have seen the naturalization of Christianity spring full-blown in certain individuals who are thoroughly Indian and irresistibly and irrepressibly Christian. In such instances, it is not a matter of self-consciousness but a matter of the expression of a gospel which intuition and insight have stripped of its Western cultural garb and reclothed in Indian dress.

I want, therefore, now to turn to some of the expressions of Christianity as illustrative of what happens when the individual is free to express himself in the way which he chooses and through the medium of his most effective presentation as he senses the reality of the Christian encounter. In doing this I would like to turn to three Indian artists. These three are chosen deliberately because of the difference in what they have to say concerning Christianity in India and what they have to say concerning their apprehension of Christian truths. I have also chosen them because at least two of them are recognized to be among the paramount painters in India and therefore have a position of influence among people who are aware of what is going on. But an introduction to these three requires necessarily some degree of background in the whole field of Indian Christian art.

"Among the many things which the Church in India feels she may offer, with not undue pride, is her native Christian art. Now, in spite of the fact that the country has to her credit one of the longest and richest art traditions, it must be confessed that Indian Christian art is still in its infancy. It would serve no useful purpose to discuss in detail why it has been so. For one thing, owing to historical circumstances, the complex of sentiment and reaction, it was very difficult for missionaries and converts to realize that the adoption of the faith, that the Christian way of life, did not necessarily involve the summary rejection of non-Christian expressions of life and culture. The process of purifying and Christianizing demands time, understanding, deep-rooted faith and other favorable circumstances. Not that the lessons of history were unknown to us, that the Church took over the wisdom of the ancient philosophers and made it minister to the incarnate work, and took over the Pagan ritual and symbols whenever such things could be Christianized and reformed. Another factor that explains the lack of sufficient progress is the poverty of our Churches and people. By sheer force of circumstances we were compelled to borrow the productions of the West. Moreover, it is hardly a few decades that the liturgical revival in the West has gained strength and importance. It is understandable in the circumstances that we should have been slow in catching up with this revival."

"There are certain circumstances special to India that may help to speed up the process. There is the variety and richness, the very character of our cultural and our artistic traditions which have an acknowledged spiritual bond. There are the vast human and natural resources of the country. Perhaps the very impatience caused by centuries of fettered national life should impel us to more strenuous and speedier efforts in rebuilding our national life in all its manifestations. This is being done by Indians, no doubt in accordance with modern trends and techniques and the adoption of what is best in all countries. But the tendency is no less strong, much stronger in fact, for many of our countrymen to do it in keeping with or by a return to the best in our age-old national tradition. What India in general is doing for the life of the country, we Christian Indians are determined not to lag behind in doing for the country itself. First of all, for our Christian way of life, for all its manifestations we could gain by being Indianized while remaining firmly Christians."

"Many of our artistic productions are still groping toward an ideal, but what art does not remain so, even in a maturer stage? This admission shows, at least, that we want our Indian Christian Art to be of the highest quality, worthy at the same time of its best traditions, both as Christian and as Indian, A better training of the artistic taste, initiated among our clergy and leading laity, the growing number of budding Christian artists, eager to translate into the best terms of Indian art their religious beliefs and ideals, the interest shown in our efforts by the leading artists and art connoisseurs in foreign countries, all that is a promise of a rich efflorescence in a not remote field." (Liturgical Arts, Indian Issue)

As all cultural expressions of Christianity must be a product of the social scene of the moment, if they are to be meaningful, it may be well to sketch something of what is going on in the various so-called mission fields, and in particular in India, at the moment. With the coming of new nationhood to many of these areas, we find a new self-consciousness in relation to the cultural history of the people. At the same time we find a very new feature which is more modern than the modern. Therefore one finds in India, particularly, very articulate expressions of what the artistic future of India is to be. There are three movements in general which may be considered, and these apply to architecture, painting, sculpture, music, all of the fine arts and expressional forms.

The first is an imitation of the old classical schools as a part of the expression of the pride in the past, I remember not so very long ago picking up a book on the *Magadha Architecture and Culture* by Sris Chandra Chatterjee. Contained in this were many designs for public buildings which were based on the designs of the Magadha period of architecture, I thought them to be very beautiful; but when I read a review of this book in *Marg* I changed my mind completely, one of the few times that a review has been able to sway me. This review analyzed the three movements I am speaking about now in relation to all of the arts of India, and it is on that which I want to base what I have to say. The essence of the review was this: We are very proud as Indians of the periods of creative activity in the fine arts of India, particularly are we proud of the Magadha period of architecture. We are living, however, in the 20th century and the things which gave rise to the beauty of the Magadha architecture were conceived under a great limitation of materials. We now do not have to confine ourselves to wood and stone, but we are free to use steel and concrete and build in a functional fashion which will be much more to the interest of the present day. "Revivalism" as they termed the imitation of the past, they would have nothing of.

Also they would have nothing of the imitation of the West, that is, the *mere* imitation of the West. One Catholic commentator has said "as for Church architecture in India, ours is a sorry story and the conglomeration of the so-called styles without adapting them to suit Indian conditions, have been the direct result of the activities of the various missionaries that have come out to India." Imitation is evident also in painting as is certainly the revivalism of the past. There are some very wonderful painters of the modern school in India who are indistinguishable from some of the western painters, Gaiatonde in Bombay is at times indistinguishable from Paul Klee. There are others who are reminiscent of Rivera and Orazco in Mexico -- notably a bold muralist, Satish Gujral, often spoken of as India's greatest painter by fellow artists, but who has not yet found himself. There are others in whom the influences of Picasso and Matisse are very evident. This is also true in architecture.

What India is seeking is those universal principles in art which have their own Indian aspects, relevant to the stark realism of the moment. Some years ago Sir Wilfred Davies in his book "*The Pursuit of Music*" had a chapter on music as the universal language which he followed immediately by a chapter on music as a local language, and there is always that local element which makes for the rebirth of a national art which India is seeking at the moment. The painters who represent the schools of the Renaissance (as opposed to imitative revivalism) of Indian painting are not those who are imitating either the West or India's own past, but those who are taking into a new synthesis those elements of technique and subject matter which make Indian art of the present moment so exciting. Such a person is K. S. Kulkarni who can paint in the modern western style, but who spends days sitting before one of the great creations of India's past and comes up with something which is distinctly Indian and yet universal enough for one-man shows in Europe and in the United States. My wife and I found some of our most exciting moments in India during this last trip as we sat with Biran De, Jaya Appasamy, Gaiatonde, Kulkarni and supremely, perhaps, Jamini Roy, dean of modern Indian painters.

Of the three painters using the Christian themes in their painting whom I wish to use as an illustration, the first shall be Francis Newton Souza, a stormy young Goanese painter, who has become known in recent years among art connoisseurs in Bombay and has become very notorious in the press. In an editorial in *Marg*, in a special issue on Goan art, this statement is made, "The dilemma of the creative artist who wishes to inherit the art of past religions as well as to face the implications of the machine age is, however, very real. As the social polity on which the great feudal religions were founded disintegrates, we find that even the artisans become unemployed and inherit only misery and nostalgia, like the sandalwood workers and carpenters of Goa who have mostly moved away from their local habitations in the face of the yawning emptiness and decay. For to inherit the past, one has to accept the social facts on which the ideas were founded. The process of accepting the facts sometimes certainly leads to the acceptance, even at a long remove, of an artificial feeling about the belief super imposed on the facts, but this leads to revivalism in art where the would-be inheritor of tradition is really looking for a Renaissance." The editorial goes on to say that the problem of how the artist of today can inherit tradition is not the problem of such an editorial but, "we believe a system of humanist values and beliefs to be essential to the creation of any genuine work in our country now." The work of Francis Newton Souza answers this description. He is a rebel of the first water. He lives in Bombay and has found that his background of Goan Christianity is not relevant in any way to the life which he leads now. Though his faith has tried to accommodate itself to its Indian surroundings in the present urban situation of India, this accommodation is hesitant and does not go beyond superficialities. Thus rebellion has perhaps been the one way out, and rebels will not submit to the paternalism of the Church. (See Paul Tillich on "Existentialist Aspects of Modern Art" in *Christianity and the Existentialist.*)

Newton was born in 1924; and his life has been one of intense struggle against social isolation, poverty, and narrow-mindedness, both Christian and Indian. He is a critic of the total social and political situation. He has had emotional difficulties, and has run the gamut of intense loves and hates, but always with a certain tongue-in-cheek outward docility. The fact that he had an early case of smallpox which left him badly scarred has not helped in his adjustment to the life around him.

Newton is fascinated by the symbols of Christianity. He is also haunted by the irrelevance of Christianity as he knows it to the present situation. There is often in his pictures of social criticism some emblem or symbol of Christianity in a setting which makes one wince. He has tried to find solutions of his problems in a leftist approach to politics, in his absorption in the movements of art and of music of which he is passionately fond. Dr. Goetz says of him "whatever Francis Newton's final style may be, in whatever manner it will be integrated into the all India tradition, his contribution will be an intensity and fierce fire which the soft escapism of modern Indian art has generally missed, but which is found in the imagery of the old Tantric seers or in the great sculptures of Ellora, Badami, etc. From where he is fetching his techniques does not matter, for all real art starts only where an artist ceases to follow anybody and dissolves all those lessons in the fire of his own vision." This is the staggering indictment of irrelevance of "Christianity" to the changing modern Indian scene that one of India's most gifted sons is presenting to those who are conscious of the realities and struggles of Modern Indian art. And Francis Newton Souza is not alone.

The second person about whom I should like to make a few critical remarks is Jamini Roy. Jamini Roy is the dean of modern Indian painters. He is the one who, more than any other, rediscovered the roots of the soil in Bengal folk art and has produced something which is distinctive, something which is representative of modern India, something which goes to the roots of the folk cultures of India. In a recent exhibition in the Metropolitan Museum, it was Jamini Roy who made the design representing India that went into the Steuben glass exhibit of designs from the East. His works appear in practically all the museums of the East and in many of those of the West. He is very prolific, very decorative; his is a stylized design in sparkling raw color and always arresting in subject matter. I myself possess six of his works, four of which are of Christian themes. Jamini Roy is a Hindu, but he has found in the Christian story something which has commanded not only his attention but his personal loyalty. It is this which perhaps gives to his works a unique interest in that he represents the modem Hindu who finds in Christianity that which he can integrate with his own faith. His Christian painting is to a certain extent confessedly the experimentation with "myths" which are not of his own background, to see whether he can fathom and present them in a form which is intelligible and beautiful.

Jamini Roy is one of the saints of the earth. He was describing to me one day a picture which I wish to possess and which, unfortunately, I do not have; and in doing so his own exposition so moved him that he was in literal tears as he told me about it. The painting was of a very strong torso of the Christ, and over His shoulder was a transparent cross. The cross was made simply with white lines superimposed upon the rest of the painting. In exposition of what he had tried to do, Jamini Roy said that he had read a story of the road to Calvary and felt in his own body all the physical agonies which pressed Jesus to the road as He carried the weight of His own cross. This haunted the painter for some days and gave him the vicarious suffering with the Christ which only so sensitive a person could feel. And then, he said, suddenly he realized that the Cross that Jesus was carrying was not the one that he had felt upon his own shoulders, that it did not have that awful weight which gave Jesus such physical agony, but the spiritual cross which Jesus bore he bore always standing straight up, and He felt its weight not at all. There was always strength adequate to the carrying of the cross.

I have in my possession a small painting which Jamini Roy made for me as a reproduction of a large mural he had of the Last Supper. In this painting we find the correct number of disciples, but they are indistinguishable one from the other. The design is magnificent and the execution extremely interesting. The respective individualities of the disciples are lost in a common turning toward the center of the composition where sits the figure of the Christ. In other words, Jamini Roy has lifted the principle of discipleship out of the historical situation in which discipleship was evidenced.

These two are illustrations enough of a man who has deep insights into things Christian, a man who has made a profound study of the New Testament, with the spirit and the soul of the artist. We certainly cannot pin him down theologically for we can pin no poet or artist completely to a systematic expression of his religious position, but these two do illustrate the fact that perhaps history does not mean as much to Jamini Roy as it does to the Christian theologian in the Divine-human encounter. There is an element here of a type of absorption into a Hindu point of view which I feel does indicate a subtle danger which the use of Christian things can have in India. Both of the pictures above can represent the Christ as the religious adept who has gone beyond history in his essential achievements and accomplishments and who is worthy to have the discipleship of the Guru. Perhaps from these two paintings alone it would not necessarily follow that this is a correct interpretation of Jamini Roy. I am reading back into these pictures the many talks that I have had with him about what his purpose is in his work, his reason for using Christian themes.

The third one that I wish to speak of is probably known to you all. He is a young Christian artist in his mid-twenties who has spent the last couple of years in Japan. He has chosen Japan as a place of study because there he feels there is more of the essentially Eastern attitude toward the transformation of nature in art for a philosophic purpose than he would find anywhere else in the world. I am referring to Frank Wesley (a referring name which is personally embarrassing to me, and I should think perhaps would be to him, although he doesn't seem to feel it so much as I do). Frank is a graduate of the Lucknow School of Arts and Crafts and has been an instructor on their staff. His major interest, however, is in Christian painting. You have all seen, I am sure, the prints of some of his paintings that have been used by the Christian Homes Movement in India, and that have been printed by the Literacy and Literature Committee of the Foreign Missions Division of the National Council of Churches. I may hasten to say here that neither Frank nor I believe that these prints represent his best work in any sense. I have said already that Christian painting in India does not consist to me in painting saris on madonnas or in the *mere* illustration of bible stories. There is something that is much more profound than that. Frank has been struggling through a maze of suggestions made by others, and the thing he dislikes most, is to be dictated to in relation to commissions. Therefore, he has developed a feeling that his best work will not be understood, but that he will be, almost necessarily, condemned to a public presentation of his lesser work which will be the result of commissions and dictation.

There are just two or three of Frank's paintings that I should like to speak about because they embody the essentials of Indian painting and convey what is to me a very profound Christian message. The first is one, which is almost impossible of reproduction because of its technique. Incidentally, Frank has used the traditional Indian classical style as his inspiration and symbolic purpose, although he has altered it a great deal for modern purposes. The first painting I want to refer to is one which is in my possession, which was given to my wife and me by Frank as a wedding gift. It is illustrative of a bible story, and yet it is considerably more than that. It is a painting of the Prodigal Son. In the faint light of the setting sun, one sees only a very dejected and despondent back. The whole center of the picture is darkness, darkness with no design, nothing in it at all to lighten the great weight of the darkness. At the very bottom of the painting are monotone pigs in a texture differing from the texture of the dark center but not differing in color. They are, in a sense, difficult to distinguish at all, except in certain lights. This has an emotional and spiritual impact which has been felt by almost everyone who has seen this painting, the dark moments of the soul when the crisis of decision is inevitable.

The second painting that I want to refer to is one which Frank will not allow to leave his possession. This one he is quite sure no one will like but himself. In that he is quite wrong. In this picture we have the beautiful torso of the Christ with an expression of very great serenity on his face. In his hands he is holding a bowl and from the inside there is a soft, rosy glow. The caption of this painting is "Conscious Maker saw His Master and Blushed." This is what happens at the moment of decision and in the presence of the Master. All conscious objects, even material ones, must change in character, must be transformed, in the presence of the Master. Here is a concept which is essentially Indian, resting probably on the transforming nature of the *darshan* -- but having a Christian significance, I think, very much beyond the usual concept of the darshan merely because the figure here is The Christ, and the transformation experiential.

Perhaps I could add just a word about another painting of Frank's that I have in my possession, one that is slightly controversial. It is *Easter Morning*. The figure of The Christ has some characteristics of Indian symbolism in a luminous forehead with the resultant semi glow behind the head. There is an almost half amused expression on his face as he is being looked at with incredulity by the faces of three women.

I had an interesting experience with this painting because many Christian Indians and Westerners have felt that the figure of Christ resembled too much that of the Krishna of some of the Rajput painting of The Christ. One day I had this painting on a dresser in my room and a Brahman secretary to a Doctor Harrison of the Bangalore Theological College, came in to take dictation. He had to go through my bedroom, and as he went through it, he stopped before the dresser and I discovered him some little time later, his hands held in an *aujali* before the picture. I said to him, "Mr. Gupta, what does that picture represent to you?" He turned around with a beaming face and said, "Oh, it's beautiful. It is some event in the life of Christ, but which one is it?" After that incident, I made it a point to show this picture to a number of Hindus. Their reaction was always the same. And yet when Christians saw it, they thought it resembled Krishna. I thought then that there was a degree of tragedy in the fact that so many mental images had been created, and they have thought that Jesus must always appear as he appeared to the medieval Italian painters, or, dare we say, in the sentimentalized Hoffman era.

I am hoping that, with his return from Japan, there will be some means by which Frank Wesley can be released to fulfill his chosen vocation of expressing to his own people, both for evangelistic purposes and for purposes of his own, creative religious philosophy, to do as he wants in painting the truths of Christianity.

These three men are illustrative of three ways in which Christian painting is being seen by the few in India. All three are recognized as significant in Indian painting (Frank less than the other two; nonetheless, his work has been highly praised in spite of the fact it has had less exposition in India than has that of the others).

This leads me to the restatement of what once was a passionate dream of mine, and which in the disillusioning years, has more or less vanished into the realm of the impossible. Years ago, I felt that one of the things that was necessary for the naturalization of Christianity in India, was the establishment of a Christian Center of Indian Culture. The proposed establishment of a research center for the study of the relationship of Christianity to the non-Christian religions is not exactly what I mean. It is an institute for the residence and mutual inspiration of those who are seeking to express Christian truths in India through all media, where they are free to create and free to offer their services to the Churches in whatever capacity they may be called upon to use them. The primary basis of such an institute would be a fundamental study of Christian Theology and what it is that should go through the mill of communication to Christian India and to non-Christian India. It would offer an opportunity for the study of Indian architecture, painting, and of music by those who are sympathetic with their use in the Christian picture. I have always felt that it would be a mistake for such an "institution" to stand on any feet other than its own, on its own merits; and therefore I would have it free of mission control or even of any single ecclesiastical control. Whether or not it should be associated with any of the theological colleges now in existence as an affiliate organization I do not know, but at least, I feel that it is necessary now that the self-conscious period of adaptation merge into one of achievement by those who are recognized as masters in their own field.

It is indeed encouraging that as part of the centenary celebration the Methodist Church has sent an Indian choir to the United States. It is also encouraging that as part of that same centenary there will be an exhibit of Christian Art in Lucknow. The next step is the aid and encouragement of those who have the talent and have the initiative to express Christianity in the ways of India, that they may be some of the finest exponents in their chosen fields, who can take their place alongside the finest flower of the vital expression of the Indian arts of the day.

And so this most inadequate paper ends abruptly, without even a suggestion concerning my supreme interest -- music. But already it is over-long, and I would choose to give music an honored place with a volume or so by itself. But if anyone felt by now he must inquire where I stand on this whole question, I should choose a text to the unconvinced the music of Lazarus, "Loose him, and let him go" – with ever-increased vitality and strength.

Issues Arising In The International Missionary Council Study On The Christian Enterprise In China

M. Searle Bates

This paper raises questions of method believed to be important for studies of other countries and for denominational studies of sufficient comprehension to involve differing areas and types of missions and churches.

The China Study of the International Missionary Council is working under the provisional title, THE CHRISTIAN ENTERPRISE IN CHINA, 1900-1950. It will probably include a brief section dealing with developments since 1950, in so far as we know them, but separated from the main text in order to emphasize the sharply differing type of information and understanding available to us for these latter years.

What is the aim of this study? Basically, to *understand* more broadly and adequately than any person or group now understands, or would be likely otherwise to understand, the work and life of the Protestant missions and churches in China during recent decades. The impulse to undertake the study arose from factors such as these:

(1) The catastrophic cessation of missionary effort in and around the year 1950;

(2) The extraordinary confusion of that period, both in events and in men's minds;

(3) The moral need to grasp the meaning of the sharp change in the Christian position in China, the home of the second or third largest

Protestant constituency in the Asian half of the world's people, long a prime area of missionary concern, and now the first major mission area to pass under communist rule;

(4) Perplexity or dissatisfaction over writings individual, controversial, or hortatory in nature, sometimes casual or dominated by a particular moment or phase of the total scene, and varying widely in quality;

(5) An earnest desire to know whether the experience in China can and should be instructive for Christian policy in other situations, including those in which opposition or restriction threatens or may threaten the continuation of missionary effort.

It was natural that in the crisis of 1949-1951 and immediately thereafter, many missionaries and others should direct their thought, speech, and writing, occasionally their study also, to the circumstances of the communist triumph and its contemporary consequences. It was also natural that not a few should attempt to follow with devoted interest the experience and the responses of Christians under the new regime, as they repudiated and were deprived of missionary aid. It was likewise to be expected that persons of these interests or other persons should pour forth admonitions and appeals of many sorts, based upon what they felt to be the failures or the warnings of China. Some such items are admirable in temper and in content, notably Victor Hayward's booklet, *Ears to Hear,* and elements of David Raton's *Christian Missions and the Judgment of God.* One of the best preliminary interpretations, establishing a plea for further study which encouraged the present effort, is Stanley Dixon's article on "The Experience of Christian Missions in China" (*International Review of Missions,* July, 1953).

Those responsible for planning the study now underway felt that concentration upon the events of 1949 and thereafter was likely to be self-defeating, failing to comprehend either Christian or general factors in the dimensions of time, change, and growth. On the other hand, a general narrative of Protestant enterprise since 1807 does not fit present needs. We have the important *History of Christian Missions in China* by Professor Latourette, carried to 1927 and naturally directing its attention, for that span of time, to missions rather than to churches. We now need a study that comes up to date, concerned deeply with the churches developing from and alongside the missions, and aimed at understanding the recent and contemporary situations. 1900 appears to be the most suitable timeline for the beginning, though the treatment should be analytical and interpretative rather than chronological.

The study is directed toward the Protestant enterprise of missions and churches, these two intertwined and interdependent, in many instances, to such a degree that neither is intelligible without knowledge of the other and of the interrelationships. Some attention will be given to the Roman Catholic undertakings, both factually and in their own interpretations of the entire situation, for possible suggestions, confirmations, comparisons, or contrasts.

Even more important is an adequate understanding of the Chinese setting and the Chinese human environment or material in which the Christian factors worked and lived. This Chinese human and total environment largely defined the problems for the Christian enterprise, and not merely resisted but continually influenced and sometimes seemed to overwhelm the visible missions and churches. It was immense, complex, and changeful. To attempt to take a true account of this setting in all its aspects is bold indeed, covering ranges such as the economic-social-political and the cultural-religious-educational. In the political framework alone, the changes run from the Manchu Empire in the Boxer Period and the late reforms; through Sun Yat-sen, Yuan Shih-kai, and the warlords; on to the new Kuomintang and the Communist Party with all their vicissitudes of the 'twenties', 'thirties', and 'forties'; through the Japanese encroachments and their consequences; and all these with the additional international factors operative throughout.

To seek an understanding of the Chinese environment on the way to a study of the Christian Enterprise raises appalling difficulties in fact and interpretation, in method, in proportions and in space. But study of these Chinese factors is imperative. If one could imagine an inquiry theological and ecclesiastical, or universally human, independent of a particular locus in space, time, society, and culture, it could not deal adequately with the Christian Enterprise in China.

Needless to say, the missionary factors are also complex as to church and nation of their origin, as to their programs and locations in China, and in their changes from 1900 to 1950.

II CRITICAL AND SELF-CRITICAL APPROACHES

A. Preliminary Note on Certain Common Judgments or Assumptions

1. *There was a widespread and vulgar assumption that the conquest of China by the Communists and the establishment of a communist regime was due to Christian failure,* or corresponded to Christian failure. Perhaps in an ultimate sense this is true. If western, missionary, and pre-communist Chinese factors had all given free course to the Spirit of Christ, there would have been no communism as we know the latter. But that is doctrinal supposition, far from historical actuality. Also, one thinks a once of the historic churches of Russia, of Germany, of Italy, of Poland. Did they prevent the triumph of communist, national-socialist, or fascist regimes? In those countries almost all the people were baptized Christians, and the culture and the leadership were prominently Christian. In China, on the other hand, the total Christian constituency was about one per cent of the population, and the culture and the leadership had never been more than tinged with Christianity. The political and military course of the communist power, and the decline and collapse of the opposing old regime, do not seem to have been significantly affected by, or to have been capable of important influence by, any Christian factor present or realistically imaginable. To assume that a Christianity ten times as extensive in China, and ten times as pure, would have altered the historic course of power, is completely visionary. The whole range, quantitative and qualitative, within which we can think, or even dream, of Christian accomplishment in China, is quite irrelevant to worldly power. Let us quietly dismiss any idea that Christianity could or should be weighed in Chinese scales against communism, a movement of political and military power. Secondary relations of these two disparates, Christianity and Communism, will appear later in our discussion.

2. *The sense of disaster was and is impressive.* Possibly the feeling of crisis and catastrophic event was too easily equated with the judgment of failure. We all know the ignorant assumption that interruption of work by overseas missions meant the disappearance of the Christian faith from China. But let us ask further as to the nature of the failure or disaster. Can it be seen essentially in the expulsion of missionaries by the communist regime? Or does the failure rest in the repudiation or partial repudiation of missionaries by the churches in China? Does the disaster consist more truly in the apparent acceptance of the communist regime by the Chinese Christians, with more readiness or less protest than many Christians

outside China approve of? Or is the sense of failure rather the product of stock-taking in a mood of discouragement at the jolting end of an era, by those now excluded from daily contact with their Chinese brethren, who see the mass of the lump and not the life in the leaven? This stock-taking tallies the weaknesses long present and frequently discussed, no longer balanced by the "feel" of spiritual life in the ongoing enterprise.

3. *But what do we mean when we speak of failure?* What is failure in the Christian undertaking? In one sense it must all be failure when sinful men are set before the will and purpose of God in Christ. Failure implies a standard of success, a dubious concept for the work of the Church in the world. And yet we all feel a real difference between growing churches and disintegrating churches, between those throbbing with life and power and those which show none. Our terms of failure are success simply mean that some churches are relatively satisfactory and others are relatively unsatisfactory, according to our poor lights. But satisfactory to whom, and relative to what? Is there a known and agreed and realizable standard of what a church should be in this actual world; and, in particular, of what a missionary enterprise and a recently developed church in a missionary situation should be? Perhaps we shall be driven toward a working statement of that sort, in order to make clear the implications of judgment or opinion necessarily involved in the present study.

B. Criticisms Raising Important Issues.

This is the heart of our subject. Although the criticisms cited are made, some of them, from the outside and by hostile opinion, they are generally accepted in some degree by thoughtful Christian opinion, that of missionaries in particular. Often stated in extreme forms, whether by communists or by other opponents, and accompanied by falsehood or distortion in detail, they point to serious weaknesses or situations that are reckoned as weaknesses. Moreover, as you will readily notice, certain of the criticisms arise from within, and are motivated by high Christian purpose.

1. *The churches lacked responsible independence.* Recognizing important exceptions of a "sect" character, seriously weak in other respects, the churches were not, in fact or in feeling, adequately self-reliant vis-a-vis Chinese society and vis-a-vis the missions. In some measure this lack is attributed to paternalism and guardianship of missions, with or without invidious sense of superiority on their part. The subject is not simple. The situation varied greatly from case to case. If Christian interests accept completely the old goal of self-government, self-support, and self-propagation, that would seem to carry the automatic elimination of any

mission relationship, however marginal and supplementary in nature. Is it right and consistent, then, to desire to continue any form of mission aid or cooperation, and at the same time condemn church and mission for failure to achieve complete independence in all its life and work? Is it right and possible to seek and to demonstrate to all a true self-reliance and self-determination, while providing the opportunity for some assistance from overseas in such form as not to weaken the material and the spiritual reality of self-reliance? It seems to be clear that missionaries did not adequately realize the unhappy position of their Chinese colleagues who felt the continual strain of needing the financial and other aid of the missions, in order to face their Christian tasks, and, at the same time, of resenting their dependence upon foreign aid ultimately resting upon forces outside Chinese society. When the attacks upon the missionary factor became too damaging to the churches, character destroying in their nature and overpowering in their volume, it was usually necessary for Chinese leaders to accept the inevitable shift to the advantages and the perils of Chinese society alone. Often they found a great relief in doing so, deliverance not only from some of the terrifying pressures of the moment but also from one major portion of the strain of the past. Any fair consideration of the subject must, of course, take account of the high degree of responsible self-direction existing in some mission-related churches before 1950, and of the considerably satisfactory forms of cooperation or transition worked out in others before 1950, in some cases long before 1950. But the ultimate problem remains as to whether partnership of missions can be combined with true spiritual independence for a comparatively young and small church in an immense ocean of non-Christian society.

2. *The missions and the churches lacked relation to Chinese culture.* They were too western in attitudes, practices, and forms. Negatively, this resulted in the charge of cultural imperialism and the lack of Christian morale through inability to deny or refute the charge. Positively, the churches and missions failed adequately to express themselves in Chinese ways, to appeal to Chinese sentiment, to enable their constituencies to feel both Christian and at home in Chinese culture. A full investigation and discussion would bring out much *pro* and *con*, but in the end would probably conclude that much more effort should have been made, and earlier, on the cultural line. The whole range of language, publication, music, art, architecture, and social customs is here involved. In particular, missionaries in considerable numbers were insufficiently concerned with the Chinese language and Chinese ways of living, keeping unconsciously too great a barrier to intimate personal and spiritual relations with their Chinese constituency, and requiring from Chinese friends too much westernization

in language and customs as the price of what the missionary could give. Once again, the subject is not an easy one. Especially in the cities, those Chinese who were readily accessible to the missionary or who tended to draw near to him, were often seeking English and modernization, and too casually confused them with Christianity.

The old Chinese culture was rapidly changing, even disintegrating, much more from secular forces than from Christian contacts. The problem can hardly be stated as relating Christianity to Chinese culture, but rather is the compound problem of relating Christianity to differing or transitional cultures, according to region, date, and social group in question. Should the churches and missions try to relate themselves to the older Confucian tradition; to a modernized form of the same -- sometimes hard to locate outside the mind of a particular critic; to the quasi-democratic nationalism of Sun Yat-sen and *The Three People's Principles* -- which were Chinese orthodoxy for a generation; to the critical scientism and humanism of the influential school of Hu Shih; to a popular nationalistic Marxism of idealistic or reformist type; or to revolutionary communism? Protagonists of every one of these cultural trends has denounced the Christian enterprise for slow and inadequate adjustment to it. Moreover, each trend required a different sort of adjustment on the several levels of intellectual leadership, of tolerably well-educated followers, of schoolboys, of the barely literate but awakening groups, and of the illiterate, lagging farmers of the interior, which last were by far the most numerous. The farm folk were still influenced, according to time and region, by the old amalgam of animism with Buddhism and Taoism in rural superstition. There were also, especially in certain regions, important bodies of Buddhists and of Moslems. Sensitiveness and effort in the cultural area were indeed demanded, but much more than their own stupidity and indifference blocked the road to significant accomplishment for missionaries and for Chinese Christians alike. What could and should be done in cultural adaptation within the complex Chinese situation or any other at all comparable?

3. *The Christian Enterprise was at fault in its relation to the political order.* Although the "unequal treaties" had been completely abolished by agreement in 1943, and had been disintegrating in desuetude for decades before that, with no significant bearing upon Christian interests as such since 1920 or thereabouts, the total history of the introduction of Christianity in the nineteenth century and the protection of foreign rights and interests in China made the Christian Enterprise vulnerable to the charge of associating with imperialism, serving imperialism, and deriving support from imperialism. In the period of Japanese aggression.

Christians and other Chinese interests had not only been more tolerant of British and American rights and interests, but had relied upon them as a means of protection and counterweight against the active enemy. But the ideologies of Sun Yat-sen, Chiang Kai-shek, and the communists all combined in their appeal to national feeling against the memory of long weakness in the face of foreign activity in China. To what extent could and should missionaries have earlier dissociated themselves and Christianity from any form of protection by outside authority? And what results might have flowed from earlier, more general, and more consistent efforts in that direction?

Missions and Christian interests generally are criticized for not supporting, with prayers, cultivation of loyal obedience and good citizenship, the government in power; also, for not actively supporting demands for reform by or in that government; and, by others, for not anticipating and supporting moves toward needed revolution, which, if successful, demands to be maintained against all pleas for radical change. It would not be simple to find the right course in *one* such situation. To do it for the Manchu regime in varying phases, for the confusion of civil war and rival regimes from 1911-1926, for the new Kuomintang and for the communists, to say nothing of the puppets of the Japanese, was beyond human wisdom. The great majority of missionaries might have their opinions about the regime of the moment, but considered that their business was something very different from politics; and many of them had religious or practical convictions that they ought, as Christian workers or as alien missionaries, to have nothing to do with public affairs. Alert Chinese attacked any foreign activity contrary to their own particular political bent, and especially that of missionaries as unwarranted interference by persons who had no business in such matters. Those Chinese who wanted Christian support of any sort were contemptuous of Christian otherworldliness and indifference to the state. Most of the Christian Chinese, in company with most of their fellow-countrymen, were passive and suspicious of government and officials. Another charge against Christianity was that of failing to speak with prophetic voice against the evils of government and on behalf of revolutionary change which promised to sweep them out.

The major case in point for several of these varied criticisms was the attitude of Christian interests toward the Kuomintang in its rise to power from 1923-1928, strongly assisted in the earlier years of that period by Russian Communist elements; then during its years of power and its years of decline and disaster. Mission interests, with some lag and difficulty, followed the lead of a growing number of Chinese Christians to support the Kuomintang in the name of nationalism and reform, despite a period of confusion caused by the communist tactics. In many provinces, the period 1928-1937 was the best in modern China, and Christian interests generally approved the relatively better order and gains in education despite the secular trends of the latter. For the most part, the communists appeared as harsh disturbers and obstacles to national progress, though the Kuomintang failed to live up to its promises and the general hopes. The long, varying, exhausting struggle against the Japanese placed Chiang and his Party in the place of patriotic defenders against cruel and greedy foes. Yet the deterioration was pervasive and there were strong undercurrents of discontent, by no means all of them associated with the craftily waxing communists. Christians tended to prefer the Kuomintang government to the harshness of the communists and their known relations with Russia, and yet to be increasingly dissatisfied with it for corruption and for ineffectiveness. The requirements of national interest and national feeling, even as recognized by Stalin and Molotov as late as the treaty of August, 1945, looked to support of Chiang against the Japanese and for national unity. Can those who blame Christians for tardy recognition of communist trends determine on just what grounds and at just what moment and with what line of action Christian interests should have withdrawn allegiance to the National Government and have transferred either active support or passive adjustment to the advancing communist power? On the other hand, could and should the Christians have been more "prophetic" in demanding and assisting radical reform within the Kuomintang? Some efforts were made in that direction, but were always subject to the suspicion that they were a form of political attack, designed to hamper the Government and to assist the communists. Indeed, public criticism of the Government was generally difficult, and private criticism was psychologically almost impossible in view of the attitude taken by the chief men. Rather, Protestants were chided for failing to enter into active political opposition to communism as did Archbishop Yu-pin and the prominent Roman Catholic dallies.

Greater alertness to need for fundamental change in the social and political order; that can be urged upon the Christian Enterprise; But there still is today, with all the advantages of hind sight, no easy recipe to reconcile the needs of (a) proper devotion to primary Christian vocations and freedom from political involvements; (b) due obedience, respect, and support for government as the organized community which maintains order, schools, and other indispensable services; (c) the prophetic functions of reforming criticism. To the extent that any of these three needs is significantly met in time of public crisis, the other needs are likely to be neglected or worsened and with sharp, perhaps paralyzing differences in conscientious judgment among responsible Christians.

4. *The Christian Enterprise lacked adequate theological concern and understanding.* It did not direct a sufficiently large part of its personnel and effort to the enlargement and nurture of the Church. The schools, medical work, and other services had their general and their Christian uses, but they absorbed too large a part of the national and missionary workers and of total strength. In understandable response to great needs, to public demand and willingness to cooperate in payment of fees, and to the desires of staffs and Christian constituency, these services tended to expand beyond the power of the leaders to maintain in and through them an effective Christian witness proportionate to the total effort made. Important elements of the missionary body and of the Chinese Christian workers tended to be social-minded rather than religious-minded, ethically concerned rather than theologically and devotionally concerned. Such tendencies may be interpreted as outworking's of the felt needs of a crowded and ill-provided society, and also of the pervasive Confucian tradition with its emphasis on human relations and its indifference toward full religion.

This great complex of criticisms involves the religious background of missionaries, and their motivation and objectives in going to China. It also involves the Chinese scene and influences the powerful playing in and through the Chinese Christian constituency. There seems to be widespread support within missionary circles for this type of judgment upon the Christian Enterprise. It must be weighed, however, against the services rendered in witness and in Christian development by the schools and hospitals, even their importance for direct evangelism in not a few instances. Extreme concentration upon evangelistic and church effort in the narrower sense would lend weight to the differing criticism of otherworldliness and lack of concern for basic human needs. Is the true judgment this, that the faults of institutionalism all too frequently appearing in schools and hospitals should have been earlier and more resolutely tackled by turning over to private Christian hands or to government such schools and hospitals as could not be adequately staffed and conducted with clear and effective Christian witness. Further, that the positive effort should have been made in those missions and related churches which tended to be weak in their working emphasis upon the church as the ongoing community of faith, to develop and assign a larger part of their best personnel to that service; and that sounder and more thorough theological teaching should have been undertaken and persistently developed throughout the working staff of the Christian Enterprise?

5. *Christianity was presented as a remedy for the nation's ills, but accomplished nothing substantial; while the communists effectively tackled them.* For many years it had been true that some of the more alert and more sensitive of Chinese youth were keenly concerned over the backwardness, ignorance, and poverty of China; over its selfish men of wealth and power. Some missionaries and Chinese pastors and teachers pointed to the advanced development of "Christian" nations, and also to the schools, hospitals, and all means of betterment evidenced in Christian activities in China. Christianity was stated in terms of moral challenge, the means of rooting out from individual lives the greed, self-indulgence, and indifference to the needs of others so conspicuous among those prominent in Chinese society. This view never prevailed over the essential Christian message. The slogan of the cooperative evangelistic movement was "China for Christ!" -- not "Christ for China!" But frequently the statement of the Christian apologetic had something of the utilitarian in it, something for individual and national welfare, which tended to confuse and to obscure the true message. Furthermore, those who took seriously the utilitarian hope might easily be disillusioned when individual and general poverty continued, when the nation persistently stumbled in weakness and the government in corruption -- headed by persons among whom advertised Christians were prominent. The number of Christian schools and hospitals did not increase, while those not Christian did increase. The number of notable communities of Christian love and character, even of notable individuals widely known for their transformed lives, did not seem to substantiate the hopes held out or seized upon.

On the other hand, the communists claimed to have the root-and-branch method of stamping out all public evil and all power to exploit; to have the record of bringing Russia from rural backwardness and poverty to leadership of the world in a single generation; and to have the appeal and the effective instruction and discipline to draw the youth into revolutionary fellowship of devotion to the common good. Moreover, the communists did this without religion, and even asserted that it was possible to achieve human well being through the proper application of science only if man renounced religion. The communist claims, their vast organization, their massive propaganda to which no counter–question could be asked, their immense resources drastically employed, their demonstration of disciplined devotion for meager material reward of the common soldier and political worker, -- all these made Christianity seem a feeble flicker before the great task of saving the people. Communists and their supporters made the comparisons on their own ground, and Christians fell into a mood of helpless failure – unless they had a clear enough grasp of their faith to know the true ground of Christianity, which many lacked, or did not have with sufficient definiteness and vigor to state convincingly to others.

6. *The Christian Enterprise was deficient in cooperation and in unity.* It is not necessary to labor for the readers of this paper the basic fact that the tiny Christian Enterprise in China was divided into more than a hundred church bodies or mission-church organizations, many of which had no spirit or experience of cooperation, and most of which had only a vague and rudimentary sense of unity in Christ poorly expressed in certain similarities of church practice. The few unions and the considerable undertakings of cooperation among some three-fifths of the Protestants were not always greatly meaningful on the local level, though they carried high values in themselves and meant much to the leadership in them. It is grimly suggestive that both the Japanese Army and the communists have been dissatisfied with the scattered frames of the churches, and have required, for their own purposes, some attempts at coordination of policies and consolidation of leadership.

On the other hand, we cannot assume with any realism that if cooperation and unity had been much more adequately developed before 1950, all the problems of the churches would have been solved. Possibly the communists would have been harder upon a unified church, as they seem sometimes to have been upon the Roman Catholics. Possibly the communists could, at some stages, have dominated or manipulated a unified church more easily than the heterogeneous miscellany which they have tried to marshall through the Three-Self Reform Committee. We may rightly ask, did the unions actually achieved before 1950 prove to be a strong witness for the truth and the sound advantages of union? Did the National Christian Council and other forms of cooperation demonstrate clearly the merits of substantial and extensive cooperation? Does the whole China experience teach any convincing lesson in regard to cooperation and unity?

III. SOME MATTERS OF METHOD

A. *Does the China experience speak to us, or do we speak to the China experience?* It is often assumed that in some unmistakable, factual, objective manner truth and instruction spring from the experience of these fateful years for the Christian Enterprise in China. Yet the experience says such different things to different people that we must be cautious about this assumption. Moreover, "the obvious lessons" of "the missionary debacle" and the communist triumph sometimes bear photographic resemblance to the views of the writer as habitually stated long before 1950. Can we try a few test queries to see whether in the facts of experience our common critical judgments are clearly supported?

1. Does a mission-church emphasizing the doctrine of the Church and its centrality, like the Episcopalian or the Lutheran, reap tangible fruits therefrom, visible in comparison with other churches and missions?

2. Can it be determined in observation of experience whether insistence on a high standard of training for the ministry has better results than more flexibility in standards and a more numerous ministry?

3. Can one discover factually whether a church-mission characterized by fundamentalist theology achieved better results than a comparable church -mission known for liberal theology?

4. Does a mission-church devoting a high fraction of its ablest personnel to new evangelism accomplish more over a period of years than a mission-church with diversified witness and program?

5. If association with imperialism had deleterious effects, is it possible to show that Scandinavian missions flourished beyond the measure of others comparable in size? Did the early action of American Board missionaries in renouncing extraterritoriality have observable results?

6. Since, up to about 1927, anti-imperialist feeling was directed most significantly against the British, were British missions actually at a disadvantage in comparison with those from the United States?

7. Did Protestant missionaries, who did not have standing as officials, fare much better than Roman Catholic missionaries, who for years had such status?

8. Did missionaries living on a lower scale, and with smaller funds for institutional and other work, have better or greater results from their service?

9. Did subsidies or lack of subsidies have any calculable relation to the growth of the churches?

B. *Is there any way to measure that which cannot be measured, the extension of the Gospel in the hearts and lives of men?* In order to provoke comment and critical suggestions, let us set down a number of criteria or indicators of Christian accomplishment in a missionary situation: (These might be used to compare across church or national lines).

1. Growth in church membership, both in net additions and in ratio to an earlier base. Query, is the total population in the field of this church a relevant factor? Also, does the ratio of missionaries to membership and to total population have relevance, and if so, what?

2. The number of national Christian workers: (a) ordained men well trained; (b) ordained men not well trained; (c) other evangelistic and church workers; (d) teachers; (e) health social workers. Also, the church's program of recruiting and training workers.

3. The quality of the Christian community, including the quality of individual transformations.

4. Outstanding leadership.

5. Indigenization, as shown by significant expression in Chinese form, whether original or adapted: (a) theological thought; (b) devotional material and practices; (c) religious education; (d) liturgy and forms of worship; (e) architecture; (f) painting; (g) literature; (h) music.

6. Responsible independence in terms of without aid from self-reliance, with or without aid from missions. This may be seen in financial support in organized self-direction and self-discipline, and in evangelistic outreach. Where aid from missions is received, the ratio of effort and accomplishment by nationals to the mission contribution in personnel and funds is certainly significant.

7. Concern for the general community and service to it. Schools, hospitals, literacy campaigns, sanitation, home and family life co-operatives, and economic betterment, neighborhood, cooperation democratic procedure, wise and honest use of resources, recreation.

C. *Can one compare church-missions in a test of objectives and theologies and policies and effectiveness,* as the Episcopalian with the Baptist, European missions with British and with American, the Methodist or Presbyterian with the China Inland Mission or the Christian and Missionary Alliance? We must point out the variables other than the element in the forefront of inquiry, and ask whether any factual or dependable result is possible. Here is a check-list of variables, thinking of the China situation:

1. Population in the area occupied.

2. Other churches in the same area, competitive or cooperative.

3. Strength of non-Christian faiths and practices.

4. Degree of anti-Christian prejudice.

5. Organized restriction or hostility.

6, Disturbance by war, revolution, inflation, or natural disaster.

7. Economic and cultural levels.

8. Ratio of urban to rural situations.

9. Rate of literacy in population.

10. Provision of governmental or other non-Christian schools.

11. Membership.

12. Number of ordained missionaries, their training and experience.

Same for other missionaries.

13. Theological tradition and outlook.

14. Number of ordained national workers and their training. Same for other workers.

15. Provision of church buildings and other significant property and equipment.

16. Provision of funds, by local contribution and by mission.

17. Number, type, size, and effectiveness of schools maintained.

18. Similarly for hospitals and other institutions.

19. Program for recruiting and training workers.

20. Share in literature and other cooperative work.

21. Degree and quality of evangelism outside churched areas.

22. Degree and quality of nurture, and development of witness through Christian community.

23. Standards of instruction before and after baptism.

24. Age and continuity of the work and policy of the mission and church.

25. Degree and age of responsibility of the Chinese church.

In view of so many variables, disregarding for the moment many others such as density of population, geographic location, and distance from centers of modernization, can a real comparison be made on the basis of one factor? Of several factors?

D. *Other far-ranging questions;* Can we learn anything significant from the general and the Christian experience with communist factors in South and Central China from 1923-1927 and in pockets thereafter, in Kiangsi Province and adjacent areas from 1928-1934, in Shensi and adjacent areas from 1935-1945, in Sinkiang and Mongolian borderlands at any time?

Just how can the study and/or comparisons or interpretations of the Roman Catholic experience be most fruitful?

In judging the Protestant Enterprise in China, what comparisons should be made with other fields? The number of missionaries per million of population; per 10,000 Protestant Christians? The development of the national ministry in numbers and in training? Are the most genuine comparisons those with other fields of great mass, of high culture and great pride of culture, of weak non-Christian religions, of foreign interference but not colonial government? Where are such fields? In any case, suggestions for useful comparisons are in order.

Finally, recognizing the intangible nature of spiritual growth, the hidden complexities as well as the visible multiplicity of the Christian undertaking, and the elaborate variety of the human material and environment in China, can we know what we are talking about, can we judge justly and speak truth? The differences of individual knowledge, interpretation, and inference are boundless. They fill great categories of opinion or judgment, such as those of Chinese Christians, of missionaries, of the general Chinese public, of communists and their echoes, from all of which we may learn something, at least as to the nature and locus of the issues. It would seem that a composite of interpretation and judgment, with emphasis on the concerned Christian and missionary understanding, facing as thoroughly and adequately as possible the ascertainable facts and learning humbly from them, is the most promising effort of the human mind upon this problem. We can be certain that real knowledge of the whole and right judgment of any part belongs to God alone.

M. Searle Bates

Missions In The Curriculum

Creighton Lacy

The assignment of this topic to one of the very newest pledges in this fraternity must have represented, for the committee, either the folly of desperation or malice aforethought. If I had taken the title literally, I should never presume to advise elder and wiser and more experienced colleagues how to teach. Those who are looking for ready-made syllabi to carry home with them might as well leave now. But as I have wrestled with these questions in my own mind, I have been increasingly convinced that some vital and urgent issues precede and underlie our pedagogical methods. And these problems seem to me to involve fundamental concepts of theological education on the one hand, and of the world mission of the church on the other. I stand here, therefore, to raise questions, not to answer them.

Many of you have been following the preliminary reports of the Niebuhr commission on "Theological Education in America." Some few of you, perhaps, have examined the recently published survey of "Theological Education in the Methodist Church," not to mention the *Christian Century* for April 25, 1956, the findings of Bates and Bangkok on Africa and Asia, and various other recent symposia. Dr. Niebuhr (Bulletin #5, April 1956) reports that 17 out of 25 seminaries include a required course in missions. The Goerner-Horner survey of 1952, or even a wider, less selective glance through catalogues, would reveal a still smaller percentage of required missions courses in theological schools as a whole. These two-thirds (of Niebuhr-studied institutions) allot a median of 3.1 credit hours to this mission requirement, in contrast to 4 hours back in 1934.

Now we are all aware of the critical pressures on academic schedules, of the proliferation in theological curricula which Niebuhr analyzes in some detail. But we need very seriously to ask ourselves whether we professors of missions are not failing first of all at the academic, curricular level to convey "the missionary obligation of the Church," even before we step into the classroom of the pulpit. If there is a "revolution in missions" as well as in the world at large, if "most congregations continue to think in 19th century terms," (as one of you wrote me), we need also to realize that many of our faculties and administrations are doing the same thing.

Without any wish to become competitive and divisive, we should reassess the relative quantity and quality of our academic program in the light of the very emphases which we presumably are making. That is, if the world mission of the Church is half as central and universal as we claim in our lectures, then it deserves a reinterpretation and a broader relation among our faculty colleagues. The mission of the church does not seem very vital when 16 out of 23 subjects get more time in the curriculum, including twice as much Hebrew and two and a half times as much Greek. According to Niebuhr, missions is now crowded out not only by social ethics (my own alter ego, so I am not making invidious comparisons) but also by sociology, not only by systematic theology but in addition by history of doctrine and pastoral theology. And very few institutions provide the type of comprehensive, correlating, and integrating examinations reported from Garrett and, I believe, Southeastern.

My concern here is not with the number of classroom hours, but with the status of missions in the curriculum. When I came to Duke, to teach both missions and social ethics, the straws in the wind were obvious. The ethics classes were to be three hours each, the missions courses two; this meant that only the former would be eligible for summer school or graduate status. Although I was offered my choice of catalogue position, I was warned not to get myself restricted to the "practical" fields lest my academic standing suffer. This was not a personal matter, but an attitude toward the field of missions as not quite respectable scholastically. I myself am not in the least afraid of being "practical"; in fact, from the start, I have offered a course in "Missionary Education in the Local Church" which students refer to as the most practical course in the entire curriculum.

A year or two ago I approached the chairman of the undergraduate department of religion (with which we in the seminary have no direct connection) to suggest that there might be a place in his curriculum for the ecumenical movement and the world mission of the church, instead of simply Bible and comparative religions. He dismissed me with the assurance that there was time enough for such subjects when the student reached seminary, and I could not get him even to understand the point that every Christian layman today should have some familiarity with these developments in world Christianity, irrespective of ministerial training.

I cite these personal illustrations not to criticize one institution or even curriculum committees in general. I cite them rather to make this shocking charge: that our primary difficulty lies in the fact that *we ourselves are not clear what it is we want to teach or how we want to teach it.* That layman in our churches, and many of our religious leaders as well, are totally ignorant of such terms as devolution, indigenization, Christianity in African culture, Younger Churches, Sangha, the Kyodan, fraternal workers, or the East Asian Ecumenical Council on Mission. Subconsciously and realistically, they know that we live in a different world since the Second World War, yet they are completely unaware of the "revolution in missions," They have not heard of any "new look" in the missionary enterprise; they have quite frankly lost interest in the old look.

This conviction lies behind many of the questions which I have circulated to some of you, and which rather puzzled and startled a few. (Let me insert parenthetically here my profound gratitude to those 15 out of 20 who so helpfully answered my inquiry. My selections of schools and individuals was largely arbitrary; I deliberately omitted such specialized institutions as Scarritt and Hartford; but this paper is far more dependent than I have indicated on the responses which have come in. It is indebted also to the magnificent inaugural address of Dean Horner on "A Theological Curriculum with International Dimensions," (which I hope you have all read).

Let us first turn to the question of terminology. This is no mere quirk or idiosyncrasy. The senior member of our Duke faculty, with perhaps the widest experience in the ecumenical movement and contemporary thought, has been urging me for some time to drop the title of missions and replace it with World Christianity, the World Mission of the Church, or some other less antiquated and criticized term. Since my own offerings in social ethics include "The Christian Critique of Communism" and "Christianity and International Relations," it would be simple and appropriate to adopt the title "Christian World Relations" used at Andover-Newton and (along with missions) at Garrett. Another of our seminaries is shifting this summer from Missions to World Christianity, although the incumbent who requested the change still holds "Missions" to be a valid term.

Only one of my 15 correspondents urged emphatically "replace it!" Far more widespread seems to be the conviction that we need a distinctive and active description of a unique and positive function of the Church. Most of us, I venture to say, are stressing the singular form, mission, instead of the scattered and uncoordinated *missions*. But the need for emphasizing a vigorous outreach and forward movement against paganism in every land far outweighs the static and institutionalized connotation of World Christianity or Christian Community. One of the causes of this dilemma is the liberal and tolerant student movement. As one who has been a participant in this trend during the past two decades, I speak with an awareness of responsibility or at least acquiescence.

We are proclaiming today -- and this is a fundamental theological issue to which we ought to return -- that every Christian is a missionary, a witness, called by God to his vocation, whatever it may be. We are seeking to remove the halo from the missionary's head and the pedestal from his feet; we are rejecting the Catholic dualism of religious and secular life. All this is both necessary and right. Yet in this process we are blunting the sharp edge of the missionary enterprise, not only for recruitment of personnel, but also in presenting the imperative call to mission and unity. With all due respect I cannot help regarding the currently popular term "fraternal worker" as dilute, spineless, and incomplete. It may imply brotherhood and cooperation. It does not imply the dynamic sharing of the Gospel of Jesus Christ, which springs from the action of Almighty God.

The original draft of this paper included a lengthy quotation from Dr. Charles Hanson's address to a recent Methodist Interfield Consultation. In it he attributed the disrepute of the terms "missions" and "missionary" primarily to the Asian and African reaction against colonialism and foreign imperialism. But it seems to me that the second interpretation of these words, which Dr. Ranson unhesitatingly accepts -- namely, "that which belongs to the unhesitatingly very nature of the Church and the word "missionary" applied to every man who loves and bears witness to Jesus Christ"-- is equally capable of becoming a stumbling block. For the teacher and preacher and money-raiser and administrator there must be some way in which the term "mission" may be kept for the distinctive *world outreach* of the Christian Church, not dissipated or bestowed too freely on every parishioner who visits the sick or brings a friend to Sunday service. I reminded a bishop of our church, who was arguing recently along these lines, that he would be most distressed to have every church member called a "minister" even though by this same logic every Christian is called to be a minister of all. Yet I and most of you I am sure, would agree with Dr. Ranson's conclusion, that "we must not abandon the essential thing for which *mission* stands... . The word missionary has got to be rehabilitated, rather than lost."

Behind this question of terminology lies for us, speaking academically, the question of content. Personally I am convinced that nowhere else has there been a greater "revolution in missions" though we have not stopped as yet to evaluate it. I had my seminary and graduate training at Yale. I chose that school primarily because Kenneth Scott Latourette personified missions and the history of Christianity in my own birthplace, Asia.

But Yale, like most seminaries in the period between the wars, offered nothing in this area beyond the *history* of the expansion of Christianity. There was no theology of missions or recognition of such a need; there was not a reference to the local church and its share in the World Church; there was no mention of the problems and policies of the missionary; the Younger Churches were abstract entities in the ecumenical movement or else heroic individual figures. That is why I have perused with intense interest and concern the statements some of you have submitted, the catalogues of certain institutions, and the growing reservoir of theological resources since the Willingen Conference. It is in these directions that the future of missionary teaching seems to lie.

At least half of the responses to my inquiry indicate the historical approach as *part* of the basic, required course in missions, although that history is often extremely sketchy. After seven volumes and at least that many courses from Dr. Latourette, I could not conceive of teaching the history and philosophy of missions in one two-hour course and insisted that they be divided at Duke, so I am frankly lost in the syllabi which indicate a couple of weeks for a history of missions. Almost every reply, however, included along with that history some treatment of contemporary problems and policies, certain areas of the world, a Biblical and theological background, the relation of Christianity to non-Christian religions, missionary motivations, and the doctrine of the Church.

When I came to Duke, the core curriculum included History of Religions, but no Missions. The exchange in position has come about not by pressure from me, but through the different and also--I hope--through emphasis of instructors recognition by the curriculum committee that for most American parish pastors "The Philosophy of the Christian World Mission" should be far more vital than the Vedanta or the Ten Gurus. In another seminary which used to require "World Religions," the new instructor has replaced it with an "Introduction to Mission Thinking". (Lest my friends in the History of Religion suspect me of discarding their studies, I shall return to that topic in a minute.)

The most striking illustration of this shift in emphasis comes from a seminary where the basic, required course is still historical (plus History of Religion).

> "But (the instructor reports) the psychological requirement in student minds is the Philosophy of Missions (with a voluntary enrollment of approximately 90% ...Why that has caught on, in spite of being an elective, is hard to say, but it has."

And the same situation has developed to a lesser degree with the Practice of Missions. In my own basic course, which begins with the philosophical and theological "Why?" of missions, students almost unanimously indicate preference for that half of the course, yet two of them (with no professional interest whatever in the foreign field) urged me last week to add a seminar on contemporary missionary problems. As one professor wrote, "The old approach does not meet their needs or attract their attention."

As a lover of history myself, I would be the first to deplore a curriculum which abandoned historical materials or methods. But I am constantly reminded that we are teachers in vocational schools (however much some faculty members may resent that designation). Our primary obligation is to prepare effective pastors and leaders in the American branch of the World Church. It is therefore more important, if a choice has to be made, to familiarize them with the ecumenical experiment of South India or the evangelism of D. T. Niles than with the Nestorians or Frumentius. No one can fail to be fascinated by the story of William Carey, vividly told, but more students today are more deeply and permanently interested in Albert Schweitzer, not for the romantic jungle (David Livingstone and Adoniram Judson had more adventures) but to discover how and why a man so often accused of wrong Christology and no theology has become the most revered missionary alive today.

Similarly at the theological level, the missionary obligation of the Church comes alive when students find that Paul Tillich and Richard Niebuhr have something to say about it, that it has vital relevance to the most influential Christian thinking of our time. My classes actually wake up when we put on a miniature and often-superficial Hocking-Kraemer debate. That issue seems to penetrate two areas of American as well as world concern: the authority and universality of the Christian faith and effective methods of evangelism. I find -- as doubtless you have found -- that though a majority of contemporary students may vote for the Kraemer theology, when they come to practical policy they advocate building on every possible point of contact with non-Christian faiths rather than accepting in program and practice the concept of "radical discontinuity."

This perhaps suggests one of several problems arising out of the new emphasis on theology of missions; namely, the study of comparative religions, or, more accurately, history of religions. In the heyday of liberalism, when Hocking and others were seeking a "world faith" the importance of understanding Buddhism and Islam and the rest appeared obvious. With the swing to neo-orthodox theology, and the Biblical realism school, one might expect an abandonment of non-Christian studies as being irrelevant to the uniqueness of Christianity. If there was a temporary leaning in that direction, the reality of the World Church, the resurgence of Oriental religions, the challenge of nationalism, and many other factors have led now to a renewed interest in other faiths.

Presumably the Christian missionary is searching for ways to challenge and win these non-Christian groups instead of to amalgamate with them. But whatever the motive, the plans for special study centers under the International Missionary Council will have repercussions and reflections in academic programs in this country, as the Christian church trains and enlists the scholars and savants who a few decades ago were often outside of the Church. As neo-orthodox theology finds paradoxical expression in the social concern of Reinhold Niebuhr or Emil Brunner, so the "radical displacement" theory of Hendrik Kraemer seems to require a deeper, clearer, and more sympathetic understanding of what Christianity hopes to displace.

As we broaden the content of a basic missions course away from the strictly historical approach, we encounter the critical problem of textbooks and other materials. Most of you who replied to my inquiry indicated that you found and used no single text in the field of missions.

To my mind Soper's *Philosophy of the Christian World Mission* is still the most comprehensive approach, but in spots his "liberation" is already dated. Lamott's *Revolution in Missions* I have found most useful in the contemporary field, but he assumes a familiarity and interest which most beginning students lack.

The Willingen Conference papers provide the most challenging theological material now available, but these are at best difficult for student assimilation and much remains to be done. For the most part I judge that we rely on a few ancient classics: Roland Allen, Leber's *World Faith in Action*, Richard Niebuhr's *Christ and Culture*, the "practical" works of

Fleming and Merls Davis, Macnicol's *Is Christianity Unique?* and then supplement with some of the contemporary studies which Dr. Price has listed. Perhaps the only reason all of us do not jump into the race to produce an adequate text is Dean Horner's sage advice in the inaugural address I mentioned:

> "There can never be a perennial textbook for the study of missions. Our minds must be constantly stretched to meet new needs, wider concepts of missionary service... The most serious danger is that of stagnating into a sterile perpetuation of routine courses of missions while the people of the world are moving into new realms of experience."

Now just a word about other, generally elective courses. Some of our seminaries are offering such specialized approaches as "The Theology of the Missionary Enterprise," "Contemporary Mission Work," "Contemporary Problems of Christian Expansion," "The Theory and Practice of Missions," "Area Studies in Christian Missions," "Missionary Biographies" and "Missionary Needs." These are all extremely valuable, and for prospective missionary candidates essential, I would go further and label them desirable for every wide-awake Christian. Yet we are faced in most theological schools with such crowded curricula that we do well to get any future pastors into more than one mission's course. This means that we need to do a great deal more missionary work among our colleagues -- to see that the missionary imperative emerges naturally and sharply in Old and New Testament, Systematic Theology, Church History, Religious Education, and Parish Work.

At least two of these areas deserve special mention. Obviously, if there is no specialized and separate treatment of the ecumenical movement, it belongs to us, both in its genealogy and function. Among the 15 instructors reporting, courses in this field ranged from "an historical and critical approach" to the so-called Hocking inclusion of "other faiths as representing full ecumenicity." In places like Princeton and Union and Yale the current ecumenical trends are given thorough independent treatment, but most of the rest of us have to struggle along with a stepchild of a step-child (not because it is unwanted or unrecognized, but because no one knows quite where it belongs). At Duke our only distinct treatment is a Senior Seminar, shared heretofore by the professors of American Thought, Historical Theology, and Missions. This fall it will be assigned to Missions and the History and Philosophy of Religion, but one of these days I am going to propose a separate course, not only to reach a wider group of students but to give the subject status and a home.

If the first thing I did to the missions department at Duke was to separate the history and philosophy of missions, the second was to insert into the curriculum an elective workshop entitled "Missionary Education in the Local Church," In the speech by Dr. Ranson previously referred to, he said:

> "One of the great failures of the organized missionary movement has been in the field of missionary education. We have got to deal with an appalling amount of ignorance in pulpits. Many Methodist preachers (and I am sure he would not limit himself denominationally) talk about the mission of the Church in rather elementary 19th century terms; or where they got beyond that, they have a sort of romanticized idea about the World Church which has very little relation to reality. We have a tremendous job of education to do in the older Christendom.

The vast majority of our students are going into the parish ministry in this country, often in small rural communities. If they know little of what the World Mission is all about, they know still less about how to convey it to their congregations. Our Methodist Discipline calls for a church-wide school of missions (not just the woman's society) once a year, yet most of our student pastors have never even seen, much less planned one, and directed such a program.

My own course (if you will forgive another personal illustration) is frankly practical and utilitarian. The students (and they average more than the optimum dozen) preach missionary sermons, criticize current mission study books, interpret the psychological and educational development of church school age groups, plan a year's program for the local church, examine basic audio-visual aids, and then actually organize and put on a two- or three-night school of missions in some local church. This should be done by the department of religious education, you say, but by and large it is not being done there, and certainly the materials and resources and even purpose of distinctively missionary education are foreign to most of our colleagues.

Some of this should be included in the basic, required course, others of you will say, I agree, at least to the extent of acquainting future pastors with personnel agencies, literature headquarters, speakers' bureaus, and the like. But the task I have in mind cannot be done in a couple of lectures, sandwiched between Shinto and self-support or between Paul and polygamy. Unless we have unusual influence with unusual colleagues in religious education, preaching, church administration, and the rest, it behooves us to descend from our ivory towers of Islamic culture and Moravian motivations to make some direct contribution toward broadening the horizons of our local church ministers and members.

There were other questions raised in my circular which I have neither time nor inclination to discuss here, such as "missions majors" and graduate courses. Let me close with the last which I listed: "Do we need a new 'theology of missions'?" Perhaps my own answer has already been obvious. Perhaps the question deserved the flippant replies which came from some of you; to wit, "Not so sure, not certain just what some would think the old to be," or more bluntly still, "If you would kindly let me know what your present theology of missions is, I should be happy to suggest whether or not you need a new theology."

The majority, however, while reluctant to accept loose phraseology, agreed earnestly that we do need "re-thinking," "she old stuff newly stated in reference to our own time and circumstances," or "reorganization of the emphases given to already accepted ingredients," At one wing there was a preference for the term "philosophy of missions as being less dogmatic;" at the other wing, a plea for more recognition and interpretation of the activity of God above man in our missionary movement. We are balancing somewhere between the "damnation of all heathen" motive and motif and the liberal amalgamation of some world faith. We are trying to combine, as I have suggested, a neo-orthodox insistence on the absoluteness of God and the uniqueness of Christ, with a recognition of the brotherhood of man and an appreciation of diverse faiths and cultures. Some deep theological reconciliation is called for.

One of our members, whom I will identify as a Southern Baptist because you would not expect the comment from that source, replied that we do need a new theology of missions and that the trouble is we missionary folks have been trying to do the job instead of calling in recognized theologians. By and large, this is true. As I have already said, there is enthusiastic response from students when outstanding theologians do speak to these matters. I could have cleared a minor fortune each year in the sale of Paul Tillich's lecture, put out by the Missionary Research library. Under the stimulus of the International Missionary Council, my own denomination is holding next month a small, intimate consultation on the theology of missions, calling together eight leading Methodist theologians (some of you probably doubt that there are such animals) and four mission board secretaries (with a thirteenth belonging to neither category), I hope other churches are doing likewise, for we are already far behind our British and Continental colleagues at this point.

As Creator, God has made from one, every nation of men and desires that each of His children should know and love and serve Him. As God Incarnate, Jesus Christ reveals not only the saving power and redemptive love of the Father, but also His concern for humanity, for the more abundant life for the whole man. As Holy Spirit, God continually leads us into deeper communion with Himself and with one another and calls us to express that unity in the universal Church. In such elements -- God's purpose for the world, his concern for the well-being of all His children, his summons to Christian community -- lies the real motivation for the world mission today, rather than in personal merit, humanitarian service, cultural transformation, redemption by our efforts, or statistical growth.

Rightly or wrongly, we are moving away from the strictly historical approach to missions and from the purely academic study of comparative religions. We need a new orientation, both theologically and academically. My own humble conviction is that that new position is to be found, first in the theological field, as we reaffirm and redefine our dependence on the activity of God, and second, in the integrated approach to all man's needs -- spiritual, physical, educational, and social. This is the Christian imperative, as Canon Warren has so vividly described it.

Let me summarize in a few sentences. We in the field of missions are lost sheep, scattered among folds of history, theology, comparative religions, and education, wandering from theological to practical fields and back again. We are so busy looking at the world revolution and the fresh strategies of the mission field that we have failed to analyze the changes required in our own teaching. We have barely nibbled at the ecumenical movement and missionary education and theology. We proclaim in our lectures and sermons that the World Mission is the central task of the Church, yet we have all too often allowed it to become peripheral in our curricula.

Even in this meeting the selection of a green and callow neophyte to present this topic at the very end of a busy schedule gives evidence that your committee had no real intention of facing these deeper issues. I can only hope that this challenge, deliberately dogmatic and provocative at certain points, will lead the new officers to put more time in abler hands two years from now to deal with curricular matters. At the very least there is always the topic I was assigned, and did not touch: "Selected Courses in Missions: Syllabi and Methods."

Two Years Of The Literature Of Missions

A REVIEW OF THE PERIOD FROM THE SPRING OF 1954 TO THE SPRING OF 1956

Frank W. Price

THE WORLD SITUATION

The missionary enterprise is carried on today in the setting of world ferment -- revolution, cold war, rising nationalisms, racial tensions, resurgent ethnic religions, aggressive communism, widespread physical and spiritual hungers. Small wonder that so many books have appeared attempting to analyze and interpret the changing world situation or the developments in particular areas and countries. Christian writers have sought to understand the changing scene and its relation to the world mission of the Church.

The book by a young Presbyterian missionary in Brazil, Richard M. Schaull, *Encounter with Revolution* (New York, Association Press, 1955) is outstanding. Friendship Press, New York, made a distinctive contribution by the publication of several excellent books on the 1955 theme for missionary education, "The Christian Mission in a Revolutionary World"; including *This Revolutionary Faith* by Floyd Shacklock; and *Revolution and Redemption* by an American and an Indian, Paul Converse and M. M. Thomas. *Christianity and the Asian Revolution*, a compilation of several scholarly papers under the editorship of Rajah B. Manikam, was first published in India in 1954, and is for sale at Friendship Press: an immense amount of valuable information is packed into its 300 pages.

In the same field, but written from a non-religious point of view, is Sidney Lens *A World in Revolution* (New York, Praeger, 1956). Leonard Hurst has made a study of the basic physical and spiritual needs that underlie revolution. *Hungry Men, A Study of Man's Need* (London, Livingstone, 1955); and he considers also their implication for Christian missions.

One of the most significant events of the past two years was the Asian-African Conference at Bandung, April 18-24, 1955; it marked a turning point in Asian history. Published documents of the Conference are available, and interpretations from various points of view: George McTurnan Kahin has written *The Asian-African Conference* (Cornell University Press, 1956); A. Appadodai of India produced *The Haidune Conference* for the Indian Conference of World Affairs (New Delhi, 1955); Carlos P. Romulo of the Philippines is author of *The Meaning of Bandung* (University of North Carolina Press, 1956); and the most fascinating account of all to me is by the American Negro writer, Richard Wright, *The Color Curtain, A Report on the Bandung Conference* (New York, World Publishing Company, 1956). Wright, one of the famous' authors of *The God That Failed*, wrote another striking book in 1954 describing his trip to the Gold Coast area of Africa, *Black Power* (New York, Harper, 1954).

Some good general books on the crucial problems of race are: *Race Issues on the World Scene* by Melvin Conant (University of Hawaii Press, 1955); *The Color Problem* by Anthony H. Richmond (Penguin Books, Middlesex, 1956), dealing largely with the British empire; and S. B. Jackman's *The Numbered Days* (London, Student Christian Movement Press, 1954). From South Africa have come three remarkable books: Professor B. B. Keet has written *An Afrikaner Speaks on Apartheid* (the original is in Dutch; the English translation by Universal Publishers and Book sellers, London, has not yet appeared in the U.S.). Another Afrikaner Laurens van der Post, has written a profound treatise in the form of a debate, *The Dark Eye in Africa* (New York, William Morrow, 1955). Just off the press here is *Naught for Your Comfort* (New York, Doubleday, 1956) by Trevor Huddleston, the Anglican priest who worked twelve years in Johannesburg, a deeply moving story. The four articles by the Reverend James Robinson, the Negro minister, first published in *The Christian Century*, have been issued in pamphlet form, *Christianity and Revolution in Africa* (Chicago, Christian Century Press, 1956).

Communism is woven into the world picture today, and its challenge is felt at every turn in world missions. New books are constantly appearing in various aspects of Communist philosophy, history, and method and their meaning for the democratic world and the Christian faith. These vary greatly in quality. Among the best recent studies which throw some new light on the problem are: *Christianity, Communism and History* by William Hardern (New York, Abingdon, 1954.); *Marxism, Past and Present* by R. N. Carew Hunt (New York, Macmillan, 1954); *The Bent World* by J. V. L. Casserley (New York, Oxford, 1955) - a theological study; *The Church Faces Communism*, a Report of the Church of Scotland Commission on Communism (London, Longmans Green, 1955); *The Appeals of Communism* by G. A. Almond (Princeton University Press, 1954); Robert Tobias, *Communist Christian Encounter in East Europe* (Butler University, Indianapolis, 1956); and Matthew Spinka's new book on the Communist-Christian confrontation behind the Iron Curtain, to be published soon by Oxford University Press. In addition, we may mention without listing them the ever-increasing number of books on conditions in Communist controlled countries. Two such books on China, with careful documentation, are *China Under Communism* by Richard L. Walker (New Haven, Yale University Press, 1955) and *The Prospects for Communist China* by W. W. Rostow (New York, John Wiley, 1954).

PARTICULAR AREAS AND COUNTRIES

Books about the environment of the Church in particular areas and countries are multiplying so fast that it is impossible to keep up with them all, or in this short paper to describe even the best ones. Only a few will be mentioned, which have appealed to me.

In a little over a year the Missionary Research Library has added nearly sixty titles on Africa. Gunther's *Inside Africa* (New York, Harper, 1955) has been a best-seller and is deservedly popular. On visiting a country Gunther is said to ask who are the real leaders; then he seeks to find the sources of their power and what are their central beliefs. The book on Africa contains an interesting chapter on Albert Schweitzer, appreciative of Schweitzer's greatness yet containing some trenchant criticisms. Other notable books on Africa are: *The Land and People of South Africa* by Alan Paton (Philadelphia, Lippincott, 1955); *Report on Africa* by Oden Meeker (New York, Scribner, 1954); *Africa in the Modern World* by Calvin W. Stillman (University of Chicago Press, 1955); *Beneath the Southern Cross* by Charlotte Crogman Wright, wife of a bishop of the African Methodist Episcopal Church, (New York, Macmillan, 1954) and translated from the German by Glyn T. Hughes is a handsome volume with many fine illustrations and color plates. A brilliant young woman author, Marvine

Howe, has written a fascinating book, *One Woman's Morocco* (London, Arthur Barker, 1956) and is preparing another on Algeria.

From the vast field of new books on Asia I would select: Marguerite H. Bro's sympathetic report on Indonesia, *Indonesia: Land of Challenge* (New York, Harper, 1954); J. E. Spencer's *Asia East by South*, a valuable reference book (New York, John Wiley, 1954); *A History of South East Asia*, an authoritative work (costing ten dollars) by D. G. E. Hall (New York, St. Martin's Press, 1955); by a British author, H. A. Wittenbach, *Eastern Horizons* (Highway Press, London, 1954); in more popular style, *Struggle for Asia* by Francis Low (New York, Praeger, 1955); *Japan's Modern Century* by Hugh Borton (New York, Ronald Press, 1955); Robert Trumbull *As I See India* (New York, Cloane, 1956); and two most readable books by father and daughter, Chester Bowles' *The New Dimensions of Peace* (New York, Harper, 1955) and Cynthia Bowles' *At Home in India* (New York, Harcourt Brace, 1956). As examples of books being produced by national scholars we may refer to: *China: New Age and New Outlook* by Kuo Ping-chia (New York, Knopf, 1956); *Korea Tomorrow: Land of the Morning Calm* by Kyong Cho Chung (New York, Macmillan, 1955); and *Hiroshima Diary* by Dr. M. Hachiya, translated and edited by Warner Wells, M.D. (University of Chicago Press, 1955).

On Latin America there is time only to name one valuable and expensive book, *A History of Latin America from the Beginnings to the Present,* by the well-known Hubert Herring (New York, Knopf, 1955. Much is being written about the Middle East and its convulsions. These two books throw much light on the problems of that area: *The Middle East; Problem Area in World Politics* (New York, Macmillan, 1954) by S. A. Morrison (New York, Harper, 1954). Within the past few months many valuable articles have appeared in secular and religious periodicals. An up-to-date bibliography on the Middle and Near East and Christianity's stake in its development is much needed.

THEORY OF MISSIONS

Now we must turn to Christian missions, its principles and methods in the tumultuous world about us.

At the meeting of this Association two years ago, the Willingen conference and its recommendations loomed large in current missionary literature. In the period since 1954 the Second Assembly of the World Council of Churches at Evanston has made an equally important contribution to missionary and ecumenical thinking. In another fact,

Evanston was another step in the growing together of missions and "ecumenics." The published reports of the Assembly and its commissions (New York, Harper, 1954) are on all theological library shelves. We know that they are being read also behind the Iron Curtain; criticisms of some portions taken not only in official meeting but also in the Visitors' Conference have been voiced by church leaders under Communist regimes. Following Evanston there has been a strong advance in the work of the Studies Division of the World Council which, in cooperation with the International Missionary Council is making significant plans for worldwide research with fresh interpretations and evaluations of "mission" and "missions" for the Church in all lands. Two books should be listed here: *The Significance of Evanston* by John Marsh (London, Independent Press, 1954) and *Evanston: An Interpretation* by James H. Nichols (New York, Harper, 1954).

Books on the theory of missions generally reflect the sociological and theological bias of the writer. *Missionary Principles and Practice* by Harold Lindsell (New York, Revell, 1955); *An Introduction to the Study of Christian Missions* by Harold R. Cook (Chicago, Moody Press, 1954); *The Unchanging Commission* by David H. Adeney (Chicago, Inter-Varsity Press, 1955) represent quite conservative points of view; nevertheless, they are full of meat and can well be used as reference books in the study of missions. Lindsell and Cook attempt to deal comprehensively with the whole field of missions: Biblical basis, history, principles, methods, missionary societies, choice and preparation of missionaries, and so on. However, one feels that they have not caught up with all the tremendous new challenges to missions and the dynamic factors in modern social change.

From the creative mind of Max A. C. Warren, Secretary of the Church Missionary Society in England, have come three new books of high quality: *The Christian Imperative - Go Preach, Go Teach, Go Heal, Go Baptize, The How of Obedience* - (New York, Scribners, 1955), *Caesar, the Beloved Enemy* (London, SCM Press, 1955), and *The Gospel of Victory*, the relevance of Galatians for the Christian Mission. Alongside the latter study should be placed a similar study several years ago of the epistle to the Hebrews in relation to world missions by William Manson (London, Hodder and Stoughton, 1951). J. B. Phillips, whose fresh translations of the Gospels and Epistles, and recently the Acts of the Apostles, have delighted so many Bible students, has produced a small but profound book for mission study in Great Britain, *The Church Under the Cross* (London, Highway Press, 1956); it is really a theology of missions. One of the new I.M.C. Research Pamphlets is a valuable study, *Toward a Theology of Missions*, by Wilhelm

Anderson. *Christian Theology: An Ecumenical Approach* by Walter Marshall Horton (New York, Harper, 1955) is the fruitful attempt by an eminent American theologian to relate the basic doctrines of Christianity to the emerging concept of a world church, but the style is heavy. *The Early Church and the Coming Great Church* written by John (New York, Abingdon, 1955) links the Church of the first two centuries and the Church that is to be, in a discussion rich with theological insights and at the same time phrased in lucid language. A similarly useful book is *The Significance of the Church*, by Robert McAfee Brown (Westminster Press, 1956).

Two German books on theory have been highly commended. One is by Thomas Ohm, *Ruhe and Frommigkeit, Ein Beitrag zur Lehre von der Missions – method*, (Kuln and Opladen, 1955). The rest and piety which the Christian Gospel offers to men are compared with the peace promised by other religions. An older book which is now receiving more attention in the U.S. is edited by J.T. Hoekendijk, a scholarly symposium, *Ker en volk in de Duitse Zendingswetenschap* in which appears the names of K. Appenzeller, W. Freytag, H. Frick, K. Hartenstien, J. Richter, G. Warneck and others (Utrecht, 1948).

Dr. Hendrik Kraemer' s *The Christian Gospel in a non-Christian World* (1938) is being republished in the United States, since the earlier edition is exhausted (Grand Rapids, Kriegel's, 1956). Dr. K. S. Latourette has written a new book embodying his philosophy of mission, *Challenge and Conformity* (New York, Harper, 1955).

The most provocative book on missionary principles that has appeared during the last two years is undoubtedly D. A. McGavran's *The Bridges of God* (London, Dominion Press, 1955). A missionary of the Disciples Church in India, McGavran compares what he calls the "people movement" with the old "mission station" approach. The people movement is not a tribe or mass movement but a movement of social groups into the Church, under the leading of the Spirit of God. Such movements in India and many other lands of younger churches are described, and from these the author concludes that the approach of the "gathered colony" around the mission compound should be discarded in favor of the more dynamic strategy. Missionary forces should be redeployed, leaving areas where little results have been achieved and moving into areas of greater fluidity and hope. McGavran tries to find a basis for people movements in the New Testament. His emphasis upon the indigenous church, self-support from the beginning, and evangelism to groups as well as to individuals and through believers to other believers, inspires widespread response. However, there is serious question whether the strategy of the people movement into the Church is as widely applicable as McGavran believes, especially in highly cultured populations. After a period of evangelistic effort people movements may come or may not come; the ingathering may be rapid or slow; those brought into the Church must still be nurtured in Christian faith and experience. One can hope and pray for the power of the Spirit at work in families, clans, groups and societies, but such movements cannot be manipulated at will. Don McGavran is right in insisting that the missionary break away from the missionary compound and static institutions to identify himself with the people and follow openings for new evangelistic witness. I question whether there is enough that is new and also practical in his proposals to justify Dr. Latourett's comment, "One of the most important books on missionary methods that has appeared in many years." But it is certain to start interesting discussions. Another good book for debate is T. S. Soltau's *Missions at the Crossroads* (Wheaton, Illinois, Van Kempe, 1954).

RELATION OF CHRISTIANITY TO OTHER WORLD RELIGIONS

Many new books on other religions have appeared but none stands out as particularly noteworthy. Valuable material is found in articles appearing in some periodicals. Irene Vongehr Vincent describes the Buddha caves in northwest China which have attracted much attention in relation to the eastern march of Buddhism, *The Sacred Oasis: Caves of Thousand Buddha's, Tun Huang* (Chicago, University of Chicago Press, 1953). Henri de Lubac's *Aspects of Buddhism* (New York, Shead and Ward, 1954) is a well written and a useful volume. Liu Wu-chi is the author of a new book on Confucius, *Confucius, His Life and Time* (New York, Philosophical Library, 1955). *Islam* by Alfred Guillaume (New York, Penguin Books, 1954); *Muhammad's People, A Tale by Anthology*, by Eric Schroeder, tr., (Portland, Maine, Bond Wheelwright, 1955); and *Islam and Christian Theology*, Part II, vol. I, by J. Windrow Sweetman (London, Lutterworth Press) are worthy of honorable mention. The *Muslim World*, published by Hartford Seminary Foundation, continues its high standard of articles, (1955).

There is a new interest in resurgent religions and their relation to culture and national life. We look forward to the results of new studies of these religions in the yeasty life of today as well as in the history of past centuries. The popular but also scholarly articles on religions of the world in *LIFE Magazine*, 1955, attracted wide attention. The Friendship Press series for general readers should also be mentioned; these include

Introducing Hinduism by Malcolm Pitt, and *Introducing Buddhism* by K. S. Latourette (1956).

Some good anthropological studies of both primitive and advanced peoples have been published. Illustrative of the former is an important work by Daryll Forde, editor, *African Worlds: Studies in the Cosmological Ideas and Social Values of African Peoples* (Oxford University Press, 1954). *Readings in Anthropology*, by E. A. Hoebel and others is a very useful reference book for students (New York, McBraw Hill, 1955). Margaret Mead has written an illuminating story of tribal change, *New Lives for Old, Cultural Transformation - Manus, 1928-1953* (New York, William Morrow Co., 1956). Another thorough study is *A Solomon Island Society* by Douglas L. Oliver (Cambridge, Harvard University Press, 1955). Last, but not least, in this list is *The Family of Man*, a book of pictures from the greatest photographic exhibition ever presented in this country, 503 pictures of "Man" from 68 countries (New York, Maco Magazine Corporation, 1955).

HISTORY OF MISSIONS

J. H. Nichols' one-volume *History of Christianity 1650-1950* (Ronald Press, 1956) contains chapters on Protestant and Catholic Missions, The Younger Churches, and the Ecumenical Movement. *Development of Modern Christianity* by Frederick C. Norwood similarly has closing chapters on Missions and the Ecumenical Church, (New York, Abingdon, 1956).

First prize for a history of missions during the past biennium should go to C. P. Groves for the completion of volumes 2 and 3 in his monumental *The Planting of Christianity in Africa* (London, Lutterworth, 1954-5). This brings the story up to 1914. It is the standard history of African missions for a long time to come, a most scholarly work with a wide range of knowledge and understanding, a truly great production.

Other definitive histories that should be in the missionary professor's library are: *Church of South India* by Bengt Sundkler of Upsala (London, Lutterworth, 1954); *The Catholic Church in Japan* by Johannes Laures (Rutland, Vermont, Charles C. Tuttle Co., 1954); *A History of the London Missionary Society* by Norman Goodall (London, Oxford University Press, 1954), *South of the Himalayas: One Hundred Years of Methodism in India and Pakistan* by James K. Mathews (New York Board of Missions of the Methodist Church, 1955); *The Meaning of Maryknoll* by Albert J. Nevins (New York, McMullen Hiljam, 1954); *Venture of Faith, the Story of the American Baptist Foreign Mission Society,* 1814-1954, by Robert G. Torbet (Philadelphia, Judson Press, 1955); *A History of the World's Alliance of Young Men's Christian Associations*, by Clarence Prouty (New York Association Press, 1956); *The Growth of the World Church*, by E. A. Payne (Edinburgh House, Macmillan, 1955).

BIOGRAPHIES

There are several new biographies of, or books about, Albert Schweitzer and David Livingstone. Erica Anderson's *Book of Photographs, The World of Albert Schweitzer,* is very attractive (New York, Harper, 1954. *Livingstone's Travels,* edited by James I. McNair is compiled from Livingstone's own diaries (New York, Macmillan, 1954). A new life of Francis Xavier has been published in Germany (Frieburg, Herder, 1955). The missionaries of more than a century ago who brought reforms to India furnish material for a unique book, *Reformers in India* (London, Cambridge, 1956). Inspiring reading may be found in John R. Weinlick's *Count Zinzendorf* (New York, Abingdon, 1956); Gordon Seagrave's *My Hospital in the Hills* (New York, Norton, 1955); Leslie T. Lyall's account of a famous Chinese evangelist, *John Sung* (London, C.I.M., 1954); W. Reginald Wheeler's recently published biography of the great missionary leader Robert E. Speer, *A Man Sent from God* (New York, Revell, 1956); and G. Sherwood Eddy's autobiography, *Eighty Adventurous Years* (New York, Harper, 1955); the autobiography of J. Leighton Stuart, *Fifty Years in China* (New York, Random House, 1954); a new edition of Dr. T. H. Somervell's story, *Knife and Life in India* (London, Living-stone Press, 1956); and the biography of the early German missionary to India, by Eric Beyneuther, *Bartholomadus Ziegenbalg* (3rd. ed., Berlin, Evang. Verlagsanstatt, 1954). I would give first place among recent biographies to *The Wise Man from the West*, the story of Matteo Ricci, by Vincent Cronin, son of the novelist A. J. Cronin (New York, Button, 1955). It was based upon the exhaustive research done by Father Pascal D'elia of Rome and others on the life of Ricci and is written in a swiftly moving, colorful style that brings the brilliant and intrepid Jesuit missionary to life.

Stories of experiences under Communist rule, especially, in China, continue to come from the press. *Four Years in a Red Hell: the Story of Father Rigney* is typical of Roman Catholic narratives (Chicago, Henry Regnery, 1956). A somewhat different type of story is *Moscow Was My Parish* by the expelled Roman Catholic priest, Georges Bissonette (New York, Mcgraw Hill, 1956). *Les Enfants dans la cille, Sory of Catholic Christian Life in Shanghai, 1949-1955* by Jean Lefeuvre (Louvain, Casterman, 1955) gathers up the experiences of thousands of humble Christians under persecution. Among Protestant stories of trials and escape from communist tyranny, the best – simply and movingly told – is written by a former British missionary in Tibet, *When Iron Gates Yield* by Geoffrey Bull (Chicago, Moody Press, 1955). Another type of book on the increase is the report of experiences and impressions by visitors to Communist countries. They are interesting, but dated, and influenced by the predilections of the writers.

OLDER AND YOUNGER CHURCHES

Here we can select only three significant titles. *Religious Freedom in Spain: Its Ebb and Flow* by J. D. Hughey, Jr., (London, Gary Kingsgate, 1955) tells a sad story of bigotry and tyranny in that once great country. A splendid example of writing from the younger churches is *Christianity in the Indian Crucible* by Eddy Asirvatham (Calcutta, YMCA Publishing House, 1955). "The world missionary," he says, "must be raceless and nationless as Jesus was." Published by the Friendship Press (1956) is a good study book, *The Church in Southeast Asia* by Rajah Manikam and Winburn Thomas.

MISSIONARY METHODS

Changes in missionary organization, administration, programs and methods are the subject of constant and lively discussion by missionary societies and groups of missionaries and Christian nationals in all parts of the world. Many missionary reports, articles and monographs reflect vigorous rethinking on these questions.

One new problem is the relation of missions to large-scale welfare programs, inter-church service, technical aid and economic cooperation between countries. Everyone in this field should read such recent books as *The Story of FAO* (Food and Agriculture Organization of the United Nations) by Gove Hambidge, (New York, Van Nostrand, 1955) and a scientific and sympathetic study by the National Planning Association, James Maddox, editor, *Technical Assistance by Religious Agencies in Latin America* (University of Chicago Press, 1955). The publications of Agricultural Missions, Inc., New York, should be in all theological libraries. The Missionary Research Library will soon publish a special bibliography on agricultural and rural missions.

In the area of Christian education a series of historic interest is being published by the United Board for Christian Higher Education in Asia, New York (formerly United Board for Christian Colleges in China).

These are stories of each of the thirteen Christian colleges in China, written by missionaries long connected with them.

A medical book that should be mentioned is *Missionary Health Manual* by Paul E. Adolph (Chicago, Moody Press, 1955). This, together with E.K. Hidgon's *New Missionaries for New Days* (St. Louis, Bethany, 1956), a study in the missionary selection and training, is evidence that increasing attention is being given to problems of turnover and loss in missionary personnel and ways of improving the quality and morale of missionaries who serve abroad.

SURVEY AND REFERENCE WORKS, BIBLIOGRAPHIES

Dr. Walter Freytag is editor of *Deutsche Evangelische Weltmission Jahrbuch* (Hamburg, 1955) with important articles and statistics about German missions. *The Japan Christian Year Book* for 1955 has been issued The Christian Councils of Korea and Burma and of Hong Kong have recently published directories of churches and missions. The third part of *Training for the Ministry in Africa*, an I.M.C. survey, has been completed and the reports of the three survey groups are now available in one volume (1955).

The bibliography of Roman Catholic missionary literature, described by Dr. Beaver two years ago, *Bibliothecan Missionum*, has now been published up to vol. 21 (Freiburg, Herder). American, Asiatic, Chinese, Indonesian, and African missions have been covered; the last volume deals with Australia and Oceania. For Protestant missionary bibliographies see the indispensable *International Review of Missions*, book reviews in various periodicals, and the *Book Lists* issued by the Missionary Research Library.

A great many very useful year books and guides are issued by different countries and international organizations. A library is limited only by its budget in the purchase of such reference materials.

John C. Thiessen's *A Survey of World Missions* (Inter-varsity Press, Chicago, 1955) is a product of theological conservatism and somewhat inadequate data; notwithstanding it contains helpful articles on conditions in each country and missionary work there and is a useful source book. We all look forward to the 1957 edition of *The World Christian Handbook* (London, Dominion Press). The Missionary Research Library will publish this summer a *Revised Directory of Foreign Missionary Agencies* in the United States and Canada, with current information and statistics about each society.

The new *20th Century Encyclopedia of Religious Knowledge*, 2 volumes (Grand Rapids, Baker Book House, 1955) contains brief but good articles on persons and places and tables of interest to the professor of mission and should be on every reference shelf.

APM

Missionary Vocation

4th Biennial Meeting
Boston University School of Theology
June 16–17, 1958

Introduction

The papers presented at each biennial meeting of the Association of Professors of Missions have been intended primarily to stimulate the thinking and study of the members, but they have proved to be useful to students of missions, to the executive staffs of mission boards, and to interested laymen. Consequently there has been a steadily-mounting demand for the Proceedings. Orders for the Proceedings of the 1956 meeting eventually totaled four times the supply. Therefore, viewing the needs in mission literature in general, as well as the concerns of the membership, the theme "Missionary Vocation" was chosen as the general subject of the 1958 meeting and of this volume.

The current practice of the Association with respect to program is to present a group of papers on one main theme and to supplement these with one additional paper on the teaching of missions in the theological curriculum and another on the literature of the biennium.

One important feature of the program is only recorded in the report of the program, but it was a most valuable instrument for unifying the program, providing inspiration, and provoking thought. This was the series of worship services by the chaplain of the meeting, Dean Harold Lindsell of Fuller Theological Seminary, Pasadena, including meditations on the Biblical basis of the Christian mission.

The grateful appreciation of the Association to those who presented papers and the criticisms of them is recorded in the minutes. The critic for the first paper was unable to be present.

Copies of the Proceedings may be obtained from the office of the secretary of the Association at $3.00 each.

R. Pierce Beaver
President, 1956–58
Secretary, 1958–60
Swift Hall 400 University of Chicago

The Missionary Calling of the Church

James A. Scherer
Lutheran School of Missions
Haywood, Illinois

In the last decade the question of the Church's missionary calling has probably received more theological attention than in any other recent period of church history. Both before and after Willingen (1952) numerous studies and reports have given articulate expression to a widespread concern to formulate the concept of the Church's missionary calling more precisely. These studies were worked out with great care and detail and it would be presumptuous to say that their results had been adequately digested. On the contrary, the Willingen Conference produced only brief statements on "The Missionary Calling of the Church" and "The Calling of the Church to Mission and Unity."[1] A proposed statement on "The Missionary Obligation of the Church" was received as a basis for further study, but not formally adopted.[2] Meanwhile, the voluminous documents and supporting papers which constitute the North American Report on Aim I - to restate the universal missionary obligation of the Church (1) as grounded in the eternal Gospel and (2) in relation to the present historical situation - remain almost wholly unpublished and are available only in mimeographed form from the Committee on Research in Foreign Missions of the Division of Foreign Missions of the National Council of the Churches of Christ in the U.S.A.[3] There has been remarkably little discussion of these studies since Willingen, though it would seem that any further discussion would regard the work done in preparation for Willingen as a requisite starting point.

---

[1] *The Missionary Obligation of the Church*. Report of the Enlarged Meeting of the Committee of the I.M.C. meeting at Willingen, 1952. London. 46 pp.

[2] *Missions Under the Cross*, ed. Norman Goodall. Published by I.M.C., London, 1953. 264; pp. Contains addresses delivered at Willingen as well as the Report. Statement referred to is entitled "The Theological Basis of the Missionary Obligation" (An Interim Report) and is found on pp. 238-245.

[3] Available through the Missionary Research Library, 3041 Broadway, N.Y. 27, NY.

Lack of a lively debate in the interim means that the present may not be greatly propitious for a restudy of the missionary calling of the Church, nor are we to await results that go much beyond the findings of Willingen. Too little time has elapsed, and in this time there has been little progress in missionary theology. At the same time, the missionary situation in the world has not radically changed in the last few years, as it did, for example, between Madras (1938) and Whitby (1947). Willingen gave rise to slogans such as "The Church is the Mission" and proclaimed that "there is no participation in Christ without participation in His mission to the world." It is not clear however that there has been any significant quickening of the missionary impulse in the churches during the interval. The actual situation remains far removed from the high sounding theological phrasing of Willingen, for the battle of translating the new formula of church-mission relationship into meaningful terms at the grass roots level still remains to be fought. In this respect, the situation in the West has scarcely changed. Missions continue to be the concern and prerogative of independent missionary societies and denominational mission boards which discharge the missionary obligation "by proxy" for the churches at large. Perhaps the real break-through and the true follow-up of Willingen will come from the lands of the younger churches.

The East Asia Christian Conference on "The Common Evangelistic Task of the Churches in East Asia" held at Prapat, Indonesia in 1957 may be the forerunner of a wider implementation of the Willingen formula as a fuller acceptance of missionary responsibility on the part of churches as churches. [4]This will not be the first occasion for the churches of the West to learn from those of the East.

Despite the somewhat inauspicious character of the circumstances, however, the unremitting search for a more adequate statement of the Church's missionary calling must go on. The unfinished task remains unfinished. Scarcely one percent of the population of Asia can be considered even nominally Christian. The world population "explosion" continues to add more non-Christians annually to the lands of Asia than there are Protestant Christians in those areas. Only in Africa and Latin America does it appear that some headway is being made. Meanwhile, repristinated pagan religious rivals grow stronger in some areas, and demonic anti-Christian ideologies threaten to engulf new territory and hinder the course of the Christian mission. In the Christian world, the

---

[4] *The Common Evangelistic Task of the Churches in East Asia.* Papers and Minutes of the East Asia Christian Conference, Prapat, Indonesia, 1957. 167 pp. Printed in Rangoon and available from I.M.C.

younger churches continue to advance in the direction of greater maturity, and the movement toward Christian unity, both locally and ecumenically, continues apace. At such a time the Church, faithful to its calling and intent upon hearing the Word of God in the present situation, cannot fail to ask herself the question about her own purpose and destiny, and to seek to recover her true nature and calling in the world. Docs the picture of the Church's missionary calling painted at Willingen offer a true description of the Christian mission and its relationship to the Church? If true, is it adequate by Biblical standards and does it give full expression to the missionary mandate of the Gospel? Or is it possible that Willingen was on the wrong track, and that further pursuit of the course set there can lead only to barren and sterile results? Inadequate though they may be, the Willingen statements represent the best guideposts that we have been given to date. The tentative character of the results of Willingen is already indicated in the report, where the editor speaks of Willingen as "a milestone, not a terminus." There it was recognized that the search for theological clarity must go on, though missionary obedience need not wait on theological understanding. Moreover, and even more important, it was a concern at Willingen that "in this present desperate world situation, the evangelization of the world might be more speedily accomplished through the power of the Holy Spirit." Such a result could not be achieved by human planning but "waits on those movements in which the obedience of man is taken up into the quickening power of the Spirit," In this spirit the event called "Willingen, 1952" was commended "to the prayers and the local missionary obedience of all who in their membership of the Church are members of "a 'worshipping, witnessing, suffering and expectant community.'"[5]

ANTECEDENTS OF WILLINGEN

The development of missionary thinking up to Willingen, and particularly through the course of the great twentieth century missionary conferences, has been sufficiently traced elsewhere and need not long occupy us here.[6] In their origins, Protestant missions have largely sprung up

---

[5] *The Missionary Obligation of the Church*, p. vi.

[6] See the following: Wilhelm Andersen, *Towards a Theology of Mission, a Study of the Encounter between the Missionary Enterprise and the Church & Its Theology.* I.M.C. Research Pamphlet #2. London, 1955. 64 pp. Eng. tr. By S. C. Neill; *Jabrbuch Eyangelischer Mission 1957*. Verlag der deutschen Evang. Missionshilfe, Hamburg, 1957. Heinz Renkewitz, "Die Missionsverantwortung der Mirche," pp. 3-25; C. Stanley Smith, "An Exploratory Attempt to Define the Theological Basis of the Church's Missionary Obligation," Parts I & II.

in Pietistic circles, and retained a strongly individualistic flavor. Missionary activities were carried on by private societies parallel to, or frequently in opposition to, the organized church. Whereas Willingen could speak of mission as the function of the Church, the first half of the twentieth century might grudgingly concede that it was at least a function of the Church, while in the centuries preceding it was scarcely conceded to be a legitimate function of the Church at all. Wilhelm Andersen in *Towards a Theology of Mission* states:

> Apart from certain exceptions, Pietism has been, up till the present century, the soil in which missionary activity has grown. The missionary enterprise regarded itself as a separate institution concerned with Christian operations overseas within, on the fringe of, in certain cases even outside, the existing Christian bodies; and in accordance with this understanding of its nature, it developed its own independent organizational structure within or alongside of the organized churches. [7]

Even allowing for wide differences in forms of organization and types of relationship between church and mission, it will be seen that the vast majority of cases -- the only likely exception being the Herrnhut (Moravian) Brethren -- fall in the "within," "on the fringe of," or "outside" categories. It is true that the American Protestant missionary enterprise stands in a somewhat more favorable relationship toward the Church than do the majority of its missionary society counterparts in Europe. Here the major church bodies have institutionalized or domesticated missions within their own houses by setting up specialized mission boards for the discharge of the Church's missionary obligation. Mission and church are regarded as belonging in some sense together, and missionary activity, instead of being the exclusive preoccupation of a few select individuals, becomes at least an institutional concern of the whole Church, albeit only one concern among many. For historical reasons missionary activity has acquired a church centered character in America rather different from the largely extra ecclesiastical status of missions in most European societies.

Unpublished mimeographed material included in supporting papers of the North American Report on Aim I; R. Pierce Beaver in *Church History* vol. XXI, pp. 345-364, "North American Thought on the Fundamental Principles of Missions during the Twentieth Century" (a survey article covering the 20th century up to, but not including, Willingen).

[7] Andersen, *Towards a Theology of Mission*, p. 15.

[8]This ought not however to obscure the fact that missionary concern remains marginal and peripheral in the life of the American churches, much the same as it does in the churches of Europe.

Two twentieth century phenomena have in a particular way prepared the ground for the rapprochement between church and mission that was to take place at Willingen. The first is the rise of the younger churches as independent entities, no longer regarded as mission dependents. This became increasingly evident in the interim between the Jerusalem (1928) and Madras (1938) conferences, where a growing proportion of the delegates came from the younger churches. World War II acted as a further catalyst to this development and Whitby (1947) dramatically signalized the emancipation of the young churches and their elevation to full equality and responsibility by coining the slogan, "Partners in Obedience." The post-Whitby era in the life of the young churches corresponds to the post-Bandung era in the life of some twenty-five new nation-states which have achieved political independence from colonial powers since 1946. The other phenomenon, borne of two world wars and the growing secularization of the West, is the breakdown of the "Christendom" concept, which has been normative for western civilization since Constantine. The abrupt breakdown of this concept through a sharp decline in church participation and institutional loyalty, particularly in Europe, has paved the way for a new recognition that the whole world, including the supposedly Christian West, is a mission field. In a fashionable phrase, the West has become "post-Christian". Distinctions between the religious situation in East and West are regarded as illusory, except that the one is characterized as "post-Christian" while the other remains largely "pre-Christian". In the West this recognition has been accompanied by a renascent interest in "evangelism," both as regards its theology, general approach, and new techniques. In accepting this new evangelistic situation the churches of the West have profited in no small degree by the accumulated experience of the missionary enterprise.

WILLINGEN -- THE ECCLESIASTICAL DIMENSION

When the Willingen meeting took place the time was thus particularly ripe for a new statement of the missionary calling of the Church. The Church not only had a mission but was a mission and must understand her nature and calling in terms of mission -- a mission that is one and the same throughout the world. A kind of inner logic had led to

---

[8]   The new relationship between church and mission in the Netherlands Reformed Church is an exception.

the selection of "The Missionary Obligation of the Church" as the principal theme for discussion at Willingen. As Andersen put it:

> Mission and church had discovered one another and through the gravest of crises had approved themselves as an inseparable unity... The mutual discovery of Church and mission had led each of the partners to a basic theological reconsideration of its own nature. Church and mission were now alike called to submit themselves to the service which theology can render, and to permit themselves to be challenged to become that which, in their dependence on God they are, and that which they are called to be in the world.[9]

For the first time the objects of the missionary enterprise came to be taken seriously by the theologians. Missions began cautiously to edge away from the sphere of practical theology and to invade the hallowed precincts of systematic theology, where it had previously found no home. A new body of theological literature under the heading of "Missionary Theology" or "The Theology of Mission" slowly came into existence and the missionary enterprise appeared to be on the way to finding a theological rationale and a new respectability. Everyone seemed satisfied that church and mission, having at last found one another through the service of theology, would never again be separated.

But the marriage gave indications of being premature. There were some who believed that the two partners were not sufficiently compatible. A dispute arose at Willingen over the interpretation of the major theme, "The Missionary Obligation of the Church," In essence the argument was between those who would have derived the missionary obligation from the nature of the Church -- i.e. as inherent in its very being and existence -- and those who insisted that the missionary obligation must be derived from something anterior to the Church, vis. the Gospel. The fact of the Gospel and of missionary obligation were not under dispute; the question raised at Willingen was whether the Church should form a middle term between Gospel and missionary obligation. The point in question may seem too infinitesimal to deserve the attention it received, for the outcome in either case is the same. Both sides to the dispute were interested only in strengthening and intensifying the sense of missionary obligation. Nevertheless, a theological impasse developed and the original statement on the missionary obligation of the Church failed to be adopted.

---

[9]   Andersen, *Towards a Theology of Mission*, p. 36.

The statement on the missionary calling of the Church as adopted by the enlarged meeting proves upon examination to be a re-write of the unacceptable original, with significant departures in the content of one section, and abbreviations elsewhere. The first four sections of the two statements correspond to one another. Section I, "The Missionary Situation and the Rule of God," affirms the triumph of the cross over all forms of pessimism. Section II, entitled "The Missionary Obligation of the Church," is the disputed section, to which we shall return. Section III, "The Total Missionary Task," states that God sends forth the Church to carry out His work to the ends of the earth, to all nations, and to the end of time. It likens the Church to an army living in tents, whom God calls to strike their tents and go forward. Section IV, entitled "Solidarity With the World," speaks of the Church as being in the world and wholly identified with it, both in sorrow and in love, thereby establishing the possibility of communicating the gospel. Section V of the approved report, "Discerning the Signs of the Times," has no precise parallel in the earlier statement. It concludes with a ringing summons to all Christians "to come forth from the securities which are no more secure and from boundaries of accepted duty too narrow for the Lord of all the earth, and to go forth with fresh assurance to the task of bringing all things into captivity to Him, and of preparing the whole earth for the day of his coming."[10]

The matter under dispute can now be indicated by a comparison of the original but disapproved version of Section II with the wording of the approved version:

Proposed but not adopted :

The missionary obligation of the Church comes from the love of God in His active relationship with men. For God sent forth His Son, Jesus Christ, to seek out, and gather together, and transform, all men... By the Holy Spirit the Church, experiencing God's active love, is assured that God will complete what He has set His hand to in the sending of His Son. This is the hope with which the Church looks forward to the goal of its existence, which in fact sets the Church marching onwards. In this sense 'mission' belongs to the purpose of the Church...

Whatever else ought to be said about the structure, life and purpose of the Church, this one thing must be said: that

---

[10]   *The Missionary Obligation of the Church*, p. 5 .

'mission' is woven into all three and cannot be separated out from any one without destroying it. When God says to the Church: 'Go forth and be my witnesses,' He is not giving the Church a commission that is added to its other duties; but a commission that belongs to its royal charter (covenant) to be the Church.[11]

Adopted:

The missionary movement of which we are a part has its source in the Triune God Himself. Out of the depths of His love for us, the Father has sent forth His own beloved Son to reconcile all things to Himself, that we and all men might, through the Spirit, be made one in Him with the Father in that perfect love which is the very nature of God...

1. God has created all things and all men that in them the Glory of His love might be reflected; nothing therefore is excluded from the reach of his redeeming love.

2. All men are involved in a common alienation from God, from which none can escape by his own efforts.

3. God has sent forth one Savior, one Shepherd to seek and save all the lost, one Redeemer who by His death, resurrection and ascension has broken down the barrier between man and God, accomplished a full and perfect atonement, and created in Himself one new humanity, the Body of which Christ is the exalted and regnant head.

4. On the foundation of this accomplished work God has sent forth His Spirit, the Spirit of Jesus, to gather us together in one Body in Him, to guide us into all the truth, to enable us to worship the Father in spirit and in truth, to empower us for the continuance of His mission as His witnesses and ambassadors, the first fruits and earnest of its completion.

5. By the Spirit we are enabled both to press forward as ambassadors of Christ, beseeching all men to be reconciled to God, and also to wait with sure confidence for the final victory of His love, of which he has given us most sure promises.

---

[11] *Missions Under the Cross* , p. 241.

"We who have been chosen in Christ, reconciled to God through Him, made members of His Body, sharers in His Spirit, and heirs through hope of His Kingdom, are by these very facts committed to full participation in His redeeming mission. There is no participation in Christ without participation in His mission to the world. That by which the Church receives its existence is that by which it is also given its world-mission. "As the Father hath sent me, even so send I you."[12]

A comparison of the two statements will show that the earlier Church centered view of missionary obligation has been displaced by a thorough going Trinitarian statement. In the Church-centered view, missionary obligation is derived from the nature of the Church and becomes the means for attaining its goal. Mission is predicated on the pre-existence of the Church. A logical corollary of this is that missionary policy is largely concerned with church extension, *plantatio ecclesiae*, and missionary activity is limited to the road from church to church, as it was in the theory of G. Wernock. It was a reaction against this view that prompted J. C. Hoekendijk to propound his now famous thesis:

Church-centric missionary thinking is bound to go astray, because it revolves around an illegitimate center ... It may well be that we are so wrapped up in our church-centrism that we hardly realize any longer how much our ideas are open to controversy. Would it not be a good thing to start all over again in trying to understand what it really means when we repeat again and again our favorite missionary text, "the Gospel of the kingdom will be proclaimed throughout the *oikoumcne*" (Matt. 24:14) and attempt to rethink our ecclesiology within this framework of kingdom-gospel-apostolate-world?[13]

Hoekendijk's penetrating critique disclosed the hidden presupposition of the proposed Church-centered formulation. At Willingen the delegates were unwilling to accept an uncritical Church-centered interpretation as adequate. In the light of Biblical theology it came to be regarded as theologically questionable. Thus ecclesiology, which initially had rendered to the theology of mission the service of providing a temporary refuge for the homeless newcomer, discovered that it could not

---

12   *The Missionary Obligation of the Church*, p. 2-3.
13   J. C. Hoekendijk, "The Church in Missionary Thinking," *International Review of Missions*, vol. 41 (1952), pp. 332-333.

comfortably accommodate the newcomer without having its own house upset. As Andersen put it, "The missionary enterprise can regard itself as an activity of the Church, only on condition that the nature of the Church itself is defined in terms of the missionary enterprise."[14] One of the chief negative services of Willingen was to show the tentative and unsatisfactory character of our ecclesiological thinking. Arising as a by-product of the discussion on the missionary obligation of the Church, the problem of the Church -- rather then that of mission -- loomed as the principal unsolved problem. To this we shall return later.

We examine now the significance of the Trinitarian statement on missionary calling. Willingen, which had convened with a Church-centered orientation toward mission as its stated presupposition, found itself compelled to renounce this presupposition for something more ultimate. This ultimate bedrock on which the missionary obligation rests is the Gospel itself, including the Biblical description of the Kingdom of God and its breaking in upon this world. This is the same as to assert that the locus of missionary obligation is found in the nature of the Triune God, revealed in the work of Father, Son, and Holy Spirit. This formulation has considerable merit, both positive and negative. On the positive side, it delineates the missionary situation which exists in the world by speaking of a universal human predicament and a universal hope for humanity in Jesus Christ. It opens with a statement of a common creation (God has created all men -- nothing is excluded from the reach of His love), continues with a common fall (all men ere involved in a common alienation from God, from which none can escape by his own efforts), and a common redemption (God has sent forth one Savior, one Shepherd to seek end save all the lost, one Redeemer who accomplished a full and perfect atonement). It concludes with a reference to the Common Body of Christ (God has sent forth His Spirit, the Spirit of Jesus, to gather us together in one Body in Him), a common mission (by the Spirit we are enabled to press forward as ambassadors of Christ) and a common expectation (we are to wait with sure confidence for the final victory of His love).

The section which begins with the assertion that "the missionary movement . . . has its source in the Triune God Himself" closes with the observation that "there is no participation in Christ without participation in His mission to the world." The Church has a missionary calling and an obligation, to be sure; nowhere does the Trinitarian formula deny or minimize this obligation. But that calling and obligation does not arise out of the Church's self-existence, nor can it be derived self-evidently from the

[14]   Andersen, *Towards a Theology of Mission*, p. 38.

Church's thinking about itself. It points back to the self revealing activity of God, who is the Author of both Church and mission. Thus Willingen stated, "That by which the Church receives its existence is that by which it is also given its World-mission," Mission can never be deduced from the pre-existence of the Church.

The negative significance of the Trinitarian formula is no less important, though it is not clearly articulated in the Willingen statement. This significance attaches to the value of the Trinitarian formula as an implied critique of traditional Church-centered missionary practice.[15] As a critique it brings a heavy judgment to bear upon our traditional arguments in justification of the continuation of Christian missions, as well as viewpoints underlying our attempts to stimulate missionary motivation. The arguments having to do with the "justification" of missions are directed primarily to the detractors of the missionary enterprise, while those having to do with "motivation" are primarily for the benefit of its potential supporters. The common presupposition of both is that the validity of the Church is self-evident, being equated with Christendom, Western civilization, and the Kingdom of God. The self-evident validity of the Church is thought to provide a sufficient foundation on which to ground missionary activity. This forms, as it were, the unspoken presupposition of every argument. On the side of justification such arguments include the demonstration of the alleged "superiority" of Christianity over the claims of non-Christian religions; the vindication of the supposed "absoluteness" of Christian revelation against the criticisms of religious relativists; the reassertion of the fundamental "spirituality" of Western civilization against the onslaughts of secularism; and the defense of the "humanity and good-will" of Western democracy against the cries of imperialism. None of these defenses has the power to convince us any longer for the spiritual foundations of Western civilization are crumbling. The Church does not possess the self-certainty it once had. The task called for is not one of mere apologetics for missions, or the justification of the right to carry on missionary activities against detractors of the enterprise. The Church's very life and existence in the world are imperiled and the facile assumptions of fifty years ago are no longer acceptable. It will therefore no longer suffice to direct the question of the Church's missionary calling back to the self-evident validity of the Church. For the question concerning the Church, like that concerning mission, must in common be redirected to the prior question concerning the meaning of the Gospel and the nature of the Triune God. Thereby the empirical Church in the world, more conscious than ever of its frailty, is relieved of a great deal of unnecessary embarrassment. But this is not mere

---

15   This is brought out clearly in the North American Reports on Aim I and II.

escapism, it is a return to the true foundation of Church and mission. For God, not the Church, is the true Author of mission, and Jesus Christ is the true Evangelist. God in Jesus Christ can and must be witnessed to; He does not need to have His ways justified before men.

So far as the arguments used to stimulate "motivation" and develop missionary support in the home constituency are concerned, it can be asserted that a serious uneasiness about the too cozy relationship between Church and mission arises when that relationship is viewed against the backdrop of the Trinitarian formula and of Biblical theology. Many of the arguments used are fraught with danger for the Christian mission lest its true nature be corrupted and perverted by recourse to motives that are manifestly un-Christian. The American missionary enterprise, at first shocked and scandalized by the cry of "religious imperialism" emanating from Christian sources in China, has been compelled to pass through a period in inner purification and self-study, as a result of which a healthy refinement in the area of motivation has taken place. "The judgment of God" as discerned in the expulsion of missionaries by a hostile Chinese Communist regime has at least had the merit of redirecting missionary thought back to ultimate theological issues. The critique of traditional missionary motivation as raised by the Willingen Trinitarian formula can be conveniently stated in terms of the "three imperialisms," as someone has put it: that mission is in danger of being politicized, of being culturalized, and of being ecclcsiasticized. Political imperialism in missionary practice is easiest to recognize. Its current appeal is seen in the fact that missions are viewed as a valuable adjunct to the government in the power struggle with Communism for the allegiance of the non-Christian neutral powers. In the minds of some they are an auxiliary weapon, in the same category with I.C.A. and U.S. I. A., in support of the major offensive, which is fought in the military sphere. Missions are viewed as "useful" or "useless" to government according to the degree that they engage in the struggle against Communism. The Kingdom of God is viewed as an irrelevance in the present power struggle.

The second variety, cultural imperialism, is much older and more deeply entrenched. It dates back to the very origins of the American Protestant missionary enterprise, and is inextricably linked with the rise of a liberal Protestant theological tradition in America. In such circles an unconscious identification between the Gospel and the American way of life has frequently led to a type of missionary motivation based on a program of exporting Western democratic culture, together with its humanitarianism and, to some extent, its standard of living. An example of this would be the instructions given by the American Board of Commissioners for Foreign

Missions to the Hawaii missionaries of that board in the early nineteenth century. Their task was,

> to aim at nothing less than covering those islands with fruitful fields and pleasant dwellings and schools and churches, and of raising the whole people to an elevated state of Christian civilization.[16]

The theological problems involved in the relationship between Gospel and culture have been increasingly brought to our attention through studies such as Prof. H. Richard Niebubr's *Christ and Culture*. But whereas the dangers have been sufficiently discerned in the theological realm, the implications of a false identification between Gospel and culture for missionary practice still require extensive attention. The question has to do with the correct norms and proper limits of what we call the "indigenization" of the Gospel. In what cases and to what extent is it necessary and desirable that the Gospel should receive a cultural expression? On the other hand, when does such a cultural expression involve distortions and become hazardous? The missionary effort cannot fairly be stigmatized with the name of "cultural imperialism" unless a constant effort in the realm of both theory and practice is made to determine the proper relationship between Gospel and culture.

The Trinitarian critique of the Church-centered missionary orientation applies most pointedly to what has been called *ecclesiastical imperialism*. It points the finger of judgment at all ecclesiastical pride, vain glory and self-sufficiency, and declares that missionary activity designed to further the worldly self-aggrandizement or satisfy the secular ambitions of a church body is false in the eyes of God. If cultural imperialism has been the bugaboo of liberal Protestant church bodies, then ecclesiastical imperialism has been the particular nemesis of conservative, tradition ridden churches. The Gospel-culture equation there is paralleled by the Gospel-church equation here. A particular doctrine, a particular form of order, a particular liturgy or some other aspect of church life is regarded as sacrosanct and shrouded with absolute significance. Missionary activity is conceived as church-extension, or *plantatio ecclesiae*. The goal of missionary effort is not simply a church, any church, but rather a church possessing a point-for-point correspondence to the features of the mother church, an exact replica in miniature of its parent. In the case of ecclesiastical imperialism, as with cultural imperialism, a modicum of truth obscures the falsity of the equation between the Gospel and something secular

---

[16]   Quoted in Deyerhaus, *Die Selbstandigkeit der jungen Kirchen als missionarisches Problem*, Wuppertal-Barmen, 1956, p. 53.

that has nothing to do with the Gospel. Just as the Gospel cannot be communicated without culture, so it cannot be proclaimed without the ministry of the Church. But so also, just as culture in the name of Gospel can displace Gospel -- while wearing the semblance thereof -- so can the Church in the name of the Gospel displace the Gospel -- while retaining the semblance thereof. The Trinitarian formula, makes the Church aware of the dangers of ecclesiastical imperialism by redirecting its gaze toward a reality beyond itself: the redemptive work of the Triune God. God, not the Church, is the Author of mission.

MISSION UNDER THE CROSS

In an otherwise evenly-proportioned Trinitarian statement regarding missionary calling, one term in the series of God's revelatory acts stood out in sharp relief and served as the focus of spiritual attention at Willingen. That single term was the Cross of Christ, which was accorded a place of prominence in missionary thinking at Willingen unlike any previous conference. For as Christology formed the key term in the new Trinitarian orientation, so the Cross played the key role in the interpretation of Christology. It was precisely at the point of the Cross, as the structural arch of the whole Trinitarian formula, that the missionary enterprise discovered its most piercing judgment and critique. But at the foot of the Cross the Christian mission also discovered its mercy seat and source of renewal. The two addresses by Canon Max Warren and Reinold von Thadden elaborated the core of spiritual meaning which the conference sought to convey to the world in issuing its addresses under the title, *Missions Under the Cross*:

> The Cross is the illuminating center of the mystery of God's redemptive purpose. It is there that we begin to look into the heart of God, begin to believe that some understanding is possible, even for us, of the mystery of redemption. And it is by way of the Cross that we are compelled to see both the necessity for showing forth that redemption and also the manner of the showing. Out of the many facets of this jewel of our redemption there are just three which I would offer to you as affording us a way of discovering some of the searching implications of this mystery of God's loving purpose as that is related to our missionary task ... (l) the cross as bearing witness to God's solidarity with man and ... to the church's solidarity with the world ... (2) the cross as a place of judgment and

mercy, where both the world and the Church receive judgment and forgiveness ... (3) the darkness of the cross, its hiddenness, its abiding summons to faith, through which we are tested and disciplined to the point where we are possessed of a hope that cannot be ashamed. The cross is the crisis of missions. There is no other crisis. [17]

Reinhold von Thadden, leader of the Kirchenteg movement, spoke as follows:

What we say of the cross primarily concerns the form of the Church; secondly, its life and, thirdly, its mission ... A church under the cross cannot present itself other than in the form of a servant ... A church under the cross is also a church of Brotherhood ... a church under the cross is an obedient church, for its Master was the One who "became obedient unto death, even the death of the cross"... In the end, such a church will also be a suffering church. It cannot be otherwise ... That the church stands under the cross of Jesus Christ is, finally, of consequence for the mission of the church ... A church under the cross should be a vicarious church ... What Jesus accomplished on His way to the cross was vicarious action. He made His own the situation of the world ... The world is waiting for the vicarious service of a church under the cross ... A church under the cross should be the exact opposite of an introverted and contemplative company. It should be a church for the world ... It must become manifest that the Church exists for the world and in the world, but is not like the world. [18]

The Cross then becomes the ultimate expression of God's redemptive purpose for the world because it is the most concrete expression. All that happens between Creation and Parousia is guaranteed by the Cross, an historic event which anchors the Christian faith to something outside the realm of speculation or hearsay. [19] Willingen could say, "We who take our stand here can never be cast down by any disaster, for we

---

[17] M.A.C. Warren, "The Christian Mission and the Cross," in *Missions Under the Cross*, pp. 25-26.

[18] Reinhold von Thadden, "The Church Under the Cross," in *Missions Under the Cross*, pp. 52-63 et passim.

[19] See Andersen, *Towards a Theology of Mission*, p. 43.

know that God rules the revolutionary forces of history and works out His purpose by the hidden power of the cross."[20] if the Cross is the crisis of missions, and there is no other crisis, then it is at the foot of the Cross and nowhere else that the believer can look for dependable freedom and security, "He has passed from death to life." (John 5:24b)

The Cross thus becomes the Biblical symbol, par excellence, for the Church's missionary calling. For the Cross represents not only the content of the Christian proclamation but also the manner of its life. As Christ became obedient onto death, even the death of the Cross, the Church which is the body of Christ will always appear before the world, if it is faithful and obedient, in the form of a servant. As He came not to be ministered to but to minister, and to give His life a ransom for many, so the Church which bears His name has no alternative, "whosoever would come after me..." is a call to true discipleship, to be sure, but it is also a call to mission.

For mission concentrates not on the sacrifice made but on the goal and object: a life given on behalf of the world, the ransoming of many souls, the accomplishment of God's redemptive purpose. The two images of the Body of Christ and the Cross of Christ stand in the most intimate relationship possible, What the Body of Christ is to the nature of the Church, so the Cross of Christ is to the nature of its mission. As Christ could not accomplish His mission without the Cross, so the Church will not participate in Christ's redemptive mission without itself accepting the Cross. The Cross is the teleological expression of the significance of the Body of Christ. The corollary of "No participation in Christ without participation in His mission" is "No participation in Christ's mission without participation in His Cross."

EVANSTON--THE ESCHATOLOGICAL DIMENSION

The second world assembly of the World Council of Churches held at Evanston in 1954 introduced a new factor into the missionary discussion: the rise of eschatological concern. Willingen had closed with a number of unanswered questions, among them the relationship between mission and eschatology:

> What is the meaning of the Christian hope in relation to the message and practice of missions? What is there in the mystery of the Last Things which must affect the character

---

[20] *The Missionary Obligation of the Church*, p. 2.

and urgency of the Church's mission? The Gospel must first be preached among all nations. Then shall the end come... How can every fulfillment by the Church of its missionary obligation become a preparing of the way of the Lord and an expression of the proclamation, "Lift up your heads, for your redemption draweth nigh?"[21]

The growing articulation of missionary concern within the ecumenical movement is seen in the records of the two world assemblies of the World Council of Churches. At the first assembly at Amsterdam (1948) the report of Section II was issued under the heading, "The Church's Witness to God's Design." Included was a sub-heading entitled "Missionary and Evangelistic Strategy." At the second assembly at Evanston (1954) the report of Section II received the name, "Evangelism: The Mission of the Church to Those Outside Her Life," indicating a disposition to assimilate evangelism and the Church's missionary calling under a single heading. Part I, "The Evangelizing Church," states that "Jesus Christ is the gospel we proclaim. He is also Himself the Evangelist. He is the Apostle of God sent to the world to redeem it. As the Father sent Him so He sends us," Part II, "The Evangelistic Dimension," notes that "everything the Church does is of evangelizing significance. Through all the aspects of its life the Church participates in Christ's mission to the world," Part III, "Communicating the Gospel," expressly recognizes that "evangelism is God's work in which we are His agents. It is not our work, and therefore we must wait upon Him in prayer... that we may learn what he would have us do." The influence of the Willingen discussion is seen in the foregoing. Part IV deals with "Exploring Frontiers" and Part V with "Non-Christian Faiths."[22] It is in Part VI, however, that the eschatological dimension of the Christian mission breaks through most clearly. The concluding part of the section on Evangelism bears the indicative title, "Come, Lord Jesus" (Part VI):

> The church partaking through the Holy Spirit in the life of its Head is assured of the fulfillment of His work. The messenger of the unlimited grace of Christ looks towards the consummation of the Kingdom in which His redeeming love shall have achieved its full intention... The time of expectation is the time of evangelism, even as the

---

21 N. Goodall, *Missions Under the Cross*, p. 21.
22 Found in *The Evanston Report*, New York. 1955. Report of Section II. pp. 98-112.

time of evangelism is the time of expectation. For He who comes as our Judge is also our Redeemer.

And again:

The time of evangelism will not last forever; it will be succeeded by the time of the Kingdom fulfilled. The good news will not remain forever a promise made; it will become a premise kept. The gospel will not be the knowledge of the privileged few: it will be revealed to all...Therefore are Christians under constraint to declare this hope to the world until the consummation of the Kingdom and the coming of the King.[23]

In this statement Evanston reaffirms the displacement of the church-centered approach to mission and evangelism which we noted at Willingen, but Evanston also moves significantly beyond Willingen. For Willingen had included eschatology in a rather unaccented way in its Trinitarian statement, to be sure, but major attention was focused upon the event of the Cross and its significance for the missionary enterprise. Whereas Willingen had looked at the Christian mission from the mid-point of the history of Revelation, the Cross, Evanston now looks at it from its end-point, the *Parousia*. An important shift in terminology also takes place. For Willingen displaced the Church-centered emphasis, to be sure, but displaced it with a traditional dogmatic statement regarding the Revelation of the Triune God. Evanston seemingly reduces traditional dogmatic terminology to a minimum and reverts to a first century Biblical language in speaking about the Christian mission. This is precisely what Hoekendijk had in mind when he advocated the adoption of the "Kingdom--Gospel--Apostolate--World" framework of Matt. 24:24.[24] In this new constellation of terms used to describe the Christian mission, the Church does not play an important part; it has all but disappeared. Only the Gospel remains a familiar term; everything else changes, and the nature of the Gospel itself changes because of its dynamic relationship to the other new (to the twentieth century) elements. For Jesus is not the herald of a Church which already belongs to past history, but of a Kingdom which is to come and is already coming. He comes not to a select portion of humanity known as Christendom but to the world as a whole, for the world is His Father's creation. His purpose in coming is not to call church members, in the traditional sense, but to create an *Apostolate*, a body of

---

[23]   *The Evanston Report*, pp. 107-108.

[24]   Hoekendijk, "The Church in Missionary Thinking," *I.R.M.*, vol. 41 (1952), p. 333.

witnesses who participate in His mission. The Christian mission moves in the direction of the twin *eschata*, or ends, of time and space. The gospel of the Kingdom must be preached throughout the whole world, i.e., to the end of space; and the mission must continue until the end of time. The present is a grace period bestowed by God for the accomplishment of the mission. "The time of evangelism will not last forever ... Therefore are Christians under constraint to declare this hope to the world until the consummation of the Kingdom and the coming of the King," Evanston concluded.

Evanston was concerned to emphasize the urgency of the Church's evangelistic mission and tried to do so by introducing into the discussion radical first-century eschatological terminology from the synoptic Gospels. To us this seems like an artificial, illegitimate, and unsuccessful attempt. Artificial, because a true eschatological sense cannot be induced by a new form of speech. Illegitimate, because in the twentieth century we are compelled to do justice to the whole sweep of Trinitarian revelation, not to mention centuries of church history, and not merely to certain apocalyptic sections of the Gospels. Unsuccessful, because while a fruitful academic discussion about eschatology was staged, no practical results for the missionary enterprise followed in terms of greater urgency or deepened conviction. Had eschatology issued in increased zeal and a greater sense of urgency, the result would have been welcome indeed. There was no apparent spiritual after-effect arising from the study of the theme at Evanston as there had been at Willingen when the Cross occupied the center of attention. In approaching the relationship between mission and eschatology Evanston raised an important question but failed to give a theologically satisfying answer.

SOME REMAINING PROBLEMS

The most elusive of the remaining problems is the need for a proper understanding of the relationship between Church and mission. Church has been displaced as the center of gravity in missionary thinking, and ecclesiology must now be re-defined in terms of its missionary concern. We have been offered two antithetical ecclesiological statements, one by the right wing and the other by the left wing, with no satisfactory middle ground. The right wing, or traditional view, finds it possible to give a complete statement of what constitutes the essence of the Church—Gospel and sacraments--without so much as a single reference to the Church's mission in the world. According to this view, mission may be regarded as a function of the Church, but it does not constitute its essence. The left wing view, as represented by Hoekendijk, asserts that "the nature of the church can be sufficiently defined by its function, i.e. its participation in Christ's apostolic ministry."[25] According to this view the Church is a mission and nothing but a mission; it arises as an epi-phenomenom of the apostolic function. It would appear that the first view is too traditionalist in failing to take into account, for historical reasons dating back to the origin of our denominations, the apostolic and missionary dimension of the Church. It does not do justice to the missionary genius of apostolic Christianity. The second view, on the other hand, is too radically reductionist in that it fails to do justice to the New Testament testimony regarding the Church, "which is His body, the fullness of Him who fills all in all."

What is indicated here is the need for a continuing dialogue between missionary theology, on the one hand, and Faith and Order studies, on the other. Faith and Order, for its part, must grant greater recognition to the question of the Church's missionary calling in its deliberations; and the missionary movement must somehow accommodate its new insights to the empirical situation in the churches. Perhaps one solution is the recognition that ecclesiological discussion can move on two levels: the one, functional level, related to problems of mission and evangelism; the other, a formal level, arising out of church history and a faithfulness to particular traditions of the past. For too long a period formal ecclesiology has dominated the field, to the exclusion of any other. Recent developments indicate that the time may be ripe for the admission of functional ecclesiology into theological discussion. Such developments as the Evangelical Academies, the theology of the laity and the newer evangelistic approaches pose far-reaching questions concerning the nature of the Church which cannot be contained within the framework of the traditional formal ecclesiology.

Another unsolved question, theologically, is the relationship between Christian missions and the activity of the Holy Spirit. The question cannot be answered simply by reference to frequent liturgical invocations of the Spirit in prayer or praise, nor can it be disposed of by a kind of attitude which reverently assigns all good effects to the prompting of the Spirit. In the Acts of the Apostles the Holy Spirit is manifestly and without a doubt the dynamic agent in the missionary out-reach of the apostolic Church. Not merely in a general way, but in many specific cases, He prompts acts of witness, inspires decisions, comforts, and up builds the Church. In the apostolic Church the Spirit is never conceived spiritualistically, as a mystically pervasive essence; He is rather the living

---

25   Hoekendijk, op. *cit.*, p. 334.

presence of the Crucified and Risen One, constantly in communication with His Church. The trinity of Resurrection, Spirit (Pentecost), Apostolate (Witness) would appear to form a constellation of entities related to the missionary situation of the early church. A proper understanding of this trinity, and a participation in its fullest depths of meaning, would release a new kind of spiritual dynamic and imbue the Church of the twentieth century with the faith and zeal of the Apostles.

Discipleship And Mission

James W. Pyke
Wesley Theological Seminary
Westminster, Maryland

No student of the missionary movement today can approach any aspect of his interest without the underlying consciousness of the kaleidoscopic nature of the times in which he and his church exist in this mid-twentieth century. Now as never before humanity, wherever it may have been, is moving with jolting speed along untried paths that may plunge it into disaster. Change and upheavel characterize our times. Great segments of the population, once quiescent and fatalistic, are now caught in a ferment of new hopes. Piece after piece of the world as we knew it is breaking off from the old sacrosanct order and re-appearing in new alignments, shaped by the demand for knowledge, for leisure, for freedom from the ravages of disease, and above all for an economic order rooted in their own wellbeing and severed from a system designed to pour profits into the laps of a wealthy few. Against this terrifying backdrop of the present day missionary movement our discussion of discipleship and mission turns back to the parallels between the first Christian age and our own, but to seek to reconstruct its urge and its passion and to recapture its vision and vitality, always with our times in mind, so that its lesson and example might be applied to our own experience.

The term "disciple" is the English form of the Latin "discipulus," which is derived from the verb "discere" to learn; so a disciple means a learner or pupil. In the English Old Testament the word occurs only once, but it is significant because it appears at the conclusion of Isaiah's autobiographical memoirs, which he composed to accompany the first recording of his oracles, saying, "Bind up the testimony, (and) seal the teaching among my disciples" (Isa. 8:16). The king and people of Israel rejected Isaiah's message at the time of the Syro-Ephraimite attack, so the prophet announced that he would speak no more, but would wait for the fulfillment of his prophecies. This is discipleship before the advent of the Messiah, Isaiah entrusting his message to followers who would preserve and publish it in days to come. The likeness here between these disciples and those of Jesus is plain.

New Testament writers are all concerned with the Christian mission, the Gospels recording the implicit, while Acts and the letters of Paul the explicit demand for missionary discipleship. In the Gospels and in Acts the word "disciple" occurs approximately 250 times, referring most often to the Twelve. In the singular, Matthew and Luke employ it in a functional sense. Jesus tells his followers that if anyone were to come to Him without hating his own father and mother and wife and family, even his own life he could not be his disciple (Matthew 10:37; Luke 14:26). Paul in his letters uses the corresponding but more specifically missionary term of "apostleship" which does not appear at all in the Old Testament and only rarely (8 times) in the Gospels.

In the sense that anyone who rejects his own life and follows Christ is a disciple, it can be maintained that there is no such thing as a distinct missionary vocation. The missionary like any believer is a follower of Christ. And the missionary movement itself in recent times has insisted that every country is a mission field. Discipleship is every Christian's vocation, and the call of God is a missionary call to everyone to the kind of work for which he is best fitted in the place where he can best do it.

Notwithstanding this essential oneness of the Christian's vocation, there is a sense in which discipleship belongs with mission, and in which the missionary calling is unique and distinct from that of the ordinary believer. Historically the missionary has always represented a breaking with the past, a going beyond the conventional and the accepted, often at times when the Church as a whole has become too complacent, too joined to the world. The missionary by his very nature has thus always had a prophetic function, the calling of the Church back to its true apostolic nature.

The missionary is further distinguished from his brother disciple in that he devotes his life to those in society who are considered the lowest in the human scale, the barbarian, the heathen, and the down-trodden. He crosses boundaries, breaks through barriers, and identifies himself with those of another race, creed, and color. He is engaged in planting the Church where it does not exist; he is the pioneer, the frontier worker of the Christian body. By so doing he is foreshadowing the reunited Church that is to be, his very existence bearing witness to that unity. The nature of his vocation demands of him also a dedication that is different from that of the follower who remains in his natural environment. Always he must be ready to forfeit his life for his convictions. His call involves a certain totality of surrender, indicated in such matters as time and privacy. His speech and the color of his skin frequently deny him the consolation of anonymity. Yet the missionary has no monopoly of the heroic; of all the servants of Christ he is apt to realize most keenly his own inadequacy, and to assert with Paul that he is the least of the apostles.

Since missionary discipleship is most explicitly revealed in the letters of Paul, it is our purpose to rely upon the great apostle for our consideration of the topic before us. We will explore four aspects of missionary discipleship, its origin and roots, the gospel it proclaims, the sphere of its work, and discipleship as awareness of the times.

THE ROOTS OF DISCIPLESHIP

What was the inception of Paul's missionary vocation and the origin of his call to discipleship? The upsurge of missionary enthusiasm that characterized the Western church in the nineteenth century has often been traced to a literal acceptance of Jesus' command to go and make disciples of all nations (Matt. 28:19), but Paul in all probability did not know this so-called Great Commission.

A. Paul's Conversion.

Paul told his Galatian readers that he had always been extremely zealous in the traditions of his fathers, until God, he concluded, had set him apart before he was born, called him through His grace, by the revelation of His Son, to preach among the Gentiles (Gal. 1:14-16). This was not so much obedience to a specific command, as a transformation of purpose that turned him from prosecutor to advocate, from destroyer to missionary. There perhaps were some other, more humanly inspired experiences that had a bearing on his missionary vocation, such as the help of Ananias at Damascus (Acts 9:10-19), the commissioning service at Antioch (Acts 13:1-3), even the conversion of the Roman proconsul of Cyprus, Sergius Paulus, and the subsequent changing of his name from Saul to Paul (Acts 13:9-12). But the one thing his transformation hinged upon was that he had seen the Lord, "Am I not an apostle? Have I not seen Jesus our Lord?" (I Cor. 9:1). In Acts, Jesus is seen after the resurrection only in the forty days before the ascension, but when Paul ends his list of the appearances of the risen Christ, he adds the affirmation that "as to one untimely born, he appeared to me also." He insists that though "last of all," he was nevertheless a witness of the resurrection of Jesus (I Cor. 15:8).

We suggest then, that if we take Paul's experience as the norm, the roots of discipleship are to be found in the personal encounter with Christ. Other factors may be found, but the taproot is the revelation from God of Jesus Christ. For Paul, the element of surprise in this experience was that it came upon him unsolicited. He refers to his mission in terms of involuntary compulsion, "Necessity is laid upon me," a necessity which left his own personal will and ambition not consulted (I Cor. 9:16-17). The love of Christ constrains him (II Cor. 5:14). He feels under obligation both to Greeks and to barbarians, both to the wise and to the foolish (Rom. 1:14). The redemptive work of Christ is an unchanging debt that rests upon his heart, making him forever no longer his own but an instrument of Christ. As a recruit joins an elite regiment of the armed forces and surrenders his will to the military tribune, so Paul feels he is no longer his own.

Paul's experience, furthermore, carries a hint of strong revulsion. He characterizes the crucified Christ as a "stumbling-block to the Jews and folly to Gentiles" (I Cor. 1:23). Before his conversion he must himself have felt this way about the religion that he was persecuting. Karl Barth is quoted as saying that to become a Christian is like drinking a bitter poison or taking a draught of medicine. The one is revolting and the other necessary to health, but after taking either, the involuntary reaction is to vomit it forth again. So the discipleship of the Cross is an offense to the mind; what is more unnatural than to hate one's own life?

B. Metaphors of Discipleship.

Paul attempts with many varying metaphors to give communicative life and meaning to his all-absorbing discipleship. He thinks of himself as an ambassador for Christ, beseeching others to be reconciled to God (II Cor. 5: 19-21); as a representative of Christ he believes that he is working together with Him in the divine work of the kingdom (I Cor. 3:9; II Cor. 6:1). The missionary has often been accused of feeling superior to the people to whom he has been sent. The effective antidote to this attitude is the Pauline conception of ambassadorship, that the missionary is the agent of the Christ whom he represents. The agent does not earn his right to be an ambassador, not is the gospel that he carries his own invention. It is the message that comes to him by way of the Cross, so the missionary is always conscious of being radically unworthy of his commission.

Another figure that Paul uses to illustrate his call to discipleship is that of slavery to Christ. He thinks of himself as the bond-servant of the Lord (Gal. 1:10), and the Greek *doulos* has the force of "slave." Christ makes Paul a slave by His own example of humiliation, taking the form of a servant (Phil. 2:6-7), so that anyone belonging to Christ must himself be a servant, not according to his own wish, but according to the will of the Lord. The love of Christ controls him, yet paradoxically it is this very slavery which makes him free and transmutes him into an heir of God (with Christ) (Gal. 4:7). Captain Mitsuo Fuchida of the Japanese Air Force tells how he was "under orders" from Tokyo to lead the attack against Pearl Harbor. But after the war by way of the witness of a devoted Christian and his own reading of the Bible, he passed under other orders, and was brought into discipleship for Christ. Like Paul his mission is now taken not from man but from the Lord, for the proclamation of the gospel to the people of Japan.

C. Implications of the Pauline Motivation for Discipleship.

It is complained that few people today experience the blinding light of the Damascus road, see the risen Christ, or hear His voice. The implication of Paul's experience of discipleship, however, is that the call which leads to missionary service must stem from a personal meeting with Christ, and that anyone may have this meeting. Undoubtedly, there are other and perhaps valid reasons for becoming a Christian, but for the missionary vocation, involving as it does dislocation, loneliness, anxiety, persecution, and possible martyrdom, Paul insists on the believer's meeting with Christ as all-important. This makes missionary recruiting a very delicate affair, for such discipleship cannot be entered upon lightly. The Moravians in their remarkable missionary history learned that it was disastrous to press missionary service upon their members. It became one of their maxims that the call to the missionary vocation must be from God alone. Missionary discipleship is a claim that each in his own way must answer in the presence of the Christ who laid the missionary vision so urgently upon the heart of Paul. Once entered upon, the missionary life fully absorbs the strength of heart and devotion, the worker always being aware of his place as a representative of Christ, even as a laborer indentured to the service of his Lord.

II. The Gospel of Discipleship

Next we must attempt to bring into focus some aspects of the gospel it is the business of the disciple to proclaim--the first three emphases of the Pauline gospel.

A. The Pauline Gospel.

Missionary discipleship, being rooted in the personal encounter with Christ, is concerned to proclaim a gospel which Paul characterized as justification not by works of the law but by faith in Jesus Christ (Gal. 2:16). Peace with God is obtained through Christ's dying for the ungodly, for since "we are now justified by his blood, much more shall we be saved by him from the wrath of God" (Rom. 5:1; 8-9), A reading of the letters to the Galatians and Romans reveals Paul's many variations on the central theme of God's salvation through Jesus Christ. We "are justified by his grace as a gift, through the redemption which is in Christ Jesus, whom God put forward as an expiation by his blood, to be received by faith" (Rom. 3:24-25). As Paul feels personally identified with Christ in His death, so he can assert that he walks with Him in newness of life, for "there is therefore now no condemnation for those who are in Christ Jesus" (Rom. 8:1). The sole reliance for salvation is on Christ; if it were not so, "Christ died to no purpose," but since Paul feels himself crucified with Christ, it is no longer he who lives, but Christ who lives in him; and the life he now lives in the flesh he lives by faith in the Son of God, who loved him and gave himself for him (Gal. 2:21, 20).

The Gospel of salvation which it is the vocation of discipleship to promulgate, secondly, involves release from the sin whose sway extends over all men (Rom. 3:9), and which is associated in Paul's mind with "death" (Rom. 5:12-13). Just as death inevitably comes to all men, so sin is inherent in all, making it impossible for any human being to justify himself before God. As Paul felt himself to be a slave of Christ, so without Christ man is under slavery to sin. Sin, therefore, is not something that a man does; it is a power that takes possession of him, a condition in which man finds himself, turning him into an open enemy of the God who loves him.

The idea of sin has been out of fashion in Christian circles for a number of decades, though recently the neo-orthodox and the existentialists have brought it back with something like Pauline clarity into the Christian picture. Even Jean-Paul Sartre, though not a Christian, in an article entitled, "Torture is a Plague of Our Era," is in fact describing the Christian conception of sin. He writes:

In 1943 in the ... Gestapo headquarters in Paris Frenchmen were screaming in agony and pain; all France could hear them. In those days the outcome of the war was uncertain and the future unthinkable, but one thing seemed impossible in any circumstances; that one day men should be made to scream by those acting in our name .... (But now) in Algiers people are tortured regularly and systematically, ... (and) appalled, the French are discovering the terrible truth that if nothing can protect a nation against itself, neither traditions nor its loyalties nor its laws, and if fifteen years are enough to transform victims into executioners, then its behavior is no more than a matter of opportunity and occasion. Anybody, at any time, may equally find himself victim or executioner.[1]

Here is a devastating admission of the depravity of human nature, which the Christian calls original sin, a condition for which Sartre has no answer, but which the missionary gospel does. The awareness of sin is of peculiar pertinence to the missionary, for not only does he know that the only solution is in Christ, but he realizes, as remarked by P. T. Forsyth, that "what goes deepest to the consciences goes widest to the world. The more completely we feel sin to be condemned in the Cross the more power and commandment we have to carry the absolution to the ends of the earth."[2]

Paul's great answer to sin and to man's helplessness is that of God's act in Christ, which reconciles all men to Himself (Col. 1:20). This cancels the legal bond which stands against them (Col. 2:14). Only in the life and death of Christ is the sacrifice made and the price paid which will put man right with God. So it is that Paul can testify that he glories in nothing except "the cross of our Lord Jesus Christ, by which the world has been crucified to me, and I to the world" (Gal. 6:14). The gospel of Paul the missionary disciple is thus "Christ crucified ... the power... and wisdom of God" (I Cor. 1:23).

It is this gospel that rescues Christian ethic from the maddeningly commonplace and relates it to a quickening energy. It places the sinful in contact with cleansing. Confession floods the subconscious with forgiveness. Hope flames upon the ashes of despair. Life succeeds death. If all religions have satisfactory roads to the divine, the Christian mission is *ipso facto* invalidated, and we are reduced to innocuous cooperation with

---

1   *Washington Post and Times Herald,* March 16, 1958.
2   P. T. Forsyth, *Missions in State and Church.*

other faiths for the attainment of religious truth. It may be a sign of our neglect of the vital core of Paul's faith, that missionary recruiting officers report candidates in these days do not know what they believe. Without a personal encounter with the Cross, Christianity is a dead-letter, and the dynamic of the Christian mission is dissipated.

B. Accommodating the Gospel.

If the Christian gospel is radically different from any other religious teaching, how is it to be accommodated to the non-Christian mind? It is at this point that the Athens speech in Acts is often referred to, and for two different reasons. Some missionary writers use the Mars Hill speech as illustrating the way in which the apostle appeals to the religious experience of his pagan hearers.[3] Others note that when Paul declares to the Corinthians that he is going to know nothing among them "except Jesus Christ and him crucified" (I Cor. 2:2), he is confessing the failure of his preaching at Athens.[4] Oscar Cullmann suggests that the very evidence of the failure at Athens is proof that the Cross is always a stumbling-block to those who do not believe, and therefore confirmation of Paul's true gospel as proclaimed to the Corinthians.[5] Any reliance on the Acts speeches for insight into Paul's mind is open to some question, however, for New Testament students inform us that these were probably the compositions of Luke rather than the utterances of Paul.[6]

In his letters, however, Paul makes it clear that he is willing to accommodate his preaching in the interest of bearing fruit for the gospel, asserting that he would gladly become all things to all men, "if by so doing he could win some for Christ" (I Cor. 9:22). If this statement is taken in conjunction with I Corinthians 2:2, it is evident that while Paul is eager to conform on almost anything, he will not compromise on his basic doctrine of salvation by faith in Christ.

This means, applied to present circumstances, that it is of great importance for missionaries today to be able to adapt themselves and their message to the people and culture where they are working. The mission boards have rightly placed great emphasis on finding the candidate who

---

[3]   Arthur T. Pierson, *The New Acts of tho Apostles*, p. 181; Karl L. Reichelt, "The Johannine Approach," *The Madras Series*, Vol. I, p. 89,

[4]   Roland Allen, *Missionary Methods*, p. 88; Andre Retif, *Foi au Christ et mission d'apres les Actes des Apotres*, pp. 140-141.

[5]   Oscar Cullman, *Christ and Time*, p. 183.

[6]   Martin Dibelius, *Studies in the Acts of the Apostles*, p. 3.

easily adjusts. The very nature of the missionary vocation, operating on the exposed frontier of the Church, demands the ability to accommodate.

Ronald Hall, Anglican Bishop of Hong Kong, has said that a successful missionary should be addicted to hobbies, for they indicate an ability to spread one's interest and relieve the intensity that is likely to characterize the missionary's personality. He himself keeps two black sows of which he is immensely proud!

So much attention has been focused on the necessity of getting along with those of other beliefs and cultures, however, that we are in danger of forgetting the second half of Paul's statement--that Jesus Christ is the only way of salvation. The missionary's position, then, is a difficult one, involving a tension between the most radical identification of himself with the conditions of the people to whom he has been sent, and a totally uncompromising attitude on the subject of man's relation to new life in Christ. Lack of the former means loss of "communication," and surrender of the latter means relinquishment of Eternal Truth.

C. The Mystical Approach.

A second appeal to the Athens speech is in the realm of mysticism, which by definition affirms that God is approachable by man. The author of Acts puts into the mouth of Paul the words of Epimenides, the Greek poet, that "in ... (God) we live and move and have our being" (Acts 17:28), whereas in the letters there is no hint of man's communion directly with God. Paul is too deeply convinced of man's estrangement from Him (Rom. 1-3), of the power of sin that sets man at enmity with God (Rom. 5:20), and of man's need of reconciliation with Him (II Cor. 5:20).

Paul often speaks of being "in Christ," but never of being "in God." All things are from God and through Him and to Him (Rom. 11:36), but hardly are they in Him. Rather the relationship with God arises only through Christ and can only be focused in Christ. Paul like John Wesley thus denies all mysticism except Christ-mysticism. He would affirm that there is no common approach to God with the Eastern religions. On the contrary he would insist that the Eastern mystic is in fact drifting farther and farther from his goal instead of nearing it. The traditional movement of the mystic is ascent of the soul to God, something inherently impossible without help. But the whole direction of missionary discipleship for the apostle is the descent of Christ, who came down to empty Himself, taking the form of a servant and being obedient unto death (Phil. 2:7). Man, for

Paul, is a bankrupt criminal and no amount of mystical or moralistic effort on his part can set him on the path to the Divine.

Mysticism no matter how ineffable is compatible with profound egotism and does not face up to the problem of how sinful man can walk with a holy God. Paul would say that unholy man cannot stand before the sinless God; only God can render this communion possible. This is the negation of all religions that depend upon any kind of legalism or enlightenment, because they all rest upon some form of self redemption.

Karl Heim tells of a Japanese of the old Samurai class who had been brought up in the severe ethic of Confucianism and the ascetic discipline of Mahayana Buddhism, but under the influence of a simple Christian the thought was borne in upon him that all of his exercises might themselves be a great sin, as long as he was estranged from God.[7] In this situation the word of Paul came to him like a ray of light, "A man is justified not by the works of the law but through faith in Jesus Christ" (Gal. 2:16).

III. THE WORK OF DISCIPLESHIP

We turn our attention next to the question of how discipleship works out in the actual business of Christian living and of mission practice. The existentialists insist that the key to the meaning of existence is involvement, that man cannot separate himself from the process of living. Paul's whole missionary career is illustration of the same principle, for he could not accept the Christian life on any other terms than complete participation in the vocation of discipleship. A modern national missionary from Brazil to this country put it this way, "If you are not a missionary, you are a mission field"; and we could add that if you are not participating in discipleship, you cease to be a disciple. Let us consider briefly three aspects of Paul's missionary practice.

A. Pauline Speed.

First, there is the speed and extent of his missionary work. Toward the end of his career he wrote to the Romans summing up in startling fashion the range of his missionary outreach: "From Jerusalem and as far round as Illyricum I have fully preached the gospel of Christ" (Rom. 15:19). In the few short years of his missionary life he had worked in

---

[7]   Karl Heim, *The New Divine Order*, p. 121.

dozens of towns and cities in four large Roman provinces, and he could say that he had "fully" preached the gospel of Christ in all this territory. For Paul to have considered his work done in the whole eastern half of the Mediterranean world in his two decades or so of itineration is not less than astonishing.

One significant difference between Paul and modern missions on this score is in the fact that Paul was moving from a poorer and subordinate culture to a richer and more dominant one, and consequently did not have to carry cultural trappings with him. The modern missionary movement, conversely, has been propagating the gospel in the cultural framework of a wealthier and technologically superior society, which tended to involve the transplanting of institutions rather than the bare preaching of the gospel. This not only deprived the mission of "Pauline dispatch," but also laid it open to the charge of "cultural imperialism." In comparison with modern missions, Paul spent only a short time in one place and yet could address the believers as the "church." Without the support of finances or the prestige of a "higher" culture he had to rely on the constructive power of the Holy Spirit and cast his young congregations at a far earlier stage upon their resources. He believed, and saw demonstrated, that where the gospel was "fully" preached, it took root in the hearts of believers, and miraculously the body of Christ was formed.

B. Pauline Pioneering.

A second principle of Paul's missionary practice was his eagerness always to pioneer in new territory. He told the Romans of his concern not to build on another man's foundation, and that he "no longer had any room to work in these regions" (Rom. 15:20, 23). Through the centuries the true missionary has followed in his footsteps, as is seen in the Irish missionaries who evangelized the European continent, in Francis Xavier who carried the gospel to India and the Far East, in the Moravians who within the space of a few short years sent missionaries to a dozen countries across the world, and in a later day by the towering figures of Carey, Morrison and Livingstone. One of the subtlest temptations of the Church is to become static and cautious, forgetting the Pauline passion to move on to virgin fields, and that, not when the existing Church has been "fully" built up, but when the gospel has been "fully" preached.

In our time geographical frontiers are disappearing, and in their place is the lure and challenge to find ever new and more persuasive ways of reaching with the Good News the vast increase in the world's population.

It is estimated that the Church in all its efforts around the world is evangelizing a maximum of two million people a year. Yet the population of the globe is increasing annually by twenty to twenty-five million. In the next few decades, at the present rate of growth, it is expected that the population of many Asiatic countries will increase fifty to one hundred percent. By 1980 China alone may reach the astounding figure of one billion people. It is very doubtful whether without serious repentance and rededication to the Pauline example of missionary pioneering, the Church will be able to meet this massive new challenge.

C. Missionary Giving.

Thirdly, Paul was much concerned about the duty of Christian giving. After the Jerusalem conference had laid upon Paul's conscience the remembering of the poor at Jerusalem (Gal. 2:10), the Apostle by letter and visit had urged upon his churches the taking of a missionary collection (I Cor. 16:1-4; II Cor. 8-9; Rom. 15:25-33). Over a period of time he evolved a procedure for encouraging the members to this task, writing the Corinthians to lay aside something every week, so that the fund would be ready when he came (I Cor. 16:2). Paul's new Christians were largely from the lower classes and the poor. Although he found he could not expect much from unplanned solicitation, he felt giving was an important part of discipleship and could not be left to chance. Discipline, it might be noted at this point, is derived from the same root as discipleship and involves steady, consistent dedication. There is a curious similarity between the first two vows of a Roman Catholic priest and those of a Buddhist monk, namely, poverty and chastity. Only in the third is there a difference, obedience for the Roman Catholic and non-violence for the Buddhist, Protestants, on the other hand, have inclined to leave the discipline of poverty and giving to the individual conscience, just as Paul held up to his Corinthian readers the example of the Macedonian churches who were giving "of their own free will" (II Cor. 8:2-4). As the supreme incentive to giving the apostle pointed to Christ Himself who "though he was rich, yet for your sake... became poor, so that you by his poverty might become rich" (II Cor. 8:9).

The imperative needs of the younger Church in Asia and Africa are the modern counterpart of the request from the Jerusalem authorities, and the Church of the West would be less than Christian, if she failed fully to respond. A practical incentive today is the tenet of the Communist movement in the lands of the East, that everyone shall have according to his need and give according to his ability. This is not far removed from

Paul's entreaty to his people to love one another "with brotherly affection … (and) contribute to the needs of the saints" (Rom. 12:10, 13).

The missionary movement has answered Paul's appeal to share in the Christian grace of giving, but paradoxically this very giving has created one of the most obstinate stumbling-blocks to the growth of the ecumenical Church. The United States with six percent of the world's population boasts sixty percent of the globe's wealth. This tremendous disparity has produced serious repercussions on the mission field, instilling in the younger church an ambition to match the economic status of the missionary. The problem is complex, for missionary giving is; on the one hand, necessary to the home Church, not as a donation after her own needs are served, but as sacrificial participation in the passion and Kingdom of her Lord. Generous as she has been, the higher standard of living of the Western Church seems progressively to have promoted forgetfulness of Paul's concern that the Corinthians "as a matter of equality" should share their abundance with their Judean brethren who were in want (II Cor. 8:14).

Missionary giving has then the problem of finding a method whereby the gift does not induce dependence. To give without stultifying growth and to receive without resentment demand much Christian grace. Because the Communist regime in China has insisted on the independence embodied in the "Three-Self Movement," the Chinese Church has apparently been more than tolerated by the new government and found added self-respect in financial separation from the West. Giving should be a two-way street. It is possible that in her material abundance, the Western Church is spiritually impoverished and needs both the prophetic insights of the younger Church, and the example of greater simplicity in living. Perhaps it will be the spiritual strategy of missions in the future to place less dependence on the material equipment for her task. Perhaps at least part of the missionary witness in the future will be living like the poor, rather than preaching to the poor, and thus demonstrate with greater sincerity obedience to the saying of Jesus, "Whoever of you does not renounce all that he has, cannot be my disciple" (Luke 14: 33).

IV. DISCIPLESHIP IN THESE TIMES

Discipleship, in the fourth place, has meaning only in the context of the time in which it exists. We look first at Paul's conception of time and its end.

A. Pauline Eschatology.

The great missionary was convinced that he was living in the shadow of the imminent end of time, and his faith was characterized by an eschatological tension between the present and the future. Eschatology was the fabric of all his life and discipleship, for Paul during much of his life believed the end of the present age was not far off. He advised in relation to the married state that each person remain as he is "in view of the impending distress" (I Cor. 7:26). The "form of this world," he says, "is passing away" (I Cor. 7: 31). Not only did Paul advise the Christian "to wait for... (the) Son from Heaven," indicating fulfillment in the near future, but he is even now living in the redemptive age; "behold, now is the day of salvation" (II Cor. 6:2). Christ has completed his work and nothing remains to be done for our salvation, except for Him to come again to receive the Kingdom. In the same way Isaiah's disciples were to preserve his message for the future, and yet make it effective in the present. The tension for faith between the actuality of Christ's advent in history and the sure hope of His return, a tension every Christian may know in his own experience, is a significant part of the incentive to complete the missionary task, and proclaim "the Lord's death until He comes."

B. Suffering and Discipleship.

Integral to Paul's eschatology is his concept of suffering which characterizes the lot of the Christian in the age between the times. Suffering for Paul is more than just enduring persecution and hardship; it is a means of grace whereby the believer is brought into fellowship with his Lord (I Cor. 12:26). Only by dying with Christ can he be raised with Him to walk in newness of life (Rom. 6:4; Phil. 3:10-11). This is the explanation of Paul's mysterious paradox of suffering, whereby he can proclaim that though "afflicted, he is never crushed, though persecuted, he is never forsaken; and though struck down, he is never destroyed" (II Cor. 4:8-9). There is a necessary connection between pain and redemption, for by his very capacity to suffer he recognizes his identity with Christ. Sufferings, moreover, are not only the hallmark of the time between the resurrection and the coming again, but without them the end will not come; they are effective as completing the sufferings of Christ and for the Church (Col. 1:24).

Martin Niemoeller has observed that the persecution of the Christian faith under Hitler brought new life to the church in Germany, and that in Eastern Germany today trials and privations are deepening the spiritual life of the Church. In West Germany, on the other hand, there has been such a return of prosperity that indifference and complacency result. An Indian superintendent of the Hyderabad district of the Methodist Church gives it as his sober and considered testimony that he is ready at any time to be a martyr for his faith. It is at this point that discipleship and mission most inexorably meet; only persecution and affliction will be the price of fulfillment of the mission. This is the final and authentic demonstration of missionary discipleship, and it is for this reason in Paul's eyes that the acceptance of the Cross must be reckoned the key word for missions in any age.

C. Our Times.

Arnold Toynbee characterizes our age as the post-Christian era and Albert Camus declares that now the human dialogue is drawing to a close. Man is only waiting in despair for the climax of time and of history. Reinhold Niebuhr likens our age to one of the great critical eras of the past:

> Our indiscriminate freedom and our tremendous productivity have made our culture soft and vulgar... We have in fact become so self-indulgent that one may raise the question whether our position vis-a-vis the Russians is not the old historic situation: the 'barbarians,' hardy and disciplined, are ready to defeat a civilization in which the very achievements of its technology have made for soft and indulgent living...We are just as effete, and probably are more vulgar than the Byzantines when the Moslems took Constantinople. [8]

Just as the West tends to defend its status-quo, so the peoples of the East are proclaiming the watchword of "self-determination," which since World War II has resulted in over twenty new republics. The common front in North Africa, the Arab Republic in the Near East, the civil war in Indonesia, a student mob in Peru, those are the outward rash of an inner fever, a frenzied effort to revive self-respect in the face of white supremacy. The missionary movement not only cannot be ignorant of these developments and exist in isolation from them, but far more basic to its discipleship is the duty of translating their meaning to the Church at large. The mission realizes that in part these events are a product of its gospel, unexpected sometimes, at times unwelcome, but nevertheless demanding

---

[8] Reinhold Niebuhr, "Christianity and Crisis," March 18, 1958.

its concern. Its effort to understand them is motivated by an unresting zeal to utilize their momentum and to seize again the initiative for the Church of Christ.

D. Eschatology and Discipleship.

The eschatology of discipleship means that not only does the Christian recognize the recalcitrance and unrepented evil of the times, but that being Christian involves participation by the disciple in history. Because history has a denouement and each moment holds within it a double destiny of life or death there is the necessity that the whole world have the opportunity to know the redemptive love of Christ. "The gospel of the kingdom will be preached throughout the whole world, as a testimony to all nations; and then will the end come" (Matt. 24:14), As the eschatological tension is a larger copy of the stress of the human situation, so the incompleteness of man's predicament can only be perfected in the final solution to the tension of the times.

Because of his exposed position the missionary stands in need of Paul's assurance that in spite of the struggle and apparent defeat in the spiritual warfare, the kingdom will be brought in when Christ comes again. Under the tension of knowing the present rule of Christ, yet realizing that the world in its present form is passing away, both the individual Christian and the missionary Church are made at every point dependent upon the grace and energy of God. It is precisely because this salvation "is nearer to us now than when we first believed" (Rom. 13:11), that it is urgent for the gospel to reach as many people as possible. Missionary discipleship does not rest for foundation upon the distress of the world, nor upon the desire of the heart for salvation; rather, it is founded upon the still unfulfilled promises of God.

V. Conclusion

Our conclusion from this study is to suggest that perhaps the most effective way in which the Church of the West can be recalled to the witness which is the reason for her being is to take seriously the Pauline prototype of missionary discipleship. The apostle believed that unless the Church is under condemnation of the world, the Cross is no longer central, and to that extent she has erred from her missionary calling. If the Church is not presently undergoing persecution, she can vicariously experience it on her missionary frontiers, for unless she takes upon herself the suffering of the world, she cannot be acceptable to God. Robert E. Speer called an unmissionary Church a "fundamental immorality"[9]; and Emil Brunner asserts that the Church lives by mission as fire exists by burning.[10] In these frightening times it is one of the foremost duties of missionary discipleship by both word and deed to awaken the whole Church to a reconsideration of her life in terms of St. Paul, her first great missionary. What are the roots of the Church's discipleship? What is the uniqueness of the gospel that she proclaims to the world? Is she performing her task in relation to the tensions of her own eschatological message and of the age in which she is called to witness?

---

[9]   Robert E. Speer, *Missionary Principles and Practice*, p. 259.

[10]   Leslie Newbigin, *The Household of God*, p, 143.

A Critique Of "Discipleship And Mission"

William J. Danker
Concordia Theological Seminary
St. Louis, Missouri

This is a good paper. The measure of its worth lies in the manner in which it stimulates us who hear it to our own thoughts and conclusions. However, one must confess to a certain impression of ambivalence conveyed by its basic structure and pattern. This treatise on missionary discipleship starts out centered around the Risen Christ and winds up in an imitation of the Crucified Christ. This seems to be indicative of a fundamental uncertainty as to the focus of the essayist's own theology of missions. One cannot help wishing that he had woven throughout his presentation the motif of the Resurrection which he so grandly began. It is true, of course, that while a missiologist like Hoekendijk puts the apostolate in the central place, Willhelm Andersen also makes the Cross of pivotal importance. But, Mr. Pyke might have gone on to say after his brave sounding of the Resurrection trumpets that the Cross has meaning only in the light of the Open Tomb. Without the Resurrection the Cross would be forgotten today. This obviously does not mean that we can dispense with the Cross. Without it there would be no reconciliation and no resurrection.

The excessive preoccupation with the Cross at the expense of the empty grave makes many missionaries, as one Japanese Christian complained, "a little too grim." Easter makes the disciple a new creature in the Risen Christ and gives his message the note of new life and joy that it deserves.

Pyke rightly contrasts the basic self-righteousness of mysticism with the Gospel way of salvation by the strength and love of another. He has this excellent sentence: "For him(Paul) the whole direction of missionary discipleship is the descent of Christ, who came down to empty Himself. taking the form of a servant and being obedient unto death (Phil.

2:7), Man in the Pauline Gospel is a bankrupt criminal and cannot ever know God; he can only be 'known by God' (Gal. 4:9)."

Yet one cannot help but feel that this kerygmatic theme of Christ's activity in making man a disciple deserves to be carried out as one discusses the making of a disciple into a missionary. There is a clear-cut difference between the Roman Catholic medieval discipleship of a Thomas a Kempis and genuine Biblical discipleship. The one is an *imitatio Christi*, the other a *conformitas Christi*, The first is the believer's activity for Christ, the second is Christ's activity in the believer. As Regin Prenter has abundantly demonstrated in his excellent *Spiritus Creator*,[1] through the Holy Spirit Christ is at work, conforming the believer to His own image. We are laborers together with God. This knowledge delivers us from frantic hysteria over our own shortcomings in personal sanctification as well as over the failure of many a well-laid scheme in the Church's missionary outreach and will instead fill us with new poise and confidence in our Divine Partner, setting us free to place our best powers in His great service, unhampered by anxiety and its inevitable paralysis of productivity. All of which is to say that, as the locus of missions is not in the Church, as both Wilhelm Andersen and Hoekendijk each in his own way have emphasized, but in God, so the locus of discipleship is not in the disciple but, likewise, in God.

This brings us to the concept of the *Missio Dei* as developed by Georg F. Vizedom in his recent book by that title which is an *Einfuehrung in eine Theologie der Mission*.[2] Since this slender volume was published in Munich only this year, it may be helpful to insert at this point my own translation of its central burden:

> *Missio Dei* declares that the mission is God's work. He is the Lord, the one who assigns the task, the possessor, the agent. He is the acting subject of missions. If we in this way ascribe the mission to God, it is withdrawn from all human whims. We must therefore demonstrate whether God wills the mission and how He Himself carries it out. Therewith all necessary limits are laid down. We cannot speak of the 'Mission of the Church.' Still less may we speak of 'our mission.' Since both the Church and the Mission have their origin in the loving will of God, we may speak of both Church and Mission only in so far as

---

[1]   Regin Prenter, *Spiritus Creator*, trans. John M. Jensen.

[2]   Georg F. Vizedom, *Missio Dei: Einfuehrung in eine Theologie der Mission*.

these are not understood as independent quantities. Both are only tools of God, instruments through which God carries out His mission. Only if the Church obediently fulfills His mission purpose, can she speak of His mission, because her mission is then contained in the *Missio Dei*.[3]

With less Teutonic systematics, if with more Scottish eloquence, the same idea is found in James Stewart's *Thine Is The Kingdom*.[4] Christ is the basis for missions. Christ is the motive for missions.

All of this is as Scriptural and Pauline as it can be. He preaches the *Missio Dei* when he says, "It is God who worketh in us both to will and to do of his good pleasure." Or, "He which hath begun a good work in you will perform it until the day of Jesus Christ." The fact that Christ is the agent of missions is averred by the greatest missionary of them all when he says, "Not I, but Christ liveth in me." (Phil. 1) In a sense Christ is also the final object of missions, for Paul says that he labors and travails "until Christ be formed in you." In Aristotelian terms, then, we could say that Christ is the material, the formal, the efficient, and the final cause in missions.

Another point at which one could wish that the essayist had followed through on his swing is in the instance of lay missions. He makes a ceremonial bow in the direction of the subject with this impeccable sentence: "... the call of God is a missionary call to everyone to the kind of work for which he is best fitted in the place where he can best do it." It would seem that the importance and relevance of the matter deserves far more than a summary sentence and a few allusions. The essayist's own statistics on the startling population increase now in progress require this. The concept of the unsalaried lay missionary cannot well be divorced from a study of the salaried professional and his activities. As the Niebuhr Commission studies have shown, one's image of the pastor can be formed only after one has structured the role of all the people of God. And if one accepts the Niebuhr picture of the clergyman as one of the people of God who trains and builds up other people of God for their ministry, as a minister to ministers, a caller of callers, a missionary to missionaries, this will vitally affect any discussion of the salaried missionary's discipleship. We are reminded here of one sentence from Bishop Krummacher's essay before the Lutheran World Federation Assembly at Minneapolis in 1957, a sentence which unfortunately did not get over into the English

---

3   *Ibid.*, pp. 12, 13.
4   James S. Stewart, *Thine Is the Kingdom.*

translation: "Die Welt evangelisieren heisst nicht die Welt klerikalisieren." -- "To evangelize the world does not mean to clericalize the world," This sentence which comes out of the Bishop's living experience in Pomerania behind the Iron Curtain in East Germany where many a pulpit is manned by a layman, where thousands of lay people have jumped into the breach to carry out confirmation instruction of the young in Christian principles, has its profound implications for the manner in which the Church sets about the mission task today.

The essayist's excellent sentence to the effect that every Christian should witness in the way he is best fitted in the place where he can best do it was, by the way, anticipated in the otherwise hostile reply given by Johann Heinrich Ursinus in the age of rigid Lutheran orthodoxy to the mission call issued by Justinianus von Weltz. Anyone who has ever read Gustav Warneck will quickly recall that German Christendom in the 17th century roundly condemned the sending out of professional missionaries, notably in the "Gutachten" or "Faculty Opinion" of the University of Wittenberg in 1651. It is perhaps not so well known that a man like Ursinus in his "Erinnerung an Justinianus," however awry his central position, emphasized the duty of those Christians who lived among the heathen to witness to their faith by word and deed. [5]

Another volume that deserves a reference in this connection is *The Art of Overseasmanship* by Cleveland and Mangone.[6] This study of a new concept will provide useful statistics and helpful background materials for the planners of missionary strategy who see the importance of enlisting the growing number of Christian men and women and families going overseas for increasingly diversified purposes.

While the above are the chief observations that occur to your critic, there are also a number of miscellaneous points which elicit various reactions.

The essayist declares that the missionary is distinguished from his brother disciple in that he devotes his life to those in society who are considered the lowest in the human scale, the barbarian, the heathen, the down-trodden. Is this really true? Is this "concern in depth" only or primarily for the professional missionary? Is it not for all Christians as the Parable of the Last Judgment also powerfully preaches?

---

[5]   Gustav Warneck, *Geschichte der Protestantischen Mission*, p. 37.

[6]   Harlan Cleveland and Gerard J. Mangone (ed.) *The Art of Overseasmanship*.

Again, while we agree with the caution that missionary service should not be pressed upon anyone, there is, however, more that can be said. If mission and Church are coextensive, if missions is of the *esse* of the Church rather than the *bene esse*, why should not every seminarian be regarded as potentially available for service anywhere in the Church and anywhere in the mission? Can we be satisfied until we have created a climate favorable to this proposition at every Christian seminary and training school?

In speaking of the uniqueness of Christianity, the essayist declares, "If all religions have equally satisfactory roads to the divine, the Christian mission would *ipso facto* be invalidated." One seeks in vain for a clear reference to the extraordinary invasion of God into history that characterizes the Christian kerygma, an invasion that reaches its climax not only in the Cross but also in the open tomb. It is in the historic event that is Jesus Christ that we must unabashedly assert the uniqueness of Christianity. Charles W. Forman of Yale properly avers:

> The exclusiveness of Christian faith, then, should not necessarily be taken as evidence of pride or self-centeredness, as Toynbee claims, and as many others certainly believe. It is rather an exclusiveness that is implicit in the very nature of history itself. Once God's redemptive self-sacrifice is regarded as historical rather than mythological, then its exclusiveness is inevitable.[7]

He goes on to demonstrate in telling fashion that any historical event, be it the Russian revolution or the resurrection of Christ, is by its very nature unrepeatable. And it is in this unrepeatability of the historical events of God's redemption in Christ--certainly not in any intrinsic superiority of the Christian himself--that the uniqueness of Christianity inescapably lies.

In his section on "Accommodating the Gospel" the essayist declares:

> Paul's so-called 'philosophical approach' in the Athens speech is sometimes referred to as an attempt by the apostle to eliminate the scandal of the Cross and to accommodate his message to the pagan mind. Critics inform us, however, that the Acts sermons are in all

---

[7]   Charles W. Forman, "The Challenge to Christian Exclusiveness," *Religion in Life*, Summer, 1958.

probability the compositions of Luke and therefore are not an entirely accurate representation of the Pauline gospel.

Again, there is more that needs to be said. We return to the Easter theme to point out that it was not the Cross but the open tomb that was a scandal to the Athenians. "And when they heard of the resurrection of the dead, some mocked." (Acts 17:32). As to the manner of accommodation exhibited in the Areaopagus sermon, it would be helpful to have a look at a book like Bertil Gaertner's *The Areaopagus Speech and Natural Revelation*, where the point is made that while Paul uses the language of Greek philosophy he presents the content of the Hebraic Old Testament.

In the discussion of mysticism, the essayist makes the statement that "Paul often speaks of being 'in Christ,' but never of being 'in God.'" This claim should be made with cautious qualifications, for in Acts 17:28 Paul quotes with approval the lines of the poet, "In him we live, and move, and have our being." Farther on in the same paragraph, there is a reference to something from Emil Brunner: "Man in the Pauline Gospel is a bankrupt criminal and cannot ever know God; he can only be 'known by God' (Gal. 4:9)." The essayist goes on to say, "This is the negation of all religions that depend upon any kind of legalism or enlightenment, because they all rest upon some form of self-redemption". However, this allows no room for the concept of general revelation to which even salty old Hendrik Kraemer has made a concession of sorts in his recent *Religion and the Christian Faith*.[8]

Under the heading of "Pauline Responsibility" the essayist says, "The imperative needs of the Younger Church in Asia and Africa are the modern counterpart of the request from the Jerusalem authorities, and the Church of the West would be less than Christian, if she failed fully to respond." While your critic has a personal preference for "Newer Church" rather than "Younger Church," a term that does not wholly avoid a patronizing after-taste, this is not the main focus of his critique. Paul was soliciting financial aid for the personal physical needs of the saints at Jerusalem in time of famine, not for the needs of an institution or organization. Further, this instance was the reverse of modern mission practice. The "Younger Church" was helping the old mother church in Jerusalem. In Pauline practice, every local church was dependent upon the Holy Spirit and the gifts He accorded diversely to the saints in that place for its spiritual and institutional needs, save for such encouragement

---

8   Hendrik Kraemer, *Religion and the Christian Faith*.

as was brought by letters and visits from him or from other Christian travelers. Therefore, we cannot quite acknowledge the parallel drawn by the essayist. We are led, rather, to ask the question whether a local church as the spiritual Body of Christ in that place really needs financial help as distinguished from full spiritual *koinonia*? Would Paul have given such financial help for brick and mortar and the support of an institutional table of organization, as distinguished from help for physical needs? Do we strengthen a local church in another land, or do we weaken it when we do that for it which Paul evidently expected each local church to do for itself? Does not this weakening process occur even more easily where financial help for organizational purposes crosses cultural lines?

In his conclusion the essayist has well said, "The apostle believed that unless the Church is under condemnation of the world, the Cross is no longer central, and to that extent has erred from her missionary calling." Perhaps while some of us look at the Church in China and Russia, wondering why there are not more martyrs there, the churches behind the Iron and Bamboo curtains are looking at us and wondering why, in the face of racial and social injustice, there are no martyrs here. Finally, if the Cross is no longer central among us, we return once more to the regrettably truncated motif of the Resurrection which the essayist sounded at the beginning, to ask, "Has this happened because in the terror and uncertainty of our time the Cross is no longer clearly seen in the light of the open tomb?"

The Vocation of the Missionary

E. Theodore Bachmann
Pacific Lutheran Theological Seminary
Berkeley, California

For one who has not himself had the distinction of serving overseas as a foreign missionary, and who has only had the privilege of living for a time amid the fruits of other men's labors in the land from which the first missionaries were sent forth, it may be presumptive to say something about the vocation of the missionary. When, however, I had accepted the invitation of our extremely able and persuasive president, Dr. R. Pierce Beaver, in which he laid stress on placing the missionary's calling in its appropriate theological context, I knew I was in for a rough assignment.

At times this presentation may appear theoretical. If it does, I hope it will not appear artificial. For you, too, may recall the character in Thackeray's *Yellow Plush Papers* who accepted an assignment on "Chinese Philosophy." Indeed, he did so unflinchingly, simply blending into an essay two articles from the encyclopedia: the one on "China," and the other on "Philosophy."

In approaching the vocation of the missionary, I was assured by discerning friends that not much had been written on the subject in recent years. There was, of course, plenty of material on recruitment; also excellent statements on the characteristics of the missionary. The importance of vital Christian experience was everywhere recognized. There were glowing accounts of the missionary vocation of the whole Church, and of the duty of each believer to be a missionary. And there were wise words about the foreign missionary vocation as a special task of some Christians who take it up as their personal responsibility. Yet I have also accumulated a small but choice file of letters in which friends at home and overseas--and this has made me suspicious--wished me well in tackling this seemingly neglected subject.

What follows is something that I can offer only as the fruit of prolonged struggle. Postwar years in Europe, especially in occasional contacts with the World Council of Churches Ecumenical Institute near Geneva, and in frequent ones with the Evangelical Academies in Germany, have made me aware of the eagerness with which people in many kinds of occupation are seeking to recover a sense of vocation, a glad awareness of being called by another, and of thus possessing once again a meaningful rather than a meaningless life. This is a life in which the individual is retrieved from the loneliness--even the sickness --of his individualism and is placed in community. If such community remains at the level of mere sociological interdependence or solidarity, it leaves life truncated and its quest for completion falls forever short. Such completion, in terms of radical reorientation and fulfillment, is available to all people in the vocation-- the calling--of the Christian Evangel.

This treatment of the vocation of the missionary is therefore an attempt to set forth the subject more by implication than by explication. It is, I think, more important at this point of search to provoke questions than to offer specifications. Indeed, what is thus said about the special vocation of the missionary may illuminate other aspects of the one vocation of all Christians.

What follows falls into four unequal parts. Firstly, the career of the missionary in our time--a brief reference to the contemporary breadth of the subject. Secondly, the missionary vocation as a special calling--a pair of biographical sketches expressing historical depth. Thirdly, the theological content in missionary vocation. Finally, the missionary vocation and the unity of the Church.

I. The Career of the Missionary in Our Time

Seldom has man been so accessible, his achievements so spectacular, his common plight so evident, his quest for community so unsparing, his need for radically good news so all-pervasive. Between the twin evils of self-destruction and self-deification there is set the task of the Christian missionary who points man's hope not to the corrupt and mortal self but to the gracious and eternal God. Yet there are many other kinds of missionaries Amid the many rival forces now claiming attention and demanding loyalty, the career of missionary--political, commercial, scientific, cultural as well as religious--is recognized as essential. The missionary of all these causes is a symbol. He operates off-stage teaching lines by which others are to live. Whether one observes a Buddhist, humanist, or communist missionary at work, there is in each a sense of commitment, a calling or vocation that appears like an alarming imitation of what the Christian missionary ought himself to possess, only to a still greater degree, by way of commitment and vocation. The alarm over this grows, at least in part, out of discordant factors among Christians themselves.

A. Sour Notes in Zion, from trumpets with uncertain sound, betray confusion in the ranks of the missionary force. The metaphor can be exaggerated, but the urgency of the Christian mission cannot. In amazing disarray this urgency breaks out in drama and procession. Now from the mass rally of sectarian enthusiasts, now from the quiet professionalism of the candidate secretary, persons are recruited and sent forth. Their destination "The ends of the earth," Their work? New or already well established. Their backing? Anything from tiny "faith mission" to proud denomination. Their unity? The Christian name--a collective term for a multiform but aggressive faith.

One of the sourest notes, unhappily, blares from the religious illiteracy of so many of today's missionary candidates. No one questions their sincerity or their Christian character. Some have had a deep experience of the grace of God. Most of them have a firm faith in Jesus Christ as Lord and Saviour. Compared, however, to earlier generations it is agreed that:

> Most missionary candidates of the present day shock their elders by their ignorance about the Bible and about missionary and church history. ...This is true, not only of medical, agricultural and educational missionaries, but also of many seminary graduates .... Few of them have read much about the missionary work of their denominations. Not many are familiar with missionary biography. Fewer still are aware of the steps which have led to the growth and development of the Younger Churches .... There is (for example) nothing today to compare with the kind of continuous missionary education received a generation ago by those who were members of Student Volunteer bands on college campuses.[1]

---

[1] "New Trends in Missionary Training in the United States," A Paper Prepared by the Secretary of the Committee on Missionary Personnel of the Division of Foreign Missions, National Council of Churches, New York: NCC, 1957, pp. 2-3.

Such disturbing observations make it all the more important to hear again what J. H. Oldham, that ecumenical and missionary veteran, had to say in 1935:

> The missionary movement... is what its representatives are. The end for which all missionary organization exists, for which funds are collected at great cost in time and labor, for which programmes of missionary education are planned, is that a certain witness shall be borne and a certain work done by persons sent out by the home churches. All depends on the character and capacity of those persons.[2]

The question of motivation thus becomes highly significant for the missionary vocation. Out of 915 denominational missionaries, in Kenyon E. Moyer's valuable survey, the personal factor accounted for five out of six decisions to enter missionary service. The influence of missionaries and their talks stands foremost. Next, comes that of parents and friends, on the one hand, and of interpersonal contacts in Student Volunteer activities, summer camps and the like, on the other. Comparatively little influence was ascribed to pastors, church school teachers, college or seminary professors.[3]

Also revealing is the fact that among those questioned nearly four out of six decisions for missionary service were made after high school, "that is, after the home church had ceased to be a major factor in the influences on their lives." Although it may be assumed that earlier Christian nurture was not without effect. Finally, in looking back, nearly five out of six felt that their preparation before being sent out was lacking in such essentials as the principles, history and methods of mission, as well as cultural orientation to the land and people they would be serving.[4]

As to the personal qualifications of the missionary, Douglas Webster's booklet, *What Is A Missionary?*, sharpens much previous discussion of the subject. He lists four priorities: (1) a personal knowledge of Jesus Christ; (2) a capacity to interpret the gospel; (3) an awareness of the kind of world in which we live; and (4) readiness to make the universal church a reality.[5] Obviously it is not easy to meet such standards. The claim that it

---

2   J. H. Oldham, ed., *The Modern Missionary*. London: SCM, 1935, p. 9.

3   "A Study of Missionary Motivation, Training, and Withdrawal (1932-1952)," by Kenyon E. Moyer. New York: Missionary Research Library, 1957, p. 29.

4   Ibid.

5   "Recruiting, Selection and Training of Missionaries in North America," A paper for study and references prepared by the Secretary of the Committee on

takes "eight volunteers or recruits to make one missionary" hardly seems an exaggeration. [6] For the person sent forth today must fit the specifications of the slot at the other end of the line. The oldtime sending of all sorts of "pioneers"--at least in the case of the older established denominations— has given way in Asia and elsewhere to requested partners in on-going tasks.

Experienced missionaries have pointed out the very practical need of gaining and holding a point of contact with the non-Christians among whom the missionary is to work. To be effective at his appointed place, the missionary must fulfill a double requirement. He must have both a keen competence in something that already has captured the interest of the non-Christians as well as a communicable commitment to Jesus Christ. For example, the late A. C. Hogg, president of Madras Christian College, put it this way: "The educational missionary must have a scholar's zest for his subject and a teacher's joy in educating as well as a longing to declare Christ."[7]

For the missionary vocation the best are none too good. If the day of the old-style missionary is over, (although some do not seem to realize this fact), the new day calls for an all-round excellence of professional talent and confessing faith such as the home churches would like to obtain for themselves--and keep. Yet the candidate secretary is in a pivotal position. He knows the church at home and also the church abroad. He has heard the sour notes in Zion echo around the world. But he also hears and shares that stronger and persistent call to mission which comes to man from another direction.

B. Who Goes Where? Those who are sent forth give an ever-fresh relevance to the map of the Christian world mission. Against the background of Latourette's monumental *History of the Expansion of Christianity* there is the ever-changing configuration of locations. Each spot is alive with missionaries and personal meaning. In the divided state of Christ's Church, some are Roman Catholic, others are Protestant, and in many places their efforts overlap and compete.

Missionary Personnel of the Division of Foreign Missions, National Council of Churches. New York: NCC, 1957, pp. 1-2.

[6] Kenyon E. Moyer, "Selection and. Training of the Overseas Personnel of the Christian Church." New York: Missionary Research Library, *Occasional Bulletin* Vol. VIII (August 15, 1957) No. 8, pp, 1, 9. [Hereafter: MRL:OB]

[7] Oldham, *op. ext.*, pp. 41, 44.

In terms of totals, the Roman Catholic Church has in its mission lands some 40 million adherents. To serve these the Propagation of the Faith, with its long-standing headquarters in Rome, has 684 "Ordinaries," responsible for some 33,000 priests, 12,000 brothers, and 75,000 sisters. Since about half of these are nationals, and half from other countries, the Roman foreign missionaries number about 60,000. Of these possibly five out of eight are women.[8]

Protestant foreign missionaries from all lands total approximately 35,000. Of these, about two-thirds (23,432) come from the United States, (Fifty years ago the United States provided only one-third of the total.) Six out of ten of those from America are women. And each year between 1,000 and 2,000 new missionaries are appointed.[9] Their support comes from 213 different missionary agencies, and they serve in about 100 countries around the globe. Asia draws over one-third of these Americans; Africa south of the Sahara nearly 30%; Latin America 26%, plus smaller contingents in the South Pacific and elsewhere. As to countries of service, India has the largest number of American missionaries; Japan is next, and the Belgian Congo third. China, with nearly 4,500 in 1925, today has one lone and unofficial American missionary, Paul Mackensen.[10]

This American agglomeration is a house divided. While the denominations cooperating in the Division of Foreign Missions of the National Council of Churches have the longest established and most extensive work, they accounted in 1956 for 43.5% of all the American foreign missionaries. In that year they also sent out 631 more missionaries than in 1952. Meanwhile, the independent societies and agencies, including so-called faith missions, in 1956 accounted for 56.5% of the American foreign missionaries, and sent out 4,170 more than in 1952.[11] Behind this visible cleavage lie theological and other differences that perpetuate the old conflict of "modernist" versus "fundamentalist" and carry it from the United States to the rest of the world.[12]

---

[8] Frank W. Price, "World Christian and Missionary Statistics." MRL:OB, IX (May 6, 1958) No. 4, p. 6.

[9] "Recruiting, Selection and Training..." p. 3.

[10] Frank W. Price and Kenyon E. Moyer, "A Study of American Protestant Foreign Missions in 1956," MRL:OB, VII (Nov, 16, 1956), No. 9, p. 1.

[11] "Recruiting, Selection and Training..." pp. 3-4.

[12] The International Review of Missions [IRM], XLVII (April 1958), No. 186. The following articles are invaluable: Harold Lindsell, "An Appraisal of Agencies not Cooperating with the International Missionary Council Grouping," pp. 202-209. David J. du Plessis, "Golden Jubilee of Twentieth-Century

C. Facing the World Divided has long been one of the major liabilities of the Christian outreach, and now it faces a day of reckoning. While the world population is booming, the number of Christians is growing only one-third as fast.[13] Moreover, the missionary today faces competition that is moving forward on many fronts with grim intensity. It is no less than the struggle for the whole man, body and soul. Its epic quality steps forth from Hendrik Kraemer's now classic work, *The Christian Message in a Non-Christian World*, as well as from such newer accounts as Rajah Manikam's *Christianity and the Asian Revolution* (1954); Keith Bridston's *Shock and Renewal* (1955); M.M. Thomas and J. D. McCaughey, *The Christian in the World Struggle* (1956), and works of comparable challenge.

His task set amid "so many and great dangers," the missionary's vocation is on the front line of Christian witness. If he is alert, he notices in such developments as the advance of Islam in Africa, the renewal of Buddhism in Southeast Asia, or the resurgence of Hinduism, certain new characteristics that did not appear to missionaries in an earlier era. The fact that some of the major changes in these ancient religions is the result of their encounter with Christianity, tells a story whose meaning demands ever higher performance in the missionary calling.[14] Along with this deep-seated religious renaissance comes also the driving force of a new nationalism. The propagandists of these changes are themselves ardent missionaries. They confront the Christian missionary with such exacting tests that he must be doubly sure of his vocation.

Nor is this all. Cutting across all ancient religions, yet with points of contact suggesting at least the possibility of a future synthesis, comes the challenge of revolutionary Communism. Born of Western secularism, this dialectical materialism professes atheism while it breathes the fanaticism of a Judeo-Christian heresy. Its apostles are missionaries for whom the one end justifies any means. In their minds is a "blueprint of world conquest" whose messianism appeals to the awaking masses, and in their lives is the iron discipline of party membership.[15] If the Party was Lenin's most

---

Pentecostal Movements," pp. 193-201, Norman Goodall, "Evangelicals' and WCC-IMC," pp. 210-215.

13   MRL, OB, IX (May 1958), p. 3.
14   Hendrik Kraemer, *Religion and the Christian Faith*. Phila: Westminster, 1956, pp. 27-30. Rajah B. Manikam, ed., *Christianity and the Asian Revolution*. Madras: Diocesan Press, 1954, pp. 185-209.
15   William Henry Chamberlain, *Blueprint for World Conquest*. Washington: Human Events, 1946, pp. 73-85, 234-45

conspicuous achievement in strategy, then the Communist cadres have become the missionary task force of this atheistic faith.[16]

Between religious renaissance and political revolution the missionary of Jesus Christ is to plant the gospel of reconciliation. This is a dangerous and costly witness to bear. It calls for a modern *martyrion* , As one missionary expressed it, in preparing for the Willingen Conference in 1952: "A missionary is called to the martyrdom of staking his life. A martyr is one who bears witness, not so much by his death as by the use of his life."[17]

II. THE MISSIONARY VOCATION IN HISTORICAL PERSPECTIVE

Besides contemporary breadth, the Protestant missionary's vocation has historical depth. This discussion can be highlighted by two lives which bracket between them the quarter millennium of continuous Protestant mission overseas. The one is Bartholomew Ziegenbalg (1683-1719), who began his missionary career in Tranquebar, South India, in 1706. The other is Rajah Bhushanam Manikam (1897-19--), who was consecrated Bishop of Tranquebar in the 250th anniversary year, 1956. In both of these men the call to mission is strong. That call is lived as a vocation involving the whole person, and it is understood as a vocation of the whole Church. Matters of theology as well as of function become personified in these men in such a way as to make each of them a symbol of the Christian world mission. On closer scrutiny we can see why.

A. Ziegenbalg was well known in the 18th century as the pioneer Protestant foreign missionary. In him Protestantism emerged belatedly on the stage of the Christian world mission, and reference to him could help to refute the Roman Catholic charge of Protestant provincialism. His letters, reports, and even personal visits from India back to Europe packed his thirteen-year missionary career with meaning for Protestants everywhere. The fact that he happened to be a pious Lutheran aided rather than hindered, and his work soon acquired an ecumenical aura.

---

16   Alfred Meyer, *Leninism*. Cambridge: Harvard University Press, 1957. See also book review of this work in *American Historical Review*, Spring, 1958. High Seton-Watson, *From Lenin to Malenkov, The History of World Communism*. New York: Praeger, 1954, pp. 343-344.

17   "The Missionary Vocation," Report of Commission II, The Missionary Obligation [a pre-Willingen study]. Division of Foreign Missions, NCC, New York, March 7, 1952, p. 20.

The geographic quadrilateral of Halle, Copenhagen, London, and Tranquebar become the design for a remarkable partnership. Men could refer to August Herman Francke in Halle as the "heart" of this venture, to King Frederick IV of Denmark as its "head," to Archbishop Tenison and the SPCK in London as its helping "hand."[18] These leaders and many others followed the reports from Tranquebar with growing interest. In young lives as well as old such news of the Kingdom summoned forth a far-reaching range of response. There was, for example, Grandmother Zinzendorf, in whose home little Nicholas first learned about the new mission in India. And while Suzanna Wesley was capturing the imagination of young John with the published translations of Ziegenbalg's letters, Cotton Mather wrote him in Latin from Boston (1717). Addressing Ziegenbalg as "the most honorable, renowned, and world famous Servant of the Gospel, dean of the Congregation in India, indefatigable missionary...and humble Servant of Christ." Mather confessed that many of the Protestant churches regard it as an offense that so little has hitherto been done for the spreading of the Christian faith. Without intending flattery, he assured Ziegenbalg:

> You have surpassed all .... The fame of your mission, and of its diligent cultivation, has echoed from East India to [our] West India. And what you have been able to accomplish by divine grace in the way of founding a Christian people among the people of India is being received in America as good news from a distant land, and is being proclaimed among American Christians to the great praise of God.[19]

The vast outflow of Protestant missionary activity in the 19th century eclipsed these cherished beginnings. But with the current re-examination of the Christian world mission, and in connection with the anniversary year 1956, Ziegenbalg's work and vocation disclose still other important features. These bear further, even if brief, notice now.

Ziegenbalg grew up in the baroque era of widening horizons and ready experimentation. Among many there moved a desire for life in full dimensional harmony: harmony with God, with the world, with the self. A basic openness in Lutheranism to the world as God's creation helped to set the tone. Even the newfound pietism--as Spener and Francke insisted -- could be harmonized with authoritative confessional orthodoxy. Indeed, piety of heart and dedication of mind were complementary elements of

---

18   Erioh Beyreuther, *Bartholomaeus Ziegenbalg*, Bahnbrecher de Weitmission. Stuttgart: Evang. Missionsverlag, 1955, pp. 65 ff.
19   Arno Lehmann, "Prioritaeten und Fernwirkungen der Tranqaebar-Mission," *Evangelische Missions Zeitschrift*, February 1956, pp. 49-50.

that faith which, like Augustine of old, confesses: *Credo ut intelligam* [I believe in order that I might know].

Son of a successful businessman in Saxony, Ziegenbalg was orphaned early, educated by friends, befriended by Spener in Berlin, and summoned by Francke to study theology at Halle, Germany's newest and fastest-growing university. His previous months of spiritual struggle had proved a season of growth, yet a recurring stomach ailment, which he called his *malum hypochondriacum*, at times severely tested his spiritual harmony with God.

At the University of Halle, August Hermann Francke introduced his students to theology by striking a missionary note. He declared:

> A hunger and thirst for righteousness and closer communion with God has come over many souls. In thousands there is a sense of need, and they are looking about for persons who will show them the way. As once from Macedonia, so today they cry: Come over and help us.[20]

Then, with an infectious enthusiasm and a conviction born of personal experience and far-flung contacts, he continued:

> One may indeed say that our Lord God is making His presence known in this world and is permitting a general shaking of the foundations far and wide, not only in Germany and Europe, but also in other parts of the world. Today such things are happening that our descendants-- when they will sometime be reading about the compassion in bodily and spiritual matters which God is showing us-- will be amazed at the blessedness of these days.

Confronting his students with a personal challenge of Scriptural power, Francke told them: "You are to become ambassadors of God! Why? For the past few years, and ahead of all others, God has been singling out the students."[21] Francke's fervor was born of evangelical piety, and his consuming activity was governed by a "kingdom-consciousness." The secret of never-failing and ever-renewing power and inspiration lay in the Kingdom that both is and is coming. Francke and his like-minded

---

[20]   Beyreuther, op. cit., pp. 10-17.
[21]   Ibid., p. 17.

contemporaries "found in the theology of the Kingdom both the will and the joy to mission."[22]

Young Ziegenbalg had caught this spirit during his single full semester at Halle. Meanwhile, a visit to Berlin coincided with the arrival there of an urgent request from King Frederick IV of Denmark for qualified men to help him conduct an experiment. The location was not yet sure, except that it would be in one of his Danish colonies, either in the West Indies, or on the African Guinea Coast, or in India. In any case, Frederick was moved to try spreading the Christian gospel among the native people. [23] Who would go?

Ziegenbalg and his older friend, Heinrich Pluetschau (1677-1746), who had been serving as a teacher in Francke's schools at Halle, hesitated. But they did not say "No." They seemed to let the decision be made for them, although there was intensive spiritual wrestling in each of them before consenting to go. Outwardly the logic of this enterprise was plain: there were chaplains for Danish seamen and pastors for Danes in the royal colonies. Then why not missionaries as a next step? After a thorough theological examination, the two were ordained in Copenhagen by the Bishop of Zeeland and pledged to the ritual of the Church of Denmark.

While en route to India, Ziegenbalg gave much thought to his vocation as a missionary. To friends in Germany he wrote:

> In the task before me I seek nothing but to serve the Triune God in gratitude for the fatherly love and constancy He has shown me since my youth, and to use whatever resources He will provide me for proclaiming His truth and spreading His kingdom. So may His name be made known and glorified among the heathen. To achieve this purpose I will gladly deny myself, relegating all earthly pleasures to the last place and accepting with great joyfulness whatever cross, sorrow, persecution and misfortune will most surely come my way. And why should I be ashamed to suffer even the most ignominious death, if thereby God be praised and my neighbor's salvation be hastened?[24]

[22] J. C. Hoekendijk, "Mission in der Krise," *EMZ*, May 1949, p. 1.
[23] Arno Lehmann, *It Began At Tranquebar, A History of the First Protestant Mission in India.* Madras: Christian Literature Society, 1956, p. 3.
[24] Arno Lehmann, ed., *Alte Briefe aus Indien.* Unveroeffentliche Briefe von Bartholamaeus Ziegenbalg, 1706-1719. Berlin: Evang. Verlagsanstalt, 1957,

Despite the hostile reception accorded the two missionaries in Tranquebar by the Danish Governor Hassius, and with the prospect of a prolonged imposition of calculated frustrations by local Europeans to whom Christian missioning was an embarrassment, Ziegenbalg's convictions remained unshaken. He was able, as he put it, "to perceive the certainty of God's call."[25]

This certitude expressed itself remarkable in Ziegenbalg's intensive application of his calling. Actually, this is the story of thirteen years of pioneering toil, full of frustration, opportunity and encouraging response. His biographer, Erich Beyreuther, has told this story well[26] and has amplified it with further studies. His letters have been gathered by Arno Lehmann and are now also available. [27]The significance of his work in India has been helpfully appraised by Hans-Werner Gonsichen.[28] Here it is enough to summarize some of their observations:

Ziegenbalg's approach was marked by patience with his Hindu critics. His refusal to return insults eventually drew their respect and, in some cases, won their interest in the Christian faith.

His desire to know all he could about Hinduism--a desire so incomprehensible, even reprehensible, to Francke and others in Europe-- grew out of his contention that non-Christians must be convinced of their sin and need of salvation in Jesus Christ not only by the Law of God but also on the grounds of their own religion.[29]

His lack of acceptance by his fellow Europeans in Tranquebar favored the acceptance of the Gospel by the Tamils and aided the beginnings of an indigenous Christian constituency.[30]

---

pp. 25-26. Z's letter from the Cape of Good Hope, 30 April 1706.

[25] Z's letter from Tranquebar, 5 September 1706, pp. 21, 33.

[26] See above, footnote 18.

[27] See above, footnotes 23 and 24.

[28] Hans-Werner Gensichen, "Die konfessionelle Stellung der daenischhalleschen Mission." *EMZ*, February 1956, pp. 1-18. Also, "Tranquebar Then and Now," *The Indian Journal of Theology*, V (October 1956), no. 2, pp. 21-26.

[29] Beyreuther, "Die Missionspredigt Ziegenbalgs," *EMZ*, February 1956, pp. 24-33.

[30] Gensichen, "Tranquebar Then and Now," *The Indian Journal of Theology*, October 1956, pp. 25-26.

In him the pietist concept of the Kingdom of God as expressed through individual conversion was balanced by a strong Reformation understanding of the Church, where specifically, in Word and Sacrament, Jesus Christ exercises his Lordship and the believer receives the forgiveness of sin.[31]

His method, tinged with a mystical intellectualism, laid much, perhaps too much, weight on disputation and education. Yet such an emphasis set sound patterns of future endeavor. Among others, it enabled his balanced and most distinguished successor, Christian Frederick Schwartz, to draw hundreds into the fellowship of the Church.[32]

His confessional Lutheranism instilled in him a concept of missionary vocation that was also actively ecumenical.[33]

His marriage and home life made a difference. Not commissioned as a missionary, but no less devoted to the work, his Maria Dorothea shared with him in demonstrating Christian family living. Roman Catholic missionaries were never able, because of their celibate ideal, to convey to the natives the reality of the Christian home, (Yet it was just at this point that Ziegenbalg's Danish mission superior, Wendt, criticized him most severely for having departed from the ideal of "apostolic simplicity.")[34]

On the whole, Ziegenbalg was far ahead of his times with his emphasis on mission as the task of the Church that leads again to the Church. Yet on this subject, as in his married estate, he got little encouragement from his pietist supporters in Denmark. [35]

In his enterprising and hopeful way, Ziegenbalg thus laid the basis for a spread of the Gospel among the Tamils and others. His deep missionary commitment found a response. Indian Christians emulated his efforts. Herein lay the test of his calling as well as that of his colleagues and successors. As Professor Gensichen concludes:

---

[31] Ibid., pp. 21-22.
[32] Beyreuther, *EMZ*, February 1956, pp. 33-36.
[33] Gensichen, "Tranquebar Then and Now," loc. cit., pp. 22-23.
[34] Beyreuther, *Bartholomaeus Ziegenbalg*, pp. 81-87.
[35] Ibid., pp. 87-92.

The great history of Protestant work in the districts of Tanjore and Tinnevelly still stands out as a lasting memorial of the fact that the road on which the Gospel went out from Tranquebar into large parts of South India was in those early days not marked by mission stations but rather by the humble meeting places and mud chapels of the unknown village Christians. This was perhaps a more lasting contribution to the integration of the mission and the church than many a deliberate strategical move on the part of the missionaries, though the latter certainly deserve credit for encouraging and promoting this process of the growth of a church to the best of their ability. [36]

B. Rajah Manikam is one of Asia's best known Christian leaders, and is a missionary at heart. In one of his last letters, Ziegenbalg conveyed the good news to Francke that the governor of the British East India Company was cooperating in the founding of a Christian school in the seaside town of Cuddaloro, one hundred air miles south of Madras. [37] Many generations later, in 1897, Rajah Bushanam Manikam was born in Cuddalore.

Son and grandson of Lutheran schoolmen, and grandson of an Anglican clergyman on his mother's side, Rajah Manikam was in 1956 consecrated fourth Bishop of Tranquebar. He thereby became the first Indian Christian to head the Tamil Lutheran Church. His consecration took place in the courtyard of Tranquebar's old Danish fort. Before the service, a procession of nearly a hundred church leaders from seventeen countries had assembled in the historic New Jerusalem Church which Ziegenbalg had built and before whose altar he lies buried. Scriptural greetings were addressed to the new bishop by churchmen from various parts of Asia, Africa, Europe and America, and each spoke in his native tongue, as a reminder of the continuing reality of Pentecost. Later, at a public meeting, Bishop Manikam boldly declared:

> We now stand on the threshold of a new era. The old missionary era with its dependence upon the superior political, economic and cultural resources of the West is over, and a new era is dawning, which demands that the Church in every land, while rooted in Christ, also be related to its own soil. The Church itself (and not a

---

[36]   Gensichen, "Tranquebar Then and Now," loc, cit., p. 24.
[37]   *Cudulur,* 28 January 1718. Lehmann, *Alte Briefe,* pp. 510-511.

foreign missionary society) must be the missionary to the nation.[38]

The boldness of these words is born of a rich and varied career. Their tone is that of a Christian leadership which is thoroughly Asian but also at home in other parts of the world. Even a brief synopsis of this man's life reveals how varied and important are the circumstances and movements compounded in the new leaders among Christians in Asia.

Neither a pastor nor a missionary in the conventional sense, Rajah Manikam prepared himself at Madras Christian College for government service. Induced to teach while working on for his M.A. degree, he presently found himself heading in an unpremeditated direction. His life would henceforth be spent for Christ and His Church. With his wife, Ruby Jesudasen, he came to the United States in 1924 and stayed for five years. Besides receiving his theological education at the Lutheran Seminary in Philadelphia, and doing further work at Union Seminary, he also earned his doctorate in philosophy at Columbia University. [39] Both he and his wife became thoroughly conversant with American life in its churches and communities. Paralleling his studies, she too had earned her degrees, including an M.A. in bacteriology, and had acquired that broad interest in health and welfare work which she was later to put to excellent use in India. The early death of their only child gave them a deepened concern for those who suffer loss. Via England, and a summer of further study at Oxford, the Manikams returned to India in 1929.

With Christian higher education as his field of specialization, Manikam's eight years of teaching at Andhra Christian College, in Guntur, were a time of growth also in administrative experience. As vice-principal under Dr. J. Roy Strock, he was closely associated with one of India's most capable missionary educators and one whose influence had worked decisively on many, including Frank Laubach. [40] In 1937 his work at Guntur presently appeared as preparatory to service in the Church at large.

---

38   *Ecumenical Press Service*, January 27, 1956, p. 1. Biographical data derived in part from "Lutheranism's Indian Bishop," News Bureau, National Lutheran Council, 57-81 (June, 1957) pp. 1-3.

39   Rajah B. Manikam, *Missionary Collegiate Education in the Presidency of Madras India; A Study of the Historical Development, the Contributions and the Religious Educational Program of Mission Colleges in the Presidence*. Lancaster, Pa.: Conestoga, 1929, 156 pp.

40   Frank Laubach, *The Silent Billion Speak*. New York: Friendship Press, 1943, pp. 104-105.

Joining the staff of the National Christian Council at Nagpur, Manikam assumed responsibility in the field of Christian higher education, cultivated contacts with the 39 associated colleges, and helped bring to completion an extensive study of the Council on the Christian college and the Christian community.[41] Both as a member of the Council's staff and as a specialist in education, Manikam became engrafted into a partnership that was deeply indebted to such student-minded and missionary-committed Christian statesmen as John R. Mott, J. H. Oldham, William Paton, and others; all of whom, either in laying the foundations or guiding its course, had helped to make the Council a vital and cooperative force. [42] When in 1938 Manikam became the Council's first Indian general secretary, his rise to responsible leadership was more than matched by the gravity of coming events. [43]

Manikam's twelve years as general secretary began in 1938 on the threshold of the International Missionary Council's crucial conference in Tambaram. Against this ecumenical backdrop, with its deep involvement in world-changing events, were set the variety of consultative and other on going functions which linked the general secretaryship in one way or another to such matters as public relations, cooperation among the several churches and missions, Christian education from village school to university, literature and publications, theological education and the training of other Christian workers, Christian-sponsored health and welfare work, social action in matters like the opium traffic, the role of the Church in the changing rural and industrial areas, the cultivation and utilization of resources in the Christian community as a whole, the place of Christians in India's aspiration for independence from Britain, and many other matters.[44]

Amid the tragedy and turmoil of World War II came further involvement in the internment of German missionaries and the care of orphaned missions, a situation in which Manikam was anchor-man for

---

[41] Manikam, *The Christian College and the Christian Community*. Madras: The Diocesan Press, 1938, 144 pp.

[42] William Richey Hogg, *Ecumenical Foundations, A History of the International Missionary Council and Its Nineteenth-Century Background.* New York: Harper, 1952, p. 213, and passim. Margaret Sinclair, William Paton. London: SCM, 1949, pp. 74-129.

[43] Cp. Sinclair, pp. 104-113. Also, Hogg, op. cit., pp. 318-334.

[44] Same, also Hogg, op. cit., 290-304 [re Tambaram]. Further background, Madras Series, vol. VII, *Addresses and Other Records*, e.g. J. R. Mott, "Supreme Obligation of the Tambaram Delegates" pp. 156-164;"A Message to All Peoples," pp. 168-171.

assistance channeled from abroad through the IMC. With war's end came the climax of the long struggle for independence, the mounting tide of nationalism, the resurgence of Islam and of Hinduism, and the breaking apart of India and Pakistan. If Christians had managed to keep free from the heat of the struggle, they were nevertheless partners in it and were generally respected for their fairness of attitude. But how responsibly would Christians now act in the new India, and how actively would they share in the duties of this Asian democracy? If as Stephen Neill observed the Christians were troubled with twin anxieties, what grounds were there to be anxious over the continued right to change freely from one religion to another, or to be apprehensive over the future of Christian schools under a secular democratic state?[45]

For Manikam this was a period of intensive personal application. Here his missionary vocation grew as it was tested by events that kept the National Christian Council ever on the alert. How effectively could he and such colleagues like Charles Wesley Ronson work? How sensitive could they be to the needs of both the Indian churches and the Western mission societies? There is more than meets the eye in W. Richie Hogg's conclusion that the India Council, like the councils in other lands, leaned heavily on subsidies from Britain and America, and were on occasion tempted to function "with something less than constant reference to member missions and churches." Nevertheless, the India Council also "served the Christian world mission magnificently."[46]

Out of this schooling in missionary vocation Manikam emerged as on able Indian Christian leader. Alongside his ecumenical duties he had remained active also within the Federation of Lutheran Churches in India. He thereby strengthened his rootage, in a spiritual heritage which, at its best, gave him evangelical freedom.[47] Then came a new challenge.

As soon as the war ended, the National Christian Councils of China and India adopted a proposal for an East Asian Regional Committee of the IMC. This committee, formed in 1945, operated under the constitution of the IMC and designated Manikam as its correspondent. Overarching these developments was the perplexing question as to the coming position of the Church and its mission among the revolution-bound peoples of

---

[45]   Stephen C. Neill, *The Cross Over Asia*. London: Canterbury, 1948, pp. 142-3.
[46]   Hogg, op. cit., p. 367.
[47]   Manikam's Christian commitment, while Lutheran in nurture, was ecumenical in outlook. To some Lutherans in India he did not appear as Lutheran enough, yet all recognized his unusual abilities and his helpfulness in rising above provincialism.

Asia. Informal discussions in London, Geneva and New York were the counterpart of those going on in Asian centers. Early in 1947 the joint committee of the World Council of Churches and the International Missionary Council cleared the way not only for a joint Commission of the Churches on International Affairs (CCIA), but also for a joint East Asian office.[48] Although the representatives from Asia counseled caution at Whitby (1917) as well as at Amsterdam (1947), it was mainly because this proposal should be solidly grounded.[49] It remained for the Eastern Asia Christian Conference, at Bangkok in 1949 to provide the regional approval and also the job description. For this new and difficult post, the man selected was Manikam. [50]

In an original way, appropriate to the new era, the East Asian office symbolized the linking of "church" and "mission" in the ecumenical movement, and the partnership of the young World Council of Churches in association with the International Missionary Council. Manikam's activities were, in this early stage, to be ambassadorial. Reluctantly he resigned his general secretaryship in India, and by April 1951 was trying out his highly specialized vocation of liaison. His duties, as defined at Bangkok, were reasonably specific. He was to give:

> his full time to visiting the Churches and Christian Councils in East Asia, helping the Churches to share more fully their thought and experience, with a view to strengthening the Churches in their evangelistic task in East Asia, and establishing closer contact than at present exists between the East Asian Churches and Councils and the world-wide movement of the Church. [51]

Central to his task in every land visited was the heart of the Church's mission, evangelism, plus its corollary, the training for Christian leadership. Everywhere Manikam has also emphasised a closer study of resurgent ancient religions. His report from the field, done with the help of co-workers, presents *Christianity and the Asian Revolution* (1954) as

---

48 Hogg, op. cit., pp. 326-27, 337, 350.
49 *The First Six Years, 1948-1954*. Geneva: The World Council of Churches, 1954, pp. 102 ff.
50 Hogg, op. cit., p. 327. *Ecumenical Review II* (Winter 1950), no. 2, "World Council Diary," pp. 198-199. *Minutes and Reports*, World Council of Churches Central Committee (Chichester), 1949, p. 111.
51 *Minutes and Reports*, World Council of Churches Central Committee (Toronto), 1950, p. 51.

a stirring call to all Christians, a call further amplified in *The Church in Southeast Asia* (1956), done in collaboration with Winburn T. Thomas.[52]

Over five years of travel and consultation, from one community and conference to another, Manikam quietly blazed a trail. His wife was often his indispensible helper on such missions. The outcome of his labors, done always jointly with others, was the East Asia Christian Conference at Prapat in March of 1957. Its theme was evangelism. If as someone has ventured, "Prapat will become one of the place-names in ecumenical history,"[53] then part of the reason is that one could be found who could personify the new era in missionary vocation. Now, as Bishop of Tranquebar, Manikam's title links his task with that of Ziegenbalg. Therein lies a reminder that historical depth in Christ's mission is always the living and hope-filled witness among people.

III. THEOLOGY IN MISSIONARY VOCATION

It is possible to popularize missionary work as a career, and to publicize it as a special vocation. But who will venture to look for theology in missionary vocation? Yet it should not escape us that the contemporary breadth and the historical depth, with which we began this study, are simply preparatory. These are human dimensions of missionary vocation. Today there is a recognized need for recovering a theology of mission. [54] This means that despite the dearth of treatment so far, an attempt must be made to delineate the necessary presence of theology in missionary vocation. This calls not simply for a deeper personal commitment but for an understanding of the context in which the missionary calling is set and the message with which he is sent by the Church.

The origin of the missionary vocation is in God, its authority is Jesus Christ, and its content is the reconciling divine grace imparted to us by the Holy Spirit. In its statement on the calling of the Church to mission and unity, the World Council of Churches has declared:

---

[52] See above, footnote 14. Rajah B. Manikam and Winburn T. Thomas, *The Church in Southeast Asia*. New York: Friendship Press, 1956.

[53] *The Common Evangelistic Task of the Churches in East Asia, Papers and Minutes of the East Asia Conference, Prapat, Indonesia, March 17-26, 1957*, p. 3.

[54] Wilhelm Andersen, *Towards a Theology of Mission*. London: SCM, 1957. The focus of attention in this striking study is on the "encounter between the missionary enterprise and the Church and its theology." Stephen Neill has made an excellent translation. R. Pierce Beaver, *The Christian World Mission: A Reconsideration*. Calcutta: Baptist Mission Press, 1957. Especially valuable is Part II, The Theological Task, pp. 20-41.

In reconciling us to Himself in Christ, [God] has at the same time made us His ambassadors beseeching others to be reconciled to Him. He has made us members in the Body of Christ, and that means that we are both members one of another and also committed thereby to partnership in His redeeming mission.[55]

This partnership in mission while remaining general to all Christians becomes specialized in some. Here, then, let us venture a few thoughts on the necessary presence of theology in missionary vocation.

A. The Missionary Is Theologically "Charged" in that he in particular must always be "prepared to make a defense. . .for the hope" he holds, and to "do it with gentleness and reverence."[56] Whatever he may say about hope today, he knows one thing surely about hope in the ancient church. "It was," as Paul Minear has said, "bitterly contested by outsiders. The world held every Christian to a defense of it." And he was to defend it with gentleness toward those who abused him, and with reverence for his crucified and risen Lord.[57]

Today again the Christian as missionary is called upon to embody the faith which the Church believes, teaches and confesses in fidelity to the apostolic testimony. This is no easy matter, and the basic simplicity of the missionary task is made complex by the contingencies of human encounter. Deeply rooted in man, and permeating all his relationships, is the reality of radical evil.

The missionary himself, like every Christian, knows himself a sinner. In the call that has come to him from Another he recognizes his own guilt, his own unworthiness to be that which God intends for him. His call is not simply a call to humility and to a sense of unworthiness, but a call to genuine repentance. One who is truly penitent, however, remains humble in the knowledge that he is no better than other men. Indeed, he stands in the same solidarity of sin with them; in the same reality of guilt; in the same condemnation of divine wrath and judgment. In short, the missionary as sinner stands solidly with his fellowmen, whatever their religion or lack of it.

---

[55] *Minutes and Reports*, World Council of Churches Central Comm. (Rolle)1951, p. 65.

[56] I Peter 3:15.

[57] Paul Minear, *New Every Morning. Bible Stady of the First Epistle of Peter, Second Assembly of the World Council of Churches, Evanston*, 1954, p. 21.

Like every penitent, however, who responds to God's high calling in Jesus Christ, the missionary in repentance and openness to divine grace is a forgiven sinner. He knows something of that unfathomable *agape* whereby, for our sake, God made His Son "to be sin for us, who knew no sin," so that in Christ we might become rightly related to God.[58]

For the missionary particularly the realization that the Christian is "sinner and saint in the same breath" (Luther) can be nothing but a sobering reminder. Once he grasps this fact about himself, his approach to others is more likely to hold than to repel. Yet all of us know that such stern self-knowledge is hard to come by, harder still to live up to. In such self-knowledge, however, is the key to the missionary's understanding of his vocation as God's gracious calling of him. He must marvel and confess that it is God alone who can use such instruments for His purpose.

The failure of the missionary to take radical evil seriously in himself encumbers his work and may also make it harder for him to practice self-criticism regarding his Western and other ways. Conversely, once he grasps the meaning of sin and the role of God's Law in convicting him and all mankind of sin, he will then have a new receptivity for the gospel in his own life. Besides, he will understand that he is sent to call others because he himself has been called to decision. While much of God's ultimate purpose has been hidden from the missionary, as from the rest of us, we may declare with the Amsterdam assembly:

> Three things are plain: All that we need to know concerning God's purpose is already revealed in Christ. It is God's will that the Gospel should be proclaimed to all men everywhere. God is pleased to use human obedience in the fulfillment of His purpose. [59]

Indeed, the keynote of this summons to obedience and self-understanding was struck long ago when Jesus himself, beginning his missionary ministry, proclaimed: "The time is fulfilled, and the kingdom of God is at hand; repent and believe the gospel."[60]

B. Seeking First the Kingdom of God is both a challenge and a temptation. It is a challenge because we are summoned to concentrate on

---

[58] II Corinthians 5:21.

[59] *The First Assembly of the World Council of Churches, Amsterdam Report*, W. A. Visser 't Hooft, ed. London: SCM, 1949, Report of Section II, "The Church's Witness to God's Design," p. 64.

[60] Mark 1:15.

doing God's will, and a temptation because we always incline to do our own. Since the kingdom of God is the central theme in the teaching of Jesus, the missionary today must have a grasp of this theme in relation to his own vocation.[61]

When "Jesus came into Galilee preaching the gospel of God" it was on the assumption that a relationship between God and the world already exists, that in the light of the Old Testament God is sovereign over His creation in general and over His covenanted people in particular. God's relationship is that of sovereignty, kingly rule, and the expression of this rule is in the law. In Israel the rule of God is formalized in the Law of Moses; among other peoples law is simply observable in the order, rather than chaos, by which "the kings of this earth" govern.

For the missionary this is a matter of first importance. He must know that even before he begins his task, wherever it may be, God is already there. Although God's sovereignty may be veiled, there is a world of difference between God-hidden and God-absent. For God-hidden, the *Deus absconditus*, is not simply an enigmatic form of presence but a dynamic and working reality?[62]

Now in Jesus, the incarnate Son of God, born under the Law, there is not simply a further manifestation of the Law-aspect of God's relationship to His creation; there is the fulfillment of the Law. Jesus is the personification of God's full intention and redemptive plan for man. In contrast to the abstract and impersonal nature of law as such, Jesus comes as the concrete and personal embodiment of God's everlasting *agape*. Jesus' presence as well as his proclamation is good news, is gospel. Good news, of course, presupposes other news -- something that man already knows. Jesus is himself the good news of God's sure promise to save errant mankind.

What missionary does not rejoice that in his vocation he is to make clear that, while the law condemns, the gospel brings life; that while the law gathers to the past, the gospel draws to the future. Yet this needs amplification. In Jesus' ministry of preaching, teaching and helping, and especially in his parables and miracles, he proclaims the sovereignty of God also over the evil and demonic power of Satan. This ministry of Jesus invites emulation today as always, and at first sight seems to reaffirm that

---

[61] *"Kingdom," A Theological Wordbook of the Bible*, Alan Richardson, ed. New York: Macmillan, 1952, pp. 119-121.

[62] John Dillenberger, *God Hidden and Revealed. The interpretation of Luther's Deus absconditus and its significance for religious thought.* Phila.: Muhlenberg, 1953, pp. 103 ff, 117 ff.

the gospel, as he proclaims it prior to the cross, is a profoundly social gospel. Yet this social aspect intensified rather than diminished the challenge with which the gospel confronts the individual.

As Jesus went about doing good, his concern for people was genuine. Yet he always met them at a deeper level than they cared to admit then -- or we now. To proclaim the kingly rule of God required the response of obedience. As obedience calls for the subordination of the personal will to the divine will, submission brings surprise. The obedience of Simon Peter in casting his nets reveals to him not only fish but also sin. As Simon discovered, and as the missionary should know, confidence in one's own way of doing things, professionally competent as this may be, needs to be transformed into confidence in God's way. To be shocked within our competence reveals the otherness of life apart from God, and the uniqueness of him who heralds the kingdom, "Depart from me, for I am a sinful man, O Lord," is the recognition of man's condition. It is also prerequisite to the forgiven life of obedient faith, A new relationship is born: "Do not be afraid, henceforth you will be catching men." Simon and his partners left everything and followed him.[63] Obedience is the precondition of faith; yet God retains the initiative, and the faith to follow comes as a gift.

Along with the first followers of Jesus, as the Whitby Conference reaffirmed, all Christians are to be "partners in obedience."[64] For obedience, as the missionary must know, is that precondition of faith which implies Another who is in charge and who is Authority. Obedience, as required, results not in a blind but in an informed faith, a faith which, because it is informed, is indeed the gift of God. It is a purposeful gift. For the faith born of repentance is the means by which we receive the kingly rule and life-giving love of God. In this faith the followers of Jesus generally, and the missionary especially, receives and is to transmit the gospel. Such transmission is at a price. Jesus foresees the time when "you will be hated by all nations for my name's sake." Nevertheless (and how many missionaries have leaned upon these words!) "this gospel of the kingdom will be preached throughout the whole world, as a testimony to all nations; and then the end will come."[65]

---

[63]   Luke 5:8-11, Cp. Dietrich Bonhoeffer, *The Cost of Discipleship*. New York: Macmillan, 1951, p. 56.

[64]   *Renewal and Advance, Christian Witness in a Revolutionary World, Whitby Report*, C. W. Ranson, ed. London: Edinburgh House, 1948. Part II, "Partners in Obedience," pp. 173 ff.

[65]   Matthew 24:9, 14.

The proclamation of the kingdom, the kingly rule of God, is a matter of setting His will over against the will of natural man. This is indeed that divine-human encounter in which the herald of the kingdom is also the victim. The Incarnation, so it appears, ends where all men end -- in death. In the Cross there stands momentarily the triumph of sinful man; he has made the Son of God equal with all men in death.

However, in the reality of the Cross man discovers something about himself. There really should be no "result" from death. Humanly speaking, death is the end and man remains what he is. Yet in the kingdom of God there is resurrection! And he who proclaims the kingdom rises to complete the proclamation that God is sovereign over sin, death and the devil. What is more, this is a self-giving sovereignty. Only God can afford not simply the patience of His law but precisely the passion of His love.

In the grace of God the missionary sees his vocation as one who stands in a succession of those who have proclaimed this gospel, this good news, of the kingdom. The proclamation is anchored in the Incarnation, in the Cross, and in the Resurrection. The kingdom is proclaimed in an emulation of Jesus' preaching, teaching and helping *diakonia* (ministry) only when these are seen as signs of the kingdom. Yet the gospel of the kingdom is more than a sign. It is the culmination of all signs in the reality of the life of the Son of God who gives all for man and who triumphs over man. In the Cross God reconciles the world to Himself. This reconciliation, like the greatest miracle of the Kingdom, touches man where he expect it least: at the point of his deepest sin and separation. It is there that God awakens the response of a new and right (righteous) relationship. The kingdom of God and His righteousness need seeking first. When this fundamental relationship is righted then all else follows; also for the missionary called and sent to proclaim that Jesus is Lord.[66]

To many, to the pious as well as to the liberal, the kingdom of God can become a dangerous temptation. For it is easy to become enthusiastic about ourselves becoming not only heralds but also builders of the kingdom in our own name and on our own terms. To do it this way means to go forth in our own uregenerate spirit instead of in God's Holy Spirit. Here, the pious or the liberal, the stay-at-home or the missionary, easily make the mistake of settling for the kingdom and neglecting the Church. Not only in the past have there been missionaries animated by a kingdom-consciousness that de-emphasized the Church. Yet today the pendulum has swung for many the other way, and there has been a mounting emphasis upon the Church, an emphasis which verges on pre-occupation.

---

[66]   I Corinthians 12:3.

"The Church is the mission," one hears people say. Whatever the case, it is necessary to distinguish as clearly as possible between Kingdom and Church, so that both may be recognized for what God intends. In Christ both Kingdom and Church are inseparably united and part of the one purpose of God.

C. *The Church of Jesus Christ* is the work of the Holy Spirit. It is the new Israel, the people of God, the Body of Christ. It is those who have been called out of the world in order to go back into the world with the Word. It is those assembled together, the *ek-klesia*, to hear and to act upon the gospel of the Kingdom. The heart of the apostolic message is the *kerygma*. It is this which Jesus entrusted to those whom he sent. They now know the meaning of the signs of the Kingdom in the earthly ministry of Jesus, For they have followed those signs to the redemptive culmination, to the salvatory deed of God, done in the Incarnation, Cross and Resurrection of Jesus Christ. [67]

Peter's sermons in the early chapters of Acts, as C.H. Dodd has pointed out, set forth this *kerygma* with a six-fold emphasis: (1) the age of fulfillment has dawned; (2) this has happened through the life, death and resurrection of Jesus; (3) Jesus, exalted to God's right hand of power, is the messianic head of the new Israel; (k) the Holy Spirit in the Church is the sign of Christ's present power and glory; (5) the messianic age will soon reach its consummation in the return of Christ; and (6) repentance is required, forgiveness is offered, and the promise of salvation is included in the gift of the Holy Spirit.[68]

The Holy Spirit, in Luther's words, is He who "calls, gathers, enlightens and sanctifies the whole Christian Church on earth, and keeps it united with Jesus Christ in the one true faith.[69] The Spirit reminds us that the Church is not our Church but the Church of Jesus Christ. And the Church exists wherever the Word, the apostolic message, is clearly communicated and the sacraments properly administered. For it is in the Word and sacraments, this two-foldness of worship in the name of Jesus Christ, that the Church grows as the Body of Christ and becomes the living, corporate and transforming community of the forgiven, that assembly of

---

[67] *Theologisches Woerterbuch zum Zeuen Testament*, Gerhard Kittel, ed. Presents illuminating insights in connection with the articles on *ekklesia, kerygma, mathetes, basileia, euangelion*, etc.

[68] "Preach," Richardson, op. cit., p. 172. Also C. H, Dodd, *The Apostolic Preaching and Its Developments*. New York: Harper, 1936, esp. Lectures I & II

[69] Martin Luther, *Small Catechism*, explanation to the Third Article of the Apostles' Creed. *Book of Concord*, H. E. Jacobs ed., p. 367.

the redeemed who are the first fruits of the new age. This Church is one, holy, catholic and, to sum it all up, apostolic. That is, the Church is sent. It is God's pilgrim people to whom He has entrusted His world-redeeming purpose while en route. The individual Christian is himself a *homo viator*, a man on his way with a message for all whom he meets. The work the Church thus does is Christ's work, and it is now done by those who are members together in His Body. This Church is not yet triumphant but it is militant in that it continues to wage Christ's struggle against the forces of evil; yet it knows that one day it will share in that victory which its Lord has Himself already secured. How this Church is organized is less important than that it does all things decently and in order; but above all, as the living apostolate, the company of those sent forth, it obediently keeps the faith and bears witness to Jesus Christ as God and Saviour. [70] In concert with the ancient Church, this confession of faith is central in the ecumenical movement today.

For the missionary in his vocation today it is necessary to know where his own task is set. First of all, he knows that the kingdom of God, both present and coming, is a reality that has to do with God's present purpose and plan. Next, he knows that the Church, both visible and hidden, is the means God uses to achieve his purpose and accomplish His plan. Third, he knows that God's purpose, the mission given the Church, is not to be derived from the Church but from God. In other words, as the German mission authority, Wilhelm Andersen, has cautioned, there is a danger today of seeking to derive our understanding of mission from the Church instead of from the gospel of the Kingdom. Thus the concept of mission becomes too narrow. [71]

From Jerusalem in 1928 to Willingen in 1952 a church-centered understanding of mission gained momentum. The churchly emphasis was well intended and rendered the service of restoring the Church to central place in the thinking of mission-minded Protestants. But church-centered mission is too easily dissociated from the gospel of the Kingdom and from the Head of the Church who expects His work to be done not behind closed doors but out in the world. Church-centered mission can become self-centered mission and therefore not Christ's mission at all, just as Kingdom-centered mission, without regard for the Church, becomes self-centered and thus contrary to God's intention.

---

70   *Constitution of the World Council of Churches*, Article I, Basis. Amsterdam Report, The First Assembly, p. 197.

71   Andersen, op. cit., pp. 38 ff.

Here we come to the serious task, also facing the missionary, of keeping Kingdom and Church together, and of neither confusing them nor exchanging one for the other. As the Body of Christ, the Church on earth is made up of penitent and forgiven sinners. With respect to the sin in its members, like the incarnate Son of God who was "made to be sin for us", the Church continues in solidarity with all the peoples of mankind. In this regard, unhappily, the Church may also give those outside as well as inside its fellowship the impression that it is neither one, nor holy, nor catholic, nor apostolic. Yet with respect to the faith of its members, focused as it must be on Jesus Christ, the Church is already set apart as the one society of that new era of the Kingdom which Christ has brought and which, at His return in judgment and glory, He will bring to consummation.

Without going to extremes as that provocative Dutchman, Professor Hoekendijk, seems at times to do, it is necessary to regard mission as part of the *esse* or being of the Church.[72] Jesus Christ promises the Holy Spirit. The Holy Spirit comes; He calls, consolidates, informs, sanctifies, and sends. People respond in faith, enter fellowship, hear the Word, grow in grace, and go forth on a God-given mission with a Christ-centered message.

Inasmuch as the Church is thus the fellowship of those called by the Holy Spirit, all Christians have one general vocation, a calling in which there is also a sending. Yet the Spirit who calls also imparts a diversity of gifts.[73] Within the company of the called, some Christians therefore have a special vocation. Such a vocation is not apart from the generality of members but is set solidly among the members. All that has so far been said about the Kingdom and the Church here comes into sharp focus in the missionary. All Christians are to be missionaries, but some are to be missionaries in a special way, specially called, specially sent forth. As this is so, the missionary is to see in his vocation a personal summation of theology that is rooted in the Word and propelled by the Spirit.[74]

---

[72]   J. C. Hoekendijk, "Die Kirche im Missionsdenken," EMZ, January 1952, pp 1-12. See also his article, "Mission – Heute!" in the symposium by that title, published by the Studentenbund fuer Mission in Germany, 1954 pp. 1-12. Note how H. is reinforced by his Dutch colleague, A.A. Van Ruler, "Theologie des Apostolates," ibid., pp. 13-33. Cp. "apostellein," etc., in *Kittel, Theologisches Woerterbuch*. Eng. tr. of Hoekendijk's first-named article above in IRM, July 1952, pp. 324-336.

[73]   I Corinthians 12.

[74]   Friedrich Meier, "'Das missionarische Amt' im Verstaendnis Karl Hartensteins" *EMZ*, December 1954, pp. 169 ff.

D. Justification By Faith for the Christian generally and for the missionary particularly is a mighty and propulsive power. This kind of faith, properly understood, is genuinely missionary faith. From Asia, for example, we are reminded that "the key point at issue is that now as never before God is calling the Church to proclaim the message of justification by faith over against [an omnipresent] justification by works."[75] For every member in the corporate life of the Church justification by faith is that crucial point at which the gospel of the Kingdom is personally received and acted upon. Justifying faith, as the gift of God and the response of man, turns believers into missionaries. At least it should do this, because it relieves the believer of perpetual preoccupation with his own salvation and places his entire future in God's keeping. In return, he lives in communion with Christ and is an instrument of God's purpose. Good works are then no longer self-seeking but seek the welfare of others. Such works are the fruit of faith and the outward sign of personal gratitude for God's unmerited grace.

Taken another way, justification by faith in the individual puts the accent on right-relatedness to God. Because God is righteous, He is always in right relationship to His creation and to His creatures. In His covenant relationship to the old Israel and now to the new. He offers His Word as true and His promise as sure in Jesus Christ, The parables and miracles of Jesus, as well as his message and life, are evidence of this tightness of relationship, a Tightness that, for man, can be gained only in repentance and faith. Yet once gained it becomes a dynamic power and expresses itself through service (*diakonia*).

To sum up: being justified by faith, the believer is both in the Kingdom and in the Church. For him this duality is both vital and crucifying. Responsible membership in the Church prevents him from escaping into a sectarian and self-gratifying "kingdom idealism"; while a living commitment to the Kingdom gives him confidence and hope despite all the trials or frustrations of the empirical Church. When regarded in this light, justifying faith enables the believer, and especially the missionary, to offer others not his own goodness but that of Christ. Justification by faith is both intensely personal and strongly corporate, for the life of all believers is comprehended in the Body of Christ.

E. The New Life Together is a partnership in obedience. This obedience focuses on faith in Christ and is sustained by *agape*, the self-giving love of God who has reconciled us in His Son. Therefore this is a

---

[75] U Kyaw Than, "The Christian Mission in Asia Today," *IRM*, April 1958, p. 159.

new life together in Christ. This living together involves self-discipline in training as well as in self-giving service. Here individualism of the self-centered sort, so common among Christians, has no place. As Ziegenbalg insisted long ago, it is in the Church specifically that Jesus exercises his Lordship in Word and Sacrament, and that the believer receives the forgiveness of sin. [76]

For the missionary called and sent by the Church today this is timely and encouraging. He may be on some lonely outpost, or he may be one of a small task force. In the face of overwhelming odds and daily frustrations he is nevertheless not alone. His vocation is like that of every responsible Christian, only more so. For him especially there are elements of the new life together which need constant cultivating. Just when he is most isolated this oneness with fellow believers in Christ is most precious and asserts itself most powerfully. For his task is that crucial instrumentation through which the Holy Spirit gathers and plants the Church in a new place through means existing in the Church as already planted. Much therefore depends on the missionary's understanding of what lies behind the life together and how he communicates it. For he has been called and sent to communicate.

Elements of the common life in Christ, as the missionary should see it, include those that have been present in the Church from the beginning. Among these we may here take note of three which are bound together in the encounter of Christ with the world:

> 1. There is the impartation of the gospel (*kerygma*) through witnessing (*martyrein*), which includes the spoken word, the preaching (*kerysein, euangeligein*) and teaching (*didaskein*) of the good news of Christ's incarnation, death, and resurrection.

> 2. There is the fellowship (*koinonia*) of the congregation for the worship (*leitourgia*) of God in the name and presence of the living Lord; united in intercession, prayer, praise, and thanksgiving; once received in baptism and ever renewed at the Lord's Table.

---

[76]   Gensichen, op. cit., *The Indian Journal of Theology*, October 1956, p. 22.

3. There is the expression of this faith in loving service (*diakonia*) to all men through the full commitment of the members.[77]

In the missionary's vocation a vivid understanding of *diakonia* is indispensible. Because "service" has suffered from today's inflation of words, *diakonia* must help us rescue the meaning. *Diakonia*, in its scriptural connotation, suggests a dual function: it challenges the Church to enter the world and it requires an examination of the theological foundation of Christian service. The theology of *diakonia*, as Anders Nygren recently pointed out, may be discerned in a four-fold form:

1. Service, or *diakonia*, in the New Testament does not stand apart from the gospel as something secondary but is in the very center of the gospel. *Diakonia* is not merely an option because,

2. Serving stands at the center of Christianity. Christ, who is at its heart, came for no other reason than to serve. Behind Jesus' oft-quoted words, "The Son of man came not to be served but to serve" (Mark 10:45) stands the testimony of Isaiah 53, in terms of which the gospels must be read; Jesus Christ steps into complete solidarity with us. Our need becomes his need. His righteousness becomes our righteousness. "The chastisement of our peace was upon him; and with his stripes we are healed" (Isa. 53:5; II Cor. 5:21). This unlimited solidarity is service in the deepest sense of the word.

3. To "live in Christ" (Gal. 2:30) is to live in the service of love. This means gratefully to accept Christ's service and to pass it on to others. It is impossible truly to accept the service of Christ and to keep it for oneself only. As he bore our burden, we are permitted to bear the burdens of others. Such service in fellowship with him is therefore a privilege and a duty. Our inclusion in the Body of Christ is something that must happen in reality. Even as Christ for our sake became a servant, a *diadonos* (Rom. 15:8), the

---

[77] Based on the report to the churches on *Policy and Strategy in Social Welfare*, adopted by official delegates at the National Conference on Policy and Strategy in Social Welfare, Atlantic City, New Jersey, May 7-10, 1957. New York: National Council of Churches, pp. 18 ff.

entire Christian life was shaped by his *diakonia* (Luke 22:27). Because this is God's world,

4. The service of the Church must be concerned not only with the spiritual but also with the physical needs of men. We distort the gospel if we spiritualize it and seek to contrast the spiritual as opposed to the physical needs of men. Christ was concerned with the whole man, and Christians are to share that concern. [78]

To these four points of Nygren may be added a fifth: As Christ continues to identify with all sorts and conditions of men, both Christian and non-Christian, his hidden presence among them is the test of our faith in him as we serve them. For, in proving God's love for all mankind, "while we were yet sinners, Christ died for the ungodly" (Rom. 5:6). Some times we are guilty of limiting the gospel. When doors are closed to evangelism as we prefer it, we may be tempted to turn elsewhere. Do we then forget that the kerygma presupposes the signs of the Kingdom, and that a test of living faith and true humility is *diakonia* exactly among "the last, the least, and the lost"? And such service looks for no reward! [79]

Indeed, *diakonia* is itself a form of disclosure that raises one of the most baffling questions of the missionary vocation. If it summons faith to action and gives expression to the new life together, what light does it throw on the relation of the Christian to the non-Christian?

F. Religion and the Christian Faith stand in disputed relationship. How shall the missionary regard non-Christian religions? He may be tempted to see too much in them, but a greater temptation is to see too little in them. Ziegenbalg, with more evangelical insight than his superiors, was purposefully curious about Hinduism. His *Genealogy of the Malabar Gods*,[80] published, alas; only 150 years after his death, represents his personal effort to carry out a basic theological demand of the missionary vocation.

This demand is to see clearly, in the very context of the missionary situation, the dialectic of law and gospel. Earlier we have noted how the

---

[78]   Anders Nygren, "The Context Within Which the Church Develops Responsible Service," Lutheran World Conference on Social Responsibility. Springfield, Ohio, August 7-10, 1957. Proceedings [to be published, 1958], Lecture on August 8.

[79]   Matthew 25:37. Cp. "Theses on Christ Frees and Unites," *Proceedings of the Third Assembly of the Lutheran World Federation*, Minneapolis, Minnesota, August 15-25, 1957. Part IV, "Free for Service in the World," pp, 88-89.

[80]   Ziegenbalg, *Genealogia der malabarischen Goetter*. Wm. Germann, ed. Madras. 1867.

proclamation of the gospel presupposes God's presence everywhere in terms of law, with order being a manifestation of the ultimate authority that is of God, "Even before the gospel is preached," as Gustaf Wingren insists, "God is at work among all nations, through the Law, through the secular power." To which Wingren adds:

> All too easily our missionary thinking is corrupted by the notion that Europe and America are the home of the Christian religion, whereas that religion is not yet sufficiently established among the [other] nations. If we see things that way, we operate with the concept of 'religion' as the dominant idea. Christianity becomes one of the 'religions.' But religion is always a human matter, at the disposal of man; and therefore when we bring the 'Christian religion' to the non-Christian world, we ourselves – and not the Word -- are in the center of our missionary activity and quite logically, though perhaps not consciously, Europe and America are seen on a higher plane than Africa and Asia. We must seriously ask ourselves if not a great part of the practically universal irritation concerning missions does not spring from the fact that we have wrongly combined or even confused the preaching of the Word of God with the spreading of European-American culture.[81]

With the resurgence of ancient religions the question of differentiation between religions and the Christian faith becomes acute. It may well be contended with Alan Richardson that God discloses Himself to all men in so-called general revelation, while in the Hebrew Christian heritage He comes to us in special revelation. This has the merit of avoiding the pitfall setting "natural" versus "revealed" religion.[82] Hendrik Kraemer, moreover, in his discussion in *Religion and the Christian Faith*, indicates that the conversation of the ecumenical Church with the renascent religions of Asia has hardly begun but must urgently be undertaken.[83] To which Rajah Manikam gives his resounding second, as he continues to plead for the closer study of these religions by Christian scholars. For Manikam notes that our missionary generation is notoriously lacking in curiosity

---

[81]   Gustav Wingren, "Lutheran Theology and World Missions," *Proceedings of the Second Assembly of the Lutheran World Federation*, Hannover, Germany, July 25-August 3, 1952, pp. 74-75.

[82]   Alan Richardson, *Christian Apologetics*. New York: Harper, 1947, pp. 110 ff, 133 ff.

[83]   Kraemer, *Religion and the Christian Faith*, pp. 27-30, 214 ff., 221 ff., 387 ff.

and competence in this regard, especially when compared with Christian scholars in this field of study a generation or more ago. [84]

For the missionary, however, this avowed openness to the resurgent ancient religions can be a serious hazard. The deepest danger may lie ultimately not in the several religions overwhelming the Christian faith but in the Church itself being tempted to pose as religion. Old as this danger is, it comes as a temptation when, so it seems, we lose our theological balance, making too little of the Kingdom and too much of the Church. Here Hoekendijk makes a timely observation: "In history a keen ecclesiological interest has almost without exception been a sign of decadence," the mark of "a race of Epigoni." On the contrary, "in the 'first generation,' in periods of revival, reformation or missionary advance, interest [is] absorbed by Christology ..."[85] Fortunately, as the work of the Faith and Order Commission of the World Council of Churches bears out, the center of theological discussion is moving from ecclesiology to christology.[86]

What, however, is the missionary in his vocation to make of the Church? Is he to follow pious or liberal enthusiasts into the camp of non-Church Christians as in Japan? By doing so he would join the flight from the hard realities of this world and of actually living together with others in Christian fellowship; he would content himself with a deceptive idealism or an insidious docetism. Not only is the missionary to take the Church seriously, but at times he must be ready to admit also to the non-Christian that, on its human side, the Church partakes of the failings common to all religions. Unlike Jesus Christ, the Head of the Church, in whom two natures, the human and the divine, were perfectly blended, the empirical Church is a paradox. For it is composed of people who, despite being the new people of God, are nevertheless "righteous and sinner simultaneously."[87]

---

[84] Manikam, *Christianity and the Asian Revolution*, pp. 185 ff. Also in personal conversation, and in the Earl Lectures, 1958, at the Pacific School of Religion.

[85] Andersen, op. cit,, p. 37. Also the EMZ and IRM articles as noted above, footnote 72.

[86] Robert L. Calhoun, "Christ and the Church," in *The Nature of the Unity We Seek*, Paul S. Minear, ed., St. Louis: Bethany, 1958, pp. bl ff. Cp. *The Third World Conference on Faith and Order*, Lund 1952; Oliver S. Tomkins, ed., London: SCM, 1953, pp. 17-18.

[87] For evangelical theology it is of first importance to re-appropriate Luther's grasp of the inter-relationship between the doctrine of the Church and the doctrine of justification by faith. For him both of these doctrines root in the Old Testament, and stand forth with special clarity in the Psalms. In them the unity of God's people at worship and of the righteousness "that

The Church is indeed the work of the Holy Spirit and the creation of the proclaimed Word. Yet while we confess it to be one, holy, catholic, and apostolic, see what we make of the Church!

In this contrite recognition the missionary joins with his fellow Christians, confesses the sins of disunity, and seeks to let himself be used as an agent of both the mission and unity of the Church. Living as he does amid the turbulent forces of the age, the missionary must confess that the Church belongs to Jesus Christ, that He builds it through people, and that from His Cross He would draw all men to Himself. To be called as His special servant thus means to be alive to theology in missionary vocation.

IV. MISSIONARY VOCATION AND THE UNITY OF THE CHURCH

The vocation of the missionary as a subject of special study presupposes that the Church corporately and the Christian individually have a mission that involves movement and unity. For it is the mission of God. It is He who is at work in the world, making known to mankind the redemption He has made available in His Son. The God who has acted once-for-all in Jesus Christ seeks and calls persons through whom this action shall become effective among all peoples.

Like a divine relay, to use the late Karl Hortenstein's simile, this mission of God comes through His Son, is passed on through the apostles, and then through the succession of witnesses in His Church until it spreads among all peoples and times, till at last the End comes. The mission of the Son, the sending of the apostles, the calling of the *ekklesia* and of its every member to bear witness, all belong inseparably together.[88]

---

alone counts in the presence of God" ("die Gerechtigkeit die allein vor Gott gilt") is unmistakable. Luther's own development of this understanding becomes apparent first in his lectures on the Psalms (1513-15), and then in his lectures on Romans (1515-16). See Karl Hell, *"Die Entsehung von Luthers Kirchenbegriff,"* pp. 288-325; and his *"Die Rechtfertigungs Lehre in Luthers Vorlesung ueber den Roemerbrief mit besonderer Ruecksicht auf die Frage der Heilsgewissheit,"* p. 111-151. Re "simul justus et peccator," p. 144. Re the role of the Psalms as Luther's starting point in justification by faith, p. 111. Holl, *Gesammelte Aufsaetze zur Kirchengeschichte,* Vol. I, Tuebingen: Mohr, 1932. See also Gordon Rupp, *The Righteousness of God,* Luther Studies. London: Hodder & Stoughton, 1953, esp. chaps. 6, 7, 8.

[88] Karl Hartenstein on "The Missionary Office," EMZ, December 1954, p. 169. See above, footnote 74.

In our enthusiasm for this dynamic unity, something may be overlooked. In certain ecumenical circles and elsewhere, too, there are those who would "leave no place for a true missionary calling of individuals [or] a calling and sending by the Church of individuals to the 'ends of the earth.'"[89] Nevertheless, between the Church's corporate and the Christian's individual responsibility there is the middle position occupied by the missionary who is specially called and sent forth.

A. The Rhythm of Calling and Sending, like the circulatory system in a growing body, is the personal side of the missioning office of the Church. That this office is not simply an elective function becomes abundantly clear from the history of the Church. Near the head of this centuries-old process stands the experience of the Church in Antioch. While the members were "worshiping the Lord and fasting, the Holy Spirit said, 'Set apart for me Barnabas and Saul for the work to which I have called them.'" After serious deliberation, prayer and more fasting, the leaders corroborated the Holy Spirit, solemnized the occasion, imposed their hands on Barnabas and Saul, and sent them off.[90] Parting with leaders who showed promise and could have been well used locally, the Church in Antioch stands not only as the gateway to Paul's first missionary journey but also as an apostolic precedent for similar action by the Church ever since.

The vocation of the missionary is the discharge in a specific manner of the general calling entrusted to the Church as the people of God. It is therefore proper to distinguish between the general vocation (*vocatio generalis*) of all Christians and the special vocation (*vocatio specialis*) of the missionary. This specialization is in that same Spirit who provides the Church with a diversity of gifts among its members. It is for the work of the Holy Spirit, for the spreading of the gospel in a not exclusively laissez faire manner that certain qualified persons are thereto set apart.

Such setting apart means assignment to special duty within the fellowship and solidarity of the Church's task. It does not mean separation from the home church. Rather it means that the home church is sharing some of its choicest leadership to help with the gathering and planting of churches-in-the-making, wherever these may be. The churches are thus comprehended in the Church, while movement is ventured and unity retained.

This setting apart for mission simply underscores the fact that the Church itself is set apart from the world. Yet such demarcation from

---

[89]   R. Pierce Beaver, letter to E. Theodore Bachmann, May 26, 1958.
[90]   Acts 13:1-3.

the world is deliberate not with respect to people as such, but from the forces of evil which, like the magician whom Paul calls a son-of-the-devil, corrupt people. These demonic forces keep people under the tyranny of sin and in rebellion against God unless they are liberated by faith in Jesus Christ. Those responding are called out of this tyrannical darkness into His marvelous light. Although they are thus set apart from the world with respect to the forces of evil, they are also set apart for the world with respect to the redemption of mankind. Mindful of this inclusive context, the setting apart of certain members of the Church for special missionary tasks becomes an act done in hope and eschatological expectation.

While the foregoing may be sound theology, it pales into theory when set over against the actual mission practice which calls and sends missionaries. Today we live with the gratifying as well as embarrassing consequences of the nineteenth century, the "great century" of missions. For us in America especially the picture is divided. On the one side are the achievements of missions and missionaries in promoting the ecumenical movement and the unity of the Church. On the other side are the still uncommitted forces, where the momentum of mission is perversely going its own way. As American Protestants we face the unpleasant fact that our missionaries form two camps. The one denotes churches cooperating in the International Missionary Council "in association with" the World Council of Churches. The other denotes three large independent combines of generally fundamentalist character, plus a number of major denominations like the Southern Baptists and the Missouri Lutherans.[91] If the case were simple, the independents might eventually be induced to cooperate. But it is complex, and before thinking of ultimate cooperation it is necessary to inquire into the nature of the churches or agencies that call and send the missionary personnel. For us in America some European experiences offer a clue to our problem.

Behind the general silence on the missionary vocation which has marked the German scene, there lurk the traumatic experiences of repatriated missionaries. As Walter Freytag reports, these men have had to ask themselves: Is our vocation for special missionary duty now done for?[92] As some since 1945 have waited in vain for an opportunity to serve at home, their repatriation came as a challenge to the church to re-think its relation not only to the missionary but also to its own missioning

---

[91]   H, Lindsell, op. cit., IRM, April 1958, pp. 202-209. See above, footnote 12. Also Norman Goodall, op. cit., pp. 210-215.
[92]   Walter Freytag to E. Theodore Bachmann, May 28, 1958.

obligation. What lies behind this returned missionary, not overseas but at home?

Unlike the pastors, and also unlike the university-trained and church ordained Ziegenbalg, this contemporary missionary had most likely been educated at a mission school. This separated him from the pastor who had studied theology at a state university. Now the mission school was also the headquarters of the mission society that had sent him. Formed in the old era of the state church, the society existed independently of the organized church on whose territory it was based. The friends who supported the mission society were active Christians, and their number included persons not only within but also beyond the immediate ecclesiastical boundaries. In effect these supporters were an *ecclesiola in ecclesia* constituting itself as a society to perform the task of mission which the territorial church appeared unable to do. The society recruited, trained and examined the candidates for missionary service. It passed upon their fitness for service and gave outward validation to their inward call. Then the society sent them forth to their appointed places, supported and encouraged them in their work, provided for them on furlough and in retirement.[93] In all this the mission society was to the missionary what the official church was to its pastors. While these parallel lines of development were frequently crossed, and the subject of "missions" had even received an official place in the theological faculties at certain universities,[94] the problem of the organized church as a missioning body long remained an enigma.

---

[93] Best overall account, including ties with England, plus interconfessional ties on the Continent, is Wilhelm Schlatter, *Geschichte der Basler Mission*, 3 vols. Basel: Missionsbuchhandlung, 1916. This is the centennial history of the oldest and in some respects most influential of the Protestant mission societies on the Continent. Its men were sent not only to Asia, Africa and the Pacific Islands, but also to the home mission front in North America. A revealing sidelight comes in a recent word of appreciation from Ghana, Mr. R. A. Quarshie, first secretary of the Ghana Embassy in Paris, pointed out "the profound influence" of the Basel mission. He said that many Ghana cabinet members "were brought up in the traditions of the Basel mission. We are a secular state and the fact that those of us who are Christian or Mohammedan or hold some other belief can work together so amicably is a tribute to the ideas of toleration instilled by the Basel mission." *Ecumenical Press Service*, No. 18/25th year, May 9, 1958, p. 7.

[94] The exhaustive work of Olaf Gottorm Myklebust, *The Study of Missions in Theological Education*, 2 vols, Oslo: Han Egede Institute, 1955-57, is a classic in this field only by intention but certainly not in achievement. Keith Bridston's critique in the *Ecumenical Review*, X, April 1958, No. 3, pp. 324-325, is sad but true. Here I would go further and say that only an academician could be content to define his subject so narrowly that he deliberately omits

Then had come the shattering encounter between the neo-paganism of the Nazis and the revived evangelical faith of the confessing Church. Suddenly a situation, presumably reserved for the overseas "mission field," turned up at home -- with a demonic totalitarianism and a missioning apologetic of its own. The struggle under Nazism and the cataclysm of World War II brought the Church closer to the people, especially in terms of a confessing and serving fellowship. All mission work, both at home (Inner Mission) and overseas, was interpreted as a living concern, a *diakonia*, of the Evangelical Church in Germany and its 29 member churches.[95]

For the key tracer in this problem, the repatriated missionary, two developments of opposite polarity shed further light. On the negative side, it happened that one of the oldest and most prominent of the mission societies was offered an opportunity to be embodied into the regional Evangelical folk church, an offer which, of course, had been possible ever since the separation of Church and State took place in 1919. But the mission society declined. Steeped in a tradition of their own, its leaders feared that "churchification" would result in a loss of freedom in missionary enterprise. On the positive side, in the spring of 1958, the Church of Luebeck, whose bishop is a former missionary in India, was the first of the German folk churches to undertake in its own right the sending of missionaries overseas. Admittedly, Bishop Heinrich Meyer was encouraged to push this matter in his own church because of his work in connection with the International Missionary Council and also with the Lutheran World Federation.[96]

In short, these developments in the homeland of the Reformation and of the first Protestant missionaries to Asia, are symptomatic of what is happening in other parts of the world as well. The growing interest in the Church and the widespread inquiry into the nature of the Christian vocation are salutary. Just as the current secular quests for the meaning in a job take the worker seriously, so it must be in the Church. What happens to certain people becomes a live clue to what is going on generally. So the missionary vocation, in terms of calling and sending, may be seen more clearly for what it means both to the person and to the whole Church

---

pre-requisite references to the role and influence of the schools of the mission societies.

[95] *Die Evangelische Kirche in Deutschland* (EKD), Grundordnung: I. Grundbestimmungen, Artikel 15 and 16. *Kirchlishes Jahrbuch fuer die Evangelische Kirche in Deutschland, 1945-1948.* Joachim Beckmann, ed,, Gueterslch: Bertelsmann, 1950, p. 99.

[96] News Bureau, National Lutheran Council, 58-60, April 15, 1958, p. 6.

when at one point, as has been noted, the process is suddenly interrupted. The dilemma of a few returned missionaries can thus become an aid to reflection and decision on the part of many Christians. Not only so, but new kinship may be disclosed in unexpected places.

One of these points of kinship lies in the functional similarity between the mission society on the European continent and the denomination in the United States. It may be no exaggeration to say that both the European mission society and the American denomination are the voluntary commitment of like-minded people to carry out an agreed purpose. As such their action embodies not only dedication in behalf of a function but also protest in behalf of a freedom essential to the task. Both sought to be free from a state-church situation. The German practice of creating societies which paralleled and supplemented the proper work of the Church was actually derived from England, the classic land of societies, The American creation of denominations, achieved after a rejection of state-church imitations in the colonial era, also drew inspiration from England. John Locke, in 1706, had given a definition to the Church which was to become determinative in American thought, when he wrote: "A church then I take to be a voluntary society of men, joining themselves together of their own accord, in order to [engage in] the public worshiping of God in such a manner as they judge acceptable to him, and effectual to the salvation of their souls."[97] While Locke's definition presupposed freedom, the application of it was far from simple. In his fascinating analysis, the thoughtful church historian, Sidney E. Mead, has shown how American Protestants were far from championing religious liberty as a pure ideal but rather lapsed into it by default. He writes:

> The true picture is not the triumph in America of right-wing or left-wing, of churches or sects, but rather a mingling through frustration, controversy, confusion, and compromise forced by necessity, of all the diverse ecclesiastical patterns transplanted from Europe, plus other patterns improvised on the spot, to form a complex pattern of religious thought and institutional life that was peculiarly 'American,' and is probably best described as denominationalism.[98]

---

[97] See Anson Phelps Stokes, *Church and State in the United States*, 3 vols. New York: Harper, 1950, I, p. 143.

[98] Sidney E. Mead, "From Coercion to Persuasion: Another Look at the Rise of Religious Liberty and the Emergence of Denominationalism," *Church History*, XXIV, December 1956, No. 4, p. 335.

"The resulting organizational form," he concludes, "was unlike anything that had preceded it in Christendom, and for purposes of distinctive clarity it is best know as the 'denomination.'"[99]

Institutionally the denomination grows out of a societal or "free church" idea which is actualized by the separation of Church and State. The denomination, as Mead shows, "is the organizational form which the 'free churches' have accepted and assumed. It was evolved in the United States under the complex and peculiar situation that there existed between the Revolution and the Civil War." Moreover, "the denomination, unlike the traditional form of the Church, is not primarily confessional, and certainly not territorial. Rather it is purposive."[100] Among its purposes three may here be singled out:

1. Differentiation in emphases and practices. This involves the justification, preservation and propagation of those things for which the denomination stands. This is its "sectarian" tendency. [101]

2. The voluntary principle. As the necessary corollary of religious freedom, voluntarism "tends to push practical considerations to the fore by placing primary emphasis on the free uncoerced consent of the individual." [102]

3. The missionary enterprise. Just as in voluntarism, a "sense of mission forms the center of a denomination's self-conscious life."[103] Not only does this then express itself in the form of revivalism and competition across the "unchurches" land, but it also provides a base "for the inter denominational and superdenominational consciousness and cooperation which has been such an outstanding aspect of American religious life."[104]

One result of denominationalism is that, while busily at work, it tends to be unreflective, to become anti-intellectual, and to harbor confused thoughts about the nature and responsibility of the Church. Each denomination "solves" the ecclesiological problem simply by calling itself "church," and doing what it considers the work of the Kingdom.

---

[99]   Ibid., p. 336.
[100] Mead, "Denominationalism: The Shape of Protestantism in America," *Church History*, XXIII, December 1954, No. 4, pp. 291 ff.
[101] Ibid., p. 295.
[102] Ibid., p. 299.
[103] Ibid., p. 302.
[104] Ibid., pp. 302, 306, 315.

The calling and sending of missionaries, as done by the denominations, not only expresses a basic functionalism but also, as in the case of the European mission societies, reminds the Church of its unfinished task. Even the far-flung independent and non-cooperating agencies, from precarious "faith mission" to imposing church body, have a place in this process, although it is often hard to see where. Ecclesiastically many of these may be "fringe" groups, yet they may also be closer to the people among whom they flourish and induce in them a stronger commitment. While a fringe group may be a denomination in process of formation, (which would understandably be denied by the group), it at least recalls features frequently found in 19th-century American life when many of today's cooperating denominations were growing up.[105]

Besides, many of these "fringers" are militantly missionary. The experiences they cultivate are bursting for communication. More than compensating for a frequent asceticism toward the "world" is the prized ecstasy in the "Spirit." Many of them, like modern Montanists, forego the Church in favor of the Kingdom whose consummation is at hand. While the message is usually one-sidedly simple, the mood of this ascetic-ecstatic apocalyptic combination is magnetic. People respond. In the Pentecostal movements, for example, many individuals and even whole families have volunteered for missionary service, sold their possessions, and started for some overseas field. Once baptized in the Holy Spirit, no sacrifice seems too great. Today, little over fifty years after the Apostolic Faith Mission of Azusa Street in Los Angeles sparked a national revival, some 3,000 men and women, half of them Americans, have been sent from Pentecostal churches into foreign fields. The Pentecostal World Conference, operative since 1947, now claims an adult constituency of over eight million in all parts of the world. [106]

At this point it may seem that the rhythm of calling and sending in Protestantism has been powered by a centrifugal force which has scattered missionaries all over the place but has failed to hold them in a "unity of the Spirit."[107] For comparison, if not for consolation, the example of the Roman Catholic Church is instructive. Far from itself being a monolithic structure, it nevertheless presents the Church as a constant factor amid many variables. Among the array of variables are the orders, many of which are or used to be ardently missionary. In them the rhythm

---

[105] Cp. Henry Pitney Van Dusen, "The Third Force in Christendom," *Life*, June 9, 1958, pp. 122-124.

[106] David du Plessis, "Golden Jubilees of Twentieth-Century Pentecostal Movements," *IRM*, April 1958, pp. 193, 195, 196-197, 201.

[107] Ephesians 4:3.

of calling and sending has repeatedly been dramatized as their "regulars" have blazed missionary trails everywhere or have revived a spirit of mission in the Church at large. Usually when the orders have pioneered some missioning enterprise they have also prepared it for consolidation into the Church. After the regulars come the seculars, and the hierarchy takes over. For Americans it may also be sobering to realize that in the methodical advance of the Roman Church, it was only in the early years of the 20th century that the United States was taken off mission status. [108]

In Roman Catholicism, moreover, there is within the hierarchical structure a dialectic of growth that encompasses Kingdom and Church. Yet the Kingdom here seems to be appropriated into the Church, leaving the Church supreme in its own foreshadowing of the glory that is to be. That this quasi inversion of the Kingdom and exaltation of Church lacks scriptural authority is really no problem in Roman Catholicism. The unity of the Church is not entrusted to a capricious preaching of the gospel of the Kingdom to all nations. As Roman Catholic missiologists are pointing out, the mission of Catholicism is Church-centered and specifically seeks the furtherance of catholicity. What is meant thereby is a progressive demonstration of the everywhereness of the Church.[109]

Perhaps, like the Roman Catholic missionary orders, both the cooperating and the independent Protestant agencies and missionaries can one day be induced to practice a greater partnership in obedience for the advance and renewal of the Church. Indeed, ever since the days of Zinzendorf and the adventuresome Moravian missionaries, Protestants have had their equivalents of the Roman missionary orders; entire denominations or faith missions have assigned themselves the missionary task. Not often, however, has it happened, as once in Greeland with the Moravians, that when a mission project was completed it was turned over to the Church. And while today it has been happening in all parts of Asia and Africa that so-called mission fields have become churches, and so-called mission properties owned by the parent church have been surrendered to the new indigenous church, the decision has frequently been prompted

---

[108] Joseph Schmidlin, *Catholic Mission History*. Techny, Ill.: Society of the Divine Word, 1933. Passim.

[109] Harald Kruska, "Zum katholischen Missionsdenken der Genenwart," *EMZ*, Maerz 1953, pp. 33-44. First published in that indispensible Protestant scrutiny of Roman Catholicism, *Materialdienst des Konfessionskundlichen Instituts* (Bensheim, nr. Heidelberg), 1953, No. 2.

by expediency and the transaction accomplished within denominational limitations.[110]

To what extent a new devotion to the wholeness of the Church may be induced among those who are called and sent forth to mission remains to be seen. The conditioning of generations and centuries here needs to be modified so as to awaken a larger understanding of the vocation of the missionary. This holds for ordained ministers and also for commissioned lay workers. Ever since the often-justified protests of left wing and other Protestants against the state churches in Europe, a protest that bore its greatest fruit in America, there has been a generally narrow and subjectivist criticism of what Europeans now call the folk church. Yet today, in keeping with the outlook of the ecumenical movement, the folk church is being understood more and more in missionary terms. Just as in Asia or Africa, so in Saxony or Sweden the gospel is here for all people. The Reformation heritage, which was more concerned for the true catholicity of the Church than later pietism and rationalism, reminds all Protestants "it is the Word and Sacraments that constitute the Church of Jesus Christ."[111] As the representatives of the cooperating North American churches have been grappling with "the nature of the unity we seek," so also must those who are called and sent as missionaries be steeped in the subject.[112] This is an exercise in the obedience of faith, and it forces us to Him who alone can deliver us from these frustrations of our own making.

B. Christ Frees and Unites for Service all those who genuinely seek deliverance from human willfulness in the doing of His work. He does this

---

[110] "The United Lutheran Church in America has turned over property valued at more that three million dollars to the Andhra Evangelical Lutheran Church at Guntur, India. [Included are] eight hospitals, a college, five high schools and training schools, 800 elementary schools. At the same time the United Lutherans are handing over 2,000 churches, chapels and other buildings. The president of the Andhra Church, Dr. G. Devasahayam, has praised the ULCA for 'inaugurating this new era of partnership.' The Andhra Church has 2,300 congregations and 250,000 members in five synods. It was begun as a mission in 1842." *Ecumenical Press Service*, No. 17, May 2, 1958, p. 4. For the life story of C. F. Heyer, who began the work in Guntur in 1842, see E. Theodore Bachmann, *They Called Him Father*. Phila.: Muhlenberg, 1942. The current transaction was carried out by Dr. Earl S. Erb, Executive Secretary of the ULCA's Foreign Board; present also was the Board's Candidate Secretary, the Rev. Frederick Neudoerffer.

[111] Wingren, op. cit., *Proceedings*, LWF, Hannover, 1952, p. 75. See footnote 81.

[112] W. A. Visser't Hooft, "The Ground of Our Unity," *The Nature of the Unity We Seek*, pp. 121 ff. See footnote 86.

by calling us, by giving us a vocation. The specific vocations of which the New Testament speaks are never considered as private affairs, but always as part of the overall call to the people of God. In a remarkable way the early Christians were reminded of this when they were pointedly admonished: "Therefore, holy brethren, who share in a heavenly call, consider Jesus, the apostle and high priest of our confession."[113]

With great penetration the World Council of Churches' general secretary, Visser't Hooft, told the Oberlin Conference last September: "We are not called to construct laboriously our unity out of a great many fragments which do not seem to fit together…What we are called to do is to manifest what is inherent in our common call, to liberate the Church of God from the man-made prisons in which we have sought to capture it."[114] But more than that, we are called to join in that mission of which Jesus Christ is the apostle and pioneer. Just as there is only one Church so there is only one call and one mission; and the mission refers to the total task of the Church.[115] Thus the missionary is a key figure, and his special vocation is one of vast concern not only to the Church but also to himself. Let us consider this personal aspect along lines sketched by the experienced director of the Basel Mission Society, the late Karl Hartenstein.[116]

The service of these called into the missionary task of the Church is founded not in enthusiasm for people far away, nor for a romanticized notion of service. It rests not on sympathy for "the poor heathen who sit in spiritual darkness," nor on the euphoristic desire to "do something for Jesus," If we have no deeper understanding of the missionary vocation than this, "we would never be in a position to persevere against the temptations and loneliness, perhaps on a doomed outpost or among great disappointments under the power of paganism."[117]

The true missionary vocation is quite different from this. It is, says Hartenstein, "a deed and intervention of God… a judgment of God which comes to a person from without and which, empowered by the inward testimony of the Holy Spirit, he accepts from within."[118] Consider this inner acceptance further. Here the same conditions hold as for our being called to salvation in Jesus Christ. For it is clear, as Luther put it, that "I

---

113   Hebrews 3:1. RSV.
114   Visser't Hooft, loc. cit., pp. 122-123.
115   Ibid., p. 124.
116   The following paragraphs summarize Karl Hartenstein's concept of the missionary office. EMZ, December 1954, pp. 169-178. See footnote 88.
117   Ibid., p. 175.
118   Ibid.

cannot by my own reason or strength believe in Jesus Christ my Lord or come to Him, but the Holy Spirit has called me through the Gospel." Vocation therefore is not simply the obedience to let oneself be sent somewhere by a mission board, even though it is important for the good order of the Church that a person be properly called. Actually, we need an inner certainty, a personal conviction that God is saying to me: I send you!

This personal conviction is reached by different persons in different ways and is hard to put in words. Yet it has a common denominator which may be described like this: The secret of my vocation to be a missionary is that I, as a sinner condemned to death, permit myself to be served by Jesus Christ; and in my being served by Him, He sends me into His service. All genuine service is thus rooted in the personal encounter of my life with the Lord Christ; and out of this encounter there arises the conviction that He has called me; and that in this calling He has forgiven my sin and taken away my guilt; and that henceforth it is He who guides and takes care of my life.

All who have been called in this special way should share the common understanding that they have become objects of God's action, Jesus Christ has taken hold of them. Therefore they can raise their voice in praise, saying: I have experienced mercy. This intervention of God into the life of the believer takes on the character of service. This is especially true in the case of the missionary. To him then comes the simple assurance: I am on the way He wants me to take, and now it is a matter of remaining faithful in my calling. [119]

If this is the vocation of the missionary as seen from within, then it also has definite features when seen from without. This outward side is no less divine in its implications than the inward side. For it is on this outward side that the Church checks and double checks the special vocation. While a candidate may with inmost conviction insist that "the Lord of the Church sends me," this very insistence presupposes that the Church also has something to say about his being sent forth. For the Church has been entrusted with the office of the missionary, and the missionary becomes the holder of an office for which the Church bears responsibility. Also the Word, through which God calls the missionary, has been placed in the Church's keeping; and the Holy Spirit uses this Word in the calling of the missionary and of all others who are to do God's work.

The Church thus has both the right and the duty to test and examine the qualifications and fitness of the prospective missionary. This

---

[119]   Ibid., p. 176.

is all in line with the Church's faithfulness in discharging its trust toward God. This must be done conscientiously even though, on occasion, the Church must decide against the qualifications of a prospective missionary. On his part, the prospect must reckon with the fact that at times God may alter the course and lead him into other paths of service. Such experience should not shatter the prospect's faith. Rather, let him remember the words of his Lord: "You have not chosen me, but I have chosen you, and appointed you that you should go and bear fruit, and that your fruit should abide."[120]

In concluding his interpretation of this special vocation, Hartenstein underscores St. Paul's conviction that the missionary is an ambassador for Christ, and that he carries out his assignment in "existential obedience." In this regard the missionary must be at least three things: a person of faith, a person of complete dedication, and a person of readiness to suffer for his vocation. Not simply by good example will he bring the gospel, nor by the most gifted rhetoric. Rather, his effectiveness as a missionary depends entirely on God's reconciling grace and redeeming action in Christ. [121]

Again, therefore, we recall that Christ frees and unites for service especially those who are called as missionaries. To see how He does this requires attentiveness not only to His calling but also to what is happening both in the Church and in the world. As the pattern and practice of the Christian world mission had been changing from paternalism to partnership, so the missionary vocation has been seeking and finding new forms of expression.

While this discovery of fresh usefulness belongs to other presentations [on "The teaching mission in the light of the ecumenical movement," on "The role of the missionary today," and on "Functional services in relation to the central task of evangelism"], we need here simply note that in this new day missionaries are wanted in new ways. When, for example, the Asia Council on Ecumenical Mission (ACEM) was formed in 1955 in Hongkong, its declared principle was this:

> We believe that the missionary task of the Church is the responsibility of the entire Church, the whole body of Christ. There are, therefore, in reality no sending churches as applied to the 'older Churches' and no receiving churches as applied to the 'younger Churches.' Both 'older' and 'younger' are sent and both have received. It is the Lord who has commissioned and sent them ... This

---

[120] Ibid., pp. 176-177. (John 15:16)
[121] Ibid., pp. 178-179.

implies a deeper sharing of resources in men and money, from all Christian agencies, and employing them in the most effective way to win the goal Christ has set before us. This means the participation of all together in the total task. [122]

The aim of this announced principle underlying the ACEM is to "shift the center of gravity in Christian mission from just one section of the world-wide church to the Church of Christ in every land," The label of Western imperialism would thus be removed and "the missionary enterprise would then become demonstrably ecumenical. [123] Thanks to the effective liaison of Rajah Manikam as East Asia Secretary of the IMC-WCC and also of others, "there is arising among the churches of Asia a strong sense of missionary responsibility . . . marked by a deep desire [to] exchange church workers and to internationalize the personnel working among the churches." [124]

The emphasis in the Asian churches is not on a divisive sectionalism but, as the IMC's president, John A. Mackay, asserted, on a practicable regionalism.[125] Therefore the sending of missionaries is by no means ruled out. As the need for more highly specialized missionary assistance is increasing, so the importance of understanding the missionary vocation in timely perspective is pressing. As in Antioch of old, Western churches must be ready to release some of their ablest workers for at least temporary duty in sister churches in Asia, Africa, and elsewhere. That this process has already begun and been found acceptable in such varied lines as journalism, agriculture, welfare, and especially theological education, speaks well for the future. [126]

As missionaries from the West continue to come to the East at the request of the churches there, so the brethren in the East must be

---

[122] *The Common Evangelistic Task*, Prapat Report, p. 87. See footnote 53.
[123] Bishop Enrique Sobrepena of the Philippines, Chairman of the Prapat Conf. Ibid., p. 93.
[124] Ibid., p. 5. Cp. U Kyaw Than, "The Christian Mission in Asia Today," *IRM*, April 1958, pp. 160-161.
[125] *Prapat Report*, p. 92.
[126] E.g., the sending of Dr. Roland Wolsey, professor of Journalism at Syracuse University, N, Y, to teach this subject at Hislop College in India; he was succeeded in this task by the Rev. William E. Dudds, who in turn is now (1958) being succeeded by the Indian, J. Victor Koilpillai, until recently editor of *The Guardian*. In time this should helpfully influence the development of an indigenous Christian journalism.

given opportunity to send missionaries to the churches in the West. To us Western Christians this would be a salutary exchange. Christian brethren among us from another part of the world would have something vital to share, and could also help us in the struggle against compromising the Christian witness with an all-pervasive secularism.

In such two-way missionary exchange lies an essential application of the Church's apostolate. For its purpose is to make the spread of the Gospel more effective and to free the Christian faith as much as possible from man-made and culturally-conditioned handicaps. Only in this way, paradoxical though it appears, can the rootage of the Gospel and the life of the Church become wholesomely indigenous. Just as the missionary is one who experiences in his own person this simultaneous identification and otherness, so he is also the indispensible agent in stimulating both the unity and the mission of the ecumenical Church. It takes many Manikams and many Newbigins to blaze this new missionary trail into the believing and doing of Christians everywhere.

Do we need to be reminded that amid the world's booming harvest of babies the number of Christians is increasing only one-third as fast? In Manikam's oft-repeated play on words there is the disturbing fact that "the birth rate is moving ever farther ahead of the re-birth rate."[127] For majority-minded Western Christians the motive for missionary vocation may be prodded by reflections on "The Common Evangelistic Task" which the Philippine chairman, Bishop Enrique Sobrepena, addressed to his fellow East Asian conferees last spring at Prapat, Indonesia. He declared:

> The summons to us is urgent … The forces in Asia arrayed against the gospel of love and righteousness are many and mighty while we who here carry the banner of Christ are few and scattered. We must consolidate our forces and our gains… And if we do so in common obedience to Christ, our Lord, then we are set to go forward under his banner. [128]

To the congregations that stand atoll-like in a vast sea of unknowing, the Lord of the Church breathes the Spirit of His confidence.

---

[127] Bishop Manikam's address, Third Assembly, Lutheran World Federation, Monday, August 19, 1957. News Release, LWF-23, The substance of this, and some of Manikam's other characteristic utterances, appear in his article, "A New Era in the World Mission of the Church," *National Christian Council Review*, (Nagpur, India), May 1958, pp. 207-216.

[128] *Prapat Report*, p. 94,

"Fear not, little flock, for it is your Father's good pleasure to give you the kingdom." To which He adds this often-overlooked beatitude. "Blessed are those servants whom the master finds awake when he comes."[129]

Finally, Christ frees and unites for service those whom He has called as His missionaries in time past, those whom He has called in our time, and those who are still to answer His call and carry forward His mission to final fruition. In Him the mission of the Church militant already partakes of the joy of the Church triumphant. For us today the vocation of missionary may be epitomized in the life of one who risked and won where others before him had failed.[130] It is Ludwig Nommensen, that pioneer of the Rhenish Mission, on the scene of whose labors of a century ago the Prapat Conference met. Might he have felt his heart strangely warmed if he could have slipped in among the representatives of the Asian churches? What might he have sensed as he heard how the vocation of the missionary was blended into the mission of the Church in the simple welcome extended precisely at Prapat by the leader of the Batak Church. The words of the Ephorus rang like a doxology as he confessed:

> It is a great miracle that we are able to meet here. In the ancient days our forefathers did not permit any foreigner to enter into our country; it was especially prohibited that any outsider should visit, or even see, Lake Toba, because the land and the lake were regarded as holy.

> But at the present time it is the greatest joy to us to have foreign guests visit the lake and have a meeting in our land as brothers ...

> [In] the Communion of the Holy Spirit ... we have the same faith, the same hope, the same love. We believe that this is not the result of man's work.

> This Communion of the Holy Spirit is the greatest gift of God that man can receive. It crosses all borders ... of nations and lands ... of human relations ... friendships ... communities and families.

> It is the kind of Communion which makes us conscious of the whole world; we realize through it the unity of all men before God ...

---

[129] Luke 12:32, 37.
[130] Johannes Warneck, *50 Jahre Batakmission*. Berlin: Warneck, n.d. Passim.

We know that our community, the community of the Church, is here to serve the world. We know that it is to be a bright and shining light in every place. As in the human body, its true gracefulness lies not in the face but in the health of the whole body, so we believe also that this is true of our relations as Churches to one another and our relation as Churches to the whole society.

We therefore pray that ... God's will may be done on earth as in heaven. His kingdom corne! Amen. [131]

---

[131] *Prapat Report*, pp. 154-155.

A Critique of "The Vocation of the Missionary"

J. L. Dunstan
Andover-Newton Theological Seminary
Newton Center, Massachusetts

This paper is a most able exposition of the missionary vocation, and it is scarcely fitting that anyone should undertake to levy criticism against it. Instead one needs to read with care and learn from its paragraphs, for there is much in it that stabs the mind awake. But if we must not criticize we can note one or two points that deserve serious consideration.

The missionary vocation is described in four sections: its contemporary breadth, its historical depth, its theological content, and its significance for the unity of the Church. The missionary must live and work in the world as it is now; he comes out of the Church as it is now in all its dividedness; and he must face the forces which now move through men and their societies. Much more could be said about this than is in the paper, but the pressure of time placed serious limitations upon the treatment. It would be interesting to ask about the role of the missionary who comes from the West and thus is a child of the cultural condition of that part of the world, and of the role of the missionary who comes from an Asian land where the search for new life has begun in excitement and hope. Both are servants of the Church and yet they are different servants working in different human settings. Once a question like this is posed a multitude of ramifications appear. The very complexity of the contemporary world affects the missionary, and the relationship between the man and his environment is never static.

The historical depth of the missionary vocation is portrayed through two brief biographies: Ziegenbalg and Manikam. Both of them had (have) within themselves the vocation of the Church, and were (are) living symbols of the world mission. Both felt the demand of God upon their lives and answered that demand by obedience; both of them faced the problems and needs of their respective positions; and both of them worked out answers to those problems and needs in ways which were to them the manner of their obedience. Thus the depth of God's continuing activity among men came alive in them.

The third and fourth sections of the paper carry the weight of the discussion. Out of those two sections two issues emerge, among others, which deserve the most careful consideration. First, there is the fact that the missionary is an officer of the Christian Church, selected, supported and directed by the Church, and at the same time an ambassador of Jesus Christ, picked out and sent by Him. These two relationships which the missionary has are not the same, nor are the alternate sides of the same coin. The early missionaries of the modern era went out as ambassadors of Christ; the Church had little interest in them or their work. Yet it is equally clear that they were Church men who heard their call because of their place in the Church and whose work brought new life to that institution.

Like a pendulum the missionary vocation swings between the two points. This, however, raises the question of the relation between the Church and the Kingdom of God; and here another swinging between two extremes appears. "For the missionary in his vocation today it is necessary to know where his task is set... he knows that the Kingdom of God is a reality that has to do with God's purpose and plan... he knows that the Church is the means God uses to achieve His purpose... he knows that the mission of the Church is derived from God." In this list of truths the missionary must know there are variables, elements which change through the years and under varied circumstances. Surely one of the tasks devolving upon the missionary in his vocation is that of finding how these variables mingle for him.

This same issue appears in the discussion of the difference between the missionary enterprise of the established churches and the enterprises launched by the free agencies or the sects; and it appears again in the resume of the problem created for the missionaries enlisted, trained and sent out by the mission boards of the Continent when circumstances forced them to return home and they found that the Church did not recognize them or assume any responsibility for them. The Church, the divinely-chosen missionary and the Kingdom of God are all involved in both discussions.

The other issue is that of the relation between the Christian missionary and the resurgent non-Christian religions. The treatment accorded this theme by the paper is cursory, as it had to be if time were to be respected, let again, there are suggestions that warrant careful discussion. Note is made of the continued lack of interest shown by missionaries in the non-Christian religions. In the early years of the modern enterprise such was not the case and today the situation is changing, but in between all was subsumed under heathendom. Now serious efforts are being made to understand other religions. But "the deepest danger (in this) may lie not in the several religions overwhelming the Christian faith but in the Church itself being tempted to pose as a religion." Yet the missionary is a religious man even as the Buddhist is a religious man, and the Christian Church is a religious institution even as is an Hongwanji temple, and the difference between them is not easily settled. So that within the missionary vocation there must be an acute awareness, not alone of his responsibility toward men of other faiths, but also of what God is doing to and for those men through other agencies than missions.

These comments have but touched a few points that were raised by the paper. An adequate critique would require a paper of equal length to the original.

Functional Services In Relation To The Central Task Of Evangelism

Herbert C. Jackson
Southern Baptist Theological Seminary
Louisville, Kentucky

For the foreign missionary task, functional services are symbolic of the understanding of God and man which underlie the Christian faith. These functional services are therefore to be viewed not as designed for effecting socio-economic transformations, nor even for alleviating the condition of individual people, but as demonstrations to "win" non-Christian peoples to the God and the faith which have produced the circumstances of said functional services. In other words, they are to be viewed not as incidentally but as fundamentally and objectively related to evangelism. In yet other words, functional services are the modern counterpart of the "signs" in the sense that the Gospel according to John uses the term, especially in 20:30. This is not to imply, on one hand, that missionaries are to perform the various functional services as mere means to an end "bait," without true, disinterested Christian love and compassion; nor, on the other hand, does it imply that those who become Christians out of other backgrounds are to have overt service as their understanding of Christianity. We are aware of the fact that almost without exception when men followed Jesus for the sake of the miracle of physical bread, for the sake of the signs themselves, He withdrew from them;

> Jesus answered them, 'Truly, truly, I say to you, you seek me, not because you saw signs, but because you ate your fill of the loaves. Do not labor for the food which perishes, but for the food which endures to eternal life, which the Son of man will give to you; for on him has God the Father set his seal.' Then they said to him, 'What must we do, to be doing the work of God?' Jesus answered them,

'This is the work of God, that you believe in him whom he has sent.'[1]

In this opening paragraph there is contained the essence of the writer's position -- for our day, at any rate. One cannot go to the Orient, it is true, without being constrained by the compassion of Christ to do something to alleviate the hunger, general poverty, ignorance and degradation of the teeming millions. It is thus that Pierce Beaver, in a treatise that is so comprehensive and so correct as to make this paper really superfluous,[2] can state of the early Protestant missionaries:

> There was little or no attempt to give a theological explanation for such activity, for it clearly appeared to be Christian duty ... Ambassadors of Christ, looking at needy humanity through the eyes of Christ, reaching out hands of compassion, knowing that inasmuch as they did it unto these least ones they were doing it unto Him their Lord. [3]

Without trying to ascertain the precise degree of credit and/or responsibility for the situation of Christian missions, on one hand, and on the other hand, of the general penetration of Western civilization and its outlook, it may be said that we are only too keenly conscious that we live in an era of "total revolution." Untold thought and attention have been given and volumes written on what this means for Christian missions, all, to the writer's knowledge, without really essaying what this revolutionary situation really should mean for the functional services of Christianity. Some generalizations have been made, such as that contained in the Report of the Methodist Conference Commission to Consider "The Missionary Obligation of the Church," which states that:

> The Christian knows that it is not only technological means that are required to make the world a fit place for the human family, but that qualities of mind and spirit are necessary ... World hunger is not only a material problem but a moral and spiritual one, and it may well be that, in the revolution of our time, God is recalling His Church from a false divorce of the spiritual from the material, and that it is His will that His people should show the

---

1   John 6:26-29 (RSV).
2   R. Pierce Beaver, *Toward a More Effective Ministry Through Missionary Institutions* (New York: Division of Foreign Missions of the National Council of the Churches of Christ in the U.S.A., 1953).
3   Ibid., p. 5.

way toward a true brotherhood among men such as the modern revolutionary spirit strives after. [4]

The Division of Foreign Missions of the N.C.C. in 1952 questioned whether institutions are ministering to real needs in the present revolutionary situation.[5]

Actually, the problem of the relationship of "functional services" to the central task of evangelism is universally recognized and universally unresolved. Typical of many indications of this from missionary statesmen both in this country and Europe are the following. Dr. Visser't Hooft says:

> The important issue that needs clarification in this connection seems to me to be whether Diakonia has only a secondary place with regard to Martyria, or whether Diakonia has its own dignity. My own feeling is that on the basis of important passages of the New Testament, and very notably of Matthew 25, we must say that Diakonia is not merely an aid to Martyria, but rather a fundamental expression of the Christian faith. The practical problem therefore becomes how Diakonia and Martyria may be constructively related to each other.[6]

The Reverend V.E.W. Hayward, Foreign Secretary of the Baptist Missionary Society in England, indicates that:

> We would all agree that the institutional work of the missionary enterprise is auxiliary to the Church's central task of proclaiming the Gospel and building up vigorous missionary-minded churches. It is indeed a very necessary adjunct. The problem is to keep it from fulfilling a major, rather than a minor, role. [7]

Dr. E. Jansen Schoonhoven, Principal of the Netherlands Reformed Church's Missionary Academy at Oegstgeest, speaks of the grappling with the problem in his country:

> The development of thinking in missionary circles in our country may be illustrated by the example of the

---

[4]   *The Report of the Methodist Conference Commission to Consider "The Missionary Obligation of the Church"* (London: The Epworth Press, 1955), pp. 27-28.
[5]   Referred to in Beaver, op. cit., p. 32.
[6]   Letter to the writer, dated Feb. 3, 1958.
[7]   Letter dated March 11, 1958.

mission of the "Gereformeerde Kerken in Nederland." This denomination, that in 1886 left the Netherlands Reformed Church and followed a stricter Calvinistic line, has a very important missionary work in Indonesia. They distinguish between "hoofddienst" (main service) and "hulpdiensten" (auxiliary services). To the first belonged evangelism and upbuilding of the Church, to the second, medical, educational and other activities. In our mission this distinction was not accepted, but the relation between the last-mentioned activities and evangelism remained a problem that did not find a satisfying answer.

After the war the distinction between main service and auxiliary services has been abandoned by the mission of the "Gereformeerde Kerken." At present they conceive of the relation by the figure of a circle that is divided into sectors: the evangelistic and church work forms an inner circle that is surrounded by the sectors of medical work, educational work, etc.

In our mission the conception of Prof. J. C. Hoekendijk of the threefold witness by kerygma, koinonia and diakonia (see his article on "The Call to Evangelism" in the *International Review of Missions*, April, 1950) has found much response. [8]

"Tomorrow is Born Today," as the title of the *Annual Report of the S.P.G.* for 1955 so aptly puts it:

> This title is one to provoke thought and to challenge response... The inheritance into which we enter has been molded by the character of the past, and what we make of it now will be the raw material upon which our successors will have to work... The use or misuse of our stewardship will leave its mark upon the future direction of the missionary enterprise. [9]

The writer is keenly conscious of his lack of qualifications to give any full answer. But as Dr. George W. Carpenter of the I.M.C. says:

---

[8]   Letter dated March 13, 1958.

[9]   Dewi Morgan, *Tomorrow Is Born Today* (London: The Society for the Propagation of the Gospel, 1956), p. 2.

Often the questions we are wrestling with lie on the frontiers between past experience and emergent new situations. As each one of us tries to think creatively and to respond to the practical issues that call for decision day by day, the new pattern gradually takes form.[10]

In part it is hoped that this paper will be a contribution to the cumulative insights forming the new pattern, and in part that it will "jump the gap" more radically than can be true of day-by-day decisions. It is hoped that a basic but radical principle may be established so that today we may lay the proper foundation for the "tomorrow" that is currently being born. This principle declares that there must be two angles for the look at functional services. For the missionary endeavor, functional services are "signs," symbolic of the Christian apprehension of existence, 'that (they) may believe that Jesus is the Christ, the Son of God, and that believing (they) may have life in His name." And in contradistinction, to those who do believe, there is an outworking of the faith that is in them, represented in functional services which evolve as concern for the total life and well-being of men in their cultural milieu, and an expression of functional services that will reflect the spirit of Christ in that environment.

I. DEFINITIONS

This statement of dual principle requires some definition of evangelism, functional services, institutionalism, and a term that is coming much to the fore in Protestant circles but which is quite unfamiliar to left wing groups such as the denomination to which I belong, namely, apostolate.

A. Evangelism. At Prapat, "evangelism was recognized as more important even than autonomy," according to James K. Mathews. [11] Against the backdrop of almost utter inertia concerning evangelistic responsibility among mission field churches and of nearly half a century of struggle, often bitter, by the so-called younger churches for autonomy from the older churches, this is startling and would of itself be reason for investigating the meaning and character of this concern for evangelism. Professor Hoekendijk calls attention to the fact that the call to evangelism in our day finds us unprepared, and he says that the ecumenical enquiry on evangelism begins by confessing that "we do not know." He declares that we need a new vision of evangelism which is "a disentanglement of all

---

10   Letter dated Feb. 18, 1958.
11   Carbon copy of an address, "What Does 'Partnership in Obedience' Mean?"

secular complexes and secret ideologies, a recovery in short, of the Biblical sense of evangelism."[12] That is to say, the understanding of evangelism must be from the point of view of the Christian faith and the theology of missions. [13]

> God acts in His world. That is where we begin.. On this view, man does not take the center of the stage in history … God wills to act for all mankind so that His redeeming love may be known by all … He redeems us from ourselves -- from our weakness, our failings, our enmity to Him, our pride and our false securities … The Old Israel failed. They had not seen themselves as chosen to suffer that others might be redeemed, but had made their calling the reason for a false, exclusive nationalism ….

> The new note that Jesus struck when He took over from John the Baptist was that the announcement of the coming of God's Kingdom, and the call to repentance because it was here, made good news to be accepted with joy. From now on the coming of the Kingdom was seen as something more than a purge of the Old Israel and of the world that Israel had been called to serve; more than putting down of evil and enthroning good. Now the mighty hand of God was stretched out in power to deliver His people from sin and trouble and distress. That hand of God which had been mighty in the Creation, which was always bringing something new to pass, was now remaking His people … This is the New Israel. Through obedience to God's call, which inevitably means suffering, it is able to go on with the work of showing God to men and of winning them for Him. [14]

Upon such foundation we can enunciate the Church of Scotland's definition of evangelism:

> By evangelism is meant the kind of attitude and impact characteristic of the witnessing Christian community as such and not the verbal message given by a particular class of people employed for this purpose. It means an emphasis on the congregation as the agency in evangelism:

---

[12] J. C. Hoekendijk, "The Call to Evangelism," *IRM*, Vol. 39, p. 167.
[13] *Report of the Foreign Mission Committee for 1951*, The Church of Scotland, p 9.
[14] *Report of the Methodist Commission*, op. cit., pp. 15-17.

a community of persons rooted in the Word of God, worshipping congregations in which human worth and mutual responsibility are acknowledged and realized and from which love goes out in the work of service to the neighborhood.[15]

In contrast there has been "a modern habit of judging Christianity by the effect that it has had upon the social order,"[16] so that the New Israel has made its calling the reason for a false and exclusive idealism (of human welfare). "Wholeness" under these circumstances is too often defined (subconsciously at least) as physical well-being and prosperity, as social and political democracy. This is most fallacious, but it is that which gives ground for the erroneous hyper-emphasis upon functional services. Hoekendijk shows that throughout the Bible evangelization is seen as possible only in a messianic context, that it is accomplished only by God, and that its objective is found in God rather than man.[17] Dr. Hoekendijk states that two obvious consequences of this view of evangelism have only very seldom been drawn:

> The first is that the Messiah (i.e. the Christ) is the subject of evangelism…The second consequence is that the aim of evangelism can be nothing less than what Israel expected the Messiah to do, i.e. He will establish the shalom. And shalom is much more than personal salvation. It is at once peace, integrity, community, harmony and justice.[18]

Thus evangelism is a relationship and a character of existence, with mundane affairs utterly subsidiary if not irrelevant. (This is at once the reason Communism can charge Christianity with being "the opiate of the people" and the reason dynamic Christianity can exist under a Communist regime.) Hoekendijk states that "this messianic conception of evangelism means a total rejection of two very well-known methods."[19] The first of these is the rejection of propaganda, however subtle. "It is not difficult to make this distinction in theory. It is, however, one of our most painful and most frequent experiences that evangelism is almost always concealed in a form of propaganda."[20] The second rejection would be of the

---

[15] Report of the F.M. Committee, Church of Scotland, op. cit., p.13 of the Report for 1951.
[16] Report of the Methodist Commission, op. cit., p. 18.
[17] Hoekendijk, op. cit., pp. 167-8.
[18] Ibid., p. 168.
[19] Ibid., p. 169.
[20] Loc. cit.

"stubborn tradition in our midst which interprets the aim of evangelism as the planting of the Church (or even the extension of the Church)."[21] There is much to support the definition of evangelism as the planting of the Church, but in our day when such hyper-emphasis is placed at this point Hoekendijk's stringent warning needs consideration: "Evangelism and churchification are not identical, and very often they are each other's bitterest enemies."[22]

This understanding of evangelism takes the three forms of expression to which reference has already been made: the kerygma (shalom proclaimed), koinonia (shalom lived out in mutual communion and fellowship), and diakonia (shalom demonstrated in humble service). [23]In this three-fold expression the koinonia is both the primary kerygmatic unit and the primary diakonic unit. Kerygmatic as the place were the shalom is really made present, diadonic because it has no other relation to the outside world than that of humble service :

> We may call it the level of the laboratory, the diakonia of a little group, living in a concrete situation, and serving each other and their environment by reforming the structure of a segment of society ... (Thus) an object lesson is given of what shalom should be. [24]

One has here a concept of evangelism which can give fuller expression to what has been termed "the spiritual revolution of today (which is) as enthralling as the material."[25] But in the end, the Word must be spoken and heard, as Mathews rightly insists, recalling Luther's statement that "Faith is an accoustical affair,"[26] "Faith comes from what is heard and what is heard comes by the preaching of Christ (kerygma)," This is the conclusion to which the Policy Group of the Foreign Mission Committee of the Church of Scotland came:

> The deepest need of the Church and Mission is not better organization or training or self-support, but a firmer apprehension of the Gospel as a glorious fact ... The Policy Group therefore would put as the primary emphasis the

---

[21]   Ibid., p. 170.
[22]   Ibid., p. 171.
[23]   Loc., cit.
[24]   Ibid., p. 175.
[25]   Morgan, op. cit., p. 3.
[26]   Quoted by Mathews, op. cit., p. 9.

possession of great and good news which it is our privilege and duty to share. [27]

This view of evangelism is seen to be in diametrical opposition to that of the Laymen's Foreign Missions Enquiry, whose conclusions have been stated in summary as that "ministry to the secular needs of men in the spirit of Christ is evangelism,"[28] It is seen, on the other hand, to issue in the "spontaneous expansion" of which Roland Allen (*The Spontaneous Expansion of the Church*) and Donald McGavran (*The Bridges of God*) speak. Thus "confronting the world with Christ is evangelism -- but only if the stress is upon Christ rather than upon the amenities that follow from being "in Christ," and only if in such confrontation there is a continual primary communication of the awareness that real confrontation means decision.

B. Functional Services. The Reformers insisted that the "ministry of the Word" and the "ministry of the sacrament" are the indispensable marks of the Church and that they should never be separated, James Mathews says:

> There is a certain sacramental character about Christian life and service. They do not stand in their own right. Rather they point to a reality beyond themselves which must finally be made clear and specific in the Word of Truth, which is the Gospel. [29]

> Deeds of Christian love are but partial witness if they do not point to the source of that love. (This) often demands selfless, endless service and suffering and sacrifice... But then most truly the service points to what great things God has done in Jesus Christ. So in the most unexpected quarters are to be found the answers to man's deepest search for meaning. [30]

Such sacrament of life and service should mark the Church wherever it be found and regardless of how recent may have been its own particular historical origin. Even in this day of ecumenicity and of such extensive interchurch aid it is necessary to point out that it is difficult to retain the sacramental quality and keep aid or services from being largely

---

[27] *Report of the Foreign Mission Committee for 1951*, Church of Scotland, p. 9.

[28] Beaver, op. cit., p, 28.

[29] James K. Mathews, "*One Lord Over All -- Let Us Proclaim Him,*" unpublished address, p. 4 of carbon copy.

[30] Ibid., p. 8 f.

social in character when one gets beyond the immediate environment. This is because, as Beaver points out in another study, diakonia proves the genuineness of koinonia and koinonia is not fully present except in directly experienced fellowship. [31]

The concern here however is with the role of functional services in the missionary endeavor. The Dutch Missionary Council's Study Committee on the Biblical Foundations of Foreign Missions declares:

> The task of missions is determined by its commission, and by its goal. The missionary commission speaks of Christ's royal authority, which is to be proclaimed all over the world, and which is to be realized in the faithful obedience of those who hear the Gospel.[32]

The Report goes on to comment that in modern Protestant missions very often no attention is paid to the goal but only to the way to the goal. [33] My concern is to call for a radical departure from emphasis upon functional services as such to a stress upon them as the sacramental signs, performed in the midst of a people who know not the God of our Lord Jesus Christ, that seeing evidence of what it means to be "in Him" they too will be drawn to commitment to Christ as Lord. The Dutch Report poses the same concern, asking, "Are missions really, in all these activities, signs of the Kingdom of God, or do they rather strive after the ideals of humanity?"[34] Despite all the amazing accomplishments of the services, the Dutch Report presses as "most important" the recognition that "life is restored, renewed, freed from devils not by modern technics and science ... but by the Crucified and Risen Lord, the source of all renewal. "[35]

When functional services are so defined for missions, not only is there the first and only real possibility of keeping services from assuming a major role and becoming ends in themselves, but only thus can they be given up or relegated to a less primary role when other agencies, as governments, take them over or the need and opportunity to render the Christian sacrament in a given form ceases to exist. That we are already on the road to this understanding of functional services in missions may be

---

[31] R. Pierce Beaver, *The Christian World Mission: A Reconsideration* (Calcutta: Baptist Mission Press, 1957), p. 35.

[32] Report of the Dutch Missionary Council's Study Committee on "The Biblical Foundations of Foreign Missions," mimeographed copy, p. 5.

[33] Ibid., p. 5.

[34] Ibid., p, 10.

[35] Loc. cit.

seen, at least in theory, in the statement on "The Christian Mission in This Hour" presented to and received by the Ghana Assembly:

> The Christian world mission is Christ's, not ours. Prior to all our efforts and activities, prior to all our gifts of service and devotion, God sent His Son into the world.... We have seen this to be the only true motive of Christian mission and the only standard by which the spirit, method and modes of Christian missionary organization must be judged. We believe it is urgent that this word of judgment and mercy should be given full freedom to cleanse and redeem our present activities, lest our human pride in our activities hinder the free course of God's mission in the world. [36]

Only thus can be resolved the paradox of which the Church of Scotland's Foreign Mission Committee spoke in 1954: the paradox that although man's material needs must be met his ultimate needs are not material, and moreover, the more his material needs are met the more he becomes "a poor man" with reference to his ultimate needs.

C. Institutionalism. Frequently the writer has had questions raised about any tendency to equate functional services with institutionalism. Yet it is his experience and observation that there seems to be inherent in man, or at least in the corporate social body, the inevitable institutionalization of function. This is peculiarly evident in Western civilization. To quote Pierce Beaver again:

> *The International Survey of the Young Men's and Young Women's Christian Associations* made a valuable contribution in pointing out that any collective undertaking tends to institutionalize itself; that is, it tends to realize itself in structure and to build itself into an external order of things. The prophets of a movement become the staff of an institution, and its message becomes elaborated into a program. Voluntary effort is trans formed into professional service. [37]

As a consequence, "institutions became as integral to Protestant missions in the 19th and 20th centuries as the Benedictine monastery had

---

[36]   *Report of the F. M. Committee for 1954*, Church of Scotland, p. 28.
[37]   Beaver, *More Effective Ministry*, p. 29.

been to the missionary conquest of Europe."[38] This characteristic was not questioned by mission societies until Edinburgh, but since then an almost complete reversal in attitude took place, until Willingen was ready to give almost wholesale condemnation to the traditional institutional approach.[39] In a direct quotation from the International Survey, attention is called to the fact that "the validity of a movement is measured not by its ability to dispense with institutional features but by its power to command them."[40] Thus the function not only becomes institutionalized but achieves a certain "guaranteed perpetuity." This tendency is powerful even in such services as Christian literature and Bible societies, Sunday School and other functions of religious education, audio-visual programs, rural missions, etc. This runs counter to one of the basic principles recognized and adopted by the Division of Foreign Missions in 1953: "Every one of the functions assumes institutional form as the Church discharges it; but it is the enduring function, not the ephemeral institutional form, which is important."[41]

D. Apostolate. Hoekendijk makes bold to declare that:

> Even theologians -- who have been in the past among the most unconquerable saboteurs of evangelism -- seem to have rediscovered here and there its theological relevance. They realize that they play away the Biblical authenticity of their thinking, if they go on refusing to acknowledge that the Church is set in this world with the sole purpose of carrying the Gospel to the ends of the earth. In some schools of Protestant as well as of Roman Catholic theology, the apostolate tends to become the all-pervading centre of thinking -- a total revolution in theology, with overwhelmingly wide perspectives. [42]

Apostolate recovers for the Church and for foreign missions their true eschatological function and stresses the character of missions as grounded in the "redemptive-historical" past, so that what is proclaimed is the fulfilled work of Christ. When this is done, "life appears in an entirely new and startling perspective. The old aeon is past, everything becomes new."[43] The "moment of fulfillment" is matched, in apostolate,

---

38   Ibid. , p. 6.
39   Norman Goodall (ed.), *Missions Under the Cross* (New York: Friendship Press, 1953), pp. 221-222.
40   Beaver, More Effective Ministry, p. 29.
41   Ibid., p. 44.
42   Hoekendijk, op. cit., p. 162.
43   Report of the Dutch Missionary Council Study Committee, op. cit., p. 3,

by the "moment of expectation," which knows that only in the future will the full truth, meaning, and victory of the Kingdom of God be realized. "One cannot escape this tension between 'already' and 'not yet,' and, what is more, one should not be able to."[44]

> From the recognition that Christ whose coming is expected is the One who has come already, missions derive the courage to fulfill their calling to preach the Gospel to the Gentiles, (and) to measure their task not by the favorability or other wise of circumstances but by the joyful certainty that Christ's power is real ... The recognition that Christ who has come already is still to be expected preserves missions from dealing with a superficial social optimism instead of the Gospel of God's grace, and also from a "comprehensive" approach where the word "comprehensive" is mainly applied to material needs and the message of reconciliation and forgiveness is lost.[45]

Both non-institutionalized services and institutions of all kinds take on an utterly different coloring, with different objectives, emphases and procedures, if the apostolate understanding should be recovered.

II. Historical Resume

The absence of the apostolate awareness in the modern missionary endeavor is well portrayed in the article, "The Meaning and Purpose of the Christian Mission,"[46] by Walter Freytag:

> A study of the modern missionary movement, of the history of missions for the last two hundred years, brings us to a significant observation. None of the waves of missionary enthusiasm and of missionary action which followed one another succeeded in adapting or preserving the full force of the missionary motive as set forth in the Bible. This fact can be seen, for instance, in the conception of the Kingdom of God. [47]

---

[44]   Ibid., p. 4.
[45]   Loc. cit.
[46]   *IRM*, vol. 39, pp. 153-161.
[47]   Ibid., p. 154.

Freytag calls attention to what he terms "four missionary streams which have emerged," each of which "reveals a characteristic contraction of the Kingdom- of-God outlook. [48] First is the Pietistic stream, which contracted the Kingdom of God to a purely spiritualized individualistic-ethical outlook, so that the Kingdom was the sum total of those "saved" out of the world. The second stream stressed the planting of the Church, until this objective supplanted the Kingdom, "Obviously," he observes, "no one taught that the churches must be identical with the Kingdom of God, and yet the idea of the Kingdom of God was so narrowed that it collapsed with the Church" His description of the third stream is so applicable to our situation, and to the topic of this paper, that we shall look at it in full:

> The third stream in missionary motivation, which gained ground earlier and over a wider field in the Anglo-Saxon countries than on the Continent, originated in the blending of the Enlightenment and philanthropy on the one hand with Christianity on the other. Here, men penetrated to the needs of mankind, and outstanding figures emerged who, with bold and practical devotion, wrestled with the misery of slavery, the lack of education, physical suffering and social distress. Here were envisaged, ingathering together all men of goodwill, the great goal and the great possibility of making "the world a better place to live in." And automatically the Kingdom of God became identified with these increasingly improved world conditions. You could call it the idealistic-socio-ethical contraction of the conception of the Kingdom of God. [49]

Freytag's fourth stream is the outlook stemming from the work of such men as Simpson, Grattan Guinness, Franson and others abroad, and from the various premillenialist groups within our country. For this outlook missions is the means of ushering in the End. Here the Kingdom of God was still a great goal to be reached at the cataclysmic close of the Age, and the motive was largely self-centered.

Most devastating of all, as Freytag indicates, was "the one thing from which they (the four streams) have all in common failed to protect themselves: they all strayed into the torrent of the propagation of Western civilization. It is a disturbing thing to contemplate, but it is not surprising. Whether the different schools of thought clung too much or too little to

---

[48] Ibid., p. 155.
[49] Ibid., p. 156.

the world, the same result ensued, that they fell victim to the influences of this world." [50]

The crux of the problem lies in understanding that it is right to render services and to promote concrete action according to the will of God, but always in the sense of being primarily concerned with God's will rather than with human needs. According to the extensive survey conducted preparatory to this paper, the most explicit implementation of this insight has been by the London Missionary Society, which reported as follows:

> Four years ago the directors took the opportunity to overhaul the policy of the Society and spent some time in examining the broad outlines of our modern work. They went on record as saying that "the first and most urgent duty of the Society in the immediate future is to do, or cause to be done, everything that is possible to build up the local churches on the field in such a way that they may more fully manifest the Divine grace within their own life and in the evangelization of their neighborhood and beyond." The report of the directors went on to list the ways in which this duty could be carried out, e.g. by training leaders and providing literature. [51]

Such an approach will avoid the inevitable consequence of viewing functional services as *preparatio evangelicae*, which is that in actuality instead of preparing the way for the Gospel there takes place an infiltration of a culture with some Christian idealism to the extent that the culture is modified but also the lines of distinction become so blurred that it is less, not more, likely that people will be "evangelized" in the sense of being brought under the Lordship of Jesus Christ. Further, mobility, and spontaneity in actual rendering of diakonia are seriously hampered, [52] and in any cut in personnel or funds the central task of evangelism always suffers first and most. [53]

In this regard, integration rather than devolution can be a means to resolving the dilemma of local (mission field church) control, which naturally looks with self-interest upon services rendered and institutions established and largely supported through foreign funds and personnel,

---

[50] Ibid.
[51] Letter from the General Secretary, dated February 13, 1958,
[52] Cf. Hoekendijk, op. cit., p. 163.
[53] Cf. letter from Hayward of the B.M.S., op. cit., p. 2.

versus the broader and less self-interested policy which a mission society might adopt. The S.P.G. provides an illustration of this potentiality, for it takes the position of adopting no particular policy beyond that of working on each specific problem with the bishop of each given local area. [54]

Since functional services so easily pre-empt evangelism, "the primacy of evangelism means a watchful eye on the institution (or service) which, as a potential ally of the greatest value, may also be like a foreign body in the Church and therefore dangerous to its health and wholeness."[55]

In our day, the route to express our Christian-rooted concern for the mundane needs of other peoples is not through vast programs of mission directed services in their midst, but rather through our government and United Nations programs. This would take the form both of urging upon our government that such welfare aids be carried on and of urging earnest Christian lay people who are technically qualified to serve in government or U.N. or private efforts. In view of the magnitude and costliness of welfare projects in this revolutionary era, we can adapt a statement by Beaver to this situation: "Missions cannot take on the whole task but can pioneer on a scale small enough for human personality to remain a major consideration."[56]

This resume could not better close than by a reiteration of the conclusions drawn from a study entitled "The Growing Edge of the Church" by the Reverend Raymond A. Dudley:

> The survey indicated that there is a "growing edge" and that lay evangelism, welling up out of a deep religious experience and fed by Bible study, plays a large part in it … It does not appear as if (institutions) were directly affecting this "growing edge."[57]

III. TOWARD MORE CORRECT EXPLICATION OF FUNCTIONAL SERVICES

Robert G. Cochrane, M.D., has succinctly stated the practical objective of functional services: not to meet need, but to demonstrate how need can be met. Christian missions, especially in functional services, must no longer expect to dominate the local scene where a given service

---

[54] Letter from the Secretary of the S.P.G., dated Feb. 3, 1958.
[55] *Report of the F. M. Committee for 1951*, Church of Scotland, p. 13.
[56] Beaver, *More Effective Ministry*, p. 23.
[57] Ibid., p. 31.

is rendered, but to be like "leaven," hidden in the meal. This is a radical reversal of the pattern of the 19th and 20th centuries, and will be no easy achievement for societies, missionaries and nationals, and if pursued would perhaps eliminate a major ground upon which national governments today are willing to permit mission work. Expediency at this point is not the answer, however. It must be realized, in the words of a tract of the Board of Ecumenical Missions of the Presbyterian Church, U.S.A., that missions "is the impact of the Christian minority and not a mass movement of the majority." Not permissiveness nor collaboration with governments, but "encounter is the order of the day." The Presbyterian leaflet goes on to say:

> Invincible under persecution as in Hungary, China, Spain, Colombia; dynamic in evangelism, even behind the "iron curtain"; sharing in suffering; vitally involved in the world spiritual struggle which will determine whether the world revolution, for which the Church is essentially responsible, will be won by the Christian or anti-Christian forces -- encounter is the order of the day.

Next to understanding the character of our situation as one of encounter rather than service, and the practical objective of functions as not meeting need but demonstrating how need may be met within the sacramental Christian context, the most important factor in explication of functional services is the element of quick adaptability and effective mobility, together with full acceptance of the expendable element. Christian missions still need to learn much from Communist techniques at this point. An amazing amount of very costly time, thought and life still goes into perpetuating services and institutions which have come down from the past, and in regard to education especially, most of the effort is almost purely administrative. The Baptist Missionary Society has, at least in theory, apprehended this:

> For all fields we are convinced of the necessity of short-term planning based on a long-term view, not because we know in relation to any of them that the time will be short, but because we know in relation to all of them (although for varying reasons) that the time may be short. We are to "discern the signs of the times," and "work while it is day," One of the obvious and impressive reasons for Communist successes is their aptitude for working in definite stages. [58]

---

[58] *Review of the B.M.S. Kork Overseas,* January 1954, p. 6.

Lessons need to be learned not only from the Communists but from Islam, which is experiencing such remarkable advance, especially in Africa. The 1956 *Foreign Mission Committee Report of the Church of Scotland* states that Islam's "strength lies in the simplicity of its creed, its ability to manage without expensive buildings or a professional ministry, and its comprehensive brotherhood open to all races. [59] Two very different illustrations may be adduced:

> One very large mission, with nine medical doctors and thirty-four nurses in three fields, after an evaluation of their long standing medical work, came to the conclusion that large, centralized hospitals are not conducive, helpful, or needed in order to develop a strong national church. It was decided that a hospital with more than twenty-five beds is not a sound policy.[60]

The other illustration is the long-standing efforts of Dr. John H. Reisner of Agricultural Missions, Inc., to get the various functional services implemented through more mobile and less institutionalized methods, particularly through programs of rural reconstruction. [61]

A novel suggestion is contained in the *Report of the Methodist Conference Commission on "The Missionary Obligation of the Church."* This suggestion is that mobile squads of missionaries -- commando units -- be trained and held ready and available for emergencies or for fitting into "planned attacks."[62]

To turn to this outlook on functional services, particularly with reference to all aspects of education, requires both a rational and an emotional acceptance of the startling (to Protestants) but very accurate observation of Daniel Fleming on the "Limitations of an Intellectual Approach in Missions." Dr. Fleming points out that:

> Westerners are apt to put too much trust in reason as a means of producing cultural change in another land ... The limitations of the approach through reason lie in assuming that facts and logic are the determining elements in the

---

[59] *The Unfinished Task: Expanding Frontiers* (Edinburgh: Foreign Mission Office, 1956), p. 12.

[60] Referred to in a letter from the Foreign Secretary of the Christian and Missionary Alliance, dated March 4, 1958, p. 4.

[61] Cf. Beaver, *More Effective Ministry*, p. 29.

[62] Original notes missing from the text.

situation... The most serious opposition to Christianity may not be from protest to its formulated thought but from its challenge to customary ways of thinking and acting. [63]

Thus again, sacramental functional service, not the improvement of the condition of people, is the role of functional services, and this is indeed an integral part of evangelism. As Fleming says, "The Cross has powerfully stirred the deepest emotions in men through all ages and in all lands. In lesser ways, also, we may well consider the use of non-rational, non-verbal ways of producing inner change."[64]

Undergirding this emphasis is the premise so well stated in the Methodist Commission's Report:

> One of the most stimulating paradoxes of the Christian faith may be expressed in the statement that "the eternal changes." By this is meant that the eternal truth of the Gospel is changing its forms in India and Africa and elsewhere in order to come nearer to the native ways of expression. In our day the practical out-working of this principle calls for nothing more urgently than for mobility in missionary strategy. [65]

James K. Mathews speaks of the contemporary missionary in a masterful piece of understatement: "His is a vocational dilemma."[66]

> Turning to the Western missionary, in many areas his frustration is more acute than ever. In some places, he feels under the threat of being eliminated by governments for nationalistic reasons or even by the church itself, distorted as the latter is by nationalistic considerations. He must carry the unhappy connotation associated with the name "missionary" in some circles both inside and outside the church. His "foreignness" which could make the valuable contribution of objectivity has become a serious hindrance. He comes eager to serve and is often given little scope for service. Though his skill may be needed, he is often made to feel he is not wanted.[67]

---

[63] See footnote 62.
[64] See footnote 62.
[65] See footnote 62.
[66] See footnote 62.
[67] See footnote 62.

It is the writer's conviction that at least much of this "vocational dilemma," as well as many other problems involved among the churches in "partnership in obedience," would be greatly reduced if all functional services were continuously rendered as the sacrament which points to the meaning behind the deed and turns men to the Christ who is Lord of the deed, thus bringing to accomplishment the central task of evangelism.

A Critique Of "Functional Services In Relation To The Central Task Of Evangelism"

Donald F. Ebright
University of Chicago
Chicago, Illinois

This paper reveals a wide reading and a wrestling with a profound topic. With Prof. Jackson's statement on page three, I can agree that the problem of functional services "to the central task of evangelism is universally recognized and universally resolved." But while we agree at this point there will be many of us who differ with the basic theme of this paper. If we look at the pattern of Jesus we will see that as long as there is one needy man in need of a cup of cold water, there will be the need for functional services.

We can range our attitudes concerning the relationship of functional services to the central task of evangelism in some such form:

1. Some missionaries would confront people with Christ to the end that they may believe and be saved from an evil world. This is called "preaching for a Verdict." It reduces education and medical aid to a bare minimum, I saw this type of missionary at work in the floods at Balliah, India, where a "faith mission" group was distributing tracts to the destitute and criticized our very worldly Methodist-Presbyterian team for taking only food and clothing to the flood area. While this group is on the decline, it is an attitude that dominates the programs of a number of societies.

2. Others would say: "Proclaim the Lordship of Christ, both to help individuals find 'life' and establish Christian churches in every land." This is an institutional interest. It is widespread and characterizes the majority of "old- line" Protestant denominations. It represents much Roman Catholic enterprise. Functional services are a necessary part of demonstrating the Lordship of Christ over all the earth.

3. A third group would define functional service relationships with the central task of evangelism as expressing through hospitals, schools and orphanages the discipleship of the Christian who supports and participates in missionary programs. This is the motive of most laymen. "It is a good thing to provide a clinic and establish scholarships."

4. Another group would make the ethical principles which are implicit in the Christian Gospel operative in the lives of men and societies, "Seek ye first the Kingdom of God."

5. At the far end of the scale would be the complete humanist who saw in education and medicine ends in themselves.

But whatever our stand we must not consider functional services as demonstrations to "win non-Christians." The Church exists as a Church only in the act of sharing its life; this includes both faith and love, both among its members and with those not members. The Church exists as His instrument – functioning as teacher, preacher, healer, welfare worker, caring for human beings regardless of their education, character or station in life. If the Church does not share its life beyond itself it is lacking in the very thing which constitutes a Church, namely, the love of Christ. For the love of Christ exists by giving itself without concern for profit or gain. Thus we share our medical skills, agricultural effectiveness and education that Christian love may be expressed.

It is obvious the functional services are essential to the central task of evangelism. In fact, there is a danger in suggesting separation. The separation of functional services and evangelism gives rise to the evil of "spiritualizing" the Christian world mission under a cloak of selfishness. We may affirm that we are not sent into the all the world to share because we are commissioned to share a greater treasure, "our Christ." This can lead to smugness. We retain the fruits of functional services [literacy, a refrigerator, and station wagon] but we will share Christ. Hence the old criticism: "the white man brought the Bible but took our land." We can tell the Good News by giving one cup of cold water in His name.

The Role of The Missionary Today

Donald McGavran
Drake University
Des Moines, Iowa

What do the tremendous changes of these times, of which we have been reminded here so often, mean for the role of the missionary in the next thirty years? What should be the relation of missionaries to younger churches? How far should missionaries be used in institutions? What does the persistent demand for identification mean for the missionary role? The subject is a broad one of vital concern to both the older and the younger churches. I start with seven introductory observations.

First, while Christian Americans employed abroad by government and corporations and while missionaries of the younger churches are important parts of the total missionary force; owing to limitations of time, we shall not discuss them. We shall confine ourselves to professional missionaries sent abroad by American churches.

Second, I read this paper in the midst of tremendous debate. The nature of the Church, the theology of mission, the relation of Christianity to non-Christian faiths, of ours to other cultures, methods of learning languages, means of communication, and even ends of mission today are all vigorously discussed. What seems to some "a concensus of enlightened opinion" seems to others "the veriest ivory towerism," Procedures into which Roman Catholics and the Assemblies of God pour millions of dollars appear to others out-moded and even reprehensible.

Professor Beaver, to whose William Carey Lectures delivered at Serampore College a year and a half ago we all owe so much, points out that while a new world mission is demanded today and many administrators are striving to find the machinery to implement it, they admittedly lack clear direction, for "no one knows just what world mission is." Consequently any pronouncement I make on the role of the missionary may to others seem questionable. When we apply to specific situations the general principles we have been talking about, we shall get lively discussion and probably some clear dissent. That is all to the good.

Third, nevertheless, forecasts on the missionary role are timely. All boards are sending missionaries and intend to continue. When we consider what is expended on education, training, travel to the fields, language study, and period of apprenticeship, we clearly see that very large expenses hang on forecasts. Even more important, the future direction of the younger churches (and hence of the Church) is being influenced by what we think the role of the missionary should be.

Fourth, my convictions about missionaries have been born in thirty years as one in intimate association in the vernacular with the actual congregations and people of mid-India. My convictions have matured in a series of investigations as to the present state of both port-city and deep interior congregations in Puerto Rico, the Philippines, Thailand, India, and Africa, and an observation of missionaries at work there. The present dissatisfaction of many younger missionaries, the high rate of return to the homeland, despite elaborate devices for selection, and the segregation of missionaries on peripheral tasks, disturbs me. I have spent a good deal of time discussing their role with them and with leaders of the younger churches.

Fifth, while the topic assigned me is "The Role of the Missionary," we all recognize that the missionary has many roles, to fit many different situations. I cannot state emphatically enough that the world mission faces multitudinous situations each one different from the others. The tasks are essentially different in each situation. We must therefore speak in the plural of the roles of the missionary.

There are, to be sure, some general trends to which I shall come in due time; but if we are to see these correctly, we need to concentrate first on the diverse roles which today demands.

Sixth, the matter is urgent. We teach missions in the midst of a blaze of opportunity. No era in the history of the Church faced a greater responsiveness to the Gospel. The part of the world revolution most significant for world mission is just this responsiveness. While debate rages on the nature of the Church, ecumenical theology, koinonia, polarity of cultural developments, the ecclesiological relation of sectarian autonomy to the world Church, and other matters, responsive multitudes who can be won to Christ, live and die without Him. Half a billion have never even heard His name. We believe that the theoretical questions need answering and will be answered, but the harvest must be reaped. We hope to be obedient in the underlying theory of mission but we must be obedient in the task at hand. There is no error greater than that of coming out of ripe fields empty handed.

Seventh, roles do not just happen. Administration creates roles in accordance with the ends of mission really sought. The Seventh Day Adventists and the Church of Rome create different roles in accordance with their basic goals. He would be a brash man who would affirm that their roles are quite wrong while ours are quite right. Roles are what we make them. Environmental factors have a bearing to be sure, but over-riding purposes play a determining part. The task of missionary administration beginning in seminaries and continuing through boards, missions, younger churches is not passively to chart immutable modern tendencies and describe what roles will fit these. It is rather to see what roles God wills, what roles our chief ends require, and what administration will create them. We are not helpless spectators watching a river in flood. We are engineers. We can divert the river, dam it, and put it to work. Administration creates the missionary roles it desires.

Eighth, and perhaps most important, the chief roles of the missionary must be seen today and tomorrow in the light of and under the judgment of the chief ends of mission. The tremendous changes of these times have not and indeed cannot change the divine ends of the Christian mission. H. D. Northfield, late warden of St. Andrews College, Selly Oak, has a fine statement on this in a recent *International Review*, He says:

> We do not think it part of God's will for His Church that men and women who go to serve the Church overseas should be only theologians, teachers, medicals or farmers. They should all be 'missionaries' over and above their qualifications. Not only should the candidate have a heart of love and regard evangelism as his main duty and privilege, but he should have had experience as an evangelist and discovered in what particular way he can best lead people to Christ.

Consideration of the chief ends of mission brings us to theology. Mission rises out of the nature of God. The God revealed by Christ is a searching, saving God. He works for the salvation of all men to the ends of the world and at the cost of His Son. The cross demonstrates His passionate desire for the redemption of men. Missionaries are precisely those who share this passionate concern which breaks through into exclamations like Paul's, "Oh for their salvation, brothers. That is my heart's desire and prayer to God."

The power of the Great Commission lies in just this: that it expresses so completely and inevitably what our God revealed in Christ and the Cross does and must command. Hence, there is no wider, deeper, and more lasting description of the chief ends of mission, unless possibly it should be Paul's great affirmation that God was in Christ reconciling the world to Himself. In either case mission becomes the Church carrying out this redemptive reconciling function. The missionary, like Paul, entreats all men: "Be reconciled to God."

According to my theology, planting churches and upbuilding those planted, that they in turn may carry out the apostolate, is what mission essentially is. I doubt if mission can profitably be defined as "the total global thrust of the Church." The Church in this wide, needy and sinful world does and should do a great many good things, which are not mission. If these be all included, "mission" becomes so thin that the Church fails to reproduce and is found barren and without children in lands flowing with milk and honey. Please do not assume, however, that this theology is unconcerned with social welfare. This theology is intensely interested in social welfare, but believes the surest way to achieve it, in lands where Christians comprise a tiny minority, is to multiply sound, thoroughly Christian churches.

The roles of the missionary are inextricably bound up with theology and that in turn with the historic processes of missions in many different situations. Missions, facing many different situations and justifying their works in each one, often arrive at theological positions very different from those with which they started out. Often also, the theological position, which the distribution of their budget shouts aloud, differs radically from that which their official statement of purpose whispers. In the light of all this I feel that the roles -- so prone to wander -- must constantly be judged by the degree to which they do reconcile men to God.

So much for introductory considerations. Let us now examine four actual situations and the roles the missionary plays in each, in the light of the chief ends of mission. As soon as we come face to face with actual fields, a good many facile generalizations will be seen for what they are -- oversimplification.

First: Jamaica

In Jamaica, a nominally Protestant land, full of highly winnable unchurched people, the Moravians started missions two hundred years ago. Today theirs is a mature church of 12,000, forty churches, five English missionary families, and twenty Jamaican ministers. It has grown little in the last thirty years.

It casts its five missionaries in the role of pastors of Moravian congregations. All have exactly the same status and duties as Jamaican ministers. One of them, a man on the point of retirement, is the bishop of the church, not because he is European, but because his Jamaican brethren thought he would make a good bishop. One successful pastor-missionary, in addition to his other duties, is principal of the Teacher's Training College. Since the five missionaries are paid from England, the contributions of their five Jamaican congregations go to the Jamaican Church Fund from which all pastors are paid.

In this Jamaican-Moravian situation, the missionary plays four roles: a continuing link with the parent church, a welcome indirect assistance in the payment of ministers' salaries, a demonstration of the inter-racial character of Christianity, and an affirmation that the primary purpose of mission is the welfare of the Church.

As we let the light of the Great Commission fall on these four good roles and gaze upon the million unchurched Jamaicans, we remember that this church has grown very little, and wonder whether she and her assisting missionaries are achieving as much "mission" as their Lord desires. Has "mission" been omitted from these missionary roles?

Second: the Philippines

In the Philippine Islands, a nominally Roman Catholic land full of winnable people, the United Church of Christ has approximately 100,000 communicants, 800 congregations, and 400 ministers. The United Church of Christ is holding its own but not growing significantly.

It is assisted by about one hundred missionaries, of whom eighty-one teach in Silliman University or theological seminaries, or do student, medical, agricultural, or administrative work. Nineteen do church work. Only two are pastors. None of the twenty-two moderators or the four bishops is a missionary. The United Church makes scant use of missionaries in the church field.

Two missionary roles are clearly seen: (1) church civil servants, not the bishop or the moderator, but the methodical civil servant who presents the Philippine heads of the departments or the bishops with the facts, records, routine decisions, and organizational planning which the church requires; (2) the specialist in student or agricultural work, or the teacher in Silliman University, theological seminary or Bible schools.

As we let the light of "mission" play on these roles, remembering both the tremendous opportunity for church growth and its necessity if the eight hundred churches are to become any kind of an Apostolate, what shall we say to the United Church? Let me tell you what I did say. My report, "Multiplying Churches in the Philippines," recommended that each of the twenty-two conferences be given two new missionary families; that these new missionaries be given eighteen months language study, instead of six; and then apprenticed to Filipino pastors under whose ministries churches were growing by conversion from the world. The new missionaries would then be located as pastors of promising but typical churches with a mandate to build and extend them.

On their return from their first furlough, the missionaries would be used throughout the churches as specialists in evangelism and church development, teachers in seminaries, pastors of churches, church administrators, student workers, college teachers, or in any other way the United Church of Christ in the Philippines desired. What I was saying, in short, was that the missionary must not be a detached specialist. First of all, he must be a successful churchman, intimately knowing the language, the churches, the peoples, and the ways in which men come to Christian faith there in the Philippines. After that, let specialization occur as it will.

Roles, I think, are not to be judged by expedience, popular fashion, or even by what the older or the younger churches desire; but by the degree to which the missionaries playing such roles do actually act in such a way that the Holy Spirit can through them build and extend the Church.

Third: Belgian Congo

In the Christian Church of Belgian Congo, we have a very different situation. With 80,000 communicant members and about 200,000 highly responsive pagans, the Church has recently almost stopped growing. In 1955 there were perhaps thirty experienced Congolese pastors whose training was that of an eighth grade graduate plus two years of Bible. The rest of the four hundred pastors were men to two to seven years of grade school education with some Bible training. No Congolese sat on the mission executive committee, nor did the Church have an effective central organization of its own.

Although on the level of the bush churches, the four hundred African pastors were in almost full control, with visits from the station missionary only once in several months, nevertheless missionaries were without question the directors of the churches, schools, and hospitals. Steps are being taken, of course, to train Africans for church, school, and hospital leadership, making them first partners and then masters of the entire enterprise, but for the next twenty years, the role of the missionary is person in charge, turning over to Africans as fast as leaders can be developed.

What should we say to this role? I suggest two answers. First, that for this band of seventy missionaries, facing this particular church, the role of trainer of leaders and directors of church and school is probably largely correct. Roles are always partly dependent on the relation of resources in a particular field, to the size of the task there. For seventy missionaries in a new Christian population of 80,000 communicants, the perfecting, rather than the discipling role may be largely correct. Second, that for the Christian Churches of America and their United Christian Missionary Society, contentment with roles which leave winnable multitudes unwon or let them go to the Church of Rome is a tragic error. In addition to this band of missionaries, the Christian Churches of America should throw another band of perhaps forty missionaries into these responsive tribes -- missionaries whose role will be not that of conserving those already Christian, but of claiming responsive populations for Christ. How different the Congo is from the Philippines! What different roles each situation requires!

Fourth: India

We now examine the India mission of the Disciples of Christ and its younger church. This is my church and my mission, which I have served for over thirty years.

The younger church has about 4,000 communicants, eighteen congregations, twenty-four missionaries, and eight ordained nationals serving as ministers. Each year in addition to about a hundred young people cut of Christian families, it baptizes a few from "the world." The church had a small spurt of growth from one responsive caste fifteen years ago, but otherwise has exhibited very little growth from the world for the last forty years. It has increased from 2,536 in 1927 to 4,037 today which is an increase of 17% per decade or slightly under two per cent a year.

Through all these years it has done much evangelistic work, maintaining a team of men and women evangelists in each of its stations. It has also emphasized educational work. It maintains 8 primary and 5 middle schools and has sent many students to Ewing, Hyslop, and Isabella Thoburn Christian Colleges. It has sent some to medical school and at least 25 to America for graduate work. It maintains two very large hospitals, one nationally famous nurses' training school, one well-known tuberculosis sanitorium, three smaller hospitals and four dispensaries.

Over 30 years ago it transferred to Indians complete control of the churches. During the last 30 years it has been turning over management of mission enterprises also. Thus at present out of 50 posts previously held by missionaries, 36 are in the hands of Indians; the committee of management has on it 9 Indians to 5 Americans.

This part of India resents conversions. The Niyogi Commission worked partly among us. The Gass Memorial was burned only 60 miles away. Christians fear to proclaim the Gospel lest they make themselves a target. In this situation, this and no other, what is the role of the missionary?

We might say, "This is a grand work. We should assign to these schools, hospitals, and churches assistants at the rate of one missionary to 150 Christians -- the present proportion. Missionaries should be institutionalists, teachers, doctors, and nurses. We cannot expect any growth for many years, but let us maintain multiple links with this fine little church and through it bear high the torch of Christianity in this part of the world."

On the other hand we might say, "This church has had tremendous assistance for over fifty years. National leaders on a great scale have been trained. Churches have been built. Property has been acquired. We cannot expect exterior growth. Further assistance now on a scale of one missionary to 150 Christians might damage self -direction. Let us turn over more and more of the enterprise to Indian management and have in effect a church which runs, with Indian and foreign money, a large institutional welfare program. Let us continue perhaps one missionary to a thousand Christians, considering the missionaries as inter-racial and international links."

This situation is radically different from those in Jamaica, the Philippines, and Belgian Congo. The roles for mid-India missionaries must be determined in relation to the mid-India situation.

A number of you have seen Dr. Rycroft's analysis of the use of missionary personnel in his excellent statement "A Strategy for the Christian Mission." He points out that in 1952, 3000 Protestant missionaries in Latin America representing 84 different United States religious agencies, were being used as follows:

General church workers and evangelists 66%

Educators, doctors, nurses, agriculturists, etc. 34%

Dr. Rycroft believes this proportion is wrong and calls for more specialists. I am not here debating whether he is right or wrong, I am pointing out that with such inclusive figures (3000 missionaries, all Latin America) totally unchecked against the growth and welfare of particular churches, any claim for rightness or wrongness is wholly subjective thinking on the one hand and much too large generalization on the other. In short, churches carrying out world mission should in the light of the Great Commission define the task in each separate situation and prepare missionaries for these roles.

We are now ready to consider eleven general roles. They are my choice from among those most frequently mentioned in this era. Other roles are also needed tomorrow. The list does not include many roles such as "Champion of the Oppressed," "Saint," "Emancipator," or "Pioneer" which have been played by missionaries of all ages. It does, I hope, focus attention on some of the roles of greatest debate and concern.

ROLE 1: MULTI-RACIAL AMBASSADORS FOR CHRIST

Since before the Throne and the Lamb will stand "a great multitude which no man can number, from every nation, from all tribes, and peoples, and tongues," there is good Christian reason for missionaries from every race. Furthermore with the rise of the younger churches in almost every land, missionaries of every nation are going to be available in large numbers. American boards can use citizens of Japanese, Negro and Mexican backgrounds as regular parts of their multi-racial teams. If we use half the imagination and zeal that goes into recruiting basket-ball teams, we shall find abundant dedicated men and women.

Korean missionaries to India, Filipino missionaries to Thailand, and Puerto Rican missionaries to Argentina, though outside the scope of this paper, would advance this good role still further.

How should teams be composed so that missionaries from many races can be most effective in extending the Christian faith? (1) Each team might be composed of persons of several races, mother tongues, and standards of living. Each team would then demonstrate inter-racial brotherhood within itself. But its inner tensions would also consume much of its energy and militate against fullest effectiveness. Or (2) each team might be composed of persons of one nationality, mother tongue and standard of living. This has been the traditional mode -- teams of Englishmen, Scandinavians, and Americans. We would now add teams of Koreans, Filipinos and Nigerians. This system would have fewer inner tensions. Teams could devote more energy to "mission." Probably both systems in varying measure should be encouraged.

ROLE 2: THE MISSIONARY AS ECUMENICAL MESSENGER

Missions today have ceased to be one-way thrusts. It is no longer the Christian West carrying the Gospel to the non-Christian East. It is instead Christians, East and West, carrying the Gospel to non-Christians, West and East. The world mission is now seen to be the task of the world Church. An apostolic Church and all her congregations is constantly in mission to the whole world with a compelling concern for the unity that constitutionally belongs to the whole Church and with a compelling passion that the world may know God in Christ. Hence, missionaries inevitably play the role of ecumenical messengers.

All American missionaries, no matter what their specific tasks, will consequently think of themselves not as Americans at work in under-privileged Eastern lands, but as missionaries of the world-wide Church of Christ. They will proclaim primarily not American culture, standards of living, or technological advance. They will proclaim primarily Him Whom to know is Life Eternal. They will be multiplying not primarily some branch of the Church of Christ, but primarily the Church of Jesus Christ itself.

The extent to which any given missionary practices this role, will depend on his situation. Should he be sent out by some church which considers itself the only valid or real church or should his field of labor lie among hundreds of rural churches in, say, Nigeria or Sumatra, he can stress this role only very slightly. If he teaches at some Union Theological

Seminary or convenes some provincial Christian Council, this role should occupy a considerable portion of his time.

Yet the basic purpose of most missionaries cannot be considered that of harmonizing churches, building up in existing congregations adequate conceptions of what the world Church really is, or bringing about an ecumenical viewpoint, desirable as all these are. Mission is the Church spending itself in proclamation by word and deed, by life and witness. Every missionary entreats men to be reconciled to God. As ecumenical messenger he makes sure that, in the process of being reconciled, men have (as far as it is possible for those particular men to have) a sound understanding of the world Church.

ROLE 3: THE MISSIONARY AS SHORT-TERM SPECIALIST

Five hundred miles south of Manila at Silliman University I met Mr. Anderson. The University had been running in the red. Mr. Anderson, a specialist in university finance, was sent out for a few years as comptroller. He pulled the accounts back into the black. On the train below Leopoldville I met Father Lievens, a highly-placed Belgian Roman Catholic priest, who was in the Congo for a couple of years "coordinating the work of Catholic missions." It is beyond question that in some situations such specialists are needed. Where American experience is immediately applicable to the younger church situation, they can be used profitably.

But the short-term specialist is not the role of the missionary. Conditions abroad are very different to those in the United States. American specialists can advise effectively in relatively few areas. The short-term specialist does not learn the language. He associates largely with the small, English-knowing section of the younger church. He often gets a distorted view of the Church's real problems and communicates it to the sending Church on his return.

The sending churches should not count the short-term specialist as a common type of missionary. When a special need arises and an American to fit it is found, special arrangements can always be made.

ROLE 4: THE MISSIONARY AS INSTITUTIONAL WORKER, TEACHER, AND TECHNOLOGIST

This role brings us at once into the heart of a vast missionary effort concerned with lifting Christians and serving non-Christians through education, medicine, and agriculture. Many writers on missions are saying, "The younger churches can handle church affairs such as worship, teaching, and evangelism, but in relieving suffering, increasing agricultural production, teaching special subjects like English literature and mathematics or launching some new emphasis like literacy, the older churches can make their greatest contribution." We have already seen that in the Philippines 81 out of a 100 missionaries were thus used. Missions which have large institutional commitments will continue to need doctors, nurses, teachers, and other institutionalists. And wherever mission becomes a kind of ecclesiastical Point Four, missionary technologists are necessary. A.H. Dammers in a recent IRM says, "It is just in these fields -- university work, teaching and research -- that the western missionary is most needed today," What shall we say to Mr. Dammers and his very common role?

In some younger church situations, I would heartily second Mr. Dammers dictum. In others I would heartily question it. In any case it seems to me we cannot naively determine roles solely on the basis of present needs or tendencies in younger and older churches. We must continually consult the chief ends of mission.

Dr. Stanley Rycroft, Secretary for Latin America for the Presbyterians, in a competent statement defines the supreme objective of the Christian mission:

> ... to make Christian disciples of all men everywhere, to seek that they accept Jesus Christ as their personal Saviour and Lord, that as baptized Christians they become active members of local congregations, seek to bring others to a knowledge of Christ, and by word and deed seek the Kingdom of God in personal and social relationships.

We must ask, "Do the roles of institutional worker, teacher, and technologist in actual situations secure this objective?" For those concerned with reconciling men to God this is the question.

Facing the tremendous revolution in missions and younger churches and the kaleidoscopic changes of the day, we must avoid generalization and ask of each specific situation: "Is this church handling worship, teaching, and proclamation so that healthy church growth occurs? In this specific church is it wise to train and manipulate missionaries so that they serve chiefly in institutions? Does such a policy advance mission? Or simply serve the existing vested interests? Is the great need of this younger church at the point of technology or victorious Christianity?"

There has been a drift in some quarters to institutional roles for missionaries, but has it been a right drift? Is it aiding these churches to vigorous, joyfully infectious, Christian life? If it is, it is right. If it isn't, must we not rule it wrong? If Protestant institutional missionaries as a matter of fact are creating fervent outreach in the churches, we should assist the swing to institutionalism. But when the institutional roles for us Protestants result in non-growing churches, spiritually impotent in the midst of multitudes of responsive men, then we should check the swing to institutionalism. I sum up my thinking about the institutional role in several propositions.

a) We shall continue to need many missionaries in institutions.

b) A great deal of nationalization of staff will and should go on. The institutions not only serve the churches but -- a highly practical consideration -- they employ Christians. Pressure will mount to put nationals into every possible post.

c) Nevertheless, contributions of missionaries to the staff, as long as paid from abroad, will be welcome. There is always a financial problem.

d) It would be a pity for the world Church to furnish the institutions just plain ordinary teachers or technologists at a cost including furlough travel of say $5000 a year when the national church could furnish these at say $1000 a year.

This is where Dr. Northfield's opinion is so pertinent. The missionary sent must not be just a "plain ordinary teacher," or "one who has a slightly higher training than the others," or "one with psychological or anthropological training." In addition to his professional requirements the missionary should "not only have a heart of love, but should have discovered in what particular way he can best lead people to Christ," The missionary on the staff should multiply redemptive passion there. That is what makes him a missionary.

Role 5: Assistant to a Younger Church

This is a widely-necessary role. Missionaries even in early stages of the establishment of churches are in reality their assistants. Today, when so many of the younger churches are in advanced stages in independent lands, the role becomes even more necessary. We do well in training and in practice to stress that the missionary is an assistant to the younger church.

However, I think two limitations of "assistantship" need to be made. First, that the missionary is an assistant to the younger church. He is not a permanent subordinate, to any and all nationals. Such an overstatement may have been necessary in the years just past when missionaries were in full control of the church-mission enterprise. But now that nationals are in full control, it is wasteful to continue to say it.

Of course, racial and national arrogance should be absent. Of course, younger missionaries will start in as assistants. But any missionary who has administrative ability, learns the language well, masters the pattern of thought of his adopted land, and really loves the people, will receive from the younger church itself abundant opportunities to manage men and churches. The very top Christian leaders in most lands will and should be nationals; but granting this, the missionary himself, as he gets into his second and third term will usually be given positions of responsibility. I look for the younger churches themselves to take vigorous action at this point. Where they do not take it, the IMC and other organizations can initiate fruitful conversations on the subject.

The second limitation to "assistantship" comes at the point of the "regions beyond." There are innumerable "regions beyond" where the American missionary, as well as the missionary of the younger church, will be starting new churches. He will quite often be "under" the younger church in only a distant way. He will be on his own. There are many examples of this kind of mission work today. Their number may diminish, but again, where Christians constitute only a percent or two of the population there is still an enormous amount of unoccupied virgin territory. We must not become romantic about the younger churches. They are still very small and weak and have many "regions beyond."

ROLE 6: THE MOBILE MISSIONARY

We live in a fast moving world. Speed is likely to increase. Doors open and shut. Evangelism is forbidden here and permitted there. Younger churches grow up and take command. The need for missionaries increases and diminishes.

All this means, I think, that a missionary must be mobile. Instead of missionaries, a few months after their arrival, being permanently assigned to life-long tasks, most missionaries should expect to be shifted according to the needs of the field. This is already being done to a limited degree. Missionaries of the United Christian Missionary Society at work in Latin America, for example, have for many years been shifted from Paraguay to Argentina, to Mexico, to Puerto Rico. And all over the world one finds missionaries who have had experience elsewhere. Some of the most effective Baptist missionaries I found in Thailand had come from Assam. Ex-China missionaries are found in many places.

But such transfers are unfortunately considered exceptional. Many transferees never get over emotional attachment to their first field. Some even manifest resentment against the second field. A good many people think it is "asking too much" to expect a missionary to learn a second language. All of which is unfortunate.

Mobility, like the other roles, of course, is not an end in itself. There are missionaries who move about too much! Only if it aids the achievement of the chief ends of mission should mobility be emphasized. In order to achieve increased mobility, the following steps will be found useful: 1) Ability at languages should receive a somewhat higher rating in choice of missionaries. 2) Their training should prepare them for possible change of field, by stressing the relative case with which second languages can be learned and the normality of such changes. 3) Missionaries should expect to establish churches and leave. The policy of permanent involvement of missions with younger churches should be modified. Only so can the missionary forces of both younger and older churches be directed to new church planting and multiplication. 4) Continuous reappraisal of the responsiveness of fields should become routine procedure in the world mission of the church. The task is not only to reach all men, but also to make sure that none who today seek to accept the Gospel are denied a hearing through the immobility of missionaries.

ROLE 7: THE MISSIONARY AS SEMINARY PROFESSOR

This good role is commonly advocated and many missionaries are used this way. The missionary is a choice gift of one church to another. He should often be used as a teacher of ministerial candidates. However, a word of caution is in place. Young missionaries fresh out of American seminaries, or German seminaries for that matter, should not ordinarily teach future church leaders. Younger churches should not deliver their most precious asset into the hands of dyed-in-the-wool Americans, who are inevitably and quite unblameably, full of American thought patterns,

American fashions, American church plans, and the latest American theology. They know what nourishes churches and multiplies them in generally Protestant, wonderfully free, scientifically-minded, ultra-modern America. They do not know what nourishes and multiplies churches in generally Roman Catholic or Hindu socially chained, pre-scientific minded, Brazil or Bombay. Training in sociology, anthropology, and supremely in the structure and growth patterns of the church to which he goes, will help to prepare a missionary to overcome this handicap. Yet any younger church which surrenders the training of its youth to foreigners or foreign-trained nationals, who have not demonstrated their ability to make local congregations flourish and actually reconcile men to God in their neighborhoods, is in danger of committing slow suicide. In the midst of winnable multitudes, such a church may stop growing and be absorbed into more virile churches.

ROLE 8: THE MISSIONARY AS CHURCH-GROWTH ACCOUNTANT

Mission boards commonly insist on full-time trained men handling incomes and expenditures. Even in this spiritual business of ours, interboard and mission treasurers are essential as far ahead as we can see.

In the same way churches in living communion with the Saviour, must keep accurately informed of how they are getting on with the Saviour's task. But such information is seldom available. For several years now, I have been making studies of church growth in Africa, India, Thailand, the Philippines, and the Caribbean. Everywhere the picture is the same: church statistics so inaccurate that as they stand they are largely meaningless. With the passage of authority to younger churches, statistics reported are increasingly of little use. Furthermore, careful accounting of church growth is specially necessary because we engage today in highly diversified missions. In the midst of the revolution, everything is being tried. All kinds of labors are advocated as "good missions." This diversification will probably increase.

Is each of these many pieces of mission work successful? It is impossible to measure some of the goals which each intends to achieve. But it is possible to measure the church growth which accompanies it. A missionary enterprise pouring thousands of lives and millions of dollars into the propagation of the Gospel needs to know what degree of propagation is occurring. Church growth is not the only end of mission, be sure of that; but it is certainly one chief end. We keep track of money. We should also keep scrupulous account of the growth of churches.

What is required is perhaps one trained statistician to each fifty or one hundred thousand communicants in the younger churches. This man will supply reliable meaningful information on membership increase to both younger and older churches. He will assemble not merely "field totals" (those deceptive figures) but exactly what groups of churches are in fact prospering most, where church growth occurs by conservation of children from within the Christian community, where by transfer of Christians from other areas, and where by conversion. Rates of growth accompanying different methods of mission work would be most useful in mapping future plans for missions and churches.

ROLE 9: THE MISSIONARY AS RESEARCHER

Even a casual perusal of the advertisements in our magazines indicates the vast amount of research being carried out by industry. The United States Post Office expends millions to discover more effective ways of delivering mail.

The multi-million dollar missionary enterprise also needs to devote an appreciable portion of its income, possibly one per cent, at finding out what modes of mission best achieve the acknowledged chief ends of mission. In the business of our Master we should use at least as much wisdom as we do in manufacture or commerce. The areas of greatest response should be kept charted and prophesied. The best ways to develop stewardship can be determined and adopted by all. Population movements involving Christians can be studied so that churches can be conserved. Procedures which multiply churches can be known. Theories about the propagation of the gospel can be checked against achievements. The causes of ingrowness and static stalemate in churches can be discovered and avoided. In education it is now common place to set up evaluative devices so that the curriculum can be constantly appraised as it is being used. Such appraisal of the growth and welfare of the younger churches and the work of their supporting missions is tremendously needed.

All this calls for missionaries who are trained in and skillful at investigating these segments of the life of the younger churches; and for younger churches and missions accustomed to use the services of research specialists to help them do their Master's will.

Role 10: The Missionary as Expert in Other Religions

Dr. Kraemer says in *Religion and the Christian Faith* (p. 202):

The Christian Church is heading toward a spiritual encounter with the great non-Christian religions ... The fast growing interdependence of the whole world thrusts these religions upon us. The Church must, therefore, manifest in new terms its spiritual and intellectual integrity and value ... Till now only 'marginal remarks' have been made to the non-Christian religions. From now on confrontation with them has to become one of the main subjects. Everything is moving in that direction as a result of the development both of the younger churches and of the non-Christian religions themselves.

Most of us cordially agree with the importance of this role. Each missionary should know a great deal about the other religion in the land where he works. Some missionaries should be highly trained in these other religions, not that they may conduct detached, scientific, "as between us scholars" conversations with them; but rather that, immersed in non-Christian faiths, indeed in living communication with them, they will continually reconcile men out of those systems to Christ.

It is to be hoped that the schools of Hinduism, Buddhism, Islam and Roman Catholicism, which are being established, will hold such intimate conversation with these other faiths on such a high level of scholarship, sympathy, and insight, that they will work out a kerygma as effective for them as Paul's kerygma was for the Jews and Greeks of his day. We missionaries follow in the steps of Paul. His greatness did not lie in being an authority on Judaism and possibly on Greek religion also, nor in his communication with Jewish and Gentile scholars. His greatness lay in using his intimate knowledge of those religions, in fully effective communication with them, to win disciples of Christ within and without the synagogues and to leave a trail of churches all over the Empire.

Role 11: The Missionary as Harvester

Many feel that missionaries in combination with nationals are called to be harvesters. True, many populations are closed to missionary evangelists; but many more are open. The success which has attended the Lacour Missions in Japan is a case in point. More remarkable is the record of the Tent Teams of the Oriental Missionary Society in Japan into which they have put half of their missionaries. Many responsive fields can be named where missionaries are being used of God to found solid churches; and there are many more populations where, were missionary-national teams to be sent, many more churches could be established. I think of the Lutheran field in Sarguja, India, the United Church of Christ field in the Philippines, the urban opportunities in Puerto Rico, the Amoy-speaking Chinese in Formosa, the Japanese in Hokkaido, great sections of the populations in Chile and Brazil, 100,000 Congolese in the one Baptist field of Vanga, the Kikuyu in Kenya, and many, many others.

"But," someone exclaims, "isn't the younger church going to take care of all these?" I wish it were, but it is rather romantic to think it will. Oh, it will aid. In some cases it will lead. In others it will simply add its blessing. In some, I fear, it will stand indifferently by. A great share of the load will fall on Western churches. God has called them into existence for just such a time as this.

The training of missionary harvesters, however, is woefully lacking. Few people know what makes younger churches grow where they are now actually growing. Very few have carefully analyzed the church growth now taking place in advanced cultures, primitive populations, among the literate, and the illiterate, and can teach churchmen the methods which God is currently blessing to the extension of His Kingdom in the very varying populations of mankind. Such teaching is greatly needed. It should receive high priority among courses in missionary training schools.

In summary and conclusion, may I say of missionary roles that the essential question is one of proportion, in each specific situation, under the judgment of the chief ends of mission. Today's proportion in missionary roles is frequently determined by the accidents of history, the surges of fashion in mission, and the pull of powerful institutions and individuals. Today's proportion is often unregulated by reference to reconciling men to God. Where this is so, it should be changed. In each of thousands of populations where the world mission is at work, the proportion of general missionaries, specialists, ecumenical messengers, teachers, harvesters or accountants should be constantly reviewed against the growth and welfare of churches in that population.

Not only should each church be an apostolate, by life and word, beseeching men to be reconciled to God, but it must know how men are answering the invitation, and then train missionaries for those roles which are measurably being blessed by God to the growth and development of His churches. The roles of the missionary we need to discover and emphasize arc those through which the Holy Spirit is actually converting men and upbuilding and multiplying churches.

A Critique Of "The Role Of The Missionary Today"

Robert T. Parsons
Kennedy School of Missions
Hartford Seminary Foundation

There is much contained in the foregoing presentation to which one would say Amen and give a strong endorsement. One would question other points; some would be revised; some enlarged and still others added to or even omitted.

First of all, one expected to find answers in the body of this paper to the question that appeared in the opening paragraph. One expected to hear something about the effect of the upheavals in the Middle East upon the roles of the missionaries, or the roles of the missionaries in those areas of Africa where there is a steadily growing consciousness among the people of human rights and basic freedoms, and what the missionary can and should do about them. One hoped to learn of the ways missionaries are coping with the issues in the ideological struggles of these times. What of the role of the missionary in the midst of this world-wide ferment in which he may be a voice for the silent people, a guide for the lost people, a spokesman for the uninformed people, an interpreter to the confused people, a champion of the causes for the unjustly-treated people.

The reply to the question could have dealt with the call for more missionaries with the spirit and courage of Father Huddleston, Michael Scott, and the Bishop of Johannesburg, For certainly there is a place today for the missionary who in the critical situations can help in redeeming, and reconciling people. It is dangerous, yet it is demanded.

One looked for something about the redemption of economic life -- the struggle for justice in trade, commerce, and honesty in business affairs;

the building of cooperatives and the establishment of new enterprises for improved standards of living. There is a role for the missionary today like that of Mr. Shepherd, the economist in Uganda.

The task of the missionary amid the turmoils in the complex processes of rapid urbanization where so few qualified persons are at work was not mentioned. Nevertheless it is an area where it seems that a major catastrophe is taking place, where so much is being left to the government or the Roman Catholic Church.

One must differ with the author when he says that it will be by the multiplication of churches that the social welfare needs of the people will be most surely achieved. It is imperative that skilled technicians who are missionaries must be used as members of the evangelistic team.

The author seemed to have a far too limited understanding of the "end of mission" found in such expressions as, "the planting of churches and the upbuilding of those planted," or "the leading of people to Christ," or "the passionate concern for the redemption of men." These definitions are excellent but they are not inclusive enough. The end of mission is the redemption of the whole man in the whole society. This seems true notwithstanding the author's insistence that for the Church to include the many good things that are not mission, the mission becomes so thin that the Church fails to reproduce itself and is found barren. A mission to save all of the people in all of their relationships and to help them grow toward an abundant life in all of their activities is a full mission productive and bearing fruit.

The writer outlined several roles for the missionary, the first, multi-racial ambassadors for Christ. The adoption of a policy to send out inter-racial teams seemed to hinge upon the question whether or not such work would cause one to live in the midst of tensions, find his energies consumed and his discipling thwarted. This role is so important that the Church must find persons fitted for it by careful selection and thorough preparation. Where tensions have arisen among missionaries there is ample evidence that the persons were not adequately tested for this role.

In discussing the role of the ecumenical messenger there seemed to be a contradiction, for in one paragraph it was stated that "the basic purpose of most missionaries cannot be considered that of harmonizing churches, building up in existing congregations adequate conceptions of what the world Church really is, or bringing about an ecumenical viewpoint, desirable as all these are." Yet a little further along he concluded, "As ecumenical messenger he (the missionary) makes sure that in the process of being reconciled, men have a sound understanding of the world Church." If this is not a contradiction, then it probably means that the ecumenical messenger is a specialist who alone may perform this task. Where are the missionaries who cannot be prepared to play this role and find it the most natural thing in their ministry to meet this need. In a day when we deplore as much as any generation has the fact of our brokenness as a Church into hundreds of segments overseas like the brokenness of the sending churches, certainly the reconciling role of every missionary is one of harmonizing churches. This task is to help make possible even more significant cooperative efforts than have yet been achieved. More than this, the role of the missionary would seem to be one of doing all within his power to stress the likenesses between all Christian groups which are so many more than their differences. The practice must cease when we pass on our peculiar ways to the persons overseas and require them to do the same.

In discussing the third role, namely that of short-term specialist, it seems to be debatable whether American specialists can advise effectively in relatively few areas. Perhaps one should say that properly-prepared specialists who know how to learn from the people overseas, how to establish rapport, will be in a position to advise in a large number of areas. So much depends upon one's understanding, humility, and approach to other people.

Much more emphasis should have been placed upon the roles of the missionary in university work, teaching, and research, where as Mr. Danners has well put it, "the Western missionary is most needed today." Much more importance should be attached to the role of the missionary as a researcher.

So very few missionaries are engaged in fall-time research. Too few are giving even a part of their time in gathering essential data. But a trickle of missionary money is being set aside for research by all of the Protestant denominations overseas.

The strongest emphasis should be placed upon the role of the missionary as assistant to the younger churches. In so many places the missionary wrestles with himself to be willing to learn how to be a true servant of the Church abroad.

The role of the mobile missionary is very fitting for some areas and at certain stages in the life of the Church. However, there are many places where the frequent movement of the missionary seems to have been the chief reason for ineffective work; for the poor command of the language; and the lack of necessary knowledge of the people.

The situation described with reference to the missionary as seminary professor points up again the need for better preparation for missionaries. If he has learned about the real worth of the elements in the culture of the receiving group, of the processes of culture change, of the limitations of his own cultural trappings, he will not be in a position to present his American fashions and plans. Instead he will be seeking to know the ways by which he may help the people to develop their own patterns of thought and action. Here again, the problem is not a matter of the role to be played, but of the type of person that is being asked to play it.

Finally, if the task before the missionary is that of helping in the redemption of all of the life of people in all of their relationships, then the roles for the missionary will be as wide as life itself.

The Teaching Of Missions In The Light Of The Ecumenical Movement

Creighton Lacy
Divinity School of Duke University
Durham, North Carolina

"The future of missions lies in the sphere of ecumenics." Thus spake Keith Bridston to the Professors of Ecumenics at Oberlin, September 2, 1957. If his assertion has any validity for the world mission of the Church, then it applies also to the teaching of missions. Revolutionary currents are lapping even at the foot of the ivory towers, and the most irresistible tide is that which surges toward manifest Christian unity. Pierce Beaver in his Carey Lecture at Serampore last year made some harsh references to professorial detachment, but he reached the optimistic conclusion that "the mission theorist is today winning recognition ... and theological encounter has become an exciting new frontier of missionary thinking." If we are to merit this new status, we must re-examine and reformulate many of our out-worn concepts. Verily, the future of mission teaching lies in the sphere of ecumenics, however diversely we may interpret that charge.

Analysis of this bi-focal relationship encounters difficulties from the start. Very shortly after the president of this group requested a paper on "The Teaching of Missions in the Light of the Ecumenical Movement," he sent the writer a two-page letter of suggestions, all of which dealt with the teaching of ecumenics, the understanding of the ecumenical movement, the interpretations of Christian unity, and so on. Apparently his thinking, like mine, had been stimulated by the Oberlin discussions last fall. But even those pundits (referred to on one page of their minutes as "Proffers of Ecumenics") failed to clarify either the priority or the dependence of the "chicken and the egg." They debated warmly whether ecumenics should be approached as a separate discipline or integrated with missions and the total curriculum. The great missionary statesman, John Mackay, even inquired whether missions should be subsumed under ecumenics. Finally, in typical ecclesiastical fashion, these gentlemen (including some of you in another hat suggested "a small committee to watch for the possibilities of meeting again, perhaps in association with professors of missions." Selah!

It behooves us, therefore, to look briefly at some definitions of the ecumenical movement and its curricular status, before we turn to the assigned theme, the teaching of missions, Dr. Visser't Hooft at Oberlin gave a comprehensive description in these terms:

> Ecumenics is the theological discipline which seeks to provide an accurate, comprehensive description of the faith, life and work of the Churches and the ways in which they cooperate; which seeks to manifest the unity of the Churches of Christ, to fulfill their common mission, to express their dynamic; and which also deals critically with the issues that arise as a result of the encounter of the Churches, for the Churches themselves and within the life of the Ecumenical Movement itself.

Traditionally the Protestant missionary enterprise has been reluctant to reach so wide and to delve so deep. Its early leaders, until well after Edinburgh, expressly disavowed any willingness to "deal critically with the issues that arise" in theological and doctrinal areas. But on one hand, the missions have found themselves increasingly involved in faith and order, in the establishment of churches with creeds and polities, in the gradual disappearance of any uncontested frontiers. On the other hand, the churches (as distinct from independent and peripheral societies) have assumed a growing responsibility for, and identification with, the world mission, thus inevitably revealing their tragic disunity. The interdependence has become so clear that John Machay could offer this succinct definition at Oberlin: "Ecumenics is the science of the Church Universal; as such, it concerns the world missionary community, its nature, mission, function, relations, and strategy."

Three years ago the National Council of Churches launched a "Survey and Study of the Needs and Resources for Ecumenical Education." Their prospectus, with which many of you are familiar, listed six phases of Christian life denoted in this country by the term ecumenical: 1) conversations among Christians of diverse backgrounds; 2) interdenominational or cooperative action; 3) the structural character of the missionary movement (whatever they meant by that -- CL);4) the work of the various councils of churches; 5) the spirit and effort toward unity among the churches, extending beyond national frontiers to what is world-wide; 6) rediscovery that the Church lives its life "in the world," i.e., in relation to all human pursuits which serve as Christian callings, and as involving the tasks of evangelism in the role of the Church in contemporary culture. One need not go that far afield, however, to see the inter-relation of unity and mission.

In many discussions today we are lifting up three traditional areas of the Church's life: kerygma (message), koinonia (fellowship), and diaconia (service). (Let us note parenthetically, as pertinent to both ecumenical and missionary movements, that the first recorded ordination, or laying on of hands, was for the diaconate, not for preachers or administrators.) The personal letter from Dr. Beaver referred to earlier suggests this same trilogy in slightly different words to describe the functions of the ecumenical movement: expansion (mission), integration (unity), and permeation (social ethics). Then he wisely and simply defines the ecumenical movement, "not as a movement for interdenominational unity, but as a movement concerned with the recognition of the Lordship of Jesus Christ over the Church and the world."

Today we take for granted, in one form or another, the inseparable character of the ecumenical movement and the world mission, "The Calling of the Church to Mission and Unity," enunciated by the Central Committee of the World Council of Churches at Rolls in 1951, has become a truism in ecumenical circles. The challenge it now poses is to create vital meaning for the local church and meaningful vitality for the world missionary program.

Both of these challenges converge on the teaching of missions. It would be rash -- and irrelevant -- to attempt to mediate here between those who favor a separate academic discipline for ecumenics and those who urge "ecumenizing the total curriculum," as Visser't Hooft put it. Both Nils Ehrenstrom and Albert Outler apparently made convincing cases at Oberlin. Most of our theological institutions, however, have neither the money and personnel nor the missionary vision to "proffer" ecumenics as a distinct department. I myself question whether that status would really allow any greater opportunity for correlating "the whole school and the whole church" or for serving as a "bond of unity within the faculty" -- in the ideal fashion which Dr. Ehrenstrom suggested. Rather I repeat what I said to this group two years ago at Naperville: "Obviously, if there is no specialized and separate treatment of the ecumenical movement, it belongs to us, both in its genealogy and in its function."

Having participated twice since then in my own denomination's Theology of Missions Consultation, I would add a third point of contact. The mission of the Church and the ecumenical movement belong together historically, practically, and theologically. It is under those three headings that I should like to approach the main issues of this paper.

I. HISTORICAL APPROACH

Pierce Beaver's aforementioned personal letter comments that "when 'ecumenics' is taught, the subject is usually confined to the history of the ecumenical movement, and more especially to the Faith and Order and Life and Work movements culminating in the World Council of Churches," Certainly these twentieth century developments should be covered in any analysis of recent mission history, emerging as they did from the cooperative efforts of missionary societies and from the rapid growth of national councils among the younger churches.

But the teaching of missions, as I said two years ago, has too often been limited to the historical narrative, thrilling though that is. We are eternally indebted as missions professors to Kenneth Scott Latourette's monumental works, and nobody possesses more ecumenical and irenic spirit than he. But the expansion of Christianity is presented by denominations and societies, even in his all-inclusive sweep. Personally I use Basil Mathew's *Forward Through the Ages* (based largely on Latourette) for the text in my History of Missions course, partly because I like the biographical approach, but his supposedly ecumenical device of mentioning no denominational affiliations whatever is sometimes as frustrating to teacher and students as the reverse would be. In other words, ecumenical missions history usually means merely avoiding sectarian labels.

The vast majority of history books, of course, are written from a completely denominational standpoint: *Christian Missions and Historical Sketches of Missionary Societies Among the Disciples of Christ, History of Southern Methodist Missions, The Foreign Missions of the Russian Orthodox Church*, and now in process a seven-volume *History of Methodist Missions*. These are all valuable for the churches concerned, for historical knowledge, and for a background to ecumenical developments. But it is high time that our teaching and our research sought to analyze the inter-relationships of Christian expansion, instead of compartmentalized units.

We all know -- and I hope teach -- that the first Protestant missionaries to Asia were German Pietists sent to India by the King of Denmark at Anglican expense. Where do we go from there? We know that

William Carey proposed a world missionary conference at Cape Town for 1800, What happened then? We may recall that Alexander Duff left the Church of Scotland for the Free Church during the Disruption of 1843, but not that he persuaded the American Methodists to open work in India. What lessons could the contemporary ecumenical movement learn from the failure of the London Missionary Society and the American Board of Commissioners to remain truly interdenominational -- especially in relation to the non-denominational faith missions which operate with such zeal and such resources today? How successful were comity agreements in the nineteenth century, and why have so many of them recently broken down? What about the innumerable daily acts of fellowship and Christian unity which take place in mission stations throughout the world, far removed from any organized ecumenicity? The history of missions might well be re-examined through ecumenical lenses.

We professors of missions keep hoping that church history will deign to notice us, although thus far there seems to be very little awareness that the history of Christianity extends outside of Europe, eastward or westward. Such a study as Dr. Latourette's is honored for its scholarship but hardly granted a place in the main stream of ecclesiastical history. We must continue to assault the bastions of academic tradition until the world Church is recognized as exactly that.

But there is another side to this, a side which more directly concerns our topic. The ecumenical movement requires that professors of missions be far more solidly grounded in church history than we have been. If we are to interpret the significance of the Church of South India, we must be familiar with the heritage of the participating confessions. If we are to evaluate the report of the Malayan Christian Council Faith and Order Commission, we need to know why the constitutional and historic episcopate, tactual transmission of Grace, immersion and affusion, and confirmation are such crucial and such controversial terms. If we are to examine, reverently and sympathetically, an indigenous creed, we must know for ourselves and others what elements in the traditional Western creeds are indispensable bulwarks against heresy and which phrases and concepts may be expendable social and cultural accretions.

The same things can be said about Biblical studies. Faith and order discussions have led all the churches to re-examine their understanding of Biblical purpose and of early Church practice. If the general consensus points to no set, exclusive pattern -- or to the use of a variety of forms in the first few centuries -- then we must not only allow but encourage a great deal more flexibility and freedom of experimentation among the younger churches today. Whatever our respective conclusions about the ministry and sacraments, it seems clear that the only divisions in the early Church were those required by geographic location. Personal loyalties (to Paul or Apollos or Cephas) were condemned as vigorously by Paul as they would be by John Wesley or Alexander Campbell. Administrative polities or even such critical decisions as circumcision were rejected as barriers to any individual's worship or fellowship in the Church of Jesus Christ.

The implications of Biblical scholarship for the ecumenical movement are presented in authoritative fashion by many recent writers. (See, for example, Albert Outler's *The Christian Tradition and the Unity We Seek.*) These implications become imperative for missions at the local level, for the sin of separation and exclusion is seen on Main Street or Mei Cha Hutung more poignantly than at Geneva or Evanston. As a recent student paper put it: "The point of togetherness is the local congregation, not at the false level of organizational charts." When a Hindu asks a missionary or a missions professor why those who profess to worship One God and represent the One Body of Christ cannot worship Him together, the answer had better be convincing! Thus, in the light of the ecumenical movement, the teaching of missions takes on new dimensions of Biblical interpretation and historical analysis.

II. Practical Approach

More immediately impelling, however, is the impact of ecumenical developments on the contemporary, practical mission scene. No longer is it possible, much less desirable, to present to our students a set of denominational statistics on budget and personnel, constituencies and institutions, embellished with biographical sketches of our own heroic pioneers. No mission station is an island anymore, even though it may be geographically remote. No group can preach the Gospel today without reference to others doing likewise -- whether the relationship be one of hostility and suspicion or of cooperation and Christian unity. The numerous aspects of this imperative can be only suggested in the time available. Let me list them under the general headings of organization and policies.

Mission boards and societies at every point on the ecumenical spectrum are confronting the problem of their relationship to ecumenical organizations. A vast majority of them had found their place, fairly comfortably, in the International Missionary Council and in its great conferences at Jerusalem and Madras. But the Second World War changed many things. Out of the urgency of humanitarian relief grew continuing agencies of inter-church aid: not only Church World Service, but Lutheran World Relief, Brethren Service Committee, the Methodist Committee for Overseas Relief.

Out of the war too came the achievement of *merdeka* for so much of Asia and ultimately Africa. The racial and regional self-consciousness which found political focus at Bandung had its Christian counterpart at Prapat, with the move to establish an Asian Christian Conference. The decision at Ghana to unite the World Council of Churches and the International Missionary Council presents to many missionary groups an acute dilemma. A number of European societies are threatening to withdraw, and a split seems likely in the Congo Protestant Council, which up to this point had preserved more comity and held together more diverse theological strains than most other cooperative mission bodies.

It is not the prerogative of this paper to weigh the arguments. Suffice it to plead that the final decisions be made not on charges and counter-charges of liberal theology or radical social ethics, not on a doctrinaire anti-conciliar stand, not on fears of concentrated power (for the World Council has no ecclesiastical sovereignty). If both Councils are "concerned with the recognition of the Lordship of Jesus Christ over the Church and the world," to repeat Pierce Beaver's phrase, then the organizational decisions should be made solely and prayerfully from the standpoint of advancing the world mission. These developments are significant because much of the momentum has come from the so-called younger churches. A short time ago many of them preferred the International Missionary Council because it was more fully oriented to their areas and to their problems; today they are determined to demonstrate that they are, in every sense, a part of the Church Universal.

One other organizational aspect of the question is becoming more acute, the formation of world-wide denominational unions: the Lutheran World Federation, the Baptist World Alliance, the World Methodist Council, etc. It is argued that oikumene, the inhabited world, did not and does not mean interdenominational. Historians (cf. Hogg: *Ecumenical Foundations*) remind us that the nineteenth century ecumenical conferences took their titles to refer to the global scope of the missionary task, not to faith and order discussions. There are those who sincerely believe that unified denominations will be more effective components of an ultimate ecumenical union than national and regional churches would be. Even some younger churches insist that they would rather feel a part of an international fellowship than be limited to a national, cultural, linguistic, or racial church. Our own Methodist Theology of Missions group will consider late this month two papers, one from England and one from this country, on the specific topic: "Should Methodist missionary efforts be directed toward service of a world-wide confessional Methodism or toward regional organic church unions?"

Again it is not the province of this paper to answer the question. The decision, however, has major implications for Congregationalists who are expanding by geometric progression, for Methodists who are negotiating mergers in North India, in Malaya, in Pakistan, in Ceylon, in Great Britain itself. Similarly it should be recognized as an extremely live issue for teachers of missions. No account of the world Church today can ignore these problems, whether we start from within full ecumenical participation or from independent external criticism. The relationship of Christian groups to one another is perhaps the most conspicuous and urgent issue affecting the missionary movement today. It can hardly be less so for professors of missions.

Clearly the ecumenical movement throws organizational stumbling-blocks, or stepping-stones, in the road of the world mission. It also scatters innumerable practical pebbles along the path of daily policies. Those who seek to interpret the evangelistic outreach of the Church to its ministers, and through them to local congregations, must be aware of the current revolution in missions. We teach, I hope, about self-government, self-support, self-propagation, about devolution and indigenization. Surely each of these is influenced by, and in turn helps to shape, the ecumenical climate of the Church. A few examples, without elaboration, will be sufficient to make the point.

Not only missionary candidates in our seminaries, but pastors whose understanding support is essential, should understand the changing role of the "fraternal worker." The Secretary of the Synod of the Church of South India was quoted (*Christian Century*, June 4, 1958) as saying: "Missionaries from overseas are beginning to occupy a different but an even more important position in the life of the church, and in several cases are pioneering in various kinds of rural service." Again a significant change has taken place. Not long ago administrators were saying that national pastors could minister more effectively to local congregations at the "grass roots" than could "foreigners," and that missionaries would have to hold down the institutional posts of training and supervision. Now the more widely-influential executive and educational offices are going to nationals, and in India and Brazil at least, it is the overseas missionary who goes out to the remaining frontiers to establish new churches.

This development has several possible ecumenical effects. Although some few nationals outdo the missionaries in denominationalism, by and large, as they assume responsibility in church councils, they are more susceptible to ecumenical pressures, less bound by Western traditions and procedures. Emotions of patriotism and independence pervade the Church too, and experiments in Christian unity in India and Japan are watched with a far greater sense of identification in Asia than in the United States. Without analyzing the process of devolution or self-government more fully, it is clear that professors of missions must recognize and interpret these trends fairly and sympathetically.

One very practical concern lies with the "mother church" in the matter of self-support. The younger churches are still desperately afraid, despite the experience of the Kyodan, that organic union will cause a reduction in funds and personnel from abroad. Some Chinese pastors quite frankly opposed joining the Church of Christ there because it might mean a lower salary or institutional budget. Here in this country it requires education to persuade local congregations to give to institutions and projects no longer in American hands; it will require even more understanding to continue contributions that are no longer directly strengthening "our denomination." Financially and emotionally, many church members in this country still react like the president of one of our major Methodist mission agencies: "I just can't stand the thought of having six hundred thousand Methodists wiped out in North India." Surely this is a challenge to pastors and professors of missions.

On the one hand, our generosity needs to find ecumenical incentive and the challenge of cooperative endeavors. On the other hand, self-support requires new wisdom in withholding or redirecting gifts. Boards which are adopting a systematic time schedule for reducing direct pastoral subsidies must explain to their constituencies at home and abroad not only the reasons but the alternatives. Contributors who may no longer provide "discretionary funds" for an individual missionary to dispense bountifully must be shown the values of helping the younger churches to send out their partners in obedience.

This in turn points to a reappraisal of missions in terms of so-called self-propagation. On the one hand, every branch of the Church needs to share in the central task of evangelism, and the interchange of non-Western missionaries, though still hardly more than a token, is one of the most significant steps of the post-war era. On the other hand, the Three-Self emphasis can too easily focus on the self, forgetting that administration, stewardship, and evangelism are all cooperative tasks. As local and regional agencies assume responsibility for Christian witness in their own areas, limitations on personnel and money (not to mention the spiritual values of unity) require increasing ecumenical partnership. Financially speaking, American churches can afford to establish competing congregations side by side; Indonesian and Burmese Christians cannot. Unity is an economic necessity if churches and institutions are to thrive.

A council of state, in preparing its report to Queen Victoria, proposed to begin as follows: "Conscious as we are of our shortcomings..," "No," protested an aged earl, "we must not lie to Her Majesty, Let us say rather, 'Conscious as we are of each other's shortcomings...'" Conscious as we are of each other's shortcomings, we all know hideous examples involving our own denominations, where sectarianism has blighted the evangelistic impact of the Christian Gospel. Those examples need not be cited here. Let us rather pay tribute to such positive witness as that of the Mar Thoma Syrian Church (report in the *Christian Century*, June 11, 1958). In two separate instances, converts won by that communion felt more at home in a different linguistic group and were allowed to join other churches, thirteen families to the Church of South India and forty English-speaking Chinese in Singapore to the Anglican Church. Now that ought to shame those who are primarily engaged in piling up denominational statistics!

The ecumenical missionary task brings together communions in Europe and America as well as in Asia. In this country we have the Interboard Committee for Christian Work in Japan. Pierce Beaver in his Carey Lecture referred to a new awareness in Europe of the Church's responsibility for mission, instead of leaving the job to the earlier independent mission society. When the Church itself is involved in mission, it cannot help but be more conscious of the need for Christian unity. We Methodists are proud of the experiment now taking place in Sarawak, where preaching, teaching and healing among the Ibans has enlisted Bataks, Filipinos, Malays, Chinese, white and Negro Americans, Britishers, Indians, a Swiss and a Swede. This is ecumenical in the sense of drawing on the inhabited world from several branches of Methodism. But in the first place, such opportunities for non competitive pioneering are almost extinct. In the second place, there are some Methodists who feel that the international, inter-racial, and inter denominational team in Nepal comes even closer to the ecumenical idea. Both of these projects represent a partnership in evangelism between younger and older churches, but the mission in Nepal has the added advantage of being rooted in an adjacent state which is closely akin, racially, culturally, politically.

This leads to one other practical field of identification. Nothing has been said specifically about the growing emphasis on indigenization, and it need take but a paragraph. Most recent missionary programs have encouraged the younger churches to develop their own music and art forms, their architecture and liturgy. Sometimes indeed it has been the missionaries who have pressed forward, and the nationals who have felt that Gothic or New England Colonial were necessary to distinguish Christian sanctuaries from pagan shrines. But we need to persevere. Today, despite the dubious frowns of a few artistic literalists, our ecumenical worship and our Christmas tables are enriched by indigenous manger scenes from Korea or Africa or India. Who knows or cares the denomination of Lu Hung-nien, Sri Oue, or Kimi Koseki? Can we really call for the development of creative theology in Asia, or the formulation of appropriate creeds for national churches, without anticipating and welcoming new and ecumenical products? Should we hail the freedom of the Church in China, from Western imperialism at least, in the very same report which mentions proudly that "the service (in Shanghai) followed completely the 1662 Book of Common Prayer"? Is no missions professor donning the mantle of Daniel Fleming in the vital area of ecumenical art and symbolism? Are we learning anything from the stimulating experiments among divergent liturgical traditions in the Church of South India?

III. THEOLOGICAL APPROACH

It is long past time to shift to the most important area of all: the theological importance of the ecumenical movement for Christian mission, and vice versa. Dr. Beaver, in the aforementioned Carey Lecture, quoted Emil Brunner as saying: "The mission is the central issue in theology, as well as in the practical work of the Church. We do not know what mission is, and until we do, we shall not know what the Church is." The doctrine of the Church (which Brunner calls "the unsolved problem of Protestantism") has become the central issue of the ecumenical movement, for the sacraments and the ministry and the structural polity are but expressions of this deeper question. As faith and order discussions, or church union negotiations, wrestle with this basic concept, the world mission has much to learn -- and even more to teach.

Dr. Visser't Hooft has said at Oberlin: "A common rediscovery of the Una Sancta and its world-wide mission means there can only be one Church... The task of the Church can only be fulfilled in unity." However we may visualize the fullest expression of that unity-- in organic union, conciliar organization, functional cooperation, or world-wide confessionalism – we cannot escape its imperative. However we may describe the Church -- as a monolithic structure, as a fellowship of individuals, as an organismic diversity of talents and functions -- we are drawn to the necessity for greater unity in Christ. It would be superfluous to reiterate here the great theological insights into mission and unity which have emerged from Rolle, from Whitby, from Willingen, from Evanston and Oberlin. They all point in the same direction.

It would be superfluous, too, to point out the relevance of ecumenical theology for the evangelistic mission of the Church. Most ecclesiastical leaders would admit today that the unity God gives us in Jesus Christ must be made manifest in our visible witness, that somehow the diverse Christian traditions must be reunited in the Christian Tradition. We are all familiar with Emil Brunner's dictum that "the Church exists by mission as fire exists by burning." Those of us who have forgotten the classic illustration from the furnace or the hearth are relearning at the suburban charcoal grill that fire does not exist by burning if the coals are scattered and isolated. Only in the unity of close association can the true warmth of the Gospel be shared among the churches and used for the purposes of Christ. As Dr. Charles Taylor, secretary of the American Association of Theological Schools, said in a letter about this paper to the chairman of this group: "Although we find our place in the whole Church of God through our several traditions, we do not really know ourselves until we know ourselves in relation to others also."

We do not really know our Christian mission until we know it in unity with others. This paper has barely suggested, superficially and pragmatically, some of the ways in which the teaching of missions must be reconceived in the light of the ecumenical movement. The history of Christian missions, the practical programs and policies of the world Church, and the theological motivation which underlies our entire *raison d'etre* -- all these are inescapably bound up with the contemporary search for the full meaning of Christian unity. To those who fear the ecumenical movement as a threat to sectarian autonomy, or to those who dilute the mission in terms of "fraternal workers" and "inter-church aid," the closing word comes appropriately from the president of this group, once more from his stimulating Carey Lecture: "The existence of churches in the *oikumene* does not signify the end of the mission but rather that the time for a world mission has come." It is our task, as professors of missions, to interpret that wider and deeper and higher mission of the Church.

A Critique Of "The Teaching Of Missions In The Light Of The Ecumenical Movement"

Robert Tobias
Christian Theological Seminary
Indianapolis, Indiana

My comments are not so much a critique as a continuation of the general line which Professor Lacy has taken; or I would have them so regarded. I rejoice in his paper and in the relation which is recognized as existing between missions and unity. I should add for some of you here who may not be aware of it that Creighton Lacy has himself done an exceptionally fine syllabus on the ecumenical movement in relation to some of his courses which has been shared with many other professors, particularly those who attended the conference on "Professors of Ecumenics" at Oberlin last year.

First, a few comments structured on Prof. Lacy's outline and then some additions. I shall begin with the least important. In paragraph one, I was struck by the reference to our "outworn concepts." It would be interesting to know how a professor of missions would define such concepts. The problem of the curriculum referred to in paragraph two seems to touch every field. Where does "ecumenics" belong? Let me correct one point or at least one indication in this paragraph: when the group of "Professors of Ecumenics" meeting in Oberlin decided to ask "a small committee to watch for the possibility of meeting again," it was not a "typical ecclesiastical fashion" which led them to this conclusion, but rather a quite strong feeling that they did not want to have any kind of new permanent association of professors.

In his fifth paragraph Professor Lacy refers in passing to the fact that one need not go that far afield… to see the inter-relation of unity and mission. Nonetheless I should like to see someone describe in more precise theological language what is that inter-relation. This is a task which some professors need to take hold of.

In the next paragraph Professor Lacy refers to kerygma, koinonia, and diaconia as "areas of activity." I am concerned at this point that we not conceive of these only in terms of activity. But what are they more than activity? And what is the inter-relationship here at this dimension? If, for example, one begins his study with a relation of missions to mission and the Church, he may speak in terms of "obligation" or "the calling" of the Church, and yet immediately he has presupposed an entity which precedes mission. Then he must first consider not simply "that the Church is mission" as Professor Beaver says, but something else about the nature of the Church; that is, the different dimensions of the being and function of the Church. At this point a quite exciting study could take place as between professors of missions and those involved in contemporary theology, i.e., to apply the categories of "relational" or "process" thought, or if one prefers the categories described as "contextual" or "Christian existentialism" or in some circles "neo-literal -- neo-Orthodox" to our understanding of the meaning of the being and function of the Church. What is the Church? What determines its shape and form? When one digs into this area he always confronts the question of the meaning of "givenness" of the Church. And I for one find that "givenness" means essentially a given relationship inherent in the nature of our created being or beings which can be described only by the word "unity" but this leads to quite different dimension than does the phrase, now becoming a slogan, "the Church is mission." Both are needed. In his section on "Historical Approach" I am delighted to see Professor Lacy's insistence that history must be studied in the light of the ecumenical movement. "It is high time that our teaching and our research sought to analyze the interrelationships of Christian expansion, instead of compartmentalized units." Let me say in passing, for Professor Lacy mentions the matter again later on that missions should be more solidly grounded in church history, that church history must also be much more solidly grounded in decent cosmology. But the point Lacy is getting at cannot be over-emphasized at this particular stage. Missions and the mission of the Church have suffered long the curse of the ecclesiastical historian who has seen history in terms of church pitted against church, Monophysite against Othodox, Constantinople against Rome, Papist against anti-Papist, Protestant against Catholic, and so on. And even the beloved Processor Latourette, Professor Lacy quite rightly I think, touches on this point. When we speak of expansion of the Church in 1900 years is it not pretty much in terms of how much the Church now has expanded beyond what the Church was 100 or 1900 years ago? The real curse hero lies in the fact that where the life of the Church is so presented that it takes its raison d'etre in terms of being different from other churches then it is no longer Gods "encounter with the world. Her missions make common cause with the ecumenical movement. For there is a hidden presupposition in the life of the ecumenical movement that is antischolastic, anti-competitive theology; namely, that it is the penetration of God in history and world through the whole of the Church which is far more important than the proper transmission of right ideas. For if God is not penetrating from generation to generation, then right ideas are nothing but a hollow mockery.

Now I come again to Professor Lacy's insistence that missions must be more solidly founded in church history. At this point I take a degree of exception. The reason being that the best history is probably now being written. Think of China, and the action of the Holy Spirit in the context of world there; or, of the mid-East, and the mission materials which have just been written concerning the mid-East. In these areas and these times where from a statistical standpoint the Church appears to have been a failure, a real attempt is being made to understand the encounter of the Church with the world. I am delighted then to see Professor Lacy calling for some "histories" to be written by mission professors as regards Malaya and other areas. Such work can be only interpretative and prophetic, not statistical and sterile. I should indeed like to see some others by mission professors: "The Mission of the Church Under Dictatorships Through the Years," or "The Mission of the Church in Eras of Conformity" or "The Mission of the Church to Organizational Man." For it is here in our Western and Protestant world that real history in terms of world-Church, in terms of penetration and encounter of God may be most lacking. Mission studies therefore can only be made by the whole Church; and we turn to China, to the mid-East and other areas for some stimulation.

In his section "Practical Approach," Professor Lacy calls for younger churches to be organizationally and structurally responsible in relation to ecumenical organizations, and at the same time for indigenization of the Church in the younger church area. There is a healthy polarity here, at the moment indigenization perhaps having the upperhand. I wonder, however, if we cannot already foresee a kind of reverse indigenization as applies to the younger churches. That is, a time when younger churches will conclude that their regional councils and the World Council of Regional Councils is really not adequate, and we in similar manner may increasingly move in the direction of making world-wide decisions in common with the whole Church. And this applies most particularly where the Church is involved in missions.

At one point Professor Lacy refers to the desirability of teaching "self-government, self-support, self-propagation" as a principle of missionary operation. I am not so sure that we haven't already passed the point when this was so important. The real danger now, it seems to me, is that in the process of "indigenization" churches may move too fast toward autonomy and from autonomy to anarchy. There may indeed be "an economic necessity" which demands indigenization, but I would expect younger churches themselves some day to come to the "mother churches" and ask why they were so readily released from their share in the total world Church responsibility at a time when they were swayed by a heavy nationalism. The pendulum swings in both cases too far, and perhaps professors of missions with younger churchmen need to get their heads together at this point to see that it doesn't swing back again too far to a kind of "momism" once the excessive "independency" insistence is past.

Professor Lacy's comment about the "global scope of the missionary task" as characteristic of the 19th century ecumenical conferences leads me to insist on a quite different emphasis which has come out of the 20th century conferences, or so I would see it, namely: the wholeness of the Church as organically visible, or to put it in other terms, the Word becoming flesh or "incarnateness" in our time. I could cite several illustrations beginning with Edinburgh and coming to Oberlin so far as conferences are concerned, the work of Gustav Tils in the Roman Catholic camp, the World Council's studies or concern for studies in "ecclesiological significance," the phenomena of councils of churches which seem to be some kind of insistent demand for "body" as over against doctrines as a unity of principle and manifest oneness of the Church, and the present stirrings of interest in the concept of world and the meaning of incarnation. This" leads into an area of theology in which missions professors will be particularly concerned, for it is in the Word's "becoming flesh" that we are concerned and that the core of the gospel is seen.

Professor Lacy refers to a transition in missionary practice from the conventional "missionary" relationship to that of the "fraternal worker." In passing, I would remark that several here have indicated their disapproval of the expression "fraternal worker." I should be glad to be enlightened as to the objection to the expression, or is it to the transition? I am not quite clear as to the difference between "fraternal workers" on the one hand and "partnerships" or "partners in obedience" on the other.

Further along Professor Lacy refers to the dilution of "the mission" in terms of "fraternal workers" and "inter-church aid." There is doubtless a transition in this direction, but does this necessarily mean it is irresponsible or "diluted"? One's answer on this point may depend somewhat on his own past experience, his orientation, and perhaps even his defense mechanisms. Perhaps the important question is what the whole of the Church feels in this matter, for most younger church leaders, it seems to me, have been quite outspoken concerning their own judgment on this point.

Professor Lacy calls our attention to a very difficult problem in his reference to the fears of younger churches that organic union in their areas would cause a reduction of interest and support from abroad. Incidentally, here is already an indication of some reverse indigenization. But that does not really say to us quite forcefully that we must begin now developing a sense of the wholeness of the Church, of our mission together in every place, recognizing that the Church in a given place has a primacy of operation in that area, but there is a general responsibility for every area which falls on the whole Church. How to do this is one of our questions. This is perhaps one of the particular areas where as Professor Lacy says, "we need to persevere," and it may well be that in the total "continuum" there may be some sharp breaks, some of which can be anticipated, all of which will require patience and the encouraging ministry of a long-range perspective.

In his section "Theological Approach," which Professor Lacy has had to condense for lack of time, I find the most stimulating area for further study. I start right off by saying that in spite of the renown authorities quoted, Dr. Brunner, Dr. Beaver, Dr. Lacy, I have some real doubt that "mission is the central issue of theology"; for it seems to me that all of these conferences and persons cited by Professor Lacy--Rolle, Whitby, Willingen, and one might add Edinburg, Angus Dun, and others -- the key issue has to do with a basic relational unity becoming visible in man's existence.

And the secondary question has been how and in what shape. Or, to state it another way, a kind of sub-conscious or conscious presupposition that there can and only will be one church in one place and that within that context "our visible witness" is not simply as from one to another within the Church primarily, but as visible to the whole world. I would assume that missions professors would be the first to say so, for certainly this is what the missionaries are about.

In conclusion may I presume to suggest some other areas of ecumenical theological interest which are being opened up or indeed are seeking the attention of professors in such fields as yours. One has to do with the question of proselytism. There is some correlation between the issues involved in proselytism as between Christian groups and in the way Christians confront persons of other faiths. We cannot discuss the issue here, but the whole process of persuasion-conversion as over against, or in relation to, the free acting of the Holy Spirit in the context of proclaiming, needs some very careful rethinking in relation to the methods of our evangelism and mission efforts. Naturally, our concepts of our own faith -- is it dogma, or the knowledge of God, or the process of revelation? -- is a key question and the present trend of interest, if it is such, toward personal encounter with God as against systematic dogmas needs to be seen in the context of the 19th century development of missions outside the churches. Here again the whole Church needs to be brought into the discussion of this process of revelation, to help discern, to evaluate and then to act. Here the conciliar process may be one of the greatest signs of God's grace in that man is enabled in a far broader way to discern to hear, to know through a far broader community what and who is the God who reveals Himself to us.

Another area is the relevance of eschatology for missions. What is the relation between the activities of the missionary and his expectation of results? What is the relevance for his "motivation"? And, what are the relative roles of the eschaton himself and of man?

Professor Lacy says it well in a brief quotation: "The existence of churches in the oikumene does not signify the end of the mission, but rather that the time for a world mission has come." It has indeed, and from where I sit, particularly in terms of depth.

Mission Literature Of The Past Biennium: From the Spring of 1956 to the Spring of 1958

Frank W. Price
Missionary Research Library
New York, New York

The old order changeth, yielding place to new;

And God fulfills himself in many ways,

Lest one good custom should corrupt the world.

- Alfred Tennyson, *Morte d'Arthur* (1842)

THE OLD ORDER CHANGETH

If Tennyson's words were true in 1842, they are certainly true, and even more pertinent, in 1958. Our time of great transition is reflected in literature, and just as much in missionary literature. In fact, we can hardly understand a great deal of missionary writing today without studying the world situation which forms its background. The Christian world mission stands in the living context of old order yielding place to new; it has a serious responsibility to conserve the best of the old and to point the way to the new order which is in harmony with God's purpose in human history.

We listen, first, to what scholars and scientists are saying about our changing world. Fifty authorities in various fields of learning have contributed to a notable survey volume, 1193 pages, *Man's Role in Changing the Face of the Earth* (University of Chicago), edited by William L. Thomas, Jr. Frederick H. Hartman brings a fresh yet sober point of view in *The Relations of Nations* (Macmillan). The well-known writer, Louis Fischer, has given us a broad perspective after a world tour, together with a study of critical issues, *This Is Our World* (Harper), Robert Strausz-Hupe ' s *The Idea of Colonialism* (Praeger) is especially relevant in view of the rising tide of nationalism and anti-colonialism on awakening continents. The eminent Swedish economist, Gunnar Myrdal, has just published what the Saturday Review calls a "seminal book," *Rich Lands and Poor; The Road to World Prosperity* (Harper); it presents an authoritative picture of economic inequalities which are due to more than economic causes. Frank Moraes, the brilliant Indian publicist, views international relations from his part of the world in an eminently readable book, *Yonder One World* (Macmillan).

The work of international organizations for the new world order is well told in a comprehensive volume, *Organizing for Peace* (Houghton Mifflin) by Cheever and Haviland. The tenth anniversary of the United Nations has stimulated several histories and evaluations of this world organization, including *UNESCO: Purpose, Progress, Prospects* (Indiana University) by Laves and Thomson. One very critical problem is that of refugees and displaced persons; a good book on this subject is *The Refugee and the World Community* (University of Minnesota) by John G. Stoessinger. Dr. Frank C. Laubach sees Christian compassion overflowing the organized Church into these international agencies and the gifts of large foundations, *The World is Learning Compassion* (Revell). This is a book of much useful information but some critics have objected to the imprisonment of the Christian ideal in organizations and systems of the moment; "the book constantly angers and at times infuriates me," says Father Huddleston.

From a considerable number of new publications on interracial and intercultural relations I select the following: *Race and Culture Contacts* (Knopf) by E. Franklin Frazier; *Christianity and Race* (St. Martin's) by Philip Mason; an excellent book, *The Kingdom Beyond Caste* (Friendship) by Liston Pope; *The Politics of Inequality* (Praeger) by Gwendolen M. Carter, which deals analytically with the South African problem; and two valuable booklets by Professor B.B. Keet, theologian of Stellenbasch University, *Whither -- South Africa*, and *The Ethics of Apartheid*, both published in South Africa and both very critical of apartheid.

If we want to be critical about American policies and attitudes in relation to world affairs these books will give us material: *America as a Civilization* (Simon and Schuster) by Max Lerner; *The Art of Overseasmanship*, published by the Maxwell School of Public Affairs at Syracuse University and edited by Harlan Cleveland and others; and H. R.

Issacs' disturbing volume about prejudices, *Scratches On Our Minds* (John Day).

Of making of books on lands and peoples near and far there is no end. The student of missions can only try to keep up with some of them. The Near and Middle East is an area of tension that continues to draw world attention; it is the subject of study this year in books published by Friendship Press, of which R. Park Johnson's *Middle East Pilgrimage* and Glora Wysner's *Caught in the Middle* should be especially mentioned. The best book I have read on this region and its challenge is Denis Baly's *Multitudes in the Valley* (Seabury). Others that should be included in this list are: *The Middle East: Its Religion and Culture* (Westminster) by Edward J. Jurji; *Bridgehead: The Drama of Israel* (Brazzilier) by Waldo Frank; *There Goes the Middle East* (Devin-Adair), strongly pro-Arab, by Alfred M. Lilienthal; *Islam Inflamed: A Middle East Picture* (Pantheon), by James Morris; *Arabian Destiny* (Essential) by Jacques Benoist-Mechin and translated from the French by Denis Weaver; *Middle East Crisis* (Penguin), a careful study, by Guy Wint and Peter Calvocoressi, and *Will the Middle East Go West?* (Regnery), strongly biased, by Freda Utley. Maxim Osward's *Asia Minor* (Morrow) is an attractive volume of 160 photographs, several in color.

Only a few books can be listed out of the many appearing on Africa and Asia in general. Heinrich Schiffers' *The Quest for Africa* (Putnam) is the story of two thousand years, magnificently told. Other fine books are *West Africa; A Study of the Environment and Man's Use of It* (Longmans, Green) by R. J. Harrison Church; *African Economic Development* (Harper) by William A. Hance; and a beautiful book of photographs, *Portrait of Southern Africa* (Collins), by Harms Reich. Similar volumes of photographs, exquisite in form and full of interest, are *Asia* (Crowell) by Hurlimann; *South America* (Crowell) by Mann; and *The Tropics* (Knopf) by Edgar Aubert de La Rue and others. *A World on the Move* (Amsterdam), is a history of colonialism and nationalism in Asia and Africa from the turn of the century to the Bandung Conference, with 674 illustrations, a fascinating but also disturbing book. On Southeast Asia we have *View to the Southeast* (Harper) by Santha Rama Rau, and *South East Asia Among the World Powers* (University of Kentucky) by Vandenbosch and Butwell, Three books on Latin America are worthy of mention here: *Latin America; A History* (Macmillan) by Alfred B. Thomas; *Fantastic South America* (Horizon), on the "continent of the future," by Henry Lionel Williams; *The Growth and Culture of Latin America* (Oxford) by Worcester and Schaeffer. A sociological study of the Caribbean area is found in *Caribbean Studies: A Symposium* (Columbia University) by seventeen contributors under the editorship of Vera Rubin. Fritz Henle and P. E. Knapp have produced *The Carribean* (Crowell) a book of 250 marvelous photographs with a fine commentary. *Archipels Polynesiens* (Hachette) is an intriguing description of the Polynesian Islands by a sensitive writer, Bernard Villaret.

Books about individual countries are even more numerous, but the best of them need to be known by missionaries going to those lands, and by students of world-wide Christianity. Interesting titles are coming out about nations behind the Iron Curtain. On Russia: John Gunther's deservedly popular new book, *Inside Russia Today* (Harper); Louis Fischer, *Russia Revisited* (Doubleday); and *RSFSR, Russian Soviet Federated Socialist Republic* (Human Relations Area Files), on Russian anthropology, economics, international relations, political developments, and social psychology. From a large number of volumes about China I select: *Chinese Thought and Institutions* (University of Chicago) edited by John K. Fairbank; *The Soul of China* (Coward-McCann) by Amoury de Riencourt, a historical survey with great breadth and a fresh approach; Earl H. Cressys *Understanding China* (Nelson); and a stirring novel of World War II in West China, *The Mountain Road* (Sloane) by Theodore H. White. The best books on Communist China have been: *From One China to the Other* (Universe), a collection of outstanding photographs with text by Han Suyin; *Communist China Today* (Praeger) by a young Chinese scholar, Peter S. H. Tang; *Im Neuen China* (Atlantis Verlag) by Lily Abegg; and Robert Guillain's *600 Million Chinese* (Criterion), an objective and well-written report by a French reporter who has visited China often. Simone de Beauvoir's *The Long March* (World), though marked by some fine insights into Chinese culture, is entirely uncritical and amusingly naive in its praise of New China. Two interesting books have appeared on Mongolia and Tibet: *Die Mongolei* (Isar Verlag) by Erich Thiel; *On the Road Through Tibet* (Spring) by V. Sis and J. Vanis, translated from the Czech. On India we have a variety of new books and must choose: *The New India: Progress Through Democracy* (Macmillan), official plans and outlook; W. S. Woytinsky's *India, The Awakening Giant* (Harper), optimistic and sympathetic; Frank Moraes' excellent biography, *Jawaharlal Nehru* (Macmillan), and Alexander Campbell's *The Heart of India* (Knopf), a second Mother India in its devastating exposure of the darker side of Indian government and society, with little sense of proportion and little compassion. An important book on Pakistan is *Pakistan, A Political Study* (Allen & Unwin) by Keith Collard.

Turning to the Far East, we call attention to these good general books on Japan: *Sources of the Japanese Tradition* (Columbia University) by Tsunoda and others; *Japan Between East and West* (Harper) by Hugh

Borton and five other authorities; *The New Japan* (University of Minnesota) by Quigley and Turner; *In the Gray Rain* (Harper) delightful personality sketches, by Hazel S. Mac-Cartney; and Philip Williams' perceptive *Journey Into Mission* (Friendship) written, said the New York Times with "enthusiasm, humility and intense sincerity," On Korea we have a fine source book, *Korea's Heritage* (Tuttle) by Shannon McGune. Representing Southeast Asia are *The Smaller Dragon* (Praeger), first political history of Vietnam, by Joseph Buttinger; *The Union of Burma* (Oxford) by Hugh Tinker; *Building a Welfare State in Burma* (I.P.R.) by Frank N. Trager; *Malaya, A Political and Economic Appraisal* (University of Minnesota) by L. A. Mills. To the books already mentioned about South Africa should be added *South Africa in Transition* (Scribner), with photographs by Weiner and text by Alan Paton. Two significant books are: *Pageant of Ghana* (Oxford) by Freda Wolfson, and Kwamo Nkrumah's autobiography, *Ghana* (Nelson). Sylvia Parkhurst's *Ethiopia, A Cultural History* (Lalibela House), is a survey of arts and culture, beautifully illustrated. A unique volume is *People of the Reeds* (Harper), describing the inhabitants of the lower Tigris in Iraq, by Gavin Maxwell. The world still watches the two dictatorships of Spain and Portugal, *Spain, A Modern History* (Praeger)by de Madariaga is a new edition of a good book first published in 1930; *The Yoke and the Arrows* (Brazziler) is a brilliantly written analysis of the continuing ferment in Spain by a noted newspaper correspondent, Herbert Matthews. Richard Wright, the Negro writer, is the author of *Pagan Spain* (Harper). The strong man of Portugal is pictured in *Salazar, An Intimate Portrait*, translated from the French (Farrar, Straus) by Christine Gamier. *Persia* (Praeger), an illustrated description by Costa and Lockhart, and *Mexico Today* (Harper) by John A. Crow contain much interesting information about the culture of these lands.

We should not end this section without a reference to the useful series of Behavior Science Monographs, Country Series and Bibliographies, published by The Human Relations Area Files (affiliated with 16 universities) at New Haven. Sixteen volumes have appeared in the last two years, covering many regions and countries. They vary somewhat in quality but should be in all libraries on world affairs. A complete list of publications may be secured from this organization.

ANTHROPOLOGY AND ETHNOLOGY

Interest in anthropological studies continues unabated. We realize more and more their significance for the missionary, A good introductory book is *Anthropology and Human Nature* (Porter Sargent) by M.F. Ashley-

Montagu. *Peasant Society and Culture* (University of Chicago), by Robert Redfield, represents the interest of anthropologists in primitive society and peasant communities. A new reference book is *Religions, Mythologies, Folklores* (Scarecrow) by Katherine Smith Diehl; it has a good annotated bibliography. Among the recent books on special groups are: *The Chiga of Western Uganda* (Oxford) by Edel; *Neuer Religion* (Clarendon), a study of the cattle –herding people of southern Sudan, by Evans-Pritchard; *Kongo, II* (Almquist & Wiksells), second part of a study by the late missionary, Karl Laman; *Kikuyu Social and Political Institutions* (Oxford) by Lambert; *The Yao Village* (Manchester University), an able study covering nearly two years of a Nyasaland tribe, by J. C. Mitchell; *Rituals of Kinship Among the Nyakyusa* (Oxford) by Monica Wilson, a missionary's daughter; *Schism and Continuity in an Indian Society* (Manchester University), a scholarly study of Ndembu Village life by V. W. Turner; *Instrument and Purpose* (Gleerup), the phenomena of Hindu rites and rituals with much new material, by Carl G. Diehl; *Where the Gods are Mountains* (Reynal), three years' observation among the people of the Himalayas by Nebesky-Wykowitz; *Leadership and Power in the Chinese Community of Thailand* (Cornell University), by G. W. Skinner; *The People of Puerto Rico: A Study in Social Anthropology* (University of Illinois) by Julian H, Steward and others; *Here Is Haiti* (Philosophical) by the trained sociologist, Ruth D. Wilson; *The Naked Aucas* (Essential), by R. Blomberg, a study of the Indian tribe in Ecuador which murdered five young missionaries in 1956; *Land of the Moon-Children* (University of Georgia) about the primitive culture of the Cuna Indians on islands off Panama, by Clyde E. Keeler; *Dawn in Arctic Alaska* (University of Minnesota), about Eskimo family life, by Diamond Jenness; and *Life Among the Aborigines* (Robert Hale) by a recognized authority on aboriginal tribes of Australia, W. E. Harney.

THE LIVING RELIGIONS OF MANKIND

Some excellent books in this field have been published since early 1956. We are all familiar with the popular, yet scholarly, articles on religions of the world which appeared in *Life* two years ago; these have been gathered now in one volume, with fine illustrations and an introduction by Paul Hutchinson, *The World's Great Religions*. Other general works are: Noss' *Man's Religions* (Macmillan), a standard text, with important revisions and additions; Edwin A. Burtt's *Man Seeks the Divine* (Harper), *Die Grossen Nichtchristlichen Religionen Unserer Zeit* (A. Kroner Verlag), by Walter Fuchs and others; and the best of them all, *The Religions of Man* (Harper), by Huston Smith, a son of missionaries, who spent the first seventeen years of his life in China and is now Lecturer at Washington University.

Arnold Toyribee has written a short and clear book from his point of view, *Christianity Among the Religions of the World* (Scribner). Christianity, he says, must give up "fanaticism and claim to uniqueness." W. E. Hocking, seemingly more conservative than he was twenty years ago, has given us a thought-provoking outlook in *The Coming World Civilization* (Harper), with special emphasis on the place of religion.

In the area of particular religions we begin with Geoffrey Parrinder's *Witchcraft* (Pelican), a study of European and African witchcraft, with a selected bibliography. On Buddhism these are my choices: *The Path of the Buddha, Buddhism Interpreted by Buddhists* (Ronald), edited by Kenneth W. Morgan; Suzuki's *Mysticism, Christian and Buddhist* (Harper), Alan Watts' *The Way of Zen* (Pantheon). Sarvepalli Radhakrishnan and Charles A. Moore have edited *A Source Book in Indian Philosophy* (Princeton University), covering three thousand years of Indian philosophical and religious thought. Gambhirananda's *History of The Ramakrishna Math and Mission* (Calcutta), commemorates the Diamond Jubilee of this movement. Swami Nikhilananda contributes the interpretation of an insider, *Hinduism, Its Meaning for the Liberation of the Spirit* (Harper). A comprehensive and imaginative history of Taoism is seen in *The Parting of the Way, Lao Tzu and the Taoist Movement* (Beacon), by Holmes Welch. Robert Bellah covers the important period of 1600 to 1868 in his *Tokugawa Religion* (Free Press).

Islam -- The Straight Path (Ronald) is a notable book, consisting of eleven articles by outstanding Muslim scholars in seven languages, all translated into English and edited by Kenneth W. Morgan. A. J. Arberry has written *Revelation and Reason in Islam* (Allen & Unwin), on the conflict within Islam and its resolution. On the relationship of Christianity to ethnic religions, especially Islam and Hinduism, three very significant books have appeared. In *The Inevitable Choice; Vedanta Philosophy or Christian Gospel* (Abingdon) the well-known Edmund Davidson Soper opposes strongly any trend toward syncretism. Hendrik Kraemer's *Religion and the Christian Faith* (Lutterworth and Westminster) is essential reading for all students of world missions and evangelism. Dr. Kraemer appears here as a dynamic classroom lecturer, strenuously defending his own orthodox position, engaging in a polemical warfare with a wide range of opponents, critics, and scholars of religion whose viewpoints vary from his, hammering continuously on the theme of the unique, incomparable, intractable disclosure of God in Christ, and making innumerable diversionary sorties. Kenneth Cragg, eminent missionary authority on Islamic studies, reacts strongly against Dr. Kraemer's rigid position in *The Call of the Minaret* (Oxford). He fears that largely theoretical and academic discussions of non-Christian faiths and a belligerent attitude toward them and their exponents may render more difficult the deeper understanding of these religions and also of the persons and societies within their systems. In his book we find a note of patient love, of tender wooing, of Christ-like yearning, of mission under the Cross, that seems to be lacking in Dr. Kraemer's magnum opus. Dr. Cragg's book has been called "the ablest ever written on the relations of Christianity to Islam," and has won high praise from Muslims as well as Christian scholars.

THE CHALLENGE OF COMMUNISM

The challenge of Communism is everywhere felt and is provoking much serious thought, discussion, and writing. Two books from within the Russian orbit should be mentioned: *Not By Bread Alone* (translation, Dutton) by Vladimir Dudintsev, a bold novel aimed at Russian bureaucracy; and the best seller, *The New Class* (translation, Praeger), by the Yugoslavian leader Djilas, who is now in prison. *The Hungarian Revolution* (Praeger), edited by Melvin J. Lasky, is a "White Book" of important documents and eye-witness accounts of that epochal uprising. Books on the Communist movement that should be on our shelves are: Kennedy's *A History of Communism in East Asia* (Praeger); Henry Wei's *China and Soviet Russia* (Van Nostrand); Lacquer's *Communism and Nationalism in the Middle East* (Praeger); George Padmore's *Pan- Africanism or Communism?* (Roy). Accounts of the Christian Church under Communist regimes are found in *The Redbook of the Persecuted Church* (Newman) by Albert Gaiter; *The Story of Mary Liu* (Farrer, Straus & Cudahy), a remarkable experience, well narrated by Edward Hunter; and two reports of deputations to mainland China, the British Quaker Mission (Friends House, London) and that of Australian churchmen (NCCC-USA, DFM). Books on the theory and practice of Communism and its meaning for Christianity include: *Marxism and the Open Mind* (Routledge and Kegan Paul) by John Lewis; *Communism and Christianity* (Devin Adair) by the English Jesuit theologian, Martin C. D'Arcy; *Theology Between Yesterday and Tomorrow* (Westminster) by the Czech theologian, Joseph L. Hromadka, who seeks to mediate between Communism and the Christian Gospel; the large new book by Charles C. West, *Communism and the Theologians; Study of an Encounter* (SCM Press, to be published in November by Westminster) heavy reading but rewarding; and my own small contribution, *Marx Meets Christ* (Westminster) by Price.

One new book of importance has appeared on religious liberty, Giovanni Miegge's *Religious Liberty* (Lutterworth Press, World Christian Books).

HISTORY AND PRESENT WORK OF MISSIONS AND NATIONAL CHURCHES

Professor C. P. Groves has completed his monumental history, *The Planting of Christianity in Africa* (Lutterworth). Volume IV, covering 1914- 1954, has just been published. Another distinguished achievement is Dr. K.S. Latourette's *World Service; A History of the Foreign Work and World Service of the Young Men's Christian Association of the United States and Canada* (Association Press). This covers YMCA service in L2 countries over almost a century. CP. Shedd's *History of the World's Alliance of Y.M.C.A's* (S.P.C.K.) appeared two years ago. *One Faith and Fellowship* (Seabury) by John Seville Higgins is the story of Anglican missionary work around the world. *Baptist World Fellowship* (Carey Kingsgate), by F. T. Lord, is a short history of the Baptist World Alliance, its missions, and younger churches. John N. Hollister has written *The Centenary of the Methodist Church in Southern Asia* (Lucknow Publishing House). In 1956 an English translation was published of E. Arno Lehmann's *It Began at Tranquebar; A History of the First Protestant Mission in India* (Madras C.L.S.).

Several denominational histories have recently come out. James A. Cogswell is author of *Until the Day Dawns* (Nashville, Presbyterian Board), story of the Southern Presbyterian Mission in Japan, which is an excellent summary also of Christian work on the islands. The Centennial Committee of the Christian Reformed Church has issued *One Hundred Years In the New World* (Grand Rapids). *Mission in Formosa and Hong Kong* (Augsburg) by Ruth Sovik and others tells about the Lutheran Church in those places. *Land of Promise* (Highway), by Mary Stuart, is a short history of Anglican missions in Uganda. H. W. Williamson has produced an extensive history, *British Baptists in China; 1855-1952*. (Carey Kingsgate). Written in Dutch and awaiting translation into English is *The Vision of Herrnhut and the Apostolate of the Moravian Brethren in Surinam* (C. Kersten) by John Marinus' Van der Linde, a scholarly and moving narrative. Another kind of history is *Proving God; Financial Experiences of the China Inland Mission* (C.I.M. Overseas Fellowship), telling how this faith mission has found support from the days of Hudson Taylor to the present, by Phyllis Thompson.

A scholar of the Eastern Orthodox Church, Cardinal Eugene Tisserant, has written the full story of *Eastern Christianity in India*; the book is now translated from the French and published by Newman Press.

Roman Catholic mission histories include: *Les Missions des Origines au XVIe Siecle* (Librairie Grund), by a group of scholars under the editorship of Monseigneur Delacroix; *Les Jesuites et 1' Extreme -Orient* (La Table Ronde), describing four centuries of Catholic work in China, Japan and India by the Society of Jesus, by Marianne Moncstier. Cary-Elwes has attempted in *China and the Cross* (Kennedy) a survey of missionary history in China from the 7th century to the present, with attention to Protestant as well as Catholic enterprise. *Martyrs in China* (Regnery) by Jean Monsterleet and translated into English is an inspiring account of persecutions and martyrdoms. The first systematic effort to collect and publish all relevant materials about Communist persecution of Roman Catholic missions in China is embodied in a book by Johannes Schutte, *Die Katholische Chinamission im Spiegel der Rotchinesischen Presse* (Aschendorffsche Verlags-Buchhandlung) -- *The Maryknoll Golden Book*, edited by A.J. Hevins, is a fine anthology of Catholic mission literature, published by the Catholic Foreign Mission Society of America. *Missiegeschiedenis* by Alphons Mulders and published by Paul Brand in Bussum is a new history of Catholic missions which makes only negative references to Protestant missions. *Digest of Catholic Mission History* (Maryknoll Publications) by Sister Mary Just is now off the press, a good example of the World Horizon Reports published at intervals by this strong missionary organization.

On the work of missions and the Christian movement today we should mention first the splendid new book by W. Stanley Rycroft, *Religion and Faith in Latin America* (Westminster). Along with this we list: Charles W. Iglehart's *Cross and Crisis in Japan* (Friendship Press) which has sold more than a hundred thousand copies; *Reconciliation and Renewal* in Japan by the young Japanese theological professor, Masao Takenaka, published by the Student Volunteer Movement and Friendship Press; *Japanese Witnesses for Christ* (Association Press), five short biographies written by Japanese; *The Tumbling Walls* (United Presbyterian Church), about North Africa and Pakistan, written by a visiting pastor and his wife, Marian and Edwin Fairman; Roland Oliver's *How Christian Is Africa?* (Highway); *Land Beyond the Nile* (Harper) by Malcolm Forsberg; *God's Fool* (Faber and Faber) by George N. Patterson, story of Plymouth Brethren missionary work in China, Tibet, and India; Constance Hallockis *East From Burma* (Friendship), about Christianity in the development of Southeast Asia nations; and *These My People* (Zondervan), an animated account by Mrs. Lillian Dickson of missionary service among the mountain tribes of Formosa. Two books, of a quite different nature, by John V. Taylor should be included: *Christianity and Politics in Africa* (Penguin), and *The Passion in Africa* (Mowbray), a story with pictures by Hans Leuenberger of a moving Passion Play using an all-African cast.

The following books will be helpful to those who are studying the expansion of foreign missionary effort by the Church of the Latter Day Saints (Mormons), and Jehovah's Witnesses: *Why I Am A Mormon* (Nelson) by Wallace F. Bennett, containing considerable information on the missionary program; Thomas F. O'Dea's *The Mormons* (University of Chicago); *Triumphant Kingdom* (Criterion) an excellent appraisal of Jehovah's Witnesses by Marley Cole; the *1956 Year Book of Jehovah's Witnesses*, published by the Watch Tower Bible and Tract Society; *Faith on the March* (Prentice-Hall), an account by life-long members of Jehovah's Witnesses; and *Thirty Years a Watch Tower Slave* (Baker), a bestselling expose by a disillusioned member.

MISSIONARY BIOGRAPHIES

This has been a great biennium for missionary biographies. At the top of the list should be George Seaverrs definitive *David Livingstone--His Life and Letters* (Harper). Based on new researches, this is a magnificent piece of work; its weakness is that it concentrates too much on Livingstone and does not give enough historical background and social context. The continued interest in Livingstone is shown by Cecil Northcott's *Livingstone in Africa* (World Christian Books) and *Livingstone the Doctor* by Michael Gelfand, M.D., a medical specialist, published by Blackwell. *The Man Who Presumed* (Holt), by Byron Farwell, is a study of motivations in the life of Livingstone's discoverer, Henry M. Stanley. Books and articles about Albert Schweitzer are endless. Robert Payne has written an excellent study of the great missionary physician, *The Three Worlds of Albert Schweitzer* (Nelson), "a work of biographical magnitude" the Saturday Review calls it. *To the Golden Shore* (Little, Brown) is a new and entrancing life of Adoniram Judson; Courtney Anderson is the author. Another biography of the apostle to the New Hebrides has appeared, *John G. Paton* (Higley), by Ralph R. Bell. *Great Lion of Bechuanaland* (London, Independent Press) is a well-written story of the life and times of Roger Price by the anthropologist, Edwin W. Smith. *The Journals of Elizabeth Lees Price* (Edward Arnold), edited by Una Long, consist of letters written by Robert Moffat's daughter who married Roger Price. Dii Arno Lehmann has edited the hitherto unpublished letters of Bartholomaus Ziegenbalg, 1706- 1719, *Alte Briefe aus Indien*, (Evangelische Verlagsanstalt), a large 552-page volume! Archibald L. Fleming has written a vigorous biography, *Archibald The Arctic* (Appleton-Century-Crofts) about a Scotch missionary to the Eskimos. Those who read and loved J. H. Oldham's biography of Florence Allshorn, missionary to Uganda, will be happy to know that the notebooks of Miss Allshorn have been edited and are now published by

SCM Press, London. Ann M. Harrison has told the story of Paul Harrison, great missionary doctor to the Arabs, in *A Tool in His Hand* (Friendship). *My Arabian Days and Nights* (Crowell), by Eleanor T. Calverley, is the autobiography of a medical missionary among Muslim Arabs.

Elizabeth Elliot wrote a very moving account of the five missionary martyrs in Ecuador, *Through Gates of Splendor* (Harper) which has had a wide sale. Alan Burgess' *The Small Woman* (Dutton) is another best seller; unfortunately this exciting story of an independent British missionary in China is as much legend as fact. The story of Pere Lebbe, the Belgian Roman Catholic missionary to China who helped to bring about a Chinese bishopric, is well told in *Thunder in the Distance* (Sheed and Ward), by Jacques Leclercq.

PRINCIPLES AND THEOLOGY OF MISSION

Dr. O. G. Myklebust has completed Volume 2 of his monumental research, *The Study of Missions in Theological Education* (Egede Instituttet); Dr. Latourette says, "All future investigations in the scientific approach to Protestant missions will find in it a comprehensive and invaluable mine of information." A distinguished contribution to mission theory, unfortunately already out of print, is the book by Johannes van den Berg, *Constrained by Jesus' Love; An Inquiry into the Motives of the Missionary Awakening in Great Britain, 1698-1815* (Kampen, J. H. Kok). *The Renewal of the Church* (Westminster) by W.A. Visser 't Hooft, and *The Unfinished Task* (Lutterworth) by Stephen Neill are solid books that will stimulate thought and discussion. A cluster of four small but most significant books should be on every missions shelf: Charles W. Forman's *A Faith For the Nations* (Westminster); R. Pierce Beaver's *The Christian World Mission: A Reconsideration, Carey Lectures, Calcutta*, Baptist Mission Press, for sale by D.F.M.); James S. Stewart's *Thine Is The Kingdom* (St. Andrew Press); and James S. Thomson's *The Divine Mission* (Toronto, United Church).

Voices challenging old concepts of missions are heard in *Revolution in Missions* (Vellore Popular Press), edited by Blaise Levai. Gabriel Hebert in an important book, *Fundamentalism and the Church* (Westminster), discusses the strength and weaknesses of fundamentalist theology and its implications for the missionary movement. An extraordinarily able study of the question of "younger churches" is found in Peter Beyerhaus' *Die Selbststandigkeit der jungen Kirchen als missionarisches Problem* (Wuppertal), soon to be published in an English translation by SCM Press, with the title *The Responsible Selfhood of the Church, A Study in Missiology*. Evangelism is considered thoughtfully and earnestly in three books of real worth: *The Communication of the Christian Faith* (Westminster) by Hendrik Kraemer; *The Preacher's Task and the Stone of Stumbling* (Harper) by D.T. Niles, first Asian to deliver the Beecher Lectures at Yale; and *Christianity and Communication* by F. W. Dillistone (Scribner's).

A noteworthy Roman Catholic contribution is *Le Probleme Cardinal de la Missiologie et des Missions Catholiques* (Holland, Rhenen), by Edouard Loffeld, a church-centered philosophy of mission. *Teach Ye All Nations* (Bonziger) is a briefer and simpler statement of Roman Catholic missionary principles.

THE ECUMENICAL MOVEMENT

The fourth and final volume of *Documents on Christian Unity*, edited by G.K.A. Bell has just been published by Oxford University Press. This valuable collection of documents covers the period 1948-1957. A Jesuit scholar, Edward Duff, is the author of a most interesting study, *The Social Thought of the World Council of Churches* (Association Press). Winifred E. Garrison in *The Quest and Character of a United Church* (Abingdon) discusses liberty and variety within the universal Christian fellowship, a fellowship which as yet is far from being a united Church. *Cooperation Without Compromise* (Eerdmans) is a severe criticism of the ecumenical movement by a leader in the National Association of Evangelicals and World Evangelical Fellowship, James D. Murch.

In the category of church union overseas we have received within the past two years: *Empty Shoes* (Protestant Episcopal National Council), an excellent report and interpretation on the Church of South India; *The Plan of Church Union in North India and Pakistan*, 3rd edition (Madras, C.L.S.); also, booklets and pamphlets on other union developments and autonomous churches. The training of leadership has received a new impetus through the I.M.C. Theological Education Fund. One survey report, *Survey of the Training of the Ministry in Madagascar* (I.M.C.) appeared in 1957.

Important conference report volumes include: *Geredja Asia Timur bertemu di Prapat* (Prapat) and the English edition of the same, entitled *A Report of the Prapat Conference* (Australian Council for W.C.C.), edited by H.L. Perkins and W. T. Thomas; another report on the Prapat Conference, *The Common Evangelistic Task of the Churches in East Asia* (Rangoon, East Asia Christian Conference); *The Listening Isles* (I.M.C.), records of the Caribbean Consultation in 1957; *The Nature of the Unity We*

Seek (Bethany), report on the North American Conference on Faith and Order of September 1957. Full reports of the I.M.C. Assembly in Ghana and of the All-Africa Church Conference in Ibadan, Nigeria, will soon be published by the International Missionary Council.

The research work of the I.M.C. and W.C.C. continues through the Division of Studies and the Departments on Faith and Order, Church and Society, Evangelism and Missionary Studies. Several publications have appeared within the past two years. Of especial concern for us are the studies in areas of social change and the I.M.C. research pamphlets. Since 1956 we have seen publication of *The Communication of the Gospel* by H. R. Weber; *The Gospel and the Religions*, by Walter Freytag; and *Processes of Growth in an African Church* by John V. Taylor, all published by SCM Press, John Taylor's booklet is being published as a big book by SCM Press in November, 1958, *The Growth of the Church in Buganda, An Attempt at Understanding*. I assume that you are familiar with the recent research monographs and papers of the Missionary Research Library.

MISSIONARY TRAINING AND METHODS

I mention three books on missionary preparation: A.T. Houghton's *Preparing to Be A Missionary* (London, I.V.F.); *Have We No Right?* (Moody), by Mabel Williamson of the China Inland Mission Overseas Fellowship; and an M.R.L. monograph, *A Study of Missionary Motivation, Training and Withdrawal*, by Kenyon E. Moyer. Many good pamphlets have been issued by the Student Volunteer Movement, NCCC-USA. Division of Foreign Missions, and denominational societies.

On the relation of missions to relief and inter-church aid we have: *The Church Is There* (Seabury) by Leslie E. Cook of the W.C.C; *Man's New Hope* (Church Peace Union) by Justin Wroe Nixon; *As Between Brothers* (Augsburg), by Richard W. Solberg, the story of the Lutheran response to world need, Frank Laubach's new book has already been listed. S.M. Kenny's *Half the World's Children* (Association Press) is a fascinating diary of UNICEF at work in Asia, in which missionaries have cooperated. *Arzte in aller Welt* (Stuttgart, Evangelischer Missionverlag) by Samuel Muller describes the invaluable contribution of medical missions. *Doctors to the World* (Viking) tells of WHO programs, which have made contact with many missionary hospitals. A former agricultural missionary to India, Arthur Mosher, has written about the place of agricultural and rural missions in his survey, *Technical Cooperation in Latin-American Agriculture* (University of Chicago). On rural missions four excellent volumes have come to the Library: *Deep Furrows* (Agricultural Missions) by Ira W. Moomaw; *Church Bells in Many Tongues* (privately published, distributed by Friendship Press) by Ralph A. Felton; *Preacher With A Plow* (Houghton Mifflin), by Samuel B. Coles, an American Negro missionary to Africa; *The Village Church in West Pakistan* (NCCC-USA, Division of Home Missions), report of a consultation in Pakistan and survey of rural churches there, by Richard O. Comfort. On the urban church and its problems we have received *The Urban Community and the Urban Church* (India N.C.C.). A splendidly illustrated book on all kinds of missionary and church work is *Christian India* (Vanguard), by Plattner and Moosbrugger, translated from the German. The use of mass media techniques in evangelism is discussed by Alan Walker in *The Whole Gospel for the Whole World* (Abingdon).

Beautifully printed and inspiring for all workers in the Christian world mission are these two devotional books: *In His Name* (Edinburgh House, St. Martin's), by George Appleton, a book of prayers; and *Meditations of an Indian Christian* (SCM Press) by M. A. Thomas.

REFERENCE BOOKS

A strict selection is necessary from the large number of reference books and bibliographies recently available. The 20th volume of *Bibliographia Missionaria* (Rome, Unione Missionaria), edited by Johannes Rommerskirchen, has been published. A reference book on Roman Catholic missions highly recommended to us is *Perspectives sur la Monde* (Quebec, L' Union Missionaire), by Abbe Adrien Bouffard. *World Religions* (Dutton), by B. Y. Landis is good for desk reference. Also, *Lutheran Churches of the World* (Augsburg), by Hans Lilje and others. The 1957 edition of *World Christian Handbook* (World Dominion) has been issued. Limits of space forbid inclusion of many good general books of reference, but I cannot forbear mention of *World Literacy at Mid-Century* (Paris, UNESCO), a comprehensive survey with statistics by countries.

Two new periodicals have recently begun publication: *Frontier*, a quarterly which takes the place of *World Dominion and Christian News-Letter*; *Worldview*, published by Church Peace Union.

APM

Conference Reports

Index of Reports

3rd Biennial Meeting (1956)

MEETING MINUTES

Thursday , June 7

1. The Third Biennial Meeting of the Association of Professors of Missions and related Fields met for devotional service in the chapel of the Evangelical Theological Seminary at 9:30a.m., Thursday, June 7.

2. Dr. Paul Eller, president of the host school, welcomed the Association and led the brief devotional period.

3. Members of the Association moved to the reading room of the library for the order of the day which President M. Searle Bates outlined as follows:
- The theme for the day centered on "Christianity and the Non-Christian Religions -- Historical Review of Thought and Literature."
- Four papers were to be presented. (Specific titles appear in the index of the total report of the meeting.)
  - *In the Far East*, presented by Joseph Kitagawa,
  - *In India*, presented by Norvin Hein,
  - *With Respect to Islam*, presented by Kenneth Cragg. (In his absence the paper was effectively read by J. Leslie Bunstan.)
  - *Present Phase of the Problem*, presented by R. Pierce Beaver.
- The President announced procedures as follows. After the presentation of papers, persons specifically assigned

would open review. Open discussion was to follow the initial interview. Reviewers were:

- *In the Far East*, Frank Price;
- *In India*, Herbert Jackson;
- *With Respect to Islam*, Leonard Wolcott and Malcolm Pitt;
- *Present Phase of the Problem*, Calvin Reber.

4. An item of business. A motion prevailed that the President appoint a nominating committee for the Association. This committee should function before the business session of Saturday morning.

Friday, June 8

5. The devotional service in the Seminary Chapel was led by Dr. Paul G. Rademacher, Professor of Systematic Theology, Evangelical Theological Seminary.

6. "The Approach of the Gospel as Seen from Within African Culture or Society," presented by Eduardo Mondlane, Mozambique, Africa. Reviewers: Leonard Gittings and George Dunger.

7. "Expression of Christianity in the Arts and Customs of Asian Cultures," presented by Malcolm Pitt, and reviewed by George Carver.

8. "Issues Arising in the International Missionary Council Study on the Christian Enterprise in China, with Request for Criticism and Suggestions," presented by M. Searle Bates, and reviewed by George Carver.

Saturday, June 9

9. Dr,. Francis W. Boelter, Professor of Old Testament Literature and Interpretation, Evangelical Theological Seminary, was the chapel devotional leader.

10. The Annual Business Meeting
- The minutes of the previous biennial meeting were read for approval and information.
- The Secretary of the Association reported briefly relative to releases and responsibilities of the past two years.

- The report of the Treasurer was presented along with the report of the auditor. The report appears following these minutes.
- It was moved that the "Association of Professors of Missions and Related Fields extend a hearty vote of thanks to the Evangelical Theological Seminary, Naperville, Illinois, for the courtesies extended. These courtesies made possible the splendid fellowship of this biennial meeting." The motion prevailed.
- It was voted that the papers presented at this third biennial meeting be mimeographed and distributed to members of the Association on payment of the biennial membership fee of two dollars. Organizations, libraries and related societies may secure copies for the sum of two dollars.
- Relationships of the Association were discussed. No action was taken. Consensus seemed to be that members present hoped for another meeting of similar nature two years hence. This is not to be construed as meaning that cooperation with the "Professors in the Practical field" is to be forgotten. It was discovered that Professors of Missions have so much in common that a meeting such as the Naperville meeting seemed a necessity.
- Suggestions for the new executive committee relative to subjects or themes of the next biennial meeting were received. They are listed as received:
  - How may missions take account of their growth and be related to churches?
  - Missions in the Curriculum of the Theological seminary.
  - The Nature of the Unity We Seek in our Missionary Enterprise.
  - What is the Relationship of "Missions in the Curriculum" to other fields of study?
- George Carver, Chairman of the Nominating Committee, reported. The Committee presented a single set of nominees.
  - President, R. Pierce Beaver.
  - Vice President, Don Holter.
  - Secretary-Treasurer, Wilber C. Harr.
  - Convener, Southern Region, Norman A. Horner.
  - Convener, Western Region, Leonard Gillings.

- The Association paused for a moment of remembrance honoring two members who passed away during the biennium: J. Wach and Stacy R. Warburton.

11. "Missions in the Curriculum", presented by Creighton Lacy, reviewed by Calvin Reber and Norvin Hein.

12. "Two Years of the Literature of Missions," presented by Frank W. Price.

13. Adjournment.

Wilber C. Harr

Secretary

TREASURER'S REPORT

As follows:

Receipts

Deposit No. 1, June 24, 1954	89.82
Carried over	67.82
Membership at Chicago Meeting	22.00
Deposit No. 2, July 9	2.00
Deposit No. 3, December 21	28.00
Deposit No. 4, Dec. 28 & Jan. 3	12.00
Deposit No. 5, January 8	4.00
Deposit No. 6, January 15	4.00
Deposit No. 7, February 7	2.00
Deposit No. 8, March 12	2.00
Deposit No. 9, June 13	2.00
Deposit No. 10, July 12	2.00
Deposit No. 11, December 5	2.00
Total	149.82

Expenditures

Order of Bank checks	2.00
Bank charge	0.10
Check No. 1: 10 reams of paper from Master Prod. Co.	13.50
Check No. 2: 100 small stamped envelopes	3.53
Check No. 3: Putting out of papers (36 stencils (4.75), secretarial time (16.50), mimeograph (20.00))	41.25
Check No. 4: (envelopes (1.83), large envelopes (3.88), postage (8.00))	13.71

Check No. 5: Refund	2.00
Check No. 6: Postage	6.00
Total	82.09

4th Biennial Meeting (1964)

Meeting Agenda

Theme: Missionary Vocation

Monday, June 16

8:30-9:30	Registration
9:30-10:00	Worship, Dean Harold Lindsell, Fuller Theol. Seminary, Pasadena
10:00-10:15	Business Items
10:15-12:15	Missionary Vocation: Paper I, "The Missionary Calling of the Church,"
	Dean James A Scherer, Lutheran School of Missions, Maywood Critic,
	Prof. T. Watson Street, Austin Presbyterian Theol. Seminary
2:30-4:30	Missionary Vocation: Paper II, "Discipleship and Mission,"
	Prof. James H. Pyke, Wesley Theological Seminary, Westminster
	Critic, Prof. W. J. Danker, Concordia Seminary

4:30-4:45	"Missions Literature of the Past Biennium,"
	Dr. Frank W. Price, Director of the Missionary Research
	Library Copies will be distributed
7:30-9:30	Missionary Vocation: Paper III, "The Vocation of the Missionary,"
	Prof. E. Theodore Bachmann, Pacific Lutheran Seminary, Berkeley Critic,
	Prof. J. L. Dunstan, Andover-Newton Theological Seminary
9:30-10:30	Worship, Dean Lindsell

Tuesday, June 17

9:00-9:30	Worship, Dean Lindsell
9:30-10:15	Business Session, including election of officers
10:35-12:15	"The Teaching of Missions in the Light of Ecumenical Movement,"
	Prof. Creighton Lacy, Duke University Divinity School Critic,
	Prof. Robert Tobias, Christian Theological Seminary
2:30-4:30	Missionary Vocation: Paper IV, "Functional Services in Relation to the Central Task of Evangelism,"
	Prof. Herbert C. Jackson, Southern Baptist Theological Seminary
	Critic, Dr. Donald F. Ebright, Federated Theological Faculty, Chicago

4:30-4:45	Business
7:30-9:30	Missionary Vocation: Paper V, "The Role of the Missionary Today,"
	Dr. Donald McGavran, School of Missions of the United Church Missionary Society
	Critic, Dean Robert Parsons, Kennedy School of Missions
9:30-10:30	Worship, Dean Lindsell

MEETING MINUTES

Monday, June 16

1. The Fourth Biennial Meeting of the Association of Professors of Missions met at 8:30 in their assigned room at Boston University School of Theology for registration and informal fellowship.

2. Members of the Association moved to the small chapel for a brief devotional period. The chaplain for all devotional services was Dean Harold Lindsell, Fuller Theological Seminary, Pasadena, California.

3. The Association members moved to their assembly room at ten o' clock. Dr. R. Pierce Beaver, President of the Association called the assembly to order. Dean Walter Muelder of Boston University School of Theology was introduced. He welcomed the professors of missions to Boston University.

4. The Association moved that the prepared program with such minor modifications as made necessary be the program of the Fourth Biennial Meeting of the Association of Professors of Missions.

Consequently, the program of the day moved forward as follows, generally stressing the theme "Missionary Vocation":
- *The Missionary Calling of the Church*, presented by Dean James A. Scherer, Lutheran School of Missions, Maywood, Illinois.
- *Discipleship and Mission*, presented by Professor James H. Pyke, Wesley Theological Seminary, Westminster, Maryland.
- *The Vocation of the Missionary*, presented by the Professor E. Theodore Bachmann, Pacific Lutheran Theological Seminary, Berkely, California.
- *Missionary Literature of the Past Biennium*, presented by Dr. Frank Price, Director of the Missionary Research Library, New York City. (This was a deviation from the convention theme as planned. It is a regular procedure

in our meetings. Dr. Price made a brief presentation and distributed the material.)

5. The day was closed with a period of corporate worship in the small chapel. The period was guided by Dean Lindsell.

Tuesday, June 17

6. Once again we moved to the chapel for prayer at 9:00 in the morning, under the guidance of the Chaplain of the assembly.

7. Following the chapel period the association moved into a business period. The morning business period extended from 9:30 to 10:15. A brief period was planned for the afternoon between 4:30 and 4:45. Items of business for the two periods were as follows:

- Dr. R. Pierce Beaver announced that he had appointed two committees to function for the Association, namely, a committee on Nominations and a Committee of Resolutions.
- The Association discussed the presentation of the papers of this meeting to interested persons and organizations. It was noted that plans of two years ago were far too limited to meet the desires of individuals and organizations. The question was raised as to whether the theme of this year "Missionary Vocation" would prove less interesting than the general one "Christian Faith and the Religions," which had been the general theme of the Naperville meeting of 1956. It was believed that the current theme would elicit even more interest. The suggestion was made that at least five hundred copies of the new report be prepared. It was further suggested that the report be made available to professors, libraries and to boards of mission.
- The Association of Professors of Missions moved to amend the constitution at one point, namely, that biennial membership dues be four dollars instead of two dollars. The membership dues entitle members to the report.
- Professors M. Searle Bates and Irven Paul presented a concern by Dr. Earl Cressy to the effect that there should be a building up of centers of scholarship in key missions areas." The matter was referred to the Executive Committee for any further consideration.

- Professor J. Leslie Dunstan of the Atlantic Fellowship of Professors of Missions spoke on the need for good textbooks for the teaching of missions. This need came as a concern of that regional association. This item was referred to the Executive Committee of the Association of Professors of Missions with the direction that the problem be explored with the objective of genuine concerned action.
- Informal plans for the 1960 biennial meetings were suggested, trusting that the new Executive Committee would make note of the mind of the assembled group.
- Dr. Robert Parsons called attention to the "African Studies Association." Secretarial Office is at Columbia University, New York City, guided from the office of Professor Gray L. Couvan. This organization will keep interested people informed concerning current programs of African studies. This includes research presently in progress and available materials in libraries.
- It was mentioned that the Directory of Professors of Missions needed revision. Dr. Frank Price is presently engaged in such revision.
- For regional representation on the new Executive Committee, it was noted that the Mid-Atlantic Fellowship and the Mid-Western Fellowship nominate individuals. Leonard Wolcott was suggested as a member of the Executive Committee from the professors in the southern area, who as yet have not organized.
- There was a brief memorial period. It was noted that at least three men who had been active in the Association had been called into the "timelessness of eternity" since we last met. The names of Professors J.C. Archer, C.N. Yocum, and A.G. Adams were placed on the Memorial Roll. The members of the Association stood for a period of prayer.
- The Nominations Committee composed of Malcolm Pitt, James Raun, Herbert Jackson, E. Luther Copeland and Harold Lindsell nominates the Following: Wilber C. Harr, President; E. Theodore Bachmann, Vice-President; R. Pierce Beaver, Sec'y- Treas. Upon motion, these men were declared elected as the officers of the Association of Professors of Missions for the Biennium 1958-1960.

- The Committee on Resolutions (Professors James Scherer, Robert Parsons, George Dunger and Searle Bates) presented two items: a) a word of gratitude to Dean Walter Muelder and the Boston University School of Theology for courtesies and facilities extended; b) the deep gratitude of the Association to the officers who served during the 1956-1958 Biennium, particularly to R. Pierce Beaver, President and Wilber C. Harr, Sec'y-Treas. Without these men the business and particularly the publishing of the last report would have been impossible. Thanks also to those who generously contributed to the duplicating of their own contributions to the report. The report was adopted.
- The Association voted that if all possible resumes of the critic's reviews be included in the published reports.
- It was noted that while twenty-eight professors of missions had officially signed the registration sheets, at least forty different individuals had been a part of the meeting.
- It was voted that the Fourth Biennial Meeting of the Association of Professors of Missions be declared adjourned following the evening devotional service.
- Papers of the day:
- *The Teaching of Mission in the Light of the Ecumenical Movement*, presented by Professor Creighton Lacy, Duke University Divinity School, Durham, North Carolina.
- *The Role of the Missionary Today*, presented by Dr. Donald McGavran, School of Missions of the United Christian Missionary Society.
- *Functional Services in Relation to the Central Task of Evangelism*, presented by Professor Herbert Jackson, Southern Baptist Theological Seminary, Louisville, Kentucky.
- The closing chapel service was led by Dean Lindsell. Professor Wilber C. Harr, the new president of the Association led the closing prayer and gave the benediction.
- Professors who signed the registration sheet at the assembly room were as follows: (This does not necessarily coincide with the list of those who registered for other meetings and who may have been present for some periods of the discussion.) E. Theodore Bachmann, M. Searle Bates, James E. Bear, R. Pierce Beaver, George Carver, E. Luther Copeland, Bruce Cummings, William J. Danker, George

Dunger, J. Leslie Dunstan, Donald Ebright, Wilber C. Harr, Norman Horner, Herbert Jackson, L. Clayton Kitchen, Creighton Lacy, Harold Lindsell, Donald McGavran, Virgil A Olson, Robert Parsons, Irven Paul, Malcolm Pitt, Frank Price, James H. Pyke, James Raun, James Scherer, Robert Tobias, Leonard Wolcott.

Wilber C. Harr

Secretary

Treasurer's Report

Receipts

Brought forward, June 9, 1956	67.73
Deposit (over the table dues) June 9, 1956	36.00
*D*eposit July 2, 1956	20.00
Deposit July 16	36.00
Deposit August 23	18.00
Deposit October 8	14.00
Deposit Nov. 26	2.00
Deposit Dec. 10	6.00
Deposit Jan. 14, 1957	23.00
Deposit Jan. 19	12.00
Deposit Feb. 26	2.00
Deposit March 23	4.00
Deposit April 18	4.00
Deposit May 2	2.00
Deposit May 13	2.00
Deposit June 11	2.00
Deposit July 15	2.17
Deposit April 21, 1958	2.00

Total Receipts	254.90

Disbursements:

Paid to Eduardo Mondlane	6.00
For stationary and stamps	10.55
Printing Biennial Report	31.15
Closed Account, due to death	2.00
Stationery	4.25
Biennial Report Equipment and Stamps	16.96
Paper from Master Products	16.56
Naperville Sun, printing covers	7.25
Kelmscott Corporation or assembling reports	8.00
100 double post cards	4.00
Naperville Post Office for stamps and cards	10.20
Mimeographing of Treasurer's Report. 1958	5.00
Total	121.92

Summarization

Total Receipts	254.90
Total Disbursements	121.92
Balance carried forward	132.98

Submitted.
Wilber C. Harr

www.ingramcontent.com/pod-product-compliance
Lightning Source LLC
LaVergne TN
LVHW051449080426
835509LV00017B/1718